THE KING OF AMERICA
JAY-Z

THE KING OF AMERICA

JAY-Z

MARK BEAUMONT

OMNIBUS PRESS

London / New York / Paris / Sydney / Copenhagen / Berlin / Madrid / Tokyo

Cover designed by Fresh Lemon
Picture research by Jacqui Black

ISBN: 978.1.78038.317.0
Order No: OP54527

Exclusive Distributors
Music Sales Limited,
14/15 Berners Street,
London, W1T 3LJ.

Music Sales Corporation,
257 Park Avenue South,
New York, NY 10010, USA.

Macmillan Distribution Services,
56 Parkwest Drive
Derrimut, Vic 3030,
Australia.

Every effort has been made to trace the copyright holders of the photographs in this book but one or two were unreachable. We would be grateful if the photographers concerned would contact us.

Typeset by Phoenix Photosetting, Chatham, Kent
Printed in the EU.

A catalogue record for this book is available from the British Library.

Visit Omnibus Press on the web at www.omnibuspress.com

Contents

Acknowledgements

As previous Jay-Z biographers will attest, writing a book about the world's biggest rap star is a lonely business. As one of the most powerful men in music, only those with long-rusted axes to grind are willing to talk about him and his history without his say-so, and my intention in writing *The King Of America* was never to revive buried beefs or air one-sided grievances. This, primarily, was to be about the music. So, in putting together the first comprehensive, in-depth biography of the man, the mogul and his music I had to rely on largely unconscious help, from those hundreds of journalists who've interviewed and reviewed him and from the contributors to such websites as rapgenius.com who've taken time to enlighten the world about the meaning behind the more obscure of Jay-Z's lyrical references.

In addition, I'd like to thank David Barraclough and Helen Donlon at Omnibus Press, my editor Lucy Beevor and my wonderful agent Isabel Atherton at Creative Authors Ltd, to whom the author politely directs any publishers of fiction who have enjoyed this book.

Introduction

MTV Video Music Awards, 2003. Host Chris Rock steps up to the podium. "What's going on in the music business? The same thing that's always going on in the music business. Black man does something; 15 years later, white man does the same thing. And makes a lot more money." Cue camera cut to an embarrassed Eminem, cringing in his seat.

Glastonbury Festival, 2008. A screenful of static, news footage broadcast on an imaginary channel, JZTV, and the voice of Oasis' Noel Gallagher. "If it ain't broke don't fix it, if you start you're gonna break it, people ain't gonna go." His words splashed across the screen as they tumbled from the speakers. "Sorry, but Jay-Z? No, I'm not having hip-hop at Glastonbury, no way man. No, no, no, no, no-no-no." Newsreel spooled through headlines of the spat – Glasto Blasto At Noel – then to a flurry of comments from public, politicians, celebrities and broadcasters. "I think Noel Gallagher definitely has a point... Jay-D? I've never heard of them; is it a pop group?... This is one step closer to equality... Glastonbury and Jay-Z is like jam and Marmite... Noel Gallagher, you've had your time, give it to somebody else... How do you mosh to Jay-Z?" Quotes on totally different subjects from Tony Blair, President Putin, Paul McCartney, Mick Jagger, Prince Charles, David Beckham, Kim Jong-il, Liam Gallagher and Hillary Clinton were culled to the cause. Gwyneth Paltrow stated: "He's the best rapper of all time, I think he'll knock it out of the park"; shots of Noel looking humiliated over a dreary, slowed-down 'All You Need Is Love'. The clips rushed ever-faster: the Queen, Gordon Brown, Kanye West, Tom Hanks, Nelson Mandela, Kate Winslet, the whole world made to appear to be talking about this controversial event, about the one final quote of the film. Noel again, summing up the feelings of a dead and dislocated old guard. "Jay-Z? Fuckin' no chance."

The lights went down.

A roar like the earth opening.

A man in a black hoodie and reams of baggy scarves sauntered out from the wings onto Glastonbury's Pyramid Stage with an electric guitar around his neck. The song being played was familiar to all 180,000 people crammed into the field to see him; guitar chords, the opening to Oasis' 'Wonderwall'. He was clearly miming. He bawled out a casual attempt at singing along, "Today is gonna be the day that they're gonna throw it back to yeeeeooooow..." The entire first verse reeled out, played by a backing guitarist, the full band kicking in, the frontman wailing along with the words as best he could, the crowd picking up the famous refrain. There may even have been some at the back who thought he'd given in to the pressure, bowed to Glastonbury tradition, gone rock for the night.

Then, as the chorus wound to its leisurely close, Jay-Z dropped his guitar, waved his arms to stop the tape, perused the monumental crowd for a moment to decide if it smelt of adoration or lynching, concluding adoration was rampant. He finally spoke.

"I just got one thing to say!" he said, and pointed at his DJ. "If you having girl problems, I feel bad for you son..."

A roar like a barrier shattering.

As Jay-Z dropped '99 Problems' in all its filth and fabulous fury upon Glastonbury 2008, the musical landscape cracked, shifted and changed forever. Word of poor ticket sales and trad rock dissatisfaction with organisers Emily and Michael Eavis' decision to book a rapper as their Saturday night headline act had looked to reinforce the (largely white) rock world's prejudices, distrust and dislocation from the (largely black) hip-hop world. Then Jay-Z, the self-proclaimed greatest rapper on the planet, killed the entire festival in the space of half a dozen rap-rock power chords, and emancipated pop culture on the spot. Two seemingly opposing cultures clashed so hard they merged. The UK rock mainstream exposed its acceptance – nay, adoration – of the world's best hip-hop, and Jay-Z proclaimed his universal crossover appeal and credibility. For decades hip-hop had sold millions but been denied the huge event status and significance of the rock dinosaurs, kicking at the fingers of new genres and generations as they clambered up into the stadium league. Now Jay-Z had shattered rap's glass ceiling. There was none of Noel's 'us and them' at Glastonbury 2008, there was only 'us'. And we loved 'us'.

"I think it's beautiful," Jay-Z said when I questioned him the following year about his part in making hip-hop as huge as rock. "Not the rap part, I love rock music as well, but I think it's beautiful, I think that's fantastic. It's humbling because if you'd asked me 10 years ago would I be here, I probably would have said (I'd achieve) half of the things, maybe a quarter of the things that I've achieved and done. I'm not jaded by the process, I enjoy it and love it and appreciate it all the time."

For Jay-Z it was the culmination of 30 years of pushing at boundaries. Boundaries of what a poor ghetto kid could make of himself, what rap music was capable of and who it could reach. His incredible story, his impossible journey, has been beaten out in countless of his rhymes, whether to inspire aspiration, awe, respect, social re-evaluation or empathy. How he started out a fatherless child of poverty, another projects statistic earmarked for jail or the grave by the age of 21. How he was inexorably drawn into crime as his only means of escape or survival, and how it brought him his first addictive taste of wealth as well as his first brushes with death and custody. How his precocious, inimitable rap talents saved his life and changed the genre. And how his immense popularity and die-hard entrepreneurial brilliance made him the head of a sprawling multimillion-dollar business empire, a friend of presidents and the most successful rapper in history with 50 million album sales, a $450 million fortune, 13 Grammy Awards and the record for the most US number one albums by a solo artist, beating Elvis into the dust –

only The Beatles are bigger. Not to mention his standing as one half of the world's most influential and loved power couples, alongside one of music's most stunning and talented women.

But Jay-Z's story is about more than the astounding numbers. It's about aspiration, determination and a constant striving to make more of himself, his family, his music, his people and his culture. It's about rich, poetic words and rhymes that speak to the very heart of the street strugglers and give them hope of luxury and high living, while gradually opening the eyes of the mainstream to the emotion, hardship and humanity writhing behind the gun crime and drug bust figures. It's about bursting society's chains, confounding what's laid out for you and blowing sky high the possibilities of life, love and music. It's about not resting until you achieve all you're capable of, and are given all the justice and respect that you and those you're speaking for deserve.

And, at the core, it's about the ascendancy of hip-hop from a Platinum-selling but exclusive niche to a chart-dominating mainstream phenomenon and spectacle to rival the behemoths of pop and rock'n'roll, and the man who was at the forefront in leading the charge. There will be gunplay and knife fights. There will be beefs and spats, friendships shattered and family members lost. There will be enough crack, cops, double-crossings, fall-outs and feuds for a dozen *Scarface* sequels. But at the story's centre is the music, some of the greatest ever recorded, and its meteoric impact on popular culture.

Okay, we've reloaded. Time to crown the new King Of America.

Chapter One

The School Of
Hard Knocks

"Saw the devil in your eyes, high off more than weed, confused I just closed
my young eyes and squeezed"

— Jay-Z, 'You Must Love Me'

The gun shook in the child's hand. He'd seen enough cop shows
and watched enough firearms being flaunted around Marcy by the
gangsta kids to know how to bear his arm. Man, he'd even seen a local
guy shot dead barely two years before. But though he tried to speak with
calm insistence, to tell Eric — his brother's eyes wide and panicked from
the crack, his lips quivering, his fingers fidgety on the jewellery — that
enough was enough, the stealing had to end, to put his ring back or he'd
shoot, his aim trembled.

Trembled enough, perhaps, as the child squeezed shut his eyes and
fired, to save his brother's life.

The shot that rang out from apartment 5C across the courtyards
of Marcy, through the maze-like walkways, down the litter-strewn
stairwells, went virtually unnoticed. The addicts on benches twitched
no more than usual; for the dealers gambling over games of cee-lo

1

against walls clogged with tags it was just more ghetto background noise. Gunfire was a common sound in the Brooklyn projects. Kids went to sleep to it, gangbangers noted it in passing, another brother biting the dust. In the crack-infested 1980s, gunshots were the heartbeat of Bed-Stuy.

The child opened his eyes, half-deafened from the blast. He dropped the gun, shocked, as his brother clutched himself, stumbled and fell, a wound pulsing in his shoulder. Suddenly Shawn Carter's short life closed down on him.* He'd never meant to shoot Eric, himself just four years older than Shawn. He'd got the gun from a friend's place (it was easy enough to find – guns were everywhere in the projects) just to wave in his face, scare him enough that he'd stop stealing his own family's possessions to feed his crack habit. Although he was the youngest of the Carter clan holed up in 5C, with his father long gone and his elder brother lost to rocks, Shawn felt he had to be the man of the house, to take responsibility for protecting his mother and two sisters. "He was doing a lot of drugs," like so many lost children of the ghettos before him, he'd one day confess to Oprah Winfrey. "He was taking stuff from our family. I was the youngest, but I felt like I needed to protect everybody."[1] Now, one flinch too far on a hair trigger, and he saw a future of bars and beatings, another projects parole pleader trapped, like so many others, in the regurgitating maw of the US penitentiary system.

As Eric was being stretchered across the lobby of a nearby hospital – again, no eyes were raised at another shooting victim prostrate on the ward trolleys of that particular dead-end corner of Brooklyn – Shawn fled to a friend's apartment, terrified. "I thought my life was over," he'd say years later, "I thought I'd go to jail for ever."[2] A restless, fear-filled

---

* Although it's widely reported that Jay-Z was 12 at the time of the shooting, he may have been older; the song which references the event, 'You Must Love Me', claims he immediately fled to rapper friend Jaz-O's place after the incident, and Jay-Z didn't meet Jaz-O until the age of 14. The Jay-Z business biography *Empire State Of Mind* by Zack O'Malley Greenburg puts Jay-Z's age as 17 at the time of the shooting.

night was endured, hours stretched out a long, lonely lifetime. When the call finally came for him, though, it wasn't a police chief requesting he turn in for questioning or social services plotting out his bleakest possible future. It was a call to say no charges would be pressed and that his brother would be happy to have Shawn visit him in his hospital bed. There, full of regret and forgiveness, Eric apologised for his weakness, addiction and theft, for the creature crack had made him, and became a man.

The young Shawn Carter sat by his brother's bedside, relieved, shaken, but he'd received a valuable but dangerous lesson: that you could do dreadful wrongs and walk away unpunished. Before long he'd be living his entire life by the creed that crime paid, and Eric's misfortunes would point his own way through his early life – crack cocaine would also take over his life, albeit from the more profitable side of the addict equation. But shooting his brother was also Shawn's first plunge into the darkest depths of himself. He'd exposed the worst excesses of anger and retribution he was capable of, and glimpsed the wasted life they could drag him down to. Perhaps – he may have thought – he could separate himself from his wickeder thoughts, create a new persona, a figure alongside Shawn Carter through which to expose and explore the growing hardships and violence on the projects' streets around him, and the frustrations, flamboyances and fears within. A character through which he could fathom out the death of his uncle, the desertion of his father, the disintegration of his wider world and the future, whatever low-down dealings and high-flying success it might bring.

An alter ego. A cipher. A superstar.

They'd call him Jay-Z. And one day he would own the world.

"I was conceived by Gloria Carter and Abnis Reid / Who made love under the sycamore tree / Which makes me a more sicker MC."

– Jay-Z, 'December 4th'

At 4.45 a.m., December 4, 1969, many more shots rang out from apartment 2337 West Monroe Street in Chicago. The first bullet struck and instantly killed one Mark Clark, the man standing guard by the door with a shotgun laid across his knees. The round Clark fired off on reflex as he died was the only shot fired by any member of the Black Panthers movement during the entire FBI raid.

The next barrage of gunshots was aimed at the sleeping body of Fred Hampton, the freshly appointed chief of staff and spokesman of the Black Panther Party, lying curled up beside his pregnant girlfriend, drugged with barbiturates earlier in the evening by an FBI plant within the BPP named William O'Neal. When the invading officers discovered Hampton was still alive after the first barrage of shooting, reports claim the still-unconscious victim was murdered with two bullets point blank to the head.

The Black Panthers were a controversial group in the late Sixties – as a militant arm of the US civil rights movement dedicated to opposing police brutality against African-Americans and enforcing black rights, they were a popular rallying banner among poor and downtrodden black communities. However, their use of violence against the police and their revolutionary rhetoric made them anathema to J. Edgar Hoover's government, a feared and dangerous enemy of the establishment and a blueprint for gang culture that Hoover devoutly wished to crush.

Hampton was the wrong scapegoat to execute, though. With little more than minor theft on his record and a history of teaching political courses in church behind him, he was widely regarded to be an honourable, non-violent man, and his death dramatically switched the public's sympathies. Jesse Jackson claimed in his eulogy to Hampton that "when Fred was shot in Chicago, black people in particular, and decent people in general, bled everywhere" and years later Chicago would declare December 4 as Fred Hampton Day. William O'Neal, for his part in Hampton's death, committed suicide. Whether the Black Panthers can be blamed for the rise of gangs in the US or not, the killing of Fred Hampton certainly made them a counterculture movement to be respected in the more rebellious and ireful of American hearts. Public Enemy, KRS-One and Tupac Shakur would all cite the Black Panthers and the group's Fight The Power creed as an influence. It could be said that the seeds of 20th century rap music were sown in those dark, bloody, early hours of December 4, 1969.

Then, some hours past dawn, 700 miles east, 21st century rap music was born.

Shawn Corey Carter slipped comfortably into the world that day despite his 10-pound bulk, giving his mother, she would later claim in song, no pain. The fourth and youngest child of Gloria Carter and Adnis Reeves*, she sensed this one would be particularly special. Like his elder brother Eric and his two sisters Michelle and Andrea before him, baby Shawn was welcomed into a loving but strictly religious family.

When he was born, Gloria, Adnis and their children all lived with Adnis' parents in Bedford-Stuyvesant, Brooklyn: young Shawn's grandfather (also named Adnis Reeves, necessitating his father being known to the family as Adnis Junior or AJ) preached at a Pentecostal church in the borough, the Church Of God In Christ, where his wife (Shawn's grandmother) Ruby was also a deaconess. Hence, the Lord's word held a heavy sway over the Reeves/Carter clan. Adnis Junior had been brought up a strict Christian, spending almost all of his spare time at his parents' church and banned from playing popular music in the house. Despite this restriction, AJ and Gloria had become avid fans and collectors of music, stockpiling stacked crates full of vinyl albums that took in every great soul, Motown, R&B and jazz record they could lay their hands on. All they needed was a place of their own to play them.

The five years Shawn Carter spent living at his grandparents' house seemed an idyllic time. Like his father, he too was expected regularly at church – his earliest memories are of watching the spectacle of Pentecostal worship with its high-spirited drummers, passionate singers and congregation members beset with bouts of speaking in tongues or holy possession. At home he ate cheap chicken as though dining at a feast of medieval kings, unaware it'd long since become the fast fuel of poverty. And when allowed to roam free around the neighbourhood,

---

* In his autobiography, Jay-Z spells his father's name as both Adnis Reeves and Abnis Reid – we've plumped here for the more widely accepted spelling.

he lost himself in childhood fantasies of adventure and glory. He and his earliest playmates discovered an abandoned boat on the block on which they'd set their imaginations a-sail every day, and by the age of four, he was already something of a local superstar.

While most of the neighbourhood kids were still teetering atop their tricycles or struggling to shed their training wheels, word spread the length of Bedford-Stuyvesant of the wonder that was the Bicycling Baby. Crowds would gather to watch this incredible spectacle, this circus-like feat. A speck of a child hoisted onto a two-wheel, 10-speed bicycle, his legs too short to reach both pedals. Yet, with a hoick of one foot on the chain he'd be off, balanced precariously on the saddle like a Wild West stuntman, one leg spiked through the frame for balance and direction. Cheers would rise as he scooted off across the street, the world's tiniest showman. That boy, Bed-Stuy agreed, sure had some talent.

Even so young, though, Shawn was no bragger. His pious grandparents instilled in him a humbleness and modesty, but also a restraint in emotional matters. "I'm not really the type of person who can sit and talk about how they feel," he'd say later in life, "we were raised to hold a lot in."[3] One day he'd find a fulfilling form of therapy to combat this tendency towards reticence, a way to express his emotions to the utmost. But for now, and throughout the dips and dives of his formative years, his inwardness would define and consume him.

That, and the bleak new world he was about to be swallowed up by.

The Marcy projects in 1974 were a warren of red brick incarceration – once you were in, you rarely got out.

Many did try, testing various escape routes. Some bought their daily tickets to oblivion central from the heroin dealers hustling on most of Marcy's corridors and corners, and took their trip away half-comatose on the projects' benches. Others leapt for freedom during police raids from their apartment windows, each of which was numbered on the street-facing side to help the police cover all possible exits and pinpoint the right perp. Still more, as gun crime, drugs and gang culture took a grip, left in cuffs or bags.

Shawn would later describe Marcy and other such poor housing schemes as "huge islands built mostly in the middle of nowhere, designed to warehouse lives".[4] These 27 six-storey blocks rising above the J and Z subway lines station at Brooklyn's Marcy Avenue – a huge complex built on the site of an old Dutch windmill in 1949 to house over 4,000 residents running the racial gamut from black to Puerto Rican to Arab to Chinese (but stopping short, notably, of the Caucasian community) – had the austerity of a penal colony, and the hope and ambition to match.

The Reeves/Carter family moved into apartment 5C when Shawn was five years old (Shawn shared a room with his brother Eric) and for him, at first, the place was a sprawling playground. With his friend DeHaven Irby from across the hall he learned the labyrinth of rundown corridors and ill-lit walkways connecting the red brick buildings, racing the fetid alleyways like a rat in a maze. He discovered dark nooks and hidden crannies for hide-outs and secret camps, crunched delighted over the glistening glass shards of the playing fields and basketball courts. He watched the hustlers throwing bills at their dice games of cee-lo, tipped unconscious addicts off their benches to laugh at them suddenly coming to from their stupors. In a world of danger and deprivation, Shawn Carter frolicked unaware.

If Marcy Houses were a new country he barely ever left – the subway only went to Queens, not Manhattan; the city seemed a world away, to be visited and gawped at only on school trips – his new apartment, too, opened up wide new horizons. Sonically speaking. Freed from the musical restrictions of Adnis Senior and Ruby, Gloria and Adnis Junior threw themselves endlessly into the floods of vinyl engulfing the apartment. Every weekend the family would shimmy through the rooms, cleaning the place along to soul grooves from Marvin Gaye, Donny Hathaway, The Blackbyrds, Average White Band or Van McCoy & The Soul City Symphony. Late at night, when their parties reached fever pitch, music flowing from the turntable and reel-to-reel teetering atop a stack of planks and crates in the front room, young Shawn would sneak from his room in his pyjamas to sit by the doorway, watch the adults dancing and listen to the sweet, soulful sounds of The Jackson

7

Five, Love Unlimited Orchestra, The Commodores, James Brown and Tavares. Shawn felt the music seep deep into his core, sitting swaying in the dark, blissed out on the honeyed voices and seductive grooves.

As the Seventies went on, Gloria and Adnis also began to play music that would influence Shawn even more fundamentally. "My mom had rap records too," he'd claim, "King James 3rd, Jimmy Spicer... I used to sneak listens to the Richard Pryor records, with him cussing all over them. Al Green... Our whole house was the party house and just stacked with records... It was overflowing!"[5]

At the time, rap music was still in an equally formative state. Block parties were taking hold in the Bronx, DJ Kool Herc and Coke La Rock had started MCing over the beats stripped from funk and soul records. The early rap collective Funky Four Plus One formed in 1976 while Afrika Bambaataa's Universal Zulu Nation, Melle Mel & The Furious Five, Kurtis Blow and Grandmaster Flash were gaining popularity and kudos among the burgeoning rap scene developing on the New York streets. Hip-hop, underground, was blowing up, but was still making few inroads into the sphere of reference of the *Soul Train*-watching, seven-year-old Shawn Carter, beyond the beats he heard creeping into his parents' collection. For his part, he was too obsessed with Michael Jackson, practising Jacko spins along to the Jacksons' tunes 'Enjoy Yourself' and 'Dancing Machine' with Michelle and Andrea acting as his backing singers. A tiny starman, seeking a scene.

In elementary school, Shawn was a smart, active child. He played little league baseball (they were a sporting family; Eric would go on to be a college basketball hotshot and the family had a hoop erected in their front room), claimed to have a photographic memory and showed signs of far outstripping his classmates as a rare Brooklyn example of a child genius (or at least, when he'd reach sixth grade, he'd be tested at a twelfth-grade level). But much of his most vital education took place on the streets.

His father Adnis was an attentive and caring man, keen to ensure his son developed the intuition and attention to detail he'd need to survive life in the pitfall-filled, unforgiving projects. He taught him to play chess to sharpen his forward thinking instincts, his sense of always thinking one step ahead of the game, and some weekends Adnis would take Shawn into Manhattan, to the sordid soul of the place, to Times Square at its most putrid Seventies depths, to observe. To observe the pimps and gangs, the hookers and bums, the seething squalor. And to recall. Over steak and fries in Lindy's diner on 53rd Street Adnis would tell Shawn to watch the people passing by on the sidewalk outside, then guess their clothes sizes. Walking back to the subway, the father would insist his son led the way – learning leadership, responsibility – and then quiz him on the wording of signs in shop windows or the attire of the people they'd passed. Adnis taught Shawn to have his eyes always open, aware of the peripheries, one watching his back. It was as if Adnis could predict for his son a life of ambush and attack, and he gave him the skills to protect himself.

The pair grew unfathomably close.

And Shawn's keen powers of observation turned to the darker forces around him, shedding a new and ominous light over the projects. He noticed the men – the hustlers, he knew – getting out of expensive cars, so much flasher and more affluent than Marcy's usual motley crew. There, perhaps, he saw his own way out. And he noticed, in the *New York Post*, the fascinating character of Vinnie Gigante, The Oddfather, a known mafia man who was considered insane, old and harmless by dint of always being pictured wandering the streets of New York in his bathrobe and slippers, muttering to himself. The persona was an elaborate ruse: as Gigante rose to positions of great power and influence in the US underworld, he escaped suspicion and conviction throughout the Seventies, deemed too mentally unstable to stand trial.* There, Shawn saw the grand benefits of disguising yourself as something you're not.

There were some instincts, however, he didn't want to trust. One December 4, Shawn sat on a bench in Brooklyn, the bench where he'd arranged to meet his father for a day of birthday treats and observation tests. An hour passed with no sign of Adnis. As Shawn trudged away

---

* The law finally caught up with Gigante in 1997, when he was given a 12-year sentence for racketeering; he died in prison in 2005.

from the meeting spot, coat curled up against the chill of the winter, he observed something new about his father.

He might not be the best guy to rely on.

1979 was the year Benny died and Slate came alive.

Marcy was changing, shifting its tone, getting edgier. Shawn Carter could sense it in the air, in the quiver of the addicts' eyes and the tension in the hustlers' holster hands. Guns were beginning to swamp the projects, gangs grew on bravado and retaliation, and the toll mounted up. "Navigating this place was life or death," Shawn would say[6], and that year he came face to face with both sides of that eternal coin.

Benny was the man who'd take the Marcy kids to play baseball. A popular guy with real talent on the mound; his young protégés swore he could make it to the majors if the right scout got wind of him. Then, one time, Shawn and a gaggle of friends caught sight of Benny running at pace through the Marcy walkways, another man on his tail. Sensing action – a fight, a showdown, a clash of fists – an excited Shawn and his entourage followed the pair into a building.

What they saw there was no game.

A hollow crack. It stopped them in their tracks, killed their giggling, dried their mouths and tightened their throats, reverberated through them carrying a chill shiver of dread and nausea. Across the floor, Benny fell to the ground. So many times he'd heard the shots from afar; never once had he been caught in their aftershock.

Benny was the first man Shawn Carter watched die.*

Slate, on the other hand, was the first kid Shawn Carter saw really *living*.

Though the shooting of Benny made him more wary around the projects, less inclined to go running towards crowds or chase commotion, the music drew him in. It was a circle of people, young kids, clapping

---

* But certainly not the last – in his interview with Alex Blimes of the *Observer* in 2008, he told of "a Sunday, 12 o'clock in the afternoon, these guys came through shooting Uzis, chasing after this other guy. And that was a normal thing."

and cheering to a deep funk beat in the summer heat. And words spread too; spitting, charging rhymes with a life, poetry and rhythm all their own. He pushed his way through the backs. In the centre of the circle stood Slate, a Marcy kid Shawn knew but had never really noticed. Only this wasn't the Slate that Shawn vaguely knew. This was Slate, superstar.

Shawn remembers the scene vividly. "He was transformed, like the church ladies touched by the spirit, and everyone was mesmerised. He was rhyming, throwing out couplet after couplet like he was in a trance... 30 minutes straight off the top of his head, never losing the beat, riding the handclaps... It was like watching some kind of combat."[7]

Shawn was entranced by the sight, this modest kid metamorphosed before his eyes into a hero, drenched in adoration, by the power of words alone. Slate rapped about the basic street furniture he could see around him, commented on the tattered sneakers or denims he spotted in the circle or simply boasted about his own attire, skills or wordplay, and the circle worshipped him for it, utterly believed his throwaway gloats that he was the best rhymer in New York. Right there, in that primitive cipher, Slate was the most famous kid in Marcy.

And, watching him agape, Shawn Carter realised he could be famous too.

Within hours he began writing his first lines in a spiral notebook, the words streaming out of him like wildfire. Within days the notepad was full, so his mother clipped together a rudimentary notebook for him, a sheaf of paper held with a paperclip. When that too was overrun with rhymes, she found him a binder full of unlined paper; before long every inch and corner of every page was a maze of lyrics for songs yet unwritten. Shawn's mind was a machine, he had a true gift and lust for this fiery, soul-searching poetry, for marking down the milestones, achievements and dreams of his young life. Suddenly, he'd found a way to make some sense of himself, to define who he was.

Next, he had to perfect his art.

The slapping and tapping became the new pulse of 5C. From windowsills, kitchen tables, desks, mattresses, any surface within reach, Shawn would keep his beats with flickering fingers and propulsive palms. Eric, Michelle and Andrea would wake in the middle of the night hearing a steady, regular drumming from the kitchen, where Shawn would be keeping the beat and pattern of the night. From the moment he woke up till the minute he dropped, he'd practise: when he wasn't hooking his rhymes to rhythms and rehearsing tongue-twisting lyrical acrobatics, determined to become the most agile and gymnastic word-spitter on the block, he was scouring dictionaries to beef up his vocabulary or honing his flow into a bulky tape recorder. If he was out in the street and a line popped into his head, he'd prop his binder against a street lamp or bench to note it down, and his schoolmates soon caught on to his new passion. Some envied him his talent, sneaking looks at his binder and performing his lyrics as their own, causing him to start writing in a miniscule script too small for others to read and hiding his book under his bed. Most, though, admired his dedication; his mother was so keen to encourage him that – much to his siblings' annoyance, you presume – she bought him a boom box to help him start freestyling, and his new 'rap name' took hold. From the age of nine onwards, his friends called him Jazzy.

Come July 1979, The Fatback Band would launch recorded hip-hop with 'King Tim III (Personality Jock)' and The Sugarhill Gang would release what's widely considered the first breakthrough rap record, 'Rapper's Delight'. Though the true underground scene resented the tune's Top 40 US success as it wasn't the work of any of the pioneering name MCs and seemed vaguely novelty in comparison to some of the more intense rappers developing across NYC, Shawn and his entire generation (including one Russell Simmons, who'd use the inspiration of the record's success to launch his own label, Def Jam) adored it. But if 1979 was the year hip-hop broke worldwide, 1978 was an equally momentous year for its eventual coming of age, and its cross-cultural mainstream acceptance.

1978 was the year Jay-Z was born.

His name alone was enough to send whispers around the battle crowds, like Wild West towns used to hiss with the names of outlaws. Jay-Z, young kid, 14 maybe, but man, the kid had skills. He was the fastest rapper in Marcy, maybe all of New York, spat rhymes like semi-automatic fire. And he knew it. Every battle he joined, he tore through his opponents like they'd barely learned to speak, left them all for dust. He'd calmly soak up every jibe, boast and taunt the other guy had in him and then – boom – he'd launch his tirade, words skipping and flipping like Ali's feet, his hands measuring out metre and rhythm like a baller's baton, the mic melting. And hey, he walked the walk; they said he stuck a slug in his own brother one time.

Across the Marcy courtyard battles of the mid-1980s – grown from those small ciphers of '78 into gladiatorial events in makeshift coliseums now, with pumped-up crowds passing judgement, digs between battlers getting so sharp and personal they sometimes ended in violence, and professional DJs sucking juice from street lamps to power their decks, pounding out beats to bulge the apartment windows – the name of Jay-Z spread with a wide-eyed respect.

Word was, the kid had some tragedy to spit, too.

In 1980, a call had come in to apartment 5C that would tear the family apart. A scuffle outside a notorious Brooklyn bar involving Adnis' brother Ray, Jazzy's uncle; a knife was pulled; Ray took it to the hilt, DOA. The community bristled with the name of the culprit – the whole city seemed to know who killed Ray – but no one would stick their hand up as a witness and the police drew a streetful of blanks.

The loss of a brother, though, wasn't something Adnis Reeves would just roll over and accept. He became sleepless, argumentative with Gloria, obsessed with hunting down Ray's murderer. "People would call in the middle of the night and tell him, 'So-and-so is out here'," Jay-Z would claim. "So my dad would get up, get his gun, and go outside to look for the guy... This was my dad's baby brother."[8]

One day, Adnis went out on one of his goose chases, and never came back. Out there in the projects, out of grief and desperation, he'd turned to alcohol and heroin, and lost himself. "My dad was in so much pain that he started using drugs and became a different person," Jay-Z recalls. "The trauma of the event, coupled with the drugs, caused him to lose his soul." No one fully explained the reasons for their parents' split to the Carter children, just that their family was fractured. "My mom prepared us more than [Adnis] did. I don't think he was ready for that level of discussion and emotion. He was a guy who was pretty detached from his feelings." At 11 years old, Shawn suddenly felt the weight of familial responsibility on his tiny shoulders, a need to protect his mother and siblings and help improve their situation. "I remember telling her, 'Don't worry, when I get big, I'm going to take care of this.' I felt like I had to step up."[9]

With the loss of his father, however – and soon the loss of a cousin too, who died falling out of a broken window in a Marcy apartment – Jazzy (as he was still nicknamed then) fell to pieces. "To me, that was basically the end of our relationship," he said to *Vibe* magazine of his father. "That was when the hurt and then the healing began for me, from that day right there." Already a soft-spoken, quiet student, at Eli Whitney High School, which he attended alongside DeHaven and a kid called Anthony Cruz (one day to be renamed AZ and become a Grammy-nominated associate of Nas and The Firm), his high grades plummeted and his interest and concentration waned. He enjoyed English lessons – anything to do with words fascinated him – but he spent the rest of his time distracted, daydreaming about sports or rapping. At home he withdrew into himself: with his mother forced to work to support the family, Jazzy was left alone after school hours. He became separated from his mother and siblings, grew angry, insular and guarded, closed off to emotional attachment in case he was ever again hurt that deeply.

"When you're growing up, your dad is your superhero," he'd explain. "Once you've let yourself fall that in love with someone, once you put him on such a high pedestal and he lets you down, you never want to experience that pain again. So I remember just being really quiet and really cold. Never wanting to let myself get close to someone like that again… I carried that feeling throughout my life… It made me not express my feelings as much. I was already a shy kid, and it made me a little reclusive. But it also made me independent. And stronger. It was a weird juxtaposition."[10]

Better to have loved and lost? That wasn't Jaz's experience. "If your dad died before you were born, yeah, it hurts, but it's not like you had a connection with something that was real. Not to say it's any better, but to have that connection and then have it ripped away was, like, the worst. My dad was such a good dad that when he left, he left a huge scar."[11]

Inevitably, he turned to the therapy that was hip-hop. By the time Jazzy had turned 14, rap had flooded Marcy (where the local talent pool of rappers was becoming formidable), the New York projects and beyond. The ground-breaking scratchings of Herbie Hancock's 'Rockit' blasted from every car stereo and skate park the summer of '83, inspiring Jaz to try his hand at DJing, scratching records himself on a couple of turntables a friend had set up across a plank of wood in his front room. Afrika Bambaataa's 'Looking For The Perfect Beat' was the backing track to his latest bedroom dance routines. He got into hip-hop radio shows by pioneering scene notaries such as DJ Red Alert, Afrika Islam and The World's Famous Supreme Team.

Then came Run-D.M.C.'s 'It's Like That'/'Sucker MCs' single, which shifted Jazzy's perspective on the possibilities of black music in the 1980s. He turned his focus from his earliest heroes, Michael Jackson and Prince, towards this group who better represented their fans and his community. The way he saw it[*], where most mainstream black artists seemed to him to be playing down their ethnicity for mass R&B acceptance or embracing eccentricity to distract from their race, the unashamedly powerful Run-D.M.C. – and 'Sucker MCs' in particular – were out to loudly, proudly and accurately reflect real street-life stories and hardships in their music, and thereby set the foundations for rap music to come. "It was going to be raw and aggressive," he believed, "but also witty and slick. It was going to boast and compete and exaggerate."[12] Like the rhymes Jazzy was becoming more and more skilful at delivering with practice, Run-D.M.C.[†] were all about being true to who you are, but also true to the roots of hip-hop – the aggressive braggadocio, the one-upmanship, the suaveness of the street player and the flaunting of freshly gained wealth and high-life trappings. Indeed,

---

[*] As dissected at length in his autobiography *Decoded*.
[†] And burgeoning hip-hop acts such as Public Enemy, Ice Cube and Rakim.

listening to Run-D.M.C., Jazzy felt the same aspiration and wonder as when he and his friends would gawp at the hustlers' expensive BMWs cruising the projects.

Meanwhile, rap had also made serious inroads into popular culture. The Funky Four Plus One had become the first hip-hop act to appear on *Saturday Night Live* to play 'That's The Joint' in 1981. That same year *ABC News* reported on the Rock Steady Crew's battle with Dynamic Rockers at the Lincoln Center, and The Sugarhill Gang stunned Jazzy when they made an appearance on his beloved *Soul Train*. Rap, he knew, was about to break big. So by the time Eli Whitney was shut down and he changed schools to George Westinghouse Career And Technical Education High School in downtown Brooklyn, Jazzy had upped his hip-hop game.

George Westinghouse was a wreck of a school; the bathrooms were blacked out and thick with dope smoke, the windows were shattered, the whole building was dense with menace, the teachers were afraid of the pupils. Jazzy was a distant, subdued attendant who kept his own company in the cafeteria most days, but these still waters ran awful deep. Word got around about his agility and sass in the mini-battles he'd conduct against other wannabe rappers in the meal hall, the beats slammed out on tables, and respect grew for him among Westinghouse's various hip-hop hopefuls – Busta Rhymes cruised those same halls, and Jazzy even got a nod or two from the larger, older kid that everyone was tipping for real hip-hop success. Kid by the name of Christopher Wallace, although most knew him as Biggie Smalls.

In the battles of Marcy, Jazzy caught both eyes and ears. By 1984 he'd developed such a strong reputation as the hottest young rapper in the projects that some friends tried to arrange for him a heavyweight title-style bout against the champion Marcy rapper of the time, Jonathan 'Jaz-O' Burks, four years Jazzy's senior. Full of bravado and self-belief, Jazzy took the challenge and showed up for the battle with a head full of rhymes and steam. Jaz-O, however, saw more of an apprentice in this young kid than an opponent: asking Jazzy to rap for him rather than battle, he saw the unrefined talent in the teenager, and decided to take him under his wing. Over months of tuition, Jaz-O turned Jazzy on to the concepts of artistic licence, of exaggeration, extended metaphor and simile, of squirming around words like a snake. Jaz-O became Jazzy's mentor, a brother figure and a provider when the younger kid went hungry. The folklore goes that, in Jaz-O's honour, Jazzy morphed his name.* From then on, he'd be Jay-Z.

And as Jay-Z, he owned the Marcy battle scene. By the time he was spotted by another of Marcy's rap ace faces, DJ Clark Kent, he, in Kent's words, "outclassed"[13] anyone he rapped with, at barely 15 years of age.

"Jaz-O was a rapper around Brooklyn," said Kent, "and his producer was Fresh Gordon, and me and Fresh were tight. Fresh Gordon was this rapper who actually knew how to make music. We would be in his crib and Jaz-O would come over and he would make Jaz-O's records... One time I'm at Fresh Gordon's house and Jaz-O comes over and he has Jay-Z with him. And Jay-Z is dumb young. He might have been 15, maybe 16. They started rhyming together and he was insane. I just kept saying 'this is the best rapper I've ever heard'. And they're looking at me like I'm crazy."[14]

Kent saw the potential to turn Jay-Z from a little league rapper on the outskirts to a real main player, and over the coming years he'd help do exactly that. But right then, Jay-Z didn't see any great appeal in being a rapper, not long term. He didn't see anyone rapping their way to fortunes around his neighbourhood. Those guys, he figured, were just puppets in someone else's expensive music video.

No, the guys making the *real* money? Jay-Z's *real* figures of hope and aspiration? Those were the hustlers...

---

* Though Jay-Z denies it himself, claiming he simply shortened 'Jazzy'.

Chapter Two

The White Menace

"There's ya ticket out the ghetto / Take flight right here"
— Jay-Z, 'Young, Gifted And Black'

However crack arrived in the United States in the 1980s – whether drifted into LA under Reagan's very nostrils on CIA-sponsored planes from the Nicaraguan Contras, or sailed into Miami from the cocaine-swamped Dominican Republic and Bahamas, where plummeting cocaine prices led dealers to convert their powder to rocks to shift in smaller chunks – it found its way to places like Marcy first. Crack spread like the contagion it was; for as little as $2.50 the users looking for an hour's escape from misery could get a hit purer than the $100 gram baggies of cocaine they could never have afforded before. Addiction was virtually instant, addicts became legion, the landscape changed forever. "What happened in the projects, especially back then during the Reagan era, it was crack wars," Jay-Z recalled. "I always think of that Public Enemy song, 'Night Of The Living Baseheads'. At night, it was like zombies walking around, very dangerous."[1]

On the subways, Jay-Z saw conductors assaulted by graffiti kids and passengers robbed by twitching thugs. On the streets he saw new, more vicious gangs evolve: the Decepticons, the Lo-Lifes and the all-girl attack squad the Deceptinettes. On corners he saw Uzis, Glocks and all their accessories openly swapping hands, and then worn like trinkets of fashion. In his own home friends of the family were suddenly concocting plans to make money quick, and his own brother started stealing things from the apartment, and would pay for it in blood.

In the projects – every day becoming more of a ghetto – he saw violence: police versus addicts, gang versus gang, children versus parents, neighbour versus neighbour. Like a smaller-scale Iran-Contra, police would become surreptitiously involved in drug deals or gun down addicts for misdemeanours or just running away. As Grandmaster Flash had noted in 1982's 'The Message', it was like a jungle where only the most alert and aware stopped themselves from going under.

But, in among all of this addiction, death and depravity, Jay-Z also saw opportunity. His generation – young teenagers – were becoming moneyed and powerful in the hustling game, supporting their families while terrifying the older generation into hiding. The kids owned the streets now, and Jay-Z wanted his slice. After all, if he was putting his life in danger just by walking to school or having to carry a gun just to safely ride the J train*, if the threat of death was always hanging over him anyway – in his face today, around the corner tomorrow – then what did he have to lose by trying to throttle some damn money out of it?

There's some disagreement over exactly what age Jay-Z started hustling drugs. Some claim it was as late as 18[†] but Jay-Z himself claims he did his first deals around Marcy at 13. Even so young, he knew the risks. "Whether you're in it from the lowest level to the top dog, you're putting your life on the line," he mused. "There's danger from the minute you make your first sale."[2]

When there was so little hope of a conventional job in his future, the introduction to hustling seemed natural. "It's so normal, you just

---

* In his book *Decoded*, Jay-Z recalls a fight on a subway home from the apartment of a girlfriend of a close friend, possibly DeHaven, in East New York with a gang of kids who didn't like his face, an event made all the more stressful by the fact that he'd given up the gun he shared with his friend back at the girl's place.

† Interviews with DeHaven by Zack O'Malley in Greenburg's *Empire State Of Mind* claim that he and Jay-Z started dealing together in 1988.

think you're coming of age. It's everywhere. The smell, the stench is in the hallway."[3] But he relished the sense of empowerment the crack epidemic gave him too. "People had lost their sense of pride... The desperation... Before, when our elders told us something, you had to listen. But now we were in power because the people who were supposed to be our support system were on crack, and they was telling us, 'I'll do anything to get it.' So we were like elders in the village, with a whole community on drugs. There was no one to police us. And we were out of control."[4]

"No one aspires to be a drug dealer," he'd tell Oprah Winfrey decades later, as the pair sat on the doorsteps of Marcy. "You don't want to bring trouble to your mother's door, even though that's what you're doing. You aspire to the lifestyle you see around you. You see the green BMW, the prettiest car you've ever seen. You see the trappings of drug dealing, and it draws you in. In my mind [I] wasn't risking a lot. You think, 'If I'm living like this, I'll risk anything to get more. What's the worst that could happen?'"[5]

The worst that could happen? He'd get to see that, all right. Throughout his years of hustling he'd see the windows of his mother's house smashed with bullets as a warning to curtail his dealings, see close friends die and almost take three bullets himself, get turned on by supposed colleagues, go broke and get rich, become insanely paranoid and overarchingly confident. Yet he never smoked crack himself (Rule Number One of the Hustler's Handbook), and always tried to do his work with the same integrity he'd later bring to a whole empire of businesses. He had to – after all, the streets had their own sense of justice. If you went back on your word or crossed someone, there was no courtroom to decide your fate, just the wronged man's barrel. A smart kid with a knack for survival, Jay-Z quickly learned the art and value of loyalty.

Even if Jay-Z's claims to being a child hustler are to be believed, it's certain he was pretty small fry in the game until DeHaven lured him to Trenton, New Jersey in his mid-teens. DeHaven had moved there to live with his aunt and become a star of the high school's basketball team but instead turned his hand to more nefarious games. He saw an opening in the New Jersey cocaine world for a couple of kids with ambition, and invited Jay-Z to come visit him to be given the low-down by DeHaven's supplier. The meeting felt like stepping into *Scarface*: the supplier sat the pair of them down and stressed that the successful hustler had to be watchful, aware and above all disciplined. Then he set them up with a supply and sent them out on the street. How watchful and aware the supplier himself would be was questionable; his career in drugs would ultimately end strapped to a chair with his own severed testicles rammed down his throat.

Such possibilities rattled Jay-Z and DeHaven, but didn't scare them off. After a stint of making regular train journeys to Trenton from Marcy posing as DeHaven's brother, Jay-Z dropped out of Westinghouse school and moved in with DeHaven's family full time, and in a New Jersey dead-end street they set up their store, dealing by night and attending Trenton High School by day, just to show off their escalating wealth to the girls there, although Jay-Z soon bored of the school and dropped out, never to graduate from high school. Though Jay-Z was well known for refusing to discount his wares by a cent for anyone, they undercut the other local crews on price and quickly grew a loyal clientele of local users and out-of-towners cruising for drugs, the first white faces Jay-Z had ever come into direct contact with.

The nights were long on the streets, the dangers many and the winters bitter.* But with their canny business sense the rewards flowed in. Jay-Z made regular drives back to Marcy to give his family money to survive – his mother could never approve of his new direction, but could also never turn away food or money in their hardest times or question him too deeply on how he could afford his shiny new jewellery. Though stricter with his sisters, she let Jay learn his own lessons, didn't ask too many questions, knew he was going to plot out his own path no matter how she tried to guide him. Jay was naturally a forthright soul. And he loved her all the more for the long leash.

---

* In his future raps, Jay-Z would regularly align the image of winter with hardship and dejection.

They worked hard, pursuing their big time dream to grow from dealing out grams to shifting ounces then kilos, and fought hard for their slice of the New Jersey action. The local crews dealing down in the parks didn't like the drop in street price Jay-Z and DeHaven had forced onto their block; one day they circled the pair in the local park to have it out, guns drawn, a real Mexican stand-off scene. Jay and DeHaven stood their ground, kept their price; the local crews backed down. They'd earned the sort of respect that makes a hustler the big money.

They started making decent money, Jay-Z got a girl, the game was treating them pretty fine. Then, one hazy Trenton afternoon, the game taught Jay-Z his first major lesson, and one that'd stay with him forever.

How to come back fighting.

A hand on his shoulder, his arm crooked in the small of his back, watched by a crowd of students and teachers, Jay-Z ducked into the back of his first police car. Such a stupid way to get caught, too – he'd literally walked right into it. He'd just snuck through the gates of Trenton High School to go pay DeHaven a visit between classes one afternoon. How was he to know he'd run into the school security and get dragged aside for trespassing? The charge turned criminal, though, once security searched him, found the bags of class As he was carrying secreted about his person and called in the New Jersey Police Department. Though the crime seemed far less serious to him than shooting his brother, the implications could be devastating. But at least to be ushered firmly but calmly into the back of a cruiser was no doubt a relief; he'd seen men get shot dead for less.

With no prior offences, no criminal record and no previous arrests, he wasn't held for long, released within hours on ROR.[*] But the confiscation of his entire stash was a major blow. He owed the proceeds from selling it to his supplier, and needed to make up the shortfall fast. He hotfoot it back to Marcy, called in a debt from a projects dealer and hit the streets for three days solid, day and night, Jay-Z running the pick-

---

[*] Released On Recognizance; the release of a perpetrator on the acknowledgement that they owe a debt to the state, in Jay-Z's case to stop hustling.

ups from the supplier and the local guy distributing on the streets. They got by on cookies and sandwiches. After 60 hours on the streets with no rest, Jay-Z drove back to Trenton to settle his debt, determined never to find himself stuck that deep again. Come downpour or drought*, he'd stay on top of his business.

Though Jay-Z had put rapping to one side as he concentrated on building up his hustling career, it was never far from his mind. The pair and their growing crew filled the cold nights arguing over the merits of their rapping heroes – Drake versus Cole, Kane versus Rakim, LL Cool J versus Run-D.M.C. – and Jay had started to develop a method of memorising his rhymes as he thought of them, boxing them into a secure corner of his brain, since he had no time or means to write them down while hustling.

On his long drives back down the I-95 to Marcy to visit and provide for his family, he'd listen to Rakim for his street poetry, Beastie Boys to admire their cross-cultural appeal, or Slick Rick; in Slick's 1988 debut album *The Great Adventures Of Slick Rick* he discovered an emotional outlet that he hadn't heard in rap before, and started incorporating more moving elements into his own rhymes. Each trip back to Marcy he'd hit Clark Kent's studio to record some verses before heading out to rap at an open mic show, or hook up with Jaz-O to write together over Cokes and ice cream – in 1986 they dropped their first joint 12-inch, the now lost cut 'HP Gets Busy'. All the while his lyrics became ever more concerned with the dangers and rewards of his life on the streets.

And it wouldn't be long before rap came round to his way of thinking.

By 1988, the gangstas had invaded. Ice-T's *Rhyme Pays* and *Power* albums had emerged from the LA ghetto laced with pimp fantasies, gun crime and drug deals used as a metaphor for musical highs. N.W.A.'s *Straight Outta Compton* went even further, redefining rap's boundaries

---

* Droughts are regular pitfalls in the hustling world, when the supply of drugs runs dry for a period, but the addicts keep needing their fix; Jay-Z took measures to ensure he always had a solid supply coming in.

with its relentless violence, unflinching depictions of South Central LA crackhouse culture, punchy profanities and anti-police rhetoric. The FBI, ignoring the real anger and concerns about police corruption and brutality Ice Cube had written about in 'Fuck Tha Police', sent N.W.A. warning letters; radio stations refused to play gangsta tracks; churches organised album burnings on a scale not seen since Lennon declared The Beatles bigger than Jesus. The confrontation escalated, the controversy took hold, the sales skyrocketed.

On the East Coast, where traditionally acts like Run-D.M.C. had avoided criminality in their songs in favour of street-life portraits and a healthy dose of self-aggrandisement, Public Enemy and Boogie Down Productions (the group moniker for KRS-One) brought political tub-thumping and social conscience to this new wave of confrontation rap. Where Boogie Down Productions' 1987 debut album *Criminal Minded* had found KRS-One and Scott La Rock on the sleeve surrounded by firearms and ammunition, Scott's murder that same year prompted KRS-One to dedicate the second album, *By All Means Necessary*, to tackling issues such as safe sex, government corruption, CIA drug trafficking and hip-hop violence. Public Enemy, meanwhile, had released their seminal albums *Yo! Bum Rush The Show* and *It Takes A Nation Of Millions To Hold Us Back*, both firebombs of black fury and power-fighting politics, from 'Don't Believe The Hype' and 'Public Enemy No. 1' to the Beastie Boys-aping 'Party For Your Right To Fight'.

In early summer 1988, into this turbulent bear pit of aggression and controversy, dropped a disc called *Long Live The Kane*, the debut album from Big Daddy Kane. Kane was a flamboyant Brooklyn character, the biggest name in the borough, a showman boasting a pre-MC Hammer wedge-fro and a love of costumery – the album sleeve pictured him as a Roman emperor waited on by a bevy of handmaidens. His first album was a grand achievement, the Marley Marl production adroitly offsetting his suave wordplay and skip-rope delivery on tracks like 'Ain't No Half Steppin'' to produce an influential sound on the late Eighties rap scene. For all his mistrust of the rap scene, Jay-Z admired Kane for his cockiness and flow.

And, crucially, Jay-Z had an in.

Fresh Gordon, at whose place Jay had first impressed Clark Kent so much, had started producing more acts than just Jaz-O, having had some mainstream success with Salt-N-Pepa's hit 'Push It'. The mix-tapes he put together and distributed across the city were the talk of New York and a major source of hype and new talent. When the opportunity to produce a track with Big Daddy Kane came up, Fresh invited Jaz-O – by now a hotly tipped name on the scene – to rap on the track, and Jaz-O suggested Jay-Z for a spot too. It was Jay's first appearance on a publicly circulated 'release'*, and it hit like a meteorite. Not just New York but the whole East Coast was buzzing with the desire to know who was the fast-stepping punk spewing the verse prior to Kane's. Suddenly, the Jay-Z name started to drop jaws outside of Marcy. Not that he was too interested. He was making good money hustling; why would he change his life's direction when all the rappers he knew who had record deals had signed on the line in return for a car?

"We'd go to events where rappers were performing and we'd all pull up in these beautiful BMWs and the rappers would have Turtle Tops," Jay-Z said. "We'd be like, 'Aren't you supposed to be rich, you're a famous performer, why you in a tight white van with 17 people?'"

But Jay was about to have his eyes properly opened to the potential rewards of the rap game.

Late in 1988, Jaz-O called Jay in New Jersey to tell him he'd been signed. Not for a car, for half a million dollars. The deal, with EMI Records in the UK, was huge for the era, and came with some serious perks. The label were flying him to London to record his debut album with producer Brian 'Chuck' New and a fresh young buck called Irv 'Gotti'

---

* There is some confusion as to which track Jay-Z was actually on – in *Decoded* he recalls being impressed by Kane rapping the line "Put a quarter in your ass/Cause you played yourself" in the verse after his, but this line appears in Kane's collaboration with the Juice Crew posse on 1988's 'The Symphony Part 1', on which no note is made of Jay-Z or Jaz-O appearing. Perhaps it was an earlier take on the track, or Fresh was recording more than one Kane track that day.

Lorenzo.* And Jaz could take a posse with him to keep him company and rap on his record. And that meant Jay-Z.

Jay-Z looked around at his wintry New Jersey patch, then looked past it to a broad new territory. London. He'd barely ever been out of the five boroughs, bar the odd jaunt to Vegas to celebrate a boom in profits; now he was being flown off to a whole other continent. Suddenly rapping had promise, glamour, money to be made. His crew mocked him for his excitement, stuck to their accepted view that rappers were just slaves and whores for white major-label fat cats, and he had his concerns. He spent a week laying the groundwork for his return, strongly suspecting this foray into music would ultimately come to nothing and he'd land from this fanciful flight straight back on the street corner. But Jay's mind was changing, his horizons widening. He'd go to London and check out how the hip-hop high life fitted.

It fitted just fine. After a six-hour flight east, Jay-Z found himself in a limo in London on the way to the New Year's Eve launch party of Jaz-O's debut album *Word To The Jaz*, barely turned 19, gawping at a whole new city's worth of bright lights. Housed in a plush flat in fashionable Notting Hill, he tagged along as De La Soul cohort MC Monie Love showed Jaz-O (under his new nom de plume The Jaz) around the city's club scene and soaked in the luxury lifestyle, half a world away from the freezing stoops and corners of New Jersey. He wasn't so dazzled that he couldn't see the downsides, though; Jaz had insisted he come along on an equal footing and gave him his first big break rapping a verse on the potential single 'Hawaiian Sophie', notable for its unique use of a ukelele in a rap song, but Jay did little else creatively on the album, felt underused and disappointed that the finished album sounded so little improved from the demos, at such huge cost.

Plus, the meetings Jay attended in Jaz's trail, his first dealings with the music industry, left him with a sour taste. The enthusiasm of the execs seemed so shallow, the integrity of the business as flimsy and fleeting as a crack high; there were scales in the label's eyes. He had less trust for

---

* The man who'd eventually go on to found Murder Inc.

26

this world than for his hustling roots – at least on the streets your word had to mean something, or it might get you killed.

The promo video for 'Hawaiian Sophie' wasn't to be Jay-Z's most extravagant cinematic experience. Dressed in leis and Hawaiian shirts on a soundstage drenched in sand, palm trees, a crashed cardboard airplane and – incongruously – a fire hydrant, or wandering around in front of a green screen that would eventually be replaced with images of airplanes arriving in Hawaii and flapping palm leaves, Jaz-O and Jay-Z treated the whole experience with the comic nonchalance this hilariously literal take on Jaz's song about meeting a Hawaiian girl on holiday and running up against her gigantic boyfriend demanded. Pouting casual lines as a bit-part sidekick, Jay-Z's head swept regularly across the front of the screen like an MTV graphic; at one point he was sent flying around the set on strings, or simply left hanging in the background of the shot for comedy effect, and his most memorable scene consisted of arguing with a beach chef over a roasting pig. An inauspicious introduction to the global viewing public indeed; it's unlikely Jay-Z is proud to remember being involved in such a comic-strip slice of hip-hop cheese.

Neither, in fact, would EMI. On its 1989 release the single flopped, as did its parent album. Undeterred, The Jaz recorded 1990's *To Your Soul*, which also featured Jay-Z, in a more prominent role. 'The Originators' featured both Jaz and Jay-Z demonstrating Jay's hyper-speed tongue-twisting rapping style over a jazzy Sugarhill trumpet groove, the words tumbling in breathtaking torrents and dotted with stuttered double words like "miggeda-more" and "siggeda-said" and perfectly timed repetitions: "I'm breaking and breaking and breaking your tongue." Jay-Z's verse acknowledges that the listener would be dazed and amazed by the technique – "It might take a couple of takes for you to clarify/ Don't lie, you coulda never got in on the first try… jaws stuck on the floor/These lyrics I pour" – before the pair declare "We are the thiggita-thiggita-thiggita-the originators" as if stamping their trademark and copyright on the style right there. Another green screen video of the couple rapping the tune superimposed over images of a funk backing band and Jaz in traditional Islamic dress exposed the real star of the song; a youthful Jay-Z seemed far more energised, charismatic and comfortable on the screen than his rather wooden mentor. It was a clip that would cause quite a stir in the hip-hop community; the Jay-Z buzz intensified.

The Jaz buzz, on the other hand, fluttered and died. With his second album failing to improve on the sales of his first, EMI dropped him, but not before sneakily trying to sign Jay-Z away from under his nose, realising where the real money was in the Jaz-O crew. Jay-Z, though, could see where the real honour lay, and it was in hustling rather than the deceitful world of music.

"The same record label tried to sign me," he said, "but Jaz was the one who'd brought me in, and I felt that signing wouldn't be loyal to him. So I told them no. I didn't want to be involved with those record guys. They weren't stand-up people."[6]

Instead, with an eye on Brooklyn credibility, Jay-Z had begun to ease his way into Kane's crew. In 1989, while Jaz's brief EMI career was stalling hard, the usually quiet Jay talked his way onto Big Daddy Kane's tour bus at a local show, using his kudos with Kane from the Fresh Gordon mix-tape the previous year. Kane remembered him, heard him rap and, naturally impressed, gave the kid a job. He could be a stop-gap guy, filling in rhymes whenever Kane had to leave the stage to change his costume, which was surprisingly often. Kane introduced him to his fellow back-up rappers on the tour: MC Serch, Queen Latifah and another fresh-faced young kid by the name of Tupac Shakur. Little could the cocky Kane have conceived that this gaggle of wannabe cameo kids he'd hired for zero cash was actually one of the greatest hip-hop collectives ever assembled, and would ultimately outshine him like a star beside a light bulb.

For four months, Jay-Z rode the Kane bus, sleeping on the floor between the bunks and nightly stealing the stage. No money, but Kane paid him in onstage respect – his entrance cue was the moment Kane would stop a track midway through, tell the DJ to cue up 'Spread Love' by Take 6 and invite Jay on to freestyle, showcasing his turbo-flow technique, a super-fast avalanche of rhymes and double meanings.

Every room exploded; Jay-Z swiftly became a blow-up hit of the show. Kane began talking about signing him to a label he was considering starting up, even though talk of contracts and advances made Jay-Z twitchy. He learned many things from watching Kane on tour in 1989: the art of showmanship, the value of the unexpected dance routine, and crowd-revving techniques such as killing one number to instantly slam on a hotter track. But he also had his suspicion that hustling was way more lucrative than rapping, backed up by the hard experience of survival on the road. After four months without the aid of a regular income from dealing, MC Serch recalls seeing Jay begging money from Kane to buy a burger. He admired a guy like MC Hammer for crossing over to the mainstream and cashing in big, even if he did it by selling out his credibility and playing on a foolish, ridiculous image. But that was still a million miles away from the relentless slog of rapping on the road.

No, if he was ever going to make it as a rapper, he'd need some serious financial backing. And that meant hustling for his life.

As the Nineties drew on, Jay-Z's two tandem empires grew. On the hustling side, he and DeHaven stepped up from pushing grams to moving serious weight. Growing their operation to include girls who'd help them scout out potential new markets out of town[*], they became cocaine frontiersmen, avoiding the big business and violence of cities like Washington in favour of starting operations in smaller towns in Maryland and Virginia, shifting the powder there in bulk to distribute via a network of pushers they themselves created.

"Everything that has ever happened has to do with a girl," Jay told journalist and friend Dream Hampton in 1998. "You meet somebody and befriend her. You need her and the most thorough nigga in town. Because girls yap, she'll tell you who that is, who has money. You meet him; you've got something for him – better prices. He'll bring everybody else in line. [There'll be] a lot of little fires. But in small towns you ain't

---

[*] Plus additional right-hand men to cover for DeHaven when he'd occasionally end up in jail for short spells.

wildin' out. You go to jail. This is like a Commonwealth; they'll lock you up for cursing. It takes a special nigga to do a small town. Anybody can do DC. You strong-arm DC. Ya'll can shoot at each other every weekend."[7]

They could ramp up the price now they were outside the influence of the NYC drug lords like Brooklyn's Calvin Klein or Fat Cat, who 'owned' Queens, and shifting their product emphasis to crack made them four times as much profit. Jay put in a lot of freeway hours, the produce hidden in a secret compartment in the roof of his car, sticking to the limits, dodging Highway Patrol. One day he wouldn't be so lucky, flagged down with enough cocaine above his head to bury him. How the cop never found the drugs, despite calling in a dog unit, would eventually become the stuff of hip-hop legend.

As money ceased to be an issue for Jay-Z – associates from the time estimate he was shifting kilos worth around $12,000 every week – so his musical ambitions were sidelined. Around the age of 20 he'd make sporadic and half-hearted attempts to shift from dealing to the music business, making the odd demo but then forgetting about rap for six months at a time when nobody bit. When he was heading a fleet of Lexuses touring Marcy to drop off cash for his mother and family (money he told her came from shows, even though, as he'd admit in 'December 4th', "nobody paid Jaz wack ass"), feeling the dead weight of hardship lifting from his shoulders (but never *quite* disappearing for good), why should he aspire to anything else? And particularly something so tough to break into?

Still, from closer to the top, the drug game was starting to get him down. The constant danger of death or arrest, the paranoia of every deal, the distrust, the need to stay constantly alert and to predict and last out those damned droughts, the endless nights, it was all so stressful and exhausting. He started to question his own humanity and decency every first and fourteenth of the month, when the welfare cheques got paid and the crackheads flocked to his door, their eyes full of desperation and captivity.

When his operation in Maryland started to look hairy he got out, just before the police busts and nightclub gang gunplay tore the whole thing down, and it set him to thinking. He couldn't stay this big in the hustling world long term and get out alive.

Besides, he just couldn't let rap go; it was his blood. And his name in the battle circuit just wouldn't die. He collaborated with a Californian producer called Three-1-Zero and won major attention from the hip-hop labels when he came out admirably against celebrated rapper Zai in a battle. Jay-Z was the hottest property in Brooklyn rap who didn't care much that he was. In fact, when Clark Kent was hired as an A&R scout for Atlantic Records in 1992, Jay-Z initially shunned his insistent invitations to sign with Atlantic, and claimed he was too busy in Virginia to guest on a remix he was putting together for rap act Troop.* But Kent wouldn't take a disinterested silence for an answer.

"As soon as I got a job in the music business," said Kent, "the first person I wanted to sign was Jay-Z because I just thought he was the best. He was saying everything. He was doing quick flows, regular flows… His rhymes were just better than everybody else's. Like head and shoulders above. When he rhymed with Kane, who I totally respect, Kane changed his style after he met Jay-Z. That doesn't happen unless you're going 'oh shit, this guy is incredible'… So I wanted to sign that guy… The one thing that made me want to sign him even more was that he didn't give a damn about it. I was like 'I just have to do this just because he doesn't care'. He had too much paper to care, and he thought that rappers were clowns. They were trying to be him."[8]

Kent kept pushing, pleading with Jay to come down to his studio in Manhattan and make demos for him, desperate to spread Jay's name by putting him on every record that came his way. Eventually, later in 1992, Jay relented, agreeing to lay down some vocals on a Clark Kent supermix of a track called 'She's Playing Hard To Get' by Hi-Five, alongside a highly respected rapper and producer called Ski from the Bronx-based Original Flavor duo, who'd released their celebrated debut *This Is How It Is* that same year. Hi-Five were a Texan R&B five-piece bedecked, on the sleeve of the original track, in garish technicolour suits and pencil moustaches like a nightmarish psychedelic Commodores,

---

* Kent had had success with a remix for Troop's 1989 hit 'Spread My Wings'.

so it's no wonder Jay-Z stole the show. Where the smooth Hi-Five boyband trills from the original clashed with Kent's crunchy new beats, Jay's confident and assured verse about being messed around by a girl who clearly likes him gelled perfectly, as though Jay's was the original track and Hi-Five had been incongruously sampled on top. "The Jay [version of the remix] was the one that everybody took to," Kent recalled. "The remix was good and Jay was going crazy on the record."[9]

Slowly, Kent chipped away at Jay-Z's defences. But he needed a more agreeable front for the Jay-Z business, a go-between who might help talk him round.

And he knew just the man.

Chapter Three

Roc The Block

The brash guy from Harlem, man could he talk. Bald-shaved and thickset in his swivel chair, he could only have been 23, maybe 24, and shorter than Jay-Z, but he dominated Clark Kent's office with the motor-mouth confidence of an oligarch of industry. Imposing and loud, the Harlem player boasted wildly about the various Harlem club nights he filled by giving away champagne to girls on entry, and the rap acts he managed and in two cases had closed deals for.* He had the front of a Manhattan mafia tough but clearly a canny business brain. In his rare pauses for breath, the two men faced each other across the afternoon sun glare of the meeting room, part in admiration of the other's chutzpah, part as suspicious and wary as rival gladiators. Though Kent had insisted they'd be a perfect business partnership, at first meeting, the overbearing Damon Dash and the retiring Jay-Z seemed like the oddest of hip-hop couples.

For his part, Dash wasn't so sure about Jay-Z that first day either. How could a kid from Brooklyn be as good as Kent said he was, when

* Some of them put under his nose by Kent for a cut of his fee when Kent, in turn, signed them to Atlantic.

there were nothing but thugs and gangbangers in Brooklyn? But this guy had the right sneakers on – box-fresh Nikes – so he couldn't be too dangerous. And once Jay had rapped for him, right there in the office, Dash, like every man with a keen eye for stardom before him, knew this was an artist he had to work with.

The pair shook on one of the most legendary partnerships in hip-hop history that same day.

Inevitably, Kent was right. Jay-Z was incredibly talented, but he lacked the determination and forceful personality that would get him a worthy deal in a music industry swarming with curs and cut-throats. And Dash had the business bullishness needed to break an act big, but needed the greatest rapper on the planet to back up his barks. Polar opposites in personality, but in partnership terms they obliterated each other's negatives.

Not one to attack any enterprise with anything but his biggest guns, Dash, as Jay-Z's new business partner and quasi-manager, set him to work. Between the joint efforts of Kent and Dash, in 1993 Jay-Z agreed to appear on an original track, 'Can I Get Open', by an act Dash was managing called Original Flavor, a street rap number that was by far a better fit for Jay than the Hi-Five remix. Introduced with the understated line from Ski – "You want a fly style Jay's about to show it" – he cut an imposing figure across 'Can I Get Open'. Not just in the video, where, now fully an adult with a certain bulk and build, he towered over Ski and his partner Suave Lover, but lyrically too. His verse burst over the track's closing half full of bravado and self-glory, detailing his dominance in the rap battle arena: "I'm shredding the track, I'm burning you back-back, like *Backdraft*." As his verse also featured the lines "who running the crack down" and "go get your gun", it was also the first publicly available example of Jay-Z delving into underworld themes that would come to dominate his early work.

Jay-Z's trademark quickstep wordplay and stammer-raps also lit up 'Many Styles' from Original Flavor's second album *Beyond Flavor*, referencing little-known horror sequel *The Rage: Carrie 2* in his flurry of immodesty about his rapping virtuosity. His slots on *Beyond Flavor* made more waves and, liking the acclaim, Jay allowed Kent to convince him to record more, working with Kent's own partner in his 3-D production company: Sauce Money.

Kent remembers the session well, for one telling moment. After Jay-Z had frittered away a few hours in the studio lounge, telling jokes and killing expensive studio time, the label executive who'd booked the session urged him to get on with laying down his vocal, concerned that after three wasted hours, Jay hadn't even heard the beat for the track, let alone written his verse. Humouring him, Jay took himself to one side, began muttering to himself, then grabbed a notepad and a pen and seemed to be scribbling frantically. Five minutes later, nodding, he placed the pad on a table, hit the mic and laid down an impeccable verse, word perfect, inspired.

Keen to capture his own little slice of the magic, Kent peeked at the notepad. It was completely blank. Ever since he built the corner of his brain where he kept his rhymes safe during the long winter hustling nights, Jay-Z never wrote down another rhyme.

Although the track Jay recorded with Sauce was never released, it further sparked his interest in making his own records. He even went as far as to invite another rising NYC rapper called Nas to work with him on a track; that Nas declined, busy working on his own highly respected 1994 debut *Illmatic*, didn't turn Jay against him, but it would be remembered.

Instead, Jay-Z hopped back on the Big Daddy Kane bandwagon. Kane was growing in sales and respect, and had kept Jay-Z on as his hype man – a role in a hip-hop show that means geeing up a crowd with call and response shouts, ramping up anticipation for the star rapper's appearance and filling in words when they have to take a breath.* Now Kane gave his protégé his big break. Alongside the Wu-Tang Clan's Ol' Dirty Bastard, a Wu-Tang affiliated kid called Shyheim, Scoob Lover and Kent's associate Sauce Money, Kane asked

---

* Although Jay-Z didn't fit this role precisely, he filled in sections of the show when Kane had to be offstage.

Jay to rap on a posse cut* called 'Show & Prove', recorded in 1993 but released almost a year later in September 1994. After Scoob's characteristically nasal verse full of comedy British accents, Sauce's sassy segment, and Shyheim spitting rhymes with a deftness and maturity beyond his (then) 15 years, Kane himself warmed up for Jay-Z's verse. Over a funk-heavy backing producer DJ Premier had forged from a sample of Grover Washington Jr's 'Black Frest', Jay opened up his lyrical range to take in a winking wit – "I'm dope like poppy seed" he spat at his usual breakneck pace, between making references to being "well endowed" (both in talent and trouser, went the implication) and unveiling the first of several alternative nicknames: "Ain't no eatin' me up/You fast fuckin' with Jigga/I'm like Prince jeans/I bring the ass out a nigga."

Though 'Show & Prove' wouldn't hit the streets for almost a year, word of Jay's innovative speed-rapping technique was spreading beyond Brooklyn, beyond New York and into the great wide open. And Jay-Z, particularly with Dash as his forceful business arm, was not a man to let an opportunity slip by. Problem was, fame and hustling mix badly. Jay had built himself a mini-empire in the hustling world by taking on Gigante's deceptive mantle, playing the quiet, humble and unflashy street kid to disguise his increasing standing in the drug world. "I was getting more money than most of the cats – than *all* of the cats I was with," he'd later claim.[1] So the more well known he became, the more dangerous it made his position as a big-time hustler. Nothing spooks a drug linchpin more than publicity.

But hustling was a life Jay was increasingly disillusioned with. Now he was seeing the likes of Ice Cube, N.W.A., Dr. Dre and Snoop Dogg making millions on the West Coast scene, his old schoolmate Notorious B.I.G. putting East Coast rap on a similar footing by hitting

---

* A term used to describe a song on which four or more rappers take turns to rap a verse. Many early hip-hop tunes took this form in order for artists to give publicity and exposure to their friends.

2 million sales of his (ironically presciently titled) debut album *Ready To Die* and Russell Simmons becoming a music mogul as CEO of Def Jam; rapping was starting to look potentially even more lucrative than shifting weight, and without the constant fear and anxiety, the forever looking over your shoulder, the threat in every hook-up, the knowledge that any random john might be undercover NYPD. The art form itself was inspiring him more too: rappers such as Too Short from California were turning him on to a more relaxed flow, and he began to work on lessening the pace of his rhymes, allowing the listener to understand his words rather than filling every inch of tape with avalanches of symbolism and significance. Plus, Kent was pushing him constantly to give up the hustling life and concentrate on developing his rap career.

The transition looked tough. He'd become addicted to the hustling lifestyle, no longer dealing solely to provide for his family but for the jewels, the wheels, the scents of it.

"In the beginning it's, 'I gotta take care of my family'," he'd tell *Vibe* magazine. "But you can't keep saying that, because in your first month, you've changed their whole situation around. Once you start living The Life it's just no stopping… It's like making the money, the sound of the money machines clicking – for some people the sensation of the coke under their nails, like dirt for construction workers – the constant hustle, everything from the living to the actual work. It's completely addictive."[2]

The downsides were becoming more and more apparent, though. His friends and associates were ending up dead or in jail. His community was disintegrating because of the effects of the drug he was distributing, girls he'd once considered cute were looking wrecked and broken on his product. For a long time he was blind to the fact that he was part of the cause. "The light slowly came on. I was like, 'This life has no good ending'… I started to realise that I couldn't be successful [in music] until I let the street life go. That was a leap of faith for me. I said, 'I have to give this everything.'"[3]

His mother had told him to get out of the game, but it wasn't just her words that whizzed in warning past his ear.

It was the bullets too.

Three bullets, fired from a TEC-9 machine gun at Jay-Z's body from no more than 10 feet away, during an ambush by an old childhood friend, some time in 1994. "That's why he got so close," says Jay. "I didn't see it coming. It was over some stupid shit, one of his houses in Trenton."[4] The muzzle flamed; Jay ran for his life; the gun jammed after only three shots were fired. That Jay-Z didn't die that day he credits to "Divine intervention, and nobody knowing how to shoot... It was one situation, three shots... no one really practises shooting a TEC-9 machine gun, right? And when you're a kid, with little bony arms – no wonder nobody could aim..."[5]

Flashbacks: Benny dropping to a dank floor, the pain and betrayal in his brother's eyes. Furious, shaken and pumping with the chemicals of death, Jay-Z lost control and ran to find a gun. A deep-hidden demon was guiding him now: instinctive retribution. "You want to shoot back. Well, maybe not everyone, but I did. I was angry."[6]

It was sheer luck that the situation didn't escalate that night, and both DeHaven and Jaz-O claim to have used their most diplomatic street skills to stop Jay-Z's assailants from hunting him down and finishing the job. "We saw each other a couple weeks later at the parole office," Jay says, "no guns allowed. We laughed about it."[7]

"It's like there was some rogue angel watching over us,"[8] Jay would say about that incident and the dozens of times he escaped arrest, but he knew that angel was on a clock. For Hova The Hustler, it was the final straw. The attack, and the news that his Virginian girlfriend of five years – the girl who'd kept him company on so many NYC trips and eased his mind over the possibility he'd be used and tossed away by the music industry just as Jaz-O had been – had suffered a miscarriage, made Jay re-evaluate what he wanted out of life, and a swift and inauspicious death by gunfire wasn't top of the list. Though he'd continue hustling for another year, he set about easing himself out of the streets and threw himself wholesale into rapping, albeit with the mindset that he'd be nobody's 'employee'; he was boss on the streets, he'd be boss in hip-hop too. His new purpose, his new future, was mapped out solidly in his mind.

His 99 problems were instantly reduced to one. All he needed was for Dash to get him signed.

"Rap right now?"

Dash looked over at him, nodding confidently. A few rhymes, he seemed to be implying, and the deal was all but inked.

"Right now?"

Jay-Z sighed deeply. Right now? Sure he could do it; he could rap anywhere, anytime, and always dominate any room. But right now he was exhausted, not just from all these endless label meetings but from a long drive to this NYC label office from Virginia, where a big, stress-inducing deal was going through that very second. And here was some mid-level A&R executive punk for some godforsaken hip-hop label, a guy by the name of Ruben Rodriguez, asking him to stand up and pump out some rhymes. Right now.

Rodriguez glanced at him expectantly. In his eyes Jay saw petty power being wielded, a man testing to see how high he'd jump when commanded. And Jay was nobody's performing monkey.

"No, man..." Jay-Z rose from his seat and walked out of the building.

When he caught up with him in the corridor, Dash would have been understanding of Jay feeling disrespected by Rodriguez's request and reluctant to jump hoops at the drop of a hat, but also tight-lipped and frustrated. They were down to very few options, and a bit of tagging along back there might have been enough to close the deal. Dash was far more hot-headed than Jay-Z about such things: Jay still wasn't life-or-death concerned about rapping – he still had another major option to fall back on. But Damon saw Jay-Z as his big break, and was starting to take the label rejections personally. Def Jam, Columbia, Uptown, no one was biting. Every time negotiations got underway for even a one-single deal with a major label, eventually the plans would fall apart – they were all impressed by his style and were used to thug life violence and guns and drug dealing references in the wake of N.W.A., but Jay-Z baffled them with the new forms of slang and impenetrable speed raps in his rhymes, and the escalation in the rivalry between the East and West

Coast acts in the rap scene was putting labels off signing acts that might add fuel to the fire. For all the credibility Jay had gained from word of Kane's 'Show & Prove', even Clark Kent and his rampant enthusiasm for the kid hadn't been enough to convince his bosses at Atlantic to sign him.

"I brought [Jay-Z to Atlantic Records]," said Kent. "Because I worked there as an A&R, I'm going to say that they didn't have enough budget [to sign him] because enough signings had happened at that precise moment, so maybe that's why... It's not like [just] one label that I worked for let him slide by him. [Atlantic] slid by him for so long that I quit and went to work for another company and they slid by him for so long, so that I was like, 'We've just got to put out our own shit.'"[9]

Whether it was Kent's suggestion or the result of observing the rise of Russell Simmons and reading books such as *Hit Men: Power Brokers And Fast Money Inside The Music Business* by Frederic Dannen, which exposed the underhand dealings within several major labels in the Seventies and Eighties and the sly methods major label recording contracts employ to rip off and tie down the artist, but the idea of being their own bosses struck an obvious chord with Jay-Z and Dash. In an unfamiliar world full of predators, they needed to be in the control of people they could trust. And the only people they could trust were each other.

Dash called in a money man associate and old school friend of his from the Bronx called Kareem Burke, nicknamed Biggs, and together they invented a company name – Roc-A-Fella, at once an attempt at gaining reflected glory from the first US billionaire John D. Rockefeller and displaying their boundless financial ambitions, and a potshot at the drug laws introduced by Nelson Rockefeller in 1973, under which the selling of two ounces of cocaine would get the perpetrator a 15-year stretch, minimum. The set-up agreed was that Jay-Z was the artist, Dash the day-to-day manager of the project and Burke the guy who (as *Vibe* would later describe him) acted as a "barometer of the streets".

Roc-A-Fella: the name was perfect, full of money, rebellion and narcotics, grit clashing with glamour. Now they needed a track to sell under it.

'Show & Prove' hit the streets in September 1994 and found Jay-Z

– credited as J.Z. on its parent album *Daddy's Home* – well reviewed, gaining his first national plaudits from AllMusic's critic John Bush. It was the sort of publicity Jay, Burke and Dash were keen to build on, so they hit Kent's personal basement studio and laid down a track entitled 'Can't Get With That'* with Kent producing the classic piano-led backing track. As the first track to name-drop Roc-A-Fella as a concept, it was the obvious choice for an introductory 12-inch – "Our Roc-A-Fella never sell-a-out" – Jay flips between boasting about his riches (claiming he'd bought a machine to count his cash since "My tongue is tired from lickin' my fingers and countin' up hundreds") and his rhymes: "More than a fluke, I'm regularly wreckin' this joint… One verse and it's a hearse/I played and I slayed yours… The Jigga is back/ You brothers are flat/I'll amaze the way that Jay rap/Now how in the hell did he say that?" It was a line that would've sounded arrogant if the rap itself wasn't so intricate and astounding, particularly a memorable line where Jay raps out the sound of his money machine counting cash. Besides publicising the fledgling brand from the outset – then little more than a smart name for an imagined collective – and dropping shouts to studio onlookers Sauce Money and Jaz-O to prove he was true to his roots, the track also worked as a showcase of Jay-Z's various rapping techniques that might help sell him to labels or investors. From cut one, Jay-Z's mind was on the promotional potential of rap music.

Dash and Burke were equally tuned in, promo-wise. Pooling their and Jay's resources, they found $5,000 to commission a video for 'Can't Get With That' from a young promo director called Abdul Malik Abbott, keen to break into music videos having worked on Spike Lee's movies *Do The Right Thing* and *Mo' Better Blues*. Abdul's video placed a sports/casual Jay-Z in street scenes around Brooklyn and New York City, expertly throwing out his skat-influenced skitter-raps over cuts to games of street dominoes, a half-naked girl listening to the track on headphones and a cameo from Dash draped in girls on the hood of an

---

* A title credited with various spellings depending on your source, including 'Can't Get Wit That' and 'Can't Get Wid Dat'.

expensive car, accompanied by the premonition "Ask this nigga Dash/ Now he don't count cause I'm making him mad rich."*

Now the fledgling Roc-A-Fella crew had a track and a video that showcased Jay as arguably the most imaginative, ground-breaking and original rapper on the East Coast, at least. The video was sent out to New York video shows on the cheap, locally owned ultra-high frequency stations, and the trio printed up copies of the 12-inch themselves to send to major radio DJs and well-respected mix-tape compilers accompanied by bottles of champagne (an old Dash trick from his Harlem club promotions). Though their independent, unknown operation had nothing like the clout with TV, media and radio as the dedicated major label promotion departments, Jay-Z knew full well the potential of building your own empire from scratch.

Their next step was to work out how to go about distributing the records they'd printed. Professional distribution companies were costly, taking a hefty fee or a substantial cut of each sale. Why on earth would a man like Jay-Z, an expert and mastermind of his own specialist form of 'distribution' across the eastern states, want to pay someone else to do a job he'd worked so hard to perfect himself since the age of 13?

No, Roc-A-Fella wouldn't 'distribute' 'Can't Get With That'. They'd *hustle* it.

"A rap record?" The barbers, bartenders and bouncers would say, turning a copy of the 12-inch in their hands quizzically. "You wanna sell a rap record, here?"

Hustling rap, compared with hustling crack, opened up wide new realms of salesmanship, a whole city of potential marketplaces. With the records and tapes stacked in the trunks of Jay-Z's Lexus and Dash's Nissan Pathfinder, the pair pushed them to people having their hair cut, buying their groceries at corner stores or drinking in Brooklyn bars. They sold to anyone, anywhere. By day they'd schmooze record

---

* The video also includes brief shots of someone who looks uncannily like Tupac Shakur.

store owners and local club DJs, hoping to secure spins in nightclubs or slots on shelves; by night they'd park up outside hip-hop clubs, gangsta hang-outs or project street corners, lay out their stall from their trunks and hustle tapes and vinyl all night long using all the same techniques and business growth plans Jay had applied to drug dealing. There was a dedicated street team working the big rap record stores too – Kareem had put together a band of assistants including Gee Roberson, Lenny Santiago and his own brother who went by the rap name Hip-Hop. Every couple of days these eager kids would hit the stores that had agreed to sell the record, dropping off fresh copies and collecting the proceeds from sales. After a round of the stores, in the first weeks, the team would bring in a bundle of notes totalling around $150.

More promotion was clearly needed. Dash decided he had to set Jay-Z a more regular performing schedule to spread his name to the wider club-going community. From being a Marcy celebrity, his name and notoriety as a crusher of battles had started to filter across the five boroughs, but outside New York was an endless country ignorant of his talents. He had to get out there and spit his rhymes directly into America's face.

Dash began booking him his first tour, Ski from Original Flavor sharing the bill and Burke acting as tour manager since, despite Burke also striking an imposing, bulky and hairless figure, he and Jay-Z had struck it off well on first meeting. Jay, Ski and Burke hit the road late in 1994, playing the club gigs Dash had secured along the East Coast, the budget ultra-tight, travelling by van and sharing rooms together. Though Jay-Z knew the highway life well, this was his first time as a travelling artist, and his first major road trip without risking a long-term prison sentence. He threw himself into the experience with a carefree enthusiasm, revelling in the shows, gaining confidence in front of a room of his own, no matter how rammed or how sparsely populated it might be, and treating the jaunt as his taste of the college life he'd missed out on. He might not have been making anywhere near the same amount of money as he was hustling, but rapping was rewarding in so many other ways. In acclaim, in enjoyment, in a new challenge and in an ease of lifestyle he was starting to yearn for more. He began to realise he'd made the right decision to worm his way out of the drug game. Hip-hop was his true calling.

By the time the van rolled back into NYC full of laughter and assurance, 'Can't Get With That' had started to infiltrate the clubs and radio shows, and Jay-Z was itching with the stage bug, a sucker for the spotlight. Eager to raise his profile as 1995 kicked in, he took every chance he could to perform, hitting open mic nights showcasing unsigned artists around Manhattan and wowing crowds with his lyrical quicksteps. If the track's eventual spoken-word intro is to be taken literally, these included rapping new number '22 Two's' at a night called Mad Wednesdays, chasing a wink to A Tribe Called Quest's slothful enquiry 'Can I Kick It?' with a maestro's weaving of words, tumbling – as the title promises – 22 variants on the word 'two' into the first verse alone. It was an early example of Jay's liking for themed raps; though his core stories would come from his soul and his history, he'd couch and engulf them in extended metaphors of sport, politics, family or just such lyrical sleight of hand as '22 Two's'.

When he wasn't grabbing mics at amateur nights, he was taking on any battler who came at him, preferably rising stars of the NYC hip-hop scene, to prove his worth against the best. He'd regularly meet up with DMX on the neutral ground of a Bronx pool hall to battle for two hours straight, standing on the baize. "Jay would battle anybody on sight," says Ski, "go to different places and just battle. He battled DMX, had a battle with Big L, he had a battle with LL Cool J. He did a lot of local shows and every time he did the show, the buzz was getting bigger and bigger because he was the best lyricist that anyone had heard and his stage presence was crazy; everything about him just transcended on stage. The word got out that Jay-Z was coming."[10]

Jay-Z didn't just battle LL Cool J, he *stalked* him. LL was a prime target for a rising New York rapper trying to make a name in a genre with competition and one-upmanship at its heart, where the apprentices are always out to snipe at and usurp the masters. From New York roots, he'd already sold 8 million albums and was the biggest name in New York rap, but with a slick and soulful style that hardcore street rappers like Jay-Z found tough to take seriously. Plus, LL Cool J had gained a reputation as the king of battle rap and was trying to emulate the West Coast gangsta scene on his most recent album *14 Shots To The Dome*. He had a target on his microphone; if Jay-Z could battle and beat LL Cool J, he'd become an instant star. And Jay-Z was virtually unbeatable.

One-time entertainment lawyer Reggie Ossé claims in his blog Combat Jack on Daily Mathematics that Dash and DJ Kent concocted a master plan to get LL Cool J to agree to let their rookie contender have his stab at rap's heavyweight title. "[Dame and Clark] figured if Jay was known as the dude that [killed] LL in battle, record labels would take note and give him that much sought after deal," Ossé wrote. "Dame and Clark had the plan laid out, whenever LL was spotted by either of them, they would page each other and Jay and get him to meet at whatever location LL was. This went on a couple of times. Once contacted, Jay would roll up to the club, bar or whatever venue and lay in the cut, waiting for his opportunity to attack LL in battle. Dame would polly with, then taunt LL about how Jay was nicer than him, was ready to take his spot even. LL's ego would result in him agreeing to go head to head against the young and then unknown challenger. They would take the battle to the parking lot, outside of the venues and away from the crowds. And battle they would."[11]

Ossé claims that not only did the battles take place on numerous occasions, but Jay-Z always won. "Dame and Clark would end up in my office the following day, laughing about how Jay lit that ass up. Every time too. They was a bit sour too, 'cause after each battle, LL would kill the vibe, crush Jay's high by flinging the 'Yo, my next record is dropping next month, uhm, when's yours coming out again, scrap?' line at him. Jay, Dame and Clark didn't like that shit. Not one bit."[12*]

Buzzing from Jay-Z's victories and the positive reception they were getting for 'Can't Get With That', Dash, Burke and Jay-Z knew they had to roll with the momentum. First they pulled in every industry

---

* When Jay-Z would eventually take over the president's position at LL Cool J's label Def Jam, LL would come to believe his career was mishandled under Jay-Z's leadership.

connection to secure Jay some more high-profile guest slots. Hence, Jay lay down a verse for a gritty urban track called 'Da Graveyard' on the 1995 debut album by Big L, *Lifestylez Ov Da Poor & Dangerous*, the laid-back but menacing tenor of the tune forcing him to slow his pace and concentrate on deftness. His verse on 'Da Graveyard', nestled between verses from Microphone Nut and Party Arty of Ghetto Dwellaz, was the most verbally accessible he'd yet recorded but still flush with cleverness: the phrase "pound for pound" becomes the sound of a scratching record and his one speed-rapped line trips by so quickly it almost invents Auto-Tune several decades early. It also set a precedent for his cautionary approach to gang and gun culture in his lyrics: "Fuck a Glock/I step through your neighborhood armed with nothing but a rep."

He also appeared on 'Time To Build', an insistent, intense track from Mic Geronimo's debut album *The Natural* with a chorus that resembled a maniac's swirl of internal voices. Revelling in the broiling tempo and hallucinogenic atmosphere of the music, Jay let loose, rhyming almost every other word, overlapping his poetry in floods of wordplay – "Niggas is moist like Duncan Hines/Choice when I'm voicing my poise/I got poison lines." This wasn't just one of the earliest examples of Jay-Z maturing his style, stepping his technique up to the level that would make his debut album a recognised rap masterpiece, it was also notable for pitting him for the first time on record against the dark, deviant flows of DMX and Ja Rule.

Next, early in 1995, Jay set about recording the follow-up to 'Can't Get With That'. Ski masterfully welded together the track itself, merging samples of Aretha Franklin's 'Oh Baby' and two Soul II Soul songs, 'Back To Life (However Do You Want Me)' and 'Get A Life'. Focusing on the stabbing lounge piano, languid beat, clicks and baritone soul moans, he formed the bedrock of 'In My Lifetime', a track that would go some way to making Jay-Z's name.

From the lyric, though, you'd think he was already made. Dedicated to a lost street soldier by the name of Danny Dan but built around the central tenet of "In my lifetime, I need to see a whole lot of dough", the tune is a virtual love song to money. Verse one sets up the scenario – Jay is a high-level hustler running an organisation that's the envy of the

New York underworld (arguably not far from the truth, by this point). "While other niggas are shooting stupid," he's playing the game smart, reasoning that if he's risking arrest anyway he may as well shift major shipments of drugs to make the most cash as fast as possible. By verse two he's running cars full of drugs around the US, making huge profits and giving his underlings a sense of ambition by showing off his material trappings, his "hundred inch screen" and luxury apartment. In the end he's high-rolling around Vegas, making the first of many name-drops of Cristal champagne* and wowing the ladies. The dice always fall his way, this money-making master of every game.

'In My Lifetime' was a pivotal recording for Jay-Z because it found him stepping up from standard battle boasting to create his first narrative, a close-to-the-bone autobiography of a life spent skipping between the crack den and the casino, openly alluding to his criminal activities even while he was, to some degree, still involved in them. This swing between high living and low dealing would come to characterise Jay-Z's writing, and help him forge his own unique niche in rap music. With 'In My Lifetime' he staked out his own territory at the precise middle point between gangsta and speed-rapping street poet; he echoed the crack culture references of N.W.A. and Ice Cube but without the alienation, black power rhetoric, threat and aggression that might put off the fans of the more personable street rapping of Run-D.M.C. or the smooth loverman style of LL Cool J. He was edgy, smart, original and dangerous, but he was also coming from an educational angle, a place of intimacy and openness.

The video for 'In My Lifetime', again shot by Abdul Malik Abbott, pressed the song's point home. Opening with images of Marcy gangs pouring Cristal into the camera and crumpled single banknotes morphing into ever-growing bundles of money, we see Jay and his crew switch from rainy Brooklyn streets to wild pool parties in Caribbean mansion houses full of girls bathing in champagne, lounging on speedboats or taking half-naked showers with Jay. The sun shines, the 50-footers scythe through the surf, the bottles pop, the girls writhe and, all the

---

* A preview of how product placement will become a cornerstone of his raps.

time, the cash stacks get taller. It was conceived as a signal of the way Roc-A-Fella were heading for the top, out to establish their own sense of sophistication as rarefied and refined rappers and imprint the image of Jay-Z as a sure-fire success story. Although Jay contends they'd got there already – his autobiography claims the speedboats, pools, champagne and bikini babes accurately reflected their party lifestyle of the time and he also argues* that none of the boats or mansions in the video were rented, they were all owned by people in and around the Roc-A-Fella crew. He was no hip-hop millionaire yet, though. Hustling, clearly, was still paying the bills.

But the boats? The girls? The Cristal? From the outside, it sure looked like Jay-Z's payday.

Payday Records were a small NYC hip-hop label with a reasonable financial clout, a far wider distribution network than Roc-A-Fella through FFRR Records and their PolyGram parent label, and its nose to the ground. Its bosses had caught wind of the street-level marketing plan set in motion by Jay-Z, Dash and Burke, heard of its success in infiltrating 'Can't Get With That' into the NYC club scene and even getting it reviewed in *Vibe* magazine (where Jay-Z was described as having "a distinctly Das EFX-type, stiggety style") and they had smelt out like minds. They contacted Roc-A-Fella with that most elusive of creatures, a record contract for Jay-Z's debut single. After so much frustration and rejection, Roc-A-Fella leapt at the offer. But, far from financing their extravagant plans for a promo video for the single, from the off the Payday push seemed woefully inadequate. On one visit to the Payday offices, Jay and Dash noticed that the entire marketing campaign they had planned for 'In My Lifetime' consisted of one box of flyers to distribute on the streets. Stunned, it was Roc-A-Fella who turned back to their own far more impressive promotional plan, contacted Abdul Malik Abbott and, off their own backs and pockets, flew to St Thomas in the Caribbean to shoot the video.

---

* In the extra footage for the *Streets Is Watching* DVD.

"[Payday] were acting shady the whole time, like they didn't know how to work a record or something," Jay said in 1999. "The things that they were setting up for me I could have done myself. They had me travelling places to do in-stores, and my product wasn't even available in the store."[13]

Its sleeve featuring a cartoon bottle of champagne to set the tone for an entire career, 'In My Lifetime' was released on July 25, 1995, backed with Kent's original version of 'Can't Get With That' and a Big Jaz remix of the single.* The remix was arguably even more pivotal and prophetic in Jay's career than the original. Firstly, Big Jaz pulled out for his repeating chorus motif the seminal hook of Soul II Soul's 'Get A Life', a soulful female coo of "What's the meaning/What's the meaning of life?", the first example of a Jay-Z song assimilating a famous melody line around which Jay can wrap his dark and dangerous dealings.

Secondly the lyrics, completely different to the original, take Jay's autobiographical narrative impulse even further, delving into the dark and desperate depths of his past. Verse one gives a potted history of Jay's slide into hustling, from craving the expensive cars he saw the dealers driving to making the leap himself, full of plans to "make the cream materialise keys to a Benz". But the life he wanted to control soon starts controlling him – "My first felony's approaching, copped my first key/ Took a freeze, now I'm frozen." Before long he's "outta control/Losin' bankrolls on blackjack" and paranoid his phone is being tapped by the FBI ("like Gregory Hines" he quips, referencing the famous tap dancer from the Eighties and Nineties). Fear and loathing creep up on him; suddenly, the game has him spinning.

Verse two envisions a future where Jay is the hip-hop hyper-hero, chewing on prime Cuban cigars and sweeping girls from his Jacuzzi each day at dawn. "The whole city's buzzin'" with his name, but still he can't quite believe it: "Is this world my world?/Am I the star of stars?" He brags of "50Gs" within easy reach, overwhelmed

---

* The remix version was the lead track on the CD release of the single, ahead of Ski's original mix.

by the rush of success. The lesson of the song, though, is to stay rooted, unaffected by money or notoriety, and not to lose yourself to a nefarious, pitfall-strewn life because, as verse three warns, disaster stalks the arrogant and foolhardy. "From the beginning we never see the ending" Jay muses, listing all of his material achievements – the Pirellis, the diamonds, the designer clothes – but concluding "the Medusa's head on Versace turned me to stone"; he was dazzled but ultimately deadened by the pursuit of materialism. And to get there, he'd submerged himself in a world of violence, death and imprisonment where "my poems just ain't poems/They bloody, when I recite 'em/Bones get disconnected like the phones" and "all my penpals' life controlled by the warden." He's in too deep, "a hardened criminal with game", and he's as much of a prisoner on the outside as his friends and colleagues on the inside. He ends with a desperate sigh: "Now I'm incarcerated for my life," positioning himself impeccably: the hot-spitting hustler with a heart.

"While at first that whole gangsta shit was shocking," he'd later explain to Pete Lewis of *Blues & Soul* magazine, "like 'Ooh! He said he shot 30 niggas on record!' – in time the shock value wore off. So it just became time for a change and for something realer. Which is why I try to show the reasoning behind some of the things these guys can do. When people commit some of these acts, a lotta people think it's just cold and callous, but you just don't know the whole situation. Like you just don't know how far that person was pushed, or what that person tried to do to avoid committing that act... Say if every day someone's messing with you or robbing you or taking your stuff, and one day you just snap... Or one day, when someone tries to take your life, you just decide you're gonna defend yourself and you react... I just try to give the whole storyline that precedes somebody's act.

"I never wanted to just glamorise the playa lifestyle and not touch on the down side. I wanted everyone who's in a desperate situation to know that, if they wanna choose that kinda lifestyle, they gotta be aware of everything that comes with it. It's not just about the cars, the ladies and the money. Instead I'm saying, 'okay, I've been down that street and there's nothing sweet about it. While there may be some jewellery behind the second door, behind the third door there's someone waiting with a bat to bang you on the head... if you want to risk your life for the material stuff – then I told you so!'"[14]

It's staggering to think his critics would eventually point to such dire warning lyrics as those of 'In My Lifetime' as 'glorifying' the lifestyle of the hustler. Even the video Abbott made for the remix came with a cautionary coda. Between re-arranged footage from the original promo, Abbott added extra scenes portraying Jay as a high-flying businessman in Lennon glasses, suits and crisp white shirts chairing high-level meetings and stopping the song to toast gatherings of fictional business associates with Cristal. It was all an extension of Roc-A-Fella's plan to set their image as a cultured, upwardly mobile hip-hop concern, but Jay still knew the risks, even when attempting to go legit. The video ends with Jay, in his smartest suit and glasses, being pulled over and manhandled into a black police car by federal agents.*

'In My Lifetime' failed to pop the US charts, but it broke Jay's life in two, at last. Catching his own video on TV while he was feeding his fish or hearing his song on the radio between tracks by Tupac and Notorious B.I.G. turned Jay-Z straight. Payday were starting to make a life in hip-hop affordable for the first time and the potential income was huge. So no more fear, no more paranoia, no more exhausting scrutiny of every encounter, scenting hints of Eau De Cop. He vowed to cut himself off from his hustling operations for the time being, and concentrate on recording his debut album. From that point on he'd be a rapper, at least for now – he claimed in his first interviews that he would only make one album, secretly planning a return to the streets when the time was right or the money turned tight. In the end, of course, the need to hustle for easy cash would never come again. "I had been trying to hold on to two branches," he said, "and I said, 'I'm going to put my all into the music, to make a legitimate life for myself.' I never turned back."[15]

---

* One of the agents was played by Abdul himself.

Jay's escape from the game was perfectly timed. Within months of sealing his last deal, the crew he left behind was cracked in a police swoop and retired to the big house. The angel watching over Jay-Z had given him one last tip-off.

So here Jay was, using the laid-bare storytelling of his lyrics as a bridge to shift from one path to another. And if Jay was going legit, Roc-A-Fella needed a respectable front. For the first time, Jay-Z was about to get a corner office...

Chapter Four

Growing... Doubt

The mice had the run of the place. Skittering and snuffling through the grime in the corners, they nibbled at the box files and rooted through the record stacks. Hoisted above the cheap rag trade stores, hot dog stalls and watch repair shops of John Street, the tiny, rundown first official office of Roc-A-Fella bowed in the shadow of the Wall Street banking blocks, hoping to drain off some dregs of their money as if by osmosis. A visiting journalist from Yahoo! would liken the street to the alleyway where Patrick Swayze was murdered in *Ghost*, but Jay-Z, Dash and Burke made the best of it they could. They installed a widescreen TV, a couch, a table to play dice on and a skeleton staff. Dara and Omoyele McIntosh would run the Jay-Z fanclub Fan Family Inc. out of there and a woman named Chaka Pilgrim held the fort through sweltering summers and icy winters – since they couldn't afford to put desks and computers in the place, an air conditioning unit was way down the priorities list.

Still, financed by the Payday advance, the John Street office was Roc-A-Fella, and it was home. For now. "I don't mind being down here in this area, because this is just a starting point for us," said Jay when questioned on his low-rent surroundings and downbeat neighbourhood. "No sense in spending a whole lot of money on office space and moving employees round if your product isn't bringing in any money yet – that's a mistake executives make."[1]

The executives at Payday Records, meanwhile, were busy making mistakes of their own. As 1995 drew on and the time was pressing to capitalise on the profile of 'In My Lifetime' by releasing Jay-Z's second single, the label was again unwilling to meet the promotional expectations of the Roc-A-Fella collective, with fractious consequences. "We shot one video, but when the time came for me to do the video for the second single, I had to be cut out," Jay explained. "They gave me the money and I started my own company. There was a little arguing back and forth, but our conflict finally got resolved. The bottom line was they wasn't doing their job, so I had to get out of there."[2]

The wrangles over the split between Payday and Jay-Z rattled on for months, delaying the release of his second single until February 1996, seven months after his debut. In the meantime, the trio began working on a deal with the Californian company Priority Records to distribute his debut album, in association with Freeze Records. Negotiating a one-album contract to give himself the freedom to seek out a more lucrative deal elsewhere if the album took off, the agreement was that Roc-A-Fella would pay for the recording and promotion of the records and Freeze and Priority would cover manufacture and sales and retain control of the master tapes. Profits would be split 50–50 between Roc-A-Fella and Priority/Freeze, an incredible deal for Jay-Z since the industry standard contract gave the artist only 20 per cent of royalties. Eventually, Payday provided Jay, Burke and Dash with enough money to start up their own label, without the need for Jay to dig in to his hustling funds. "We didn't need dirty money to start Roc-A-Fella, because we had Payday's money," said Jay, "and just so you know, I didn't want to ask Priority for shit. They would have kicked in some money [for overhead expenses], but I wanted to do this on my own so the profit was mine, free and clear. At a certain point, if you ain't livin' right you want to do things legally. You want to leave your past behind and start looking for the future."[3]

Hence, the amorphous concept of Roc-A-Fella became the solid business Roc-A-Fella Records. And its very first release would be considered one of the greatest rap songs ever recorded.

On its release on February 20, 1996, 'Dead Presidents' caused a meteoric splash in New York hip-hop. With a title reflecting Jay-Z's obsession with the acquisition of money – the dead US presidents on banknotes gave money its rap nickname – and a soulful piano-led backbeat concocted by Ski from samples of two Lonnie Liston Smith tracks, 'A Garden Of Peace' and 'Oh My God (Remix)'*, Jay-Z delivers a virtuoso rap developing the 'In My Lifetime' theme of the hazards and insecurities of the hustler's lifestyle, particularly the inexperienced dealers, the "little monkey niggas turned gorillas" who "aside from the fast cars/Hunnies that shake their ass at bars/You know you wouldn't be involved," the guys who, the minute they get caught, are "ready to start snitchin'". Holding back on his stutters, the rhythm and cadence of his flow, his rests and his line links seemed to add a whole new level to the art of hip-hop; it sounded like rap entering a new realm of wordplay, a bar being raised. It's still considered, by hardcore Jay-Z fans, his best track ever.[†]

It would bring trouble down on the house of Roc-A-Fella, though. Even keener to work with Nas since his *Illmatic* album had broken big, Jay had invited him to re-rap a sample from his highly respected tune 'The World Is Yours (Tip Mix)' on the chorus of 'Dead Presidents' that Ski had used as the song's pivotal hook – a sample of Nas singing "I'm out for dead presidents to represent me" – and make a cameo appearance in the song's video. The collaboration was designed as a precursor to offering to sign Nas' group The Firm to the new Roc-A-Fella Records label. Again Nas declined to appear, but with promises to record a verse or two on Jay's album when the time came. Jay-Z and Ski went ahead and used the sample anyway, a decision that would ultimately lead to credit and payment issues between the two rappers and escalate into one of the most legendary feuds in hip-hop history.

---

* Ski filtered out the high frequencies on the piano melody to boost the bass.

† 'Dead Presidents' would go on to be covered by a host of hip-hop luminaries including Lupe Fiasco, Drake, Lil Wayne and Chamillionaire.

'Dead Presidents' was a true grassroots success. The biggest and best Roc-A-Fella hoped for the track at the start of the campaign was to get a play or two from Funkmaster Flex on the Hot 97 hip-hop station, an influential show by the biggest name in NYC rap DJing circles. To Roc-A-Fella, getting plays from Flex would have been a coup worth major celebration. At first Flex wasn't interested, but by now Jay-Z had built up some important contacts – from his stint in London with Jaz-O he'd met and maintained the support of Irv Gotti, a producer with ties to Universal Records (under whose umbrella he'd launch his own The Inc. record label) and a good friend of Flex. Gotti loved the single, and was so keen to help Jay-Z push it that he sang its praises to Flex, and also arranged a clandestine meeting at a petrol station to pass it into the hands of another influential figure in NYC hip-hop, DJ Clue. It's fitting that Jay-Z's breakthrough was shifted and dealt between main players like narcotics, and the song hit the underground's bloodstream like a hot fix.

Adding it to their hottest radio and club playlists, between them Flex and Clue spread the word of 'Dead Presidents' like wildfire. But it was the flip-side cut that had the real deep impact. In 1995, while taking a break from recording his early singles, Jay-Z had hit the Palladium club to check out the current hip-hop scene, and been staggered by the whoops and wildness that met a gangsta-style new track from LL Cool J called 'I Shot Ya'. One voice stood out, a sassy girl holding her own against LL, Prodigy and Fat Joe on the track with a sneer to her flow, a ballsiness to her stance and her lyrics oozing sex, money and designer name tags. He'd heard word of this young kid, Foxy Brown, plucked from a Brooklyn talent show at the age of 17 by producers for LL's forthcoming *Mr Smith* album to rap over 'I Shot Ya'. She'd become a part of Nas' The Firm collective, and Jay was so entranced he had to have her.

The call went out; Foxy made the record. A song called 'Ain't No Nigga', destined for the B-side of 'Dead Presidents'. Funked up for the dancefloor by producer Big Jaz from a sample of 'Seven Minutes Of Funk' by The Whole Darn Family and with Foxy singing a rewritten line from The Four Tops' 'Ain't No Woman (Like The One I Got)' for the chorus, it was Jay-Z's catchiest song yet, a modern hip-hop battle of the sexes about an unfaithful hustler and the cash-obsessed, long-suffering woman who made him. Brimming with wit (Jay-Z mocks his own bedroom performance with the lines "They say sex is a weapon/ So when I shoot, meet your death in less than eight seconds") and wisdom (Foxy reflects on the lot of many a hustler's girl with the forlorn admission that her partner "sleeps around but he gives me a lot"), 'Ain't No Nigga' was both funny, funky and true, and it lit up the dancefloors.

A huge underground NYC club hit, it was an irrepressibly danceable cross-gender anthem: the guys loved it for Jay's shameless womanising and sexual bragging, the girls loved it for the high-ground balling Foxy gives him in return. It's a relationship in which each boldly stakes their claim on the other, although Foxy's character comes out with the upper hand, responding to her man's cheating with a bitter disregard and demands for the security he owes her. The Jay character may think he's in control here, promising an attempt at monogamy but casually flouting his vow in the very next line, but it's Foxy's who wields the real power – emotional, moral and financial.

The song wasn't only controversial because of the sexual politics involved – the implication many read into the lyrics that a woman should dutifully accept a man's infidelities and deal with the heartache as her inevitable lot – but also because of its title. The word 'nigga' was in common use throughout hip-hop, but was still a taboo for radio audiences and a phrase most on-air DJs wanted no association with, refusing to play the track under that title. "For now," wrote Janine McAdams in *Billboard* that June, "'Ain't No N-G-A' has radio production rooms working overtime. None of the stations contacted for this story advocate the use of the n-word over the air, but their solutions are varied: some edit the word out; others substitute 'brother' or 'player'." Realising they had a potentially huge radio hit on their hands that should definitely be released as a single in its own right, Roc-A-Fella saved the stations the effort, recording a radio edit that removed the offensive word with the intention of releasing the track as 'Ain't No Playa' on March 26, 1996.

The record made just as big a splash overseas; Nick Raphael, an A&R scout for Sony BMG, signed Jay-Z to a UK record deal after being sent the track. "Will Socolof of Freeze Records sent me a CD and a video and said to me, 'This guy is incredible, but he needs a bigger label to take over. Are you interested?' The record he sent to me was 'Ain't No Nigga' and I went crazy, thinking that I had to sign him! Not only was he a brilliant recording artist, he was also a very bright business person. The way he and his manager Damon Dash ran their business and their label was very logical."[4]

Logic was screaming in Jay-Z's ear right then. 'Dead Presidents' had hit radio. 'Ain't No Nigga' had made him a club smash and got him an overseas major label deal. The single had gone Gold, creating such a swirl of interest that the major mix-tape compiler Ron G was apparently planning to call his first compilation tape 'Dead Presidents'. Jay-Z had to capitalise on all this by writing and recording a debut album, and fast – his debut needed to be on the shelves by the summer of 1996 at the latest, he reckoned, before the buzz died off. He had four months, maximum.

It was time this playa started playing.

Off the streets, going legit, and still Jay-Z gets ambushed. Double-crossed by his own right-hand man.

The guy that came out of the shadows at him this time was more imposing than any gangbanger or hustler's hitman. And not just for the sheer bulk of the man. In the years since they'd nodded to each other in the hallways of George Westinghouse school, Biggie Smalls had gained a notorious reputation in East Coast rap, selling 2 million copies of his 1994 debut album *Ready To Die*, and now here he was, invading Jay-Z's own studio stronghold, secreted inside by the shadowy go-between, DJ Clark Kent.

And now, face to face across the mixing desk like some serious David and Goliath shit, Jay was going to have to take Biggie on, man to mountain.

It was a twisted plot to get Jay-Z and Notorious B.I.G. on a track together, concocted between Kent and Dash. As Biggie's touring DJ, on the road Kent would taunt Biggie with a tape of 'Dead Presidents' before its official release, playing it over and over and claiming, half-jokingly, that Jay was the better rapper. "Everybody was mad at me," he remembers. "On the bus, I was like the alien for even trying it. But after Big heard that... he was like, 'Clark, that dude got it. He got it. He got it.' That let me know that I wasn't crazy."[5]

Biggie was so impressed by the record he accepted an invitation to appear in its video, cameoing in a high-stakes dice game scene at the end, the dice rattling between empty bottles of Cristal. In a break from filming, Dash approached Biggie as he and Jay were chilling out with D-Roc and Lil' Cease with an offer that was half suggestion, half challenge. "Damon approached Biggie, like, 'What's up with that record? You gonna do something with Jay?'," recalls Roc-A-Fella's promotion officer Lenny Santiago. "Big was like, 'Whatever, nigga. I'm waitin' on y'all. Whatchu sayin'?' Dame was like, 'I'm sayin', though, we could do it right now...' Dame was trying to put him to the test."[6]

Damon and Biggie drank almost five bottles of Cristal together to seal the deal, matching each other shot for shot. Before Dash reeled outside to vomit, he made Biggie promise to call the Roc-A-Fella office at five the next day to arrange a joint session. Through the afternoon hangover haze, sure enough, the Roc-A-Fella phone painfully rang.

Though no plan for a recording was set right there, communication was open and the seed of the idea was planted. Now Kent had to water it. Off the road, Kent had begun putting together beats for the Junior M.A.F.I.A. record that Biggie was overseeing. He'd play his formulative beats to Biggie in the studio from a tape machine. One session early in 1996, Kent had accidentally let the tape run on to a beat he'd intended to save for a Jay-Z track, 'Brooklyn's Finest', destined for Jay's first album.

"What's that track, man," Biggie urged. "I love it."

"That's for Jay-Z, this hot new kid."

"I gotta rap on that beat."

"I can try to make it happen," Kent told Biggie, "but be warned, this guy could hold his own against you..."

Biggie relished the challenge to take on this talented young rapper Kent had been mocking him with, so Kent acted as middleman, suggesting to Jay-Z that he should essentially battle Biggie on the record. The idea was tossed back and forth. Kent was excited about the possibility, but Jay-Z and his advisors had concerns; Irv Gotti phoned every day to discourage Jay from having as heavyweight a name as Biggie on the track as it'd make Jay look like a bit-player rather than the main star of the tune, it'd no longer be Jay's song. "I did not want that record to happen," Gotti says. "I was adamantly against it. I said, 'What I'm scared of is you doin' [a record] with Biggie and you comin' off like his little man.'"[7]

Jay was confident he could hold his own against Biggie, but the Roc-A-Fella crew weren't crazy about the idea of the respect and acclaim they might end up giving to Biggie's label Bad Boy Records and their cocky impresario founder Sean 'Puffy' Combs, aka Puff Daddy. Roc-A-Fella were East Coast body and blood, but the rising tensions between Bad Boy Records and Death Row out west (since Tupac Shakur had become convinced Biggie and Combs were behind his robbery and shooting in a New York studio lobby in 1994) made any association with Bad Boy feel like stepping into a minefield. Combs was also under attack at the time from Death Row boss Suge Knight, who'd used his Source Awards speech in August 1995 to criticise Puffy's tendency to randomly appear on his artists' records and dance in their videos. When Suge was shot in the arm at a Jermaine Dupri party in Atlanta that Combs also attended, suspicion immediately fell on the Bad Boy camp.

Connected or not, trouble seemed to love Combs in 1996. And trouble was something Jay-Z was well skilled in avoiding.

At one of the many intense recording sessions Jay-Z rattled through at D&D Studios in West 37th Street in Manhattan to record his debut album, the debate raged in earnest, Kent keen to convince Jay to take on Biggie, Jay uncertain whether it was the right move for him and Dash adamant he wouldn't pay any huge sums for Biggie's appearance. Eventually, the decision still unmade, Jay hit the recording booth to lay down his verses. But Kent had other ideas. He snuck down to the street where Biggie was holed up in a waiting car, and ushered him surreptitiously upstairs. "I go get Big, bring him upstairs, and they met each other the right way, properly. And everybody was like, 'Well, if you're going to do it for whatever...'"[8]

Though Jay-Z was shocked to suddenly find himself being introduced to this Herculean figure in NYC rap in his own studio, he was never a man to step down from a challenge to rap against the greatest. The first stand-off came over paper and pen. A pad between them on the table, Jay pushed it towards Biggie to write his verse. Biggie pushed it straight back. "Go ahead," said Biggie, gesturing to Jay. "Nah, you're alright," Jay replied, signalling Biggie to take the paper. After a few moments they realised one major and significant similarity between them. Neither rapper wrote his rhymes down.

While Biggie sat smoking blunts in the control room, nodding along to Jay's rhymes with eyebrows arched in admiration, Jay-Z spat his confrontational battle cries out at him. "You think your little bit of rhymes can play me?... I twist your shit/The fuck back with them pistols/Blazin' hot like Cajun... I rhyme sick/I be what you're trying to do". Planting himself on one side of an imagined violent rivalry and throwing out gunplay death threats ("So you sent your little mans to come kill me/But on the contrilli, I packs the mack-milli... left them paramedics breathing soft on him"), Jay wasn't holding back, he was firing both barrels. Over sparky nu-soul scratches taken from 'Ecstasy' by The Ohio Players and 'Brooklyn Zoo' by Ol' Dirty Bastard, this was an all-out assault that on one level tackled Biggie as his direct opposition but, on another, sided with him in the growing East Coast/West Coast rivalry by shouting the glory of Brooklyn and New York and celebrating their collaboration: "Jay-Z and Biggie Smalls, nigga shit your drawers."

Taken aback by the conviction and bite of Jay-Z's verses, with gaps left for him to fill in his own, Biggie puffed once more on one of his many blunts of the afternoon and decided he'd take his time in replying to Jay's shots at him. "We had Biggie come and smoke 60 blunts," says Burke. "Biggie lay down like a line or two, then he said he couldn't finish, he had to go home and finish it."[9]

Jay assumed that was the last he'd hear of the collaboration happening at all. Still, they toasted the effort – that night Biggie, Jay and the Roc-

A-Fella crew hit the town together, catching a comedy show by Bernie Mac at Radio City Music Hall and bonding over Cristal flutes.

Sure enough, Biggie's verses for 'Brooklyn's Finest' arrived at Kent's mixing desk two months later; a firestorm. With the benefit of knowing in advance what he was up against lyrically, he'd made his words vicious and uncompromising, full of personal digs at Jay's drug dealing reputation, hints of having high-level mafia links and images of violent retribution ("Fuck fist fights and lame scuffles/Pillow case to your face, make the shell muffle/Shoot your daughter in the calf muscle"). He even couldn't resist dropping in a shit-stirring pop at Tupac, as if to drag Jay-Z into the fray: "If Fay had twins she'd probably have two-pacs".* But what the verses belied was that, following their night at Bernie's, Jay and Biggie had become close friends – Jay had even invited him down to Miami that March to make another cameo in the video for the proper release of 'Ain't No Nigga'.

In Miami, between recreating scenes from *Scarface* as intro links, filming at poolside art deco bars and revving sports cars along Ocean Drive†, Roc-A-Fella played as hard as they worked. Biggie even contrived to get Jay-Z stoned on set, handing him a joint far stronger than Jay expected. Within a few minutes Jay realised he was too high to perform properly and, ever the control freak, decided never to lose focus on his work like that again.

Back in the mixing studio, Kent rifled Biggie and Jay-Z together on the track between the chorus he'd built with vocals from the recently Grammy-winning Mary J. Blige, with whom Kent had been working on Biggie's new album. Blige's appearance was another coup for the team working on Jay-Z's debut album, since she was riding high on the huge US hit 'Not Gon' Cry'. But, with the clock ticking, the track was still missing a vital hook.

---

* A reference to Tupac's claim that he'd slept with Biggie's wife Faith in 'Hit 'Em Up'.
† Scenes from the video which were intercut with snippets from *The Nutty Professor* movie.

"Me and Clark Kent had to make up a hook," says Dash. "We had to hand it in like the next day."[10] As the hours clicked by towards dawn at Giant Studios and the deadline loomed, gradually the players disappeared – Burke and Jay both heading out the door with promises to return to finish the elusive hook. "They leave me there and never come back," says Kent. "So it's like three in the morning, I decided to write a hook, and I performed the hook. That's my voice."[11]

Biggie Smalls was far from the only collaboration that Jay-Z worked on in his long hours at D&D that spring, the adrenalin keeping him awake for weeks on end. He pulled together a strong team of producers to provide his beats, each working between other sessions and competing to get their tracks on Jay-Z's record. His team were encouraged to delve into Seventies soul for samples and inspiration, a rich source of emotion and meaning for Jay; old tracks by Isaac Hayes, The Stylistics and The Four Tops had a glow of childhood magic for him, and he craved the satisfaction of feeling he was continuing the lineage of those immortal acts of his father's record collection, paying them the honour of re-imagining.

So Knobody* gave him a slinky backing for 'Can't Knock The Hustle' he'd pieced together alongside co-producers Sean C and Dahoud Darien from samples of 'Much Too Much' by Marcus Miller, Meli'sa Morgan's 'Fool's Paradise' and Eric B. & Rakim's 'I Know You Got Soul' at his mother's house back in 1994.† Irv Gotti, likewise, turned to the Isaac Hayes classic 'The Look Of Love' as inspiration for 'Can I Live', while in a studio elsewhere recording with Camp Lo, Ski Beatz produced and

---

* An NYC producer who'd gained acclaim for his work on 'Funky Piano' from the *New Jersey Drive* movie soundtrack, and who'd impressed his nearby neighbour Dash and Jay-Z with the first beats he'd made since his group had disbanded.

† The track would also end up featuring Mary J. Blige, recording her vocals for 'Can't Knock The Hustle' alongside Jay during a string of gigs out of New York, in Tampa, Florida. Reworking the vocal hook from 'Fool's Paradise' for 'Can't Knock The Hustle' had been Blige's idea.

submitted the Ahmad Jamal-sampling 'Feelin' It', a song that was never even meant for Jay-Z initially, as Ski explained. "It was me and Geechi Suede from Camp Lo, it was my hook and everything. Jay heard it and was like, 'I want that record. I don't care what you do, I want that record.' I didn't want to give it to him, but I had to because I knew he was going to be the man at the time. So I said, 'Fuck it, take the record.' He killed it in his own way."[12]

If that sounds mercenary, it merely reflects the competitive edge and exacting standards Jay-Z instilled on the sessions. For example, in the space of one afternoon Ski beat Kent to the punch with his version of 'Politics As Usual', deploying a sample from Jay-Z's beloved Stylistics which Kent was also, by coincidence, working on at exactly the same time. "I was riding in the car with my baby's mama," Ski recalls. "I had it on the oldies-but-goodies station, and I hear 'Hurry Up This Way Again' by The Stylistics. I said, 'Yo, this shit is crazy. If I sample this here, and chop it up right and let Jay hear it, he got to hear that shit and love it.' That same day, she took me to the old record store, and I took it home that night and chopped it up and played it for Jay the next day. He was going crazy for it. A funny thing is, at the same time, Clark actually found the sample too and did it. But I think the one I did was just a tad bit hotter."[13]

Kent disagrees. "I brought him the same beat like an hour later. Jay was like, 'Dag, I think yours is a little better... [but Ski] gave it to me first'."[14]

Sean C recalls Roc-A-Fella's unusual method of paying the record's participants. "They paid niggas with the shoe box of money. It was either fives or ones... it was three people counting the money. It wasn't a lot. It was less than 10 Gs, put it like that."[15]

Just as recording was hitting its intense peak at the start of April 1996, the single release of 'Ain't No Playa' shifted the whole machine up a gear. The song had been picked up for the soundtrack to the new Eddie Murphy movie *The Nutty Professor* and was a smash, hitting number 50 on the *Billboard* Hot 100 and topping the Hot Dance Music chart. Suddenly Jay-Z was hot property and his calls to major rap players were getting answered in a ring. This huge new respect was most noticeable through the involvement of DJ Premier, aka Primo, a Brooklyn mix-tape contact considered among the best hip-hop producers of all time thanks to his work with Ice-T, Cookie Crew, Soul II Soul, Biggie and Nas. Premier supplied Jay-Z with three tracks, 'Friend Or Foe'*, 'Bring It On'† and 'D'Evils', for which he used his West Coast connections to secure permission to rework lines and use samples from Dr. Dre and Snoop Dogg. But his overall gift to the project was far greater, his name and endorsement. The fact that Primo was on board made Jay-Z big time.

In fact, pretty much the only big name collaboration that didn't go as planned was with Nas. When Jay-Z finally convinced him to guest on a track for the album, 'Bring It On', along with his Firm cohort AZ, Nas and AZ didn't show up for the recording. Jay-Z called in some old friends to fill the gap, Big Jaz and Sauce Money. But Nas' no-show wouldn't be forgotten.

So Jay-Z had a hit song in the charts, a hot album in the works, his own buzz-heavy record label, a major international record deal and a host of superstar rappers and producers adding weight and kudos to his record. His fledgling rap empire was almost complete. All he needed now was an apprentice.

He had the song for them already. It was called 'Coming Of Age', one of Kent's numbers hooked around a blaxploitation kind of groove from Eddie Henderson's 'Inside You', and the rhyme Jay wrote over it was a conversation between a wannabe hustler and the mentor interviewing him for the job. Jay-Z's mentor figure character in the song, seeing a bit of himself in the ambition of the young kid who's been "clockin' my rocks", senses a loyalty in his keen-ness, and outlines to him the dealer's career path from pushing eight balls to shifting weight, all while keeping his profile under the radar. The ultimate test, though, is one of greed versus commitment. Jay offers the kid a thousand dollars to ride with

---

* Built on a sample of Brother To Brother's 'Hey, What's That You Say'.
† Sampling D&D Allstars' '1, 2, Pass It'.

him; the kid turns it down: "I want the long-term riches and bitches."
The kid starts Monday.

Jay had a young rapper in mind for the role of the trainee in this
scenario – Shyheim, who he'd rapped with on Kane's 'Show & Prove'.
But Shy's first album *AKA The Rugged Child* had been a number seven
hit in the R&B chart by this point, and Shyheim's people didn't see
their rising star as anybody's apprentice. "I'm honored that I had an
impact on [Jay] like that," Shyheim would later claim. "I never really
had no clue to the extent of how I was viewed. It's kind of disturbing
because being an artist when you're young and things, people make
decisions for you, and [not appearing on that record] was a decision that
I don't know who made that call... but I personally didn't say no. If
someone would have been like, 'Yo, Shy', then maybe we would have
had that dialogue and it would've been a different outcome... Coulda
shoulda woulda, but it is what it is."[16]

So Jay-Z went hunting for a kid with the same sort of fire and attitude
he'd seen in the young Shyheim, someone to mentor from nothing, to
rear through rap. And where better to find him than back in the Marcy
projects, where the hungry young battlers tore at each other's throats
nightly.

The day after Shyheim's rejection came through, Jay was out there
in the courtyard circles again, this time watching from the edges rather
than stealing the scene. He spotted a skinny teenage rapper with a flow
like fireworks and a ravenous gleam in his eye, an 18-year-old by the
name of Malik Cox who'd lived two floors down from him in his Marcy
block. The teenager was keen but, in keeping with the spirit and story
of the song, Jay tested him. He gave Malik 24 hours to learn his parts
to 'Coming Of Age', then sent him away with a sheet of handwritten
lyrics that was purposefully illegible, impossible to read. The next night,
in Jay-Z's apartment, Malik arrived wired and sparking to rap. Jay
offered to buy him fast food; Malik ordered six bacon cheeseburgers and
wolfed down the lot. Belly full but still pumped with a hunger, he then
ricocheted through his verses of 'Coming Of Age' like a caged lemur;
he was exactly what Jay-Z wanted. Within hours they'd laid down the
vocals at Kent's basement studio and Malik's name had been stretched

and contorted to fit the hip-hop legend Jay was intent he'd become. Goodbye Malik Cox, hello Memphis Bleek.*

By the end of the recording, Jay was flooded with relief. "It wasn't even like I was making music," he said. "The studio was more like a psychiatrist's couch for me. All the shit I'd been through, and all the shit I wanted to say, just came out. It was like 'phew!'"[17]

Come May 1996, bang on schedule, the album was ready to ship out to Platinum Island studios on Broadway for mixing. And any unreasonable doubt over Jay-Z's brilliance was about to be wiped out.

Mafia style.

---

* On future tours, when Jay-Z and Memphis Bleek would re-enact the story of 'Coming Of Age' live, Jay-Z would hand Bleek a fistful of fake dollars on the line "Here's a thou'…" and Bleek would throw them into the audience with the casual aside "A G? I ride wit you for free…"

Chapter Five

Streets Is Watching

"Okay, okay, okay, big man, you wanna make some big bucks, huh? Let's see how tough you are. You know something about cocaine? There's a bunch of Colombians coming in Friday, new guys, they say they've got two keys for us for openers, pure cocaine. I want you to go over there and if it's what they say it is you buy it and you bring it back. You can do that, you make five grand."

– Pain In Da Ass reciting the *Scarface* script, *Reasonable Doubt*

The four girls in the car, parked outside the tenement in broad daylight, were getting antsy.

"He's in there right now," said the driver, riled. "You know what he doing? Wassup?"

From the back seat, a second girl fumed. "I say we go in there and bust a cap in his lying, cheating ass. We going in there to bust his cap or what? He's playing you, girl. He. Is. Playing. You."

Mary J. Blige, the jilted party in the front seat, lifts her leopard-print sunglasses and peers across the street. She catches the eye of Jay-Z, in black fedora, Michael Corleone suit and white *Godfather* scarf, as he emerges from the suspect building, a mistress leaning in to kiss his neck.

A knowing smirk.

As the tremulous silent movie piano soundtrack gives way to a smooth soul groove, Jay-Z pushes his mistress to safety, dives for cover.

Then, from the car, the bullets start flying.

So, with the introductory quotes from *Scarface* recreated by Pain In Da Ass and with the opening skit in the video for its first track 'Can't Knock The Hustle', the tone was set for Jay-Z's debut album *Reasonable Doubt*. Here was a record intended to blur the boundaries between hustling fact and cinematic fiction, to imprint a sense of myth, mystery and cult crime classicism onto a very real life story. *Reasonable Doubt*, in the tradition of Raekwon's *Only Built 4 Cuban Linx...* album and AZ's *Doe Or Die*, was a mafioso rap record, cartooning Jay-Z's world of Lexuses, Cristal and hustling hardships by framing it within the celluloid anti-glamour of organised crime. It was fact folded within a fantasy.

Besides the Biggie battle of 'Brooklyn's Finest', the rhyming somersaults of the plaintive '22 Two's' and the rap row of 'Ain't No Nigga', *Reasonable Doubt* was made up almost entirely of semi-autobiographical missives from Jay-Z's life on the streets. Jay arranged it to tell a story, trace the hustler's arc from being a cocky player on the rise to a paranoid maniac at the top of the tree. So 'Can't Knock The Hustle', oozing along on a lush funk throb and Blige's sizzling soul diva choruses, pictured an ambitious and successful hustler new to the game, "making short-term goals" and good money, "six digits and running", keeping enough cash to hand to make his own bail and spewing the rest on dice games, fast cars, diamonds and champagne. There were hints of some distant danger, but they were crushed and swept aside by the feelings of invincibility brought on by unlimited supplies of banknotes – "let's get together and make this whole world believers at my arraignment".

The disco-tinged 'Politics As Usual', with its hook of swirling siren Stylistics, found that same dealer getting in a little over his head. Now he was having to check into the backgrounds of potential buyers, work day jobs to throw the IRS off his scent, warn his enemies not to underestimate him. He was realising that once you're lost to the criminal life the ties can never fully be cut: "Sucking me in like a vacuum/I

remember telling my family 'I'll be back soon'/That was December
'85/Then Jay-Z rise 10 years later/Got me wise, still can't break my
underworld ties." And for all his "hittin' towards a mil'" in the bank,
he could feel a shift in himself as he was dragged further inside – "The
game changed, it's like my mind just ain't right."

'Dead Presidents' never made it onto *Reasonable Doubt*; in its place sat
'Dead Presidents II', the same track with different lyrics on the verses.
Where the original feared the snitch, the sequel felt the Feds' net closing
and the rival gangs loading their clips. Referencing Jay's own near-fatal
shooting – "I had near brushes/Not to mention three shots close range/
Never touched me" – this hustler knew now that "factions from the
other side would love to kill me/Spill three quarts of my blood into
the street" and that "the Feds is buggin' my life". Honour still ruled the
streets: Jay swore to "slay" the killers of one of his crew shot in a drive-
by, but as much as the money was mounting and the bad guys kept
winning*, he knew it was time to move up or move out.†

First, he considered moving out. The piano-led lounge cut 'Feelin' It'
was a vision of the high-flying hip-hop lifestyle that Jay-Z was starting
to become accustomed to. Here success bred success, the crew closed,
made sure everyone in their circle became rich so that "nobody will
fall cause everyone would be each other's crutches". Now the superstar
rapper could look back on his old hustling ways with a hushed relief
and a twinge of regret for the damage he'd done, sending shouts out to
"all the towns like Cambridge that I killed wit shit" and to his mother
who "prayed I'd stop/Said she had nightmares snipers hit me with a fatal
shot." Though in this scenario Jay was out, his freedom is hard bought.

Then, following the darker parallel universe, Jay explored the
trajectory of the hustler who sinks deeper into the game. Set to Premier's
redemptive Snoop-esque slink, 'D'Evils' was a litany of desperation and

---

* "I'll tell you half the story, the rest you fill it in/Long as the villain win" Jay rapped,
  suggesting a half-truth to this story. An interesting and deceptive aside, since later
  he asserted his credentials as a 'real' ex-criminal: "You fake thugs is *Unplugged* like
  MTV/I empty three, take your treasure, my pleasure."
† 'Dead Presidents II' became the definitive version of the track, voted the 16th best
  rap song by About.com.

violence from a dealer overtaken by his lust for profit, despairing of himself that "for the love of money I'm giving lead showers". He turned against a childhood friend as they fought over territory, kidnapping, bribing and finally attempting to murder the guy's "baby's mother" to uncover his whereabouts. By the end of the song he was robbing and stripping people in the streets, a maniac as out of control as any crackhead, firm in the grip of these inner 'D'Evils'. By the jazzy big band epic 'Can I Live', the character had recognised he was dealing "out of a sense of hopelessness, sort of a desperation... sorta like the fiends we accustomed to serving" and had moved up the ranks to protect himself from "every nigga watching me closely" and to allay his fears and psychoses, watching from a distance as his workers sealed the deals on the front line. But even at this level he couldn't sleep, constantly on edge, his mind was "fried to a fricassee" and he was still defiantly in fear for his life, hence the now legendary line "I'd rather die enormous than live dormant". His life flitted from high-roller presidential suites in Vegas and trips to Maui to knowledge of the "atrocities" he'd had to oversee on the streets to maintain it all. In the end, though he claimed to be living a dream, he was still begging to be allowed to simply exist, without fear.*

For the rest of the album, Jay-Z dealt in hustling minutiae, playing out the sort of set piece scenes a hustler runs into daily. After a short skit in which a rival gang armed up to tackle Jay-Z's operation over money, Premier's brass-heavy 'Friend Or Foe' found Jay facing down out-of-town invaders muscling in on his turf in a stand-off of guts and guns; his calm but cold-blooded threats saw off the competition for good and Jay even scared them into giving him the keys to their hotel room, where their drugs and guns were presumably stashed, as they fled.

'Coming Of Age', a sparky soul roll from DJ Clark Kent, had him recruiting an apprentice in Memphis Bleek. And after he played the purring pimp in 'Cashmere Thoughts', likening his rhymes to top-end goods – cashmere, gold, mink, fine wines, Persian rugs, diamonds, filet

---

* In his autobiography *Decoded*, Jay-Z claims he taught himself to mentally segregate and dispose of such thoughts, thoughts "that sabotage".

mignon and pearls – and fronted wildly about money, charisma and weight with Sauce Money and Big Jaz on 'Bring It On', the album ended with a stark triptych of the damage dealing can do.

'Regrets', a twitchy groove full of twinkling triangles and a looped acoustic guitar refrain pieced together by producer Peter Panic from 'It's So Easy Loving You' by jazz masters Earl Klugh and Hubert Laws, painted three scenarios: the first a drug boss watching, through a telescopic lens from his BMW, a police sting that may have left one of his apprentices dead; the second a rising hustler finding himself pointing a shaking gun at his first bum deal; and the last a gang feud between old friends, similar to that in 'D'Evils'. All three characters were cracking under emotional pressure and full of regrets – the boss for putting his crew in life-threatening situations, the young hustler for the guilt he'll carry with him and the pain he'll cause to his mother for shooting a man, and the feuding gangbanger, well, he was wrestling with the "suicidal tendencies", the eternity in hell guaranteed for him and the loss of a father which may have set him off on this path of loneliness and retribution. The message of 'Regrets' was that whichever road the hustling life draws you down, it can only end in death, anguish and a tortured conscience that blights a lifetime.

It was this open-hearted blaze of truth from inside the game, combined with a brutal personal honesty, emotional vulnerability and wisdom – all wrapped in the familiar blankets of classic Seventies soul and funk – that made *Reasonable Doubt* an instant rap benchmark. Though it put on all the surface toughness and braggadocio of the very in vogue gangsta rap, lavished with grotesque hustling detail, it simultaneously undermined that very image with hints of fear, regret, desperation and humanity. Rather than an impenetrable, prickly ghetto underworld figure such as those portrayed by Ice-T, N.W.A. or the burgeoning Wu-Tang Clan, or Chuck D's belligerent freedom fighter, Jay-Z was the laid-back, assured and human face of mafioso rap, his rhymes as sharp as modernist poetry and his beats as familiar and trustworthy as *Shaft*.

Though the album's seminal status would take decades to fully establish – it would be 2003 before *Rolling Stone* and *Blender* magazines would include it in their lists of the 500 Greatest Albums Of All Time and 500 CDs You Must Own Before You Die respectively, 2004 when *Vibe* would include it in their ranking of 51 Albums Representing A Generation, A Sound And A Movement, and 2007 when MTV would declare it the sixth greatest hip-hop album ever made – the initial reviews were very favourable. *Entertainment Weekly*'s Dimitri Ehrlich awarded the record a B+ rating, praising Jay's "irresistible confidence, a voice that exudes tough-guy authenticity, and unadorned but suitably militant beats". *The Source* marked it four out of five mics, their reviewer Charlie Braxton remarking "[Jay-Z] flows like he's conversing with you at a party or on the street, telling tales of male conquest or simple stories of street survival" while also admonishing Jay's apparent disrespect for women on the album.

It would take time for critics to recognise the cultural shift in rap the album's lyrics would spark. "MC's had definitely touched... on hustling," Dream Hampton would claim, "but Jay talks about what it can do to a person's inner peace, and what it can do to their mind." In *Vibe* magazine in 2011 she'd expand her comments to expound *Reasonable Doubt* as belonging to an "era we only now understand to be a zenith in hip-hop", positioning the album alongside Tupac's prolific recordings and the peakings of Biggie, Mary J. Blige and Nas: "Jay could say in three bars what it took other writers three verses to communicate... What he didn't say seemed as important as what he did, his pauses had gravity, he dealt with space like a hot block, dipping in and around a beat, painting pictures with inflections as often as vocabulary... Jay filled in the details, and more importantly, profiled the psychic collateral damage of the lifestyle... Paranoia, envy, greed and addiction were the price of success." AllMusic's Steve Huey stated that Jay's lyrical deftness "helps *Reasonable Doubt* rank as one of the finest albums of New York's hip-hop renaissance of the Nineties... He's cocky bordering on arrogant, but playful and witty, and exudes an effortless, unaffected cool throughout... Jay-Z waxes reflective, not enthusiastic, about the darker side of the streets." In 2001 Steve Juon from RapReviews would claim it "not only the definitive album from H To The Izzo's catalogue, it's one of the 10 most important rap records of the entire Nineties. It's possible to live without having heard it – but after you do, you'll wonder how you ever managed without it." Pitchfork's Ryan Schreiber would call it, simply, "one of hip-hop's landmark albums".[*]

Even in 1996, however, many immediately noted how he was bringing a high-class refinement to rap and how well Jay fared against Biggie on 'Brooklyn's Finest', quoting the track as a blistering standout. As a result, the two friends began talking about further collaborations, perhaps on a rap supergroup called The Commission which would also include Sean Combs, a female MC called Charli Baltimore and a host of others, in the style of an East Coast version of the Death Row collective of Tupac Shakur, Snoop Dogg and Dr. Dre. Over brandy nights and Cristal afternoons, conquering entire back rooms of up-market Manhattan restaurants, Biggie would urge him to strive for Multi-Platinum status and fill arenas, become the first hip-hop arena superstar. But even as *Reasonable Doubt* hit the streets on June 25, 1996 and shot to number 23 on the *Billboard* Hot 200, heading for 420,000 sales in its first year[†], Jay was still insisting his Gold-status album would be his last, that he'd retire from rapping to focus on running his business. It was an attitude fuelled, one suspects, by his lack of reach far outside New York City in 1997, or by the death threats he was getting whenever he was booked to play out on the West Coast because of his close connection to Notorious B.I.G., the LAPD often forcing him to cancel Californian gigs. The promoter of Jay-Z's first gig in Vegas – Andreas Hale, who'd eventually become Editor-In-Chief of HipHopDX rap website – reported that his record store signing there shortly after *Reasonable Doubt*'s release out west drew around 10 fans, and the gig in the overambitious Huntridge Theater brought in around twice that number, despite the bargain $10 ticket charge.

But as the album fed out into New York, becoming an East Coast classic, and as 'Can't Knock The Hustle' – released as a single on August

---

[*] The record's influence in hip-hop would become widespread too – The Clipse recreated the vibe of *Reasonable Doubt* for 'We Got It For Cheap' in 2006 while the likes of The Game, Jean Grae, Chubb Rock, Termanology, Apathy, Mary J. Blige and De La Soul would sample or name-drop the album in song.

[†] And Platinum status within a decade, racking up 1.5 million sales by 2006.

27 – and its cinematic *Godfather*-inspired video directed by Hype Williams cemented his standing by hitting number 73 on the *Billboard* chart and number 30 in the UK*, the reception from the kids on the street grew more and more intense, started to effect him. He began to see he was moving people, affecting lives.

"There were cats coming up to me," he told *Vibe* magazine, "like, 'You must have been looking in my window or following my life'… It was emotional. Like big, rough, hoodlum, hardrock, three-time jail bidders with scars and gold teeth just breaking down. It was something to look at, like, I must be going somewhere people been wanting someone to go for a while."[1]

As his reputation on the East Coast exploded, however, Jay-Z was about to find that the hip-hop life could be just as back-stabbing, cut-throat and deadly as the upper echelons of the hustling world.

And once again, the sights were trained directly on him.

"I'm a Bad Boy killer/Jay-Z die too"
– Tupac, 'Bomb First (My Second Reply)', recorded August 1996

The dense desert air whooping down the Strip was hot on his chest; the roar of the boxing crowd resounded in his ears, crowing him a champion. Tupac Shakur stood stoutly through the sunroof of Suge Knight's brand new black BMW 750 sedan, soaking in the casino neon of Las Vegas blurring by. The night had held mishaps already, detained by a motorcycle cop for a few minutes for playing the car stereo too loud and keeping their licence plates in the trunk, but now they were on the move, away from the Tyson vs Seldon fight at the MGM Grand and into the endless night.

As he flirted with a couple of girls in a car that pulled up beside the BMW at Flamingo Road at 11.10 p.m. that September 7, inviting them to join his entourage at Club 662, owned by his record label

---

* Where Jay-Z's records were being released by Northwestside Records.

Death Row, he'd probably already forgotten about his own post-fight altercation in the lobby of the Grand.

An altercation with a member of the Southside Crips gang. A 21-year-old guy called Orlando 'Baby Lane' Anderson, who'd robbed a Death Row crew member earlier in 1996 in a Foot Locker. Tupac had been told Anderson was in the vicinity and, with the support of Suge and his entourage, had piled in to hammer the kid. Retribution, the Death Row way.

The hot air on his chest. The bellow of the fight. Invincible.

The white four-door Cadillac pulling up to the right of the BMW.

The window rolling down.

The glint of black metal.

When Tupac Shakur died, aged just 25, from internal bleeding in the critical care unit of Las Vegas University Medical Center on the afternoon of September 13, having survived five days of emergency surgery, the removal of a pierced lung and further death threats from the drive-by shooters, who'd called the Death Row offices promising to invade the hospital to "finish him off", fingers pointed wildly. Crips associates of Anderson were prime suspects, jealous boyfriends of the girls Tupac had chatted up were wild possibilities; maybe it was even a belated hit from someone upset that he'd had a number one album with *Me Against The World* in 1995 while serving time for sexual assault.

But, little knowing he had only weeks to live, Tupac had unwittingly left his own list of suspects.

A list some may have come to take far too seriously.

"Resources tell me a number of less fortunate rappers have joined together in conspiracy to assassinate the character of not only Mr Shakur, but of Death Row Records as well," said a spoof news reporter in a skit introducing 'Bomb First (My Second Reply)', recorded just days before his death for the opening of Tupac's fifth album *The Don Killuminati: The 7 Day Theory*. "Nas, the alleged ring leader of it, is furious at Tupac, excuse me, Makaveli's verbal assault on Mobb Sleep, Notorious P.I.G., and several other New York rappers, Jay-Z, from 'Hawaiian Sophie' fame, Big Little whatever and several other corny-sounding motherfuckers are understandably shaken up by this release."

Rumours that Biggie Smalls was behind Tupac's shooting were rife in the press and on the streets within hours of it happening, but were also the most spurious and speculative of all, based solely on the pair's lyrical beef. In 2002 an article by Chuck Phillips, a Pulitzer prize-winning investigative reporter for the *Los Angeles Times*, claimed to have evidence linking Biggie to the murder via anonymous Crips members Biggie was alleged to have hired as security during his West Coast appearances, but the paper retracted all claims in 2008 after discovering the evidence was based on fake documents. No firm link from Biggie to the Vegas shooters has ever been established and the Wallace family, to this day, strenuously deny that Biggie was in any way involved in Tupac's death.

None of which was any consolation to Jay-Z as he stood alone among the weeping throng of Biggie Smalls' funeral, March 1997. Confusion, loss and disbelief at the tragedy laid out before him left him speechless and reticent for the whole day. The convoy of GMC Suburbans away from an after-party for the Soul Train Music Awards at LA's Petersen Automotive Museum on March 8, Biggie in the lead car's passenger seat; the black Chevrolet Impala SS pulling up beside his Suburban at a stop light 50 yards from the party; the shooter in the blue suit and bow tie with the blue-steel 9mm; the door peppered with holes. It seemed so unreal, so Hollywood, so *Scarface*, he couldn't believe his friend had been hit, so young. The man who only months before had sat with him at the Bad Boy studio Daddy's House listening to the cinematic swirl of 'Streets Is Watching'*, the first track recorded for Jay's second album, insisting Jay play this intense streak of hustler's paranoia 20 times in a row, frustrated and challenged that it was so good and fretting that Jay's second album, if it all hit the same standard, might blow Biggie's own planned 1997 second album clean off the scene. "We played it so much I just gave it him," Jay remembers. "I was like, 'Just keep it'."[2]

The man who'd been so unwilling to escalate an argument that, at a nightclub that very same night, he'd balked at confronting some kids with a beef against him, heading home instead.

---

* Produced by Ski from samples of Labi Siffre's 'I Got The', a continuation of the soul vibe of *Reasonable Doubt*.

The man who'd encouraged him to embrace a wider, more mainstream appeal by slowing his raps and recording with Puffy, and who'd invited him to contribute a typically cash-flashing verse to 'I Love The Dough' for his forthcoming album *Life After Death*.* The guy who'd backed Jay to the hilt as he broke away from his Freeze Records distribution deal because record label procedures were slowing up his money, used his street dealing toughness to negotiate his way out while keeping control of his master tapes and the rights to his music† and then set about re-selling *Reasonable Doubt* in a bidding war between Sony and Def Jam, eventually selling one-third of Roc-A-Fella to Def Jam for $1.5 million at the start of 1997.‡ And, most poignantly, the man who'd reassured him that Biggie's on-record feud with Nas over a personal slight he read into Nas' 'The Message'§ was a harmless, good-natured beef.

That guy, his big lisping Brooklyn rock, had been snatched away. Jay's life seemed tossed into turmoil, fear, anger and upset. He spoke to virtually no one at the service and left the wake early. "Going to Big's funeral was a big deal for me," he says in his defence. "I don't go to funerals, period. I don't want that to be my last memory of them."[3] His tribute to Biggie would be made in the studio, recording a verse for Puffy's 'Young Gs' to go alongside that of his dead friend: "Solemnly we mourn all the rappers that's gone... I told my nigga Big I'd be multi before I die."

* Ironically released three weeks after Biggie's death.
† A scenario that was practically unprecedented in rap at that time, such was Jay-Z's bargaining power, and his hustler-style approach in the boardroom.
‡ The deal broke down as follows: Def Jam gained the rights to release a second run of *Reasonable Doubt* and Jay's second album and bought one-third of Roc-A-Fella plus a percentage of the rights to any future Jay-Z master recordings. Def Jam were to cover production and video costs with all profits from the records shared with Roc-A-Fella – Dash, Jay and Burke taking 67 per cent of profits after some hardcore negotiation from Dash, whom Def Jam boss Russell Simmons credits as being behind the Jay-Z phenomenon.
§ "There's one life, one love, so there can only be one king," Nas rapped, challenging Biggie for the title of king of New York rap; in the posthumous 'Kick In The Door', Big responded "ain't no other kings in this rap thing/They siblings, nothing but my children."

After the shock and the anguish, and a fortnight of self-imposed seclusion and mourning on a Caribbean island where no one could reach him, Jay returned having taken a sense of steadfast determination from the death of Notorious B.I.G. As if in honour to his fallen friend, he swore to make his business a success – he'd already begun delving into A&R by signing acts such as Sauce Money, The Rangers, Ruffness, Michelle Mitchell and Christión to Roc-A-Fella. Plus, the experience of discussing million-dollar deals across a luxury office desk with his role model Russell Simmons at Def Jam had inspired him to a vaulting ambition. He negotiated with Simmons so hard to keep his major stake in Roc-A-Fella so as one day to also be in Simmons' position, at the head of his own multimillion-dollar label empire.

But most of all, Jay returned from the Caribbean desperate to exorcise his pain and confusion onto tape. His oath to only make one album would have to be broken – he'd use the grief of a period he'd come to describe as one of the hardest of his life to pen rhymes of his youthful hardships, his poverty and hard knocks. And, of course, the measures he took to escape.

Even as the fourth single from *Reasonable Doubt*, 'Feelin' It', was released on April 15, 1997 destined for number 79 in the *Billboard* chart, accompanied by a low-budget video of luxury beach living and big-money dealings in Miami[*], Jay threw himself back into the studio with Combs, as his executive producer, overseeing the work of the slicker, pop-centric hit-makers Combs recommended from his Bad Boy stable such as Teddy Riley, The Hitmen and Trackmasters. Ski, Premier and Big Jaz would contribute too, but this time Jay was seeking a more accessible mainstream sound, a slice of Bad Boy's commercialised pie. The nigh-on-half a million sales of *Reasonable Doubt* seemed small cheese compared with the 4 million units Biggie's *Ready To Die* had shifted. With New York dizzy from the loss of its hip-hop king and desperate to crown his successor, Jay-Z wanted to step up to Biggie's throne before

---

[*] The chorus of 'Feelin' It' would later be pilloried by 50 Cent on the 2002 track 'Be A Gentleman'.

anyone crowned Nas in his place. And Big Boy, in his eyes, were the keepers of the sceptre.

If his loyal, competitive and hard-working circle of producers felt a little shunted aside by this new swarm of big names, Jay in turn found his own disciples spurning him. Keen to foster him further, Jay invited Memphis Bleek to rap on a track for the album, only for Bleek, a little full of himself now he'd gained a reputation around Marcy, to no-show the session. Jay called his apartment; Bleek's mother claimed he was too ill to come out to play. So Jay jumped in his Lexus and drove to Marcy, knocked on Bleek's door and found him in his bedroom with a girl. Furious that Bleek had learned nothing from him about loyalty and priorities, Jay cut him off from the album and its subsequent tour on the spot. Bleek, like so many apprentices of the street, was going to have to learn the hard way.

Instead, Jay turned to more reliable accomplices. To regular names like Foxy Brown and Sauce Money, and to Bad Boy affiliates Lil' Kim – Biggie's girlfriend and a member of the Junior M.A.F.I.A. crew that Biggie had encouraged – Blackstreet, his highway hero Too Short, Kelly Price and Puffy himself. He also hooked up with R&B stalwart Babyface for the commercial gloss pop of '(Always Be My) Sunshine', a track producer Daven 'Prestige' Vanderpool pieced together from samples of Alexander O'Neal, Kraftwerk and the Fearless Four.

The sessions for the album were stressful and wrought with emotion for Jay. Battling with the loss of Biggie and wary of the industry figures closing in around his work, he ploughed through the recording with his creative blinkers firmly on, got through it the best he could. Working characteristically fast, the album was in the can within months and the first new material was showcased just five weeks after the release of 'Feelin' It'.

'Who You Wit' was the perfect track as a bridge between *Reasonable Doubt* and his forthcoming new direction: produced by Ski from a sample of Jeff Lorber Fusion's 'Night Love' it was funk-heavy, catchy as hell and as fun as any mainstream pop. The lyrics were suitably cocksure, with Jay cast as the consummate seducer of both "bitches" and businessmen, neither of whom would rob him of his freshly gained riches. "Givin' a chick half my trap like she wrote half my raps?/Yeah, I'm having that/You be the same chick when you leave me/The bankbook and the credit cards and take everything you came with" he warned any potential gold-digging future ex-wives. And while he was affirming his position as a music industry hotshot with hustling firmly part of his history, in keeping with his more mainstream approach he exuded a generous gregariousness, treating girlfriends to foreign holidays and playing the hip-hop peacekeeper in the wake of the Biggie murder – "frivolous beef, please, we lookin' past that". As he turned away from his criminal life for good, he built a more approachable persona here, recognising his own maturity: "Had beef of all sort but I turned it around/Chose my steps more wisely, I'm learning the ground/I was so gung-ho when I earned my first pound/Now it's million dollar deals, straight turning 'em down."

But there was also a playful humour to the mood of the track, fitting since it was rush-released on May 20, 1997 to coincide with the comedy movie *Sprung*, which it soundtracked.* The video was a riot too – a gathering of cartoon pimp types from across the country to compete in the final of a Playa Of The Year competition, the towering trophy for which Jay-Z predictably wins. If his videos to date had been a chance for Jay-Z to indulge in *Scarface* homages and tongue-in-cheek recreations of yacht life, here was his first all-out slab of comic chutzpah (at least since 'Hawaiian Sophie'), another revealing glimpse of the human being behind the gangsta grimace.

If 'Who You Wit' was a stop-gap single redolent of *Reasonable Doubt*'s soulful splices, the shock of Jay's real stylistic swerve was only a summer away. '(Always Be My) Sunshine' 'dropped' on September 16, accompanied by an eye-blitzing video filmed largely inside a huge light-up Rubik's Cube, with routines from brightly dressed dancers intercut with shots of Jay and his rap accomplice Foxy Brown superimposed onto fairground rides. The video reflected the synthesised disco-pop vibe of the track, with Babyface providing a slick R&B chorus of chart-friendly romance and George Fontenette adding keyboard blasts more attuned

---

* The single reached number 84 on the *Billboard* chart.

to Grandmaster Flash's 'The Message' than the prevailing menace of mafioso rap.

Jay-Z and Foxy's verses, however, displayed a depth greater than the music's pop varnish. Jay played the same distrustful moneybags we met in 'Who You Wit', but this time Foxy won him over, and the song followed his tests of her dedication to him as their relationship grows. At first he needed to "double-check your story" to ensure she wasn't "purely out for the bucks", then, a year later, he was lavishing her with gifts to the point of criminality to keep her happy – "Risked a four to life bid to keep that shit on her arm." But, faced with the men trying to steal her from him, his insecurities wouldn't fade and he kept testing her devotion. Would she "hit the block" for him if all the money went, forgive him cheating on her, share his criminal convictions, even give him her kidneys if he needed them? Beneath this shiny pop gleam lurked a song of obsession and possession, but one that ended, Jay's character finally appeased, with as firm an oath of commitment as any gangsta could make. "Me and you ballin', from the heavens or the hell/ Won't let you hit the ground if I'm fallin' myself."

'… Sunshine' was a sideswipe at his fans' preconceptions; *In My Lifetime… Vol. 1* was the full-force sucker punch. Any diehard fans of *Reasonable Doubt* who were surprised or disappointed by the populist sheen of the single* would be disgusted by the album on its November 4 release, swathed as it was in glistening R&B hooks and radio-friendly pop samples. The Seventies soul grooves of the debut had given way to a modern synthetic electronica that, to the ear of some supporters, sounded like a cool and credible artist selling out to the mainstream. He'd even backtracked on his purist plan to stop rapping after one album, the '… Vol. 1' of the title suggesting a whole string of follow-ups. His introductory mutterings didn't even offer an apology: "I did it again niggas/Fucked up, right?/I know what you niggas asking yourself/Is he ever gonna fall off?/No." Here he was, in typical second-album fashion, complaining about the trappings of success – the bad-mouthing press write-ups, the repetitive interviews, the gold-digging girls and the ease

---

* And there were undoubtedly a few, since the single reached only number 95.

with which he can "snatch" them – and the uncredited spoken-word intro[*] even seemed to mock the faithful, with its whispers of "look at these suckers, I ain't a rapper, I'm a hustler, just so happens I know how to rap". There was much here to annoy the *Reasonable Doubt* devotees, and Jay was coming out biting.

Look past Puffy's production polish, though, and … *Vol. 1* was a rewarding listen. With five of its 14 tracks contributed by *Reasonable Doubt* alumni Premier, Ski and Big Jaz, it provided a solid bridge between the debut and Jay's new commercial direction by including tracks like 'A Million And One Questions/Rhyme No More', 'Streets Is Watching' and the direct continuation of the gangland rumble of 'Friend Or Foe' in Premier's 'Friend Or Foe '98'. Simultaneously, in the style of the 'In My Lifetime Remix', it cemented what would become a Jay-Z trademark – shamelessly reclaiming very well-known choruses from classic pop hits or even Broadway musicals and surrounding them with stories of violence, drugs and destitution to ingrain familiar hooks with a fresh gravity and danger. He'd become the man who draped the murk around the mainstream.

His first attempt was arguably his least successful. Puffy and his co-producer Ron 'Amen-Ra' Lawrence from The Hitmen brought him a beat that assimilated a glam rhythm from 'A Fly Girl' by Boogie Boys – resembling an electro update of Queen's 'We Will Rock You' – with the catchy chorus hook from new wave band The Waitresses' 1982 hit 'I Know What Boys Like'. Around it Jay and Lil' Kim rapped a crude seduction routine called 'I Know What Girls Like', Jay appreciating Kim's style in a brutish, footballer's fashion ("I never seen a face like yours before/And I been around some cute whores before/That either me or my boys tore it up before") and Kim not caring what he thinks of her so long as she gets her slice of his money ("When chickens cluck give up the buck… you can call me a slut, who gives a fuck?… fuck a pre-nup, give me half up front"). The pair ended up living in a multi-million dollar mansion penned in with Rovers, Benzes, Rembrandts

---

[*] Probably by Pain In Da Ass, since he would provide the intro to several Jay-Z albums of the era.

and jet skis on the private lake. It was a low-rent sort of high-end romance, but one that could have made for an enjoyable throwaway pop novelty if Combs hadn't wrecked it with his own superfluous hisses and asides throughout the track and several choruses of his intentionally atonal singing. Of Jay-Z's recording career so far, it was a low point.

Luckily, 'I Know What Girls Like' was in classier company. The album's 'old skool' opening track 'A Million And One Questions/ Rhyme No More'* found Jay-Z asserting his street dealing credentials against critics and interviewers who doubted that his backstory could be so gritty or that he could really have as much money as he boasted about on his records. Spinning more tales of his (possibly exaggerated) hustling past over Premier's piano-led funk crunch, he told of how "I used to be O.T., applying the force/Shoot up the whole block, then the iron I toss... Started from the crack game and then so sweet/Freaked it to the rap game." History affirmed, he turned the wearying interrogations of the interviewers asking those million questions† to his favour, claiming that the invented pasts of any fake hustlers in the rap game would buckle under the sort of questioning he handled with only a minor fluster. "Motherfuckers can't rhyme no more 'bout crime no more/Til I'm no more/Cause I'm so raw my flow exposes holes that they find in yours."

Having set the album off on a familiar track, Jay dropped his first bombshell. 'The City Is Mine' was Jay-Z lauding his rise, mocking his imitators and critics and staking his claim on the throne of New York hip-hop in Biggie's wake‡, but he did it against the backdrop of an invigorating funk disco track compiled by pop producers Teddy Riley and Chad Hugo from The Jones Girls' 'You Gonna Make Me Love Somebody Else' and the MOR rock hook of 'You Belong To

---

* A two-part track put together by DJ Premier from samples of Aaliyah, Latimore, Main Ingredient, Ferrante & Teicher and Isaac Hayes.

† "Can you really match a Triple Platinum artist buck by buck by only a single going Gold?... Do you really have a spot like you said in 'Friend Or Foe', and if so, what block?"

‡ "You held it down long enough, let me take those reigns/And just like your spirit the commission remains... I'm the focal point, like Biggie in his prime... the city is mine."

The City' by ex-Eagles songwriter Glenn Frey, as sung on this track by R&B superstars Blackstreet. Some reviewers would claim 'The City Is Mine' veered too close to the sounds Nas had used the previous year under his guise as Escobar on The Firm's debut, especially for a rapper trying to usurp Nas' claim on New York, but it was undeniably an inspired, genre-straddling song merging rock, R&B and rap to ultra-commercial effect. A sign that Jay-Z saw no musical territory as beyond his boundaries.

After 'I Know What Girls Like' cemented the album's attitude of pop experimentation upfront, … *Vol. 1* took some time to consolidate, to revive the hustle. We were back in slinky *Shaft* territory for Prestige's 'Imaginary Player', a title that would spawn many a theory that Jay-Z's hustler persona was all an act, despite Jay's admission that "I got blood money, straight up thug money/That brown paper bag under your mattress drug money." In fact, the pretend gangsters here were the "young cats" ripping off Jay's style and "talking about how they funds stack" without proving it with Hummers, diamonds and Rolex watches. It was a key track in Jay's canny brand marketing at the luxury end of hip-hop; in his world, status is nothing without its symbols.

'Streets Is Watching' – the track that had so impressed and concerned Notorious B.I.G. – and 'Friend Or Foe '98' plunged us back into the violence and paranoia of the drug trade. The first had Jay, as a high-level hustler too well known to work the streets any more, watching his back knowing there's a price on his head and a street-level prestige for anyone taking him down. His fear of rival gangs, kidnappers, psychopaths or ambitious underlings eyeing him for any mistake that they could use to destroy him bristled through Ski's tense cinematic strings and urgent bass, Jay hissing "It's like a full-time job not to kill niggas, can't chill" as if from under his desk, hugging a shotgun. Sure enough, drug droughts, arrests and death decimated his crew in the end, and Jay's conscience bit. "Was this a lesson God teaching me?… I'm playing the game straight from hell from which few came back… Public apologies to the families of those caught up in my shit… the life and time of a demonic mind excited with crime."

Then 'Friend Or Foe '98' revisited the story of Jay running a rival gang out of town in the original 'Friend Or Foe', except this time his adversaries had marshalled arms and returned to exact revenge, to take over the patch for good. Not a problem for the ever-alert Jay-Z – he ambushed their ringleader in the motel where the gang's goons are "lined up in adjoining rooms/Like some wild cowboys coming to get me at high noon" and blew the guy away, after a moralistic final speech. Suitably, Premier mustered* the sound of a pack of mobsters on the march.

'Lucky Me' was a prime example of Jay's new knack for pulping the edges of pop. Karen Anderson's sultry soul chorus and Stevie J and Buckwild's smooth R&B production couldn't be more accessible, a tune that would ooze like honey from radio speakers. But on their outskirts Jay was still in fear for his life, outlining how he was just as much of a target as a rapper as he was as a hustler, except rather than Feds and bullets now he was dodging sexual harassment lawsuits, "girls with ulterior motives", jealous competition and murderous haters: "Niggas wanna strip to the bone for shit you own." By verse three he was readying himself to kill or be killed once more, but knew his raps would live on "like a dart from the speaker to your heart". After a mid-section of the album so sunk in neuroses and dread, the lighter-hearted relationship squabbles of '... Sunshine' and 'Who You Wit II' – an exact re-run of 'Who You Wit' with the final verse about treating girls to holidays and fine wines replaced with an explicit sex scene too X-rated to have ever made the single version – came as much-needed relief.

But the most brutal and broken was yet to come. Pinballing lines back and forth between them like girls at a gangbang, Jay-Z and Sauce Money played ungracious lotharios on 'Face Off', sharing conquests disdainfully around their crew and screwing pick-ups in bathrooms. Though Trackmasters' chick-a-chick-a disco backbeat, complete with a horn note like a passing Forties cop car, was reassuring, 'Face Off' was Jay's first all-out slump into misogyny after treating women with

---

* From a sample of 'Car Of Love' by Seventies R&B act Main Ingredient.

Roc-A-Fella at its most harmonious: Damon Dash, Shawn "Jay-Z" Carter and Kareem "Biggs" Burke.

The young Jay-Z, though he'd never actually graduate from High School. WENN

Jay Z and his mentor Jaz-O at BT's Lounge in Trenton, NJ.

Girls, Girls, Girls: Jay-Z, Aaliyah, Bijou Phillips and Kidada Jones at the Bar North in Los Angeles, California.
JEFF VESPA/WIREIMAGE

Jaz-O and Jay-Z. AL PEREIRA/MICHAEL OCHS ARCHIVES/GETTY IMAGES

Enjoying a Cristal with Biggie's girlfriend Lil' Kim.
DAVE ALLOCCA/DMI/TIME LIFE PICTURES/GETTY IMAGES

East Coast playas - Jay-Z & Sean "Puffy" Combs.
JEFF VESPA/WIREIMAGE

Recording an MTV interview at Riverside Park NYC, 1997. MONIQUE BUNN/RETNA LTD

Rocking the collegiate sports look on the Hard Knock Life tour, 8th April 1999, Las Vegas, Nevada. SCOTT HARRISON/HULTON ARCHIVE/GETTY IMAGES

Ludacris and Jay-Z play scissors, paper, um, stick backstage at an Outkast, Ludacris and Foxy Brown show at Madison Square Garden. THEO WARGO/WIREIMAGE

Building the empire from the Roc-A-Fella offices. AL PEREIRA/MICHAEL OCHS ARCHIVES/GETTY IMAGES

Promoting *'Bonnie & Clyde '03'* with Beyonce Knowles at Spankin' New Music Week on MTV's "TRL" - November 21, 2002 at MTV Studios Times Square in New York. K.MAZUR/WIREIMAGE

Music' biggest power couple-to-be onstage at the 2003 MTV Video Music Awards, Radio City Music Hall, New York.
JEFF KRAVITZ/FILMMAGIC

ashing two of his four 2004 MTV Video Music Awards in Miami (Best Rap Video, Best Direction, Best Editing and Best nematography). LISA O'CONNOR/ZUMA/CORBIS

ooking up to Magic Johnson at the Caesars Hotel & Casino in Atlantic City, New Jersey. MYCHAL WATTS/WIREIMAGE

Throwing the Roc-A-Fella diamond backstage at the MTV Europe Awards 2001 in Frankfurt, Germany, November 8, 2001.

a mixture of suspicion and devotion for the rest of the album, and it would be the most often recited track when critics pointed to the record's lyrical triteness, its repetitive obsession with easy sex, violence and consumerism.

Similarly, both Anthony Dent's laid-back, West Coast style 'Real Niggaz' and Big Jaz's scratchy, crack-skittery 'Rap Game/Crack Game' followed another of the album's recurring themes, likening rapping to hustling. In the first, Jay-Z and Too Short told of having "flipped the script" from drugs to music, but still found themselves surrounded by the same kinds of predators and enemies, the labels no less mercenary than drug gangs and the police still hard on their case, convinced they must still be selling to afford the luxury lifestyle they lay claim to. In the second Jay used drug dealing as a direct metaphor for rapping: from cooking up their record to scouting out the market, getting radio hooked on their product, building up a client base, maximising demand and then watching the expansion explode, the tune filling listeners with a thrill as wild, euphoric and fleeting as any crack hit, leaving them desperate for "another fix". But the two tracks had widely different intentions. 'Real Niggaz' ended with Jay-Z playing the peacemonger, arguing that East and West Coasts alike were living too well to ruin it with acrimony – "How sweet niggaz' lives can get/Put beef aside, the East and Westside connect... I want Biggie to rest in peace as well as 'Pac/How real is that?" 'Rap Game...' on the other hand, mischievously sampled another line from Nas – "somehow the rap game reminds me of the crack game" – from the *Illmatic* track 'Represent'. An act probably intended to stir up the growing animosity. After all, with Biggie and Tupac's beef tragically concluded, there was surely space for another, less deadly rivalry to snatch the headlines.

So far, ... *Vol. 1* had been an enjoyable but inconsistent creature. It flicked between the familiar and the unexpected, the crude and the sublime, magnanimity and misogyny, paranoia and security, bravado and despondency, the horrors of hustling and the irritations of rap, soothing soul and prickly pop, sex and death. It could have seemed, to the more critical ear, overtly commercial and lyrically vapid. But in its closing couplet ... *Vol. 1* finally illuminated its depths. After the album's numerous surface-value references to crack dealing, the brooding but melodic 'Where I'm From'* was where Jay truly dug into the dirt of his Marcy upbringing. A lyric of panoramic scope, it took in the skewed dystopian politics and religion of projects poverty – the streets that "politic themselves", where news crews never ventured to report black crime, the police only appeared in dawn swoops, and faith in any God or church faded along with money and hope. But its real devils were in its details: the boys lost to the morgue and the girls lost to boys from better neighbourhoods; the teenagers writing wills; the dumped stashes at the whir of a siren; the stolen goods traded half-price; the court cases caught and lost; the bullet-proof vests you can't leave home for a day; "the pimps, prostitutes and the drug lords". And, at the heart of it all, a sense of hard-earned honour and truth. Jay-Z stated some rules here – you don't rap about what you haven't lived through and, if the platform is ever yours, it's your duty to tell the world every terror of the ghetto. "Promise fulfilled": in hip-hop terms, this was the stuff of Don DeLillo.

For 'You Must Love Me', the final track on ... *Vol. 1,* Jay-Z drew his vision inwards, from macro to micro, political to personal. Over solemn, funereal church bells, strings and epic soul choirs† he calmly and regretfully laid bare three confessional open letters to those close to him, as if trying to make amends for all the ill he'd done in his life. The first verse went out to his mother, who he'd tormented "since my date of birth" with his petty theft, court hearings and drug dealings. The song even went as far as to suggest he sold crack to Gloria to help her escape the pain of his father leaving, a (quite possibly fictional) story expounded in heart-wrenching detail on record but never spoken about in interviews: "All you did was motivate me/Don't let 'em hold you back/What I do, I turned around and I sold you crack/I was a bastard for that/Still I'm drowning in shame." When he "ran across this memory... it stung the

---

* A Hitmen production incorporating samples from Yvonne Fair and Fat Joe alongside lines Jay raps from Puffy's own 'Young Gs'.

† Put together by The Hitmen's Nashiem Myrick from samples from The O'Jays' 'What Am I Waiting For' and original vocals from rising soul star Kelly Price.

brain"; the thought of such an act, that he could "ever destroy the beauty from which one came", tormented him, particularly since he admitted he'd be nothing without his mother's love and encouragement. In the end he was thankful his mother pulled through her troubles, and grateful and amazed she could still find love for him.

Verse two detailed the shooting of his brother Eric, brought on (the song explains) by an entire childhood of the two room-mates rowing and sharing or stealing each other's clothes and possessions. The lyrics added details to the scene – the presence of "Mickey, Andy and the girl that bought [the ring]" and Jay asking his brother to get out of the house but shooting him on his way down some stairs – but the lingering image is of the boy overtaken with rage, "ya drillin' it and my ego hurt combined/Drove me bezerk, saw the devil in your eyes... confused I just closed my young eyes and squeezed." Eric's forgiveness of him in hospital the next day seems all the more poignant and good-hearted for the madness of the moment itself.

The final verse addressed a girl Jay had strong feelings for and had tried hard to protect from the perils of his hustling, but still, on the girl's insistence, allowed himself to use as a drug mule. After the cynical and uncaring front he'd exhibited towards women for the rest of the album, it was a rare moment of tenderness, albeit one laced with exploitation. But, more than any other lyric to date, it cut to the heart of the dealer's dilemma: that the pursuit of money can become so all-engrossing that, in the heat of it, the dealer doesn't care who or what he'll sacrifice. It was a hot nugget of shame that Jay, the ex-criminal, here wrestles with deeply, and it closed an often cold and heartless album with a redemptive pulse of humanity.

Initially, ... *Vol. 1* was met with a rush of acclaim and success on its November 4 release. Keen to keep up the critical impetus of *Reasonable Doubt*, the reviews were glowing. "A rock-steady set with both street and pop appeal," said Steve Jones of *USA Today*. "Arrogant yet diffident, ruthless yet cute – a scary original," claimed Robert Christgau from *The Village Voice*. "Jay-Z established himself as that rare underground rhymer with commercial appeal," went Soren Baker of the *Chicago Tribune*. The public were swept along on the Jay-Z wave too, sending the album to number three on the *Billboard* chart, Gold on its way to eventual Platinum. The third single from the album, 'The City Is Mine', would also improve on its predecessors' placings, hitting a respectable number 52 in the US and number 28 in the UK in February 1998 with the help of another filmic video intercutting shots of Jay-Z as a New York linchpin with a recreation of Kevin Spacey's scenes from *The Usual Suspects* movie, blazing spoilers and all.

Among the mainstream press plaudits, though, there were grumblings. Soren Baker also passed comment on the alienating effect of Puffy's involvement, and *Vibe*'s incognito reviewer The Blackspot picked at this wound further. "The key word here is 'inconsistency'. In some songs Jay-Z fires rhymes with fully automatic intensity; while on others, he throws punches with the impact of hip-pop marshmallows. For instance, 'The City Is Mine' sinks to lows one would never imagine Jay would reach. Here our hero goes for Puff fluff by using a popular Eighties hit for a hook."[4]

Chris Norris from *Spin* also laid into Combs for tarnishing the Jay-Z magic, claiming "without one sure, guiding vision, the Combs blueprint comes off as either mundane or embarrassing". It was an opinion that, as the album was dissected over time, became the prevailing one, even to Jay-Z himself. "I think 85 per cent of it is solid," he told *Vibe*'s Dream Hampton, "and that 85 per cent was better than everybody's [sic] else's album at the time."[5] But as the album crept rather than raced towards Platinum, Jay-Z started to agree that it was (in his eyes) underselling due to a botched or rushed job.

"What I did with *In My Lifetime... Vol. 1* was I tried to make records," he'd later state. "I had just made *Reasonable Doubt...* it wasn't successful in music industry terms. It was a cult classic on the streets, but it wasn't successful in the music business and I tried to blend the two. If you look back on *In My Lifetime... Vol. 1*, there were songs on there that were brilliant. I don't listen to that album because I think I messed it up... You got 'Where I'm From', 'Streets Is Watching', 'You Must Love Me' and 'Lucky Me'. It's so many incredible records on there that I think I missed having two classics in a row [by] trying to get on the radio. It really hurt me because that album was so good; I can't listen to it.

When that record comes on it just irks me. I don't have any regrets but musically, the album [is] the one that got away."[6]

He would be less swayed, though, by criticism from the specialist rap critics that he'd slowed his raps down in order to gain a wider fanbase. The life experiences he was trying to convey, he'd argue, meant that he had to slow down his style to get the message across clearly. "In the beginning it was all technique," he said. "I was like a trickster, dribbling behind my back, just really trying to impress people. But as I started to get life experiences, I had to tell a story, so the technique had to slow down a bit. It had to make way for the story and the emotion... I was enunciating and making clear points. I think people connected to a real truth."[7]

Ironically, it would be by slowing his raps further and ignoring The Blackspot's major criticism of 'The City Is Mine' that Jay-Z would make the first of his hip-hop fortunes.

And he'd make it within a widescreen 12 months, too. And all thanks to a lovable ginger orphan of legend...

Chapter Six

Annie Get Your Gun

"'Stead of treated, we get tricked! / 'Stead of kisses we get kicked!"

The bellyful roar of men singing a young girl's song rocked the boat. Twenty-dollar bills flung in mushroom clouds from the table flicked on the air just beyond the Norfolk State college girls' fingertips and floated off over the edge to settle like green grease on the Atlantic Ocean. The Roc-A-Fella party slammed their palms on the table in time to the beat, tipping champagne flutes and cognac shots to the deck, laughing and bellowing along triumphantly to the track the DJ was spinning. The corny-ass track and its hard-luck chorus that had made them all rich.

The elated holler, ironically, of the high life.

"It's the hard-knock life for us! It's the hard-knock life…!"

Labor Day weekend, 1998, and aboard the two-decked boat that Timbaland had hired off the coast of Virginia to celebrate the holiday, Jay-Z and the Roc-A-Fella posse were in raucous spirits, tossing back shots and bawling their successes to the high seas. As Jay-Z's biggest radio hit to date gave way to another of his tunes that had owned the airwaves all summer, the Jermaine Dupri collaboration 'Money Ain't A Thang', the crew started peeling banknotes from their wallets and flinging them into the air for the students to scramble for. It was only

September but already 1998 had proved a proud and productive year for Roc-A-Fella and Jay-Z. As the rap world still rocked in the wake of the Tupac and Biggie killings, the genre was split: DMX had managed two US number one albums that year with his doom rap violence reflecting murderous times, while The Fugees' Lauryn Hill had produced one of the year's best-selling albums by soothing rap into a soulful gospel stew on *The Miseducation Of Lauryn Hill*, as if calming the decade, forcing hip-hop to take a deep breath and count to 10.

And straddling the two camps – the soul and the street – towered Jay-Z.

Unprepared to leap straight into a third album following the shaky reception afforded to ... *Vol. 1*, Roc-A-Fella had started the year concentrating on expanding their empire. Jay had signed up an impressive roster of acts and was looking for a way to showcase them; Dash, on the other hand, had become obsessed with branching out into cinema, envisioning himself as a hotshot movie producer, perhaps for Roc-A-Films. Having already made one drastic career swerve, Jay wasn't crazy about the idea of moving into pictures, but they were doing well enough from ... *Vol. 1* to indulge Dash's inner Spielberg for a while. They concocted a project that would answer both of their needs, without resorting to any blockbuster budgets.

Streets Is Watching, billed as 'A long form music video movie by Abdul Malik Abbott', was Dash's concept to link Jay's existing videos and new shoots by Abbott for non-single tracks into a cohesive story based around the more cinematic and narrative-based of Jay's raps so far. With a micro-budget attached, its production values were inevitably cheap, its storyline half-baked and its interpretations of Jay's songs painfully literal. Opening with a to-camera rant from a gun-toting Pain In Da Ass proclaiming Jay's *Scarface*-style reputation, over 40 minutes it follows an exaggerated and fictionalised story of Jay-Z's hustling life. There's an unexpected ambush of his gang in the Marcy projects, gat barrels flaming wildly to the backing of 'Where I'm From', suggesting the start of the sort of low-level turf war not uncommon among hustling crews in the projects. Next, a faithful acting out of the face-offs from both editions of 'Friend Or Foe' shows Jay's crew casually killing or chasing off the competition and becoming top dogs, only for the psychosis of the original 'Streets Is Watching' video to bring the most coherent thread of the film's narrative to an unsettling end.

From here, Abbott merely turns Jay-Z's tracks into filmic set pieces. The emotionless sexuality of 'Face Off' is an excuse for a gratuitous and incongruous scene of occasionally explicit soft porn set in a private mansion strip club just for Jay and his crew, which ends in Jay and Dash inexplicably shooting a guy making out with one of the many topless girls. 'Imaginary Player' is precisely recreated in a nightclub scene where a bunch of wannabe big shots goof around at one table, scraping together enough money for one glass of Cristal between them, while Jay-Z, Dash and the Roc-A-Fella party get the girls, guzzle the champagne and leave the no-marks to drink up their dregs when they hit the limos.

The final track featured, 'You Must Love Me', finds Jay on a church pew remembering the evils he's done, from a re-enactment of shooting his brother to strapping a belt of drugs to his girlfriend's waist and sending her off to jail. With shots of crack being cooked and cut and of a child actor playing a young Jay admonishing his elder self for his crimes, it makes for quite a moving piece, offset by a random, pointless coda scene in which two groups of girls in Marcy fight over Jay and his gang.

For all its crude nudity, casual macho gun violence and low-budget attempt to recreate gangbanger films such as *Boyz N The Hood* and *Menace II Society* – ironically making Roc-A-Fella the imaginary players of the gangsta movie world – *Streets Is Watching* does have its poignant moments. Opening shots of the Marcy projects in autumn make the red brick buildings and tree-lined courtyards seem a deceptively idyllic place, as Jay testifies to its hidden horrors in voice-over. And the closing credits contain a hidden gem in the form of a new Jay-Z and Memphis Bleek track called 'It's Alright', built by Dash and a co-producer called Mahogany from a slowed-down sample of Talking Heads' classic 'Once In A Lifetime' warped into the glass-shattering tinkles of Kraftwerk's 'Hall Of Mirrors', another example of Jay and his producers reclaiming a cult hit hook for their own raw hip-hop ends.

'It's Alright' formed the opening salvo of Jay-Z's side of the *Streets Is Watching* bargain: the soundtrack. This album was basically a way to expose the acts that Jay had signed to Roc-A-Fella, but under the umbrella of his name. So he rapped alongside Memphis on 'It's Alright', Rell on 'Love Is Free', Christión on 'Your Love' and Sauce Money, Wais and Memphis again on 'Celebration'. Elsewhere, Roc-A-Fella signings contributed tunes that had acted as musical interludes between Jay's songs in the film – Christión's 'Pimp This Love', 'The Doe' by Diamonds In Da Rough and 'Crazy' by Usual Suspects. For extra credibility Jay roped in DMX, a rising Ja Rule, and established NYC acts including M.O.P. and DJ Clue and Noreaga to add weight to the release.

Though the straight-to-video release of *Streets Is Watching* racked up 100,000 sales and made Roc-A-Fella $2 million, artistically the album was far more worthwhile, if only for 'It's Alright'. The lyric was a typical first-generation Jay-Z boast about his money, jewels, jets, rap skills and ability to avoid the Feds and wipe out rivals, all adorned with gambling metaphors, Memphis Bleek, now forgiven for his second album faux pas and allowed back into the Roc-A-Fella fray, played the street-level apprentice "taking nine to the chest" for Jay's overlord. But the tune was an exuberant bounce embedded with cultish cool and space-age synthetics, the perfect amalgam of *Reasonable Doubt*'s peerless flows and … *Vol. 1.*'s pop edge. It sounded like a hit, and before long it would be.

Of Jay-Z's other appearances on the soundtrack, there were several standouts. His cameo on Rell's R&B loverman tune 'Love For Free' as the womaniser from whom Rell steals an impressionable girl is slickly played out in a video heavily branded with Roc-A-Fella logos. His own 'You're Only A Customer'* finds him, as a newly moneyed man, reminiscing about the foolish impetuosity of his young hustlings and aspiring to Triple Platinum, the Forbes rich list and the Fortune 500 – a key first indicator that Jay was considering expanding his rap exploits

---

* An assured, pounding rhythm put together by Irv Gotti and including a chorus sample from Mary J. Blige and LL Cool J's 'All Night Long Remix'.

into other streams of business revenue. It also makes his boldest claim to rap supremacy yet (warning pretenders that taking him on is "like spitting to God") and describes the speed and awe with which Jay-Z's fame was then spreading in some of his most poetic lines: "I shoot through the city like a rumour... paper heading read 'Jay-Z breathes, 80 degrees'." Yet still the police stalk him, looking for continuing signs of his old criminal ways – "Can't stop for the Feds, say cheese/ You know they wanna take a nigga picture/Pray for the day to get ya/But I'm a parlay and stay richer for now/Jigga hasn't done dirt for a while."

The cruel combination of Jay, Ja Rule and DMX made the killer clash of 'Murdergram' the most ominous and scary track in Jay-Z's canon yet, a feral treatise on the art of killing*; the huge, joyous funk horns of 'Celebration' closed the record in a flurry of energised speed-spits that Jay, Sauce, Memphis and Wais must've been breathing through their eyeballs to deliver. The *Streets Is Watching* soundtrack gave its fair share of bang per buck, not least when Jay set in stone one of his most lasting nicknames, rolling out rhymes like Ali: "I'm the God MC, me, Jay-hovah."

As legendary as his God MC/Hova persona would ultimately become, it wasn't what made Jay's fortune that year. It wasn't what prompted him to toss money in the air like confetti and bawl his own songs from Timbaland's starboard.

No, the fortune had been seeded earlier that year, borne of an epiphany he wished down from the disco heavens.

"I'm wishing on a star/To follow where you are..."

The voice cut like crystal, soared like songbirds. Made perfect sense. He'd rapped around samples and re-recordings of classic tunes before – Soul II Soul's "What's the meaning of life?", The Waitresses' 'I Know What Boys Like' – but now a new avenue of association with the past

---

* Fictionally, of course – as late as 1998 Jay was insisting to *Vibe*'s Dream Hampton that he'd never killed anyone himself.

was opening up to him. Watching Gwen Dickey from Rose Royce through the glass of his studio recording booth recreate the star-gazing chorus from her 1978 ballad 'Wishing On A Star', Jay knew he was onto something big. No longer did he have to borrow history's greatest tunes, now he could stand alongside them.

On a mellow groove produced by Trackmasters that predicted the crossover potential of Eminem's 'Stan' two years early, Jay reminisced wistfully on his youth, on the girls he never connected with because he was too caught up in his dealing, on the lost games and poverty of childhood, his first battles, the friends who "passed right in front of my eyes", the stars they wished on. Accompanied by a black and white video of a young actor playing a pre-teen Jay-Z as he grows up admiring the hustlers' rides and strides, fighting in the streets, making his first dollars dealing, trying to impress the project girls, witnessing his first shooting and performing his first raps, the track didn't make any major dents on the US charts but it was a Top 20 hit in the UK, reaching number 13.* Facing his biggest international chart placing yet, a major breakthrough, Jay realised he was onto something big. And started looking around for an even grander crossover concept.

As the summer of 1998 progressed, Jay-Z invaded the airwaves with greater and greater intensity. First, in May, with his sassy, cash-flashing collaboration with producer Jermaine Dupri on 'Money Ain't A Thang'†, a reworking of the glory horns from 'Weak At The Knees' by Eighties soul minister Steve Arrington that had both rappers tripping out catchy rhymes about their sports cars, their hundred grand jewellery and even their diamond-studded bullets, and came with a video of Ferrari racing, high-end gambling and bills flying like ticker-tape, the inspiration for the flying wallets of Timbaland's Labor Day boat. It's a song that also included a telling premonition, as Jay rapped about how the million-selling rapper would "hit an R&B chick and she fit the bill". Then, in

---

* It was included on the UK release of *In My Lifetime… Vol. 1*.

† For which Jay would earn his first Grammy nomination in 1999 for Best Rap Performance By A Duo Or Group.

July, the radio waves throbbed along to the single release of 'It's Alright', complete with the obligatory high-times video shot on the beach at Mexican luxury retreat Cancun. But behind the scenes he was laying the groundwork for an even bigger radio bomb.

But first, he'd really have to invent a fake past for himself.

DJ Mark The 45 King gave him the track. The 45 King was an old Flavor Unit cohort of Queen Latifah making a comeback after drug addiction had seen a production deal with Warner Bros. collapse in the early Nineties. Kid Capri – one of Jay's latest production recruits for his third album alongside such rising names as Ruff Ryders' in-house producer Swizz Beatz and a fresh young kid called Timbaland, who'd done great jobs on the debut albums from Missy Elliott and Aaliyah – first played it to him while Jay was on the road touring … *Vol. 1* around the US. The tour bus soundtrack was wide-reaching that year, taking in Alanis Morissette, Sarah McLachlan, Scarface and Jay's then favourite song 'I Don't Want To Miss A Thing' by Aerosmith, but this new track stretched the boundaries to breaking point. Comprising only the beat and a sample of the hook at the time, Jay adored it so much he hunted down The 45 King and convinced him to hand over the track rather than keeping it for his own compilation album.

It wasn't just the laid-back ghetto beat with its bouncing rubber bassline, nagging piano plinks and the odd crash of Broadway timpani that had Jay hooked. Crucially, it was the fact that it revolved around a central chorus instantly recognisable to any listener. The keynote chorus from the musical *Annie*, in which the lead character and her fellow orphans bemoan their tragic situation and traumatic upbringings: "It's the hard knock life for us/It's the hard knock life for us/'Stead of treated we get tricked/'Stead of kisses we get kicked."

A corny song, an audacious sample, but it struck so many chords with Jay-Z. He'd had success and gained attention by utilising famous populist hooks, and there were few more famous or populist than 'Hard Knock Life'. It was a chorus ingrained into the public conscience like a genetic memory handed down from generation to generation, as automatically recognised as 'Consider Yourself' or 'Over The Rainbow'.

It transcended genre and criticism by coming from so far outside rap it was unimpeachable, chargeless of musical meddlings or meanders, yet it spoke directly to the heart and roots of hip-hop, its political punch all the more powerful for its stark simplicity. As Jay-Z would tell *People Weekly*, "These kids sing about the hard knock life, things everyone in the ghetto feels coming up... That's the ghetto anthem."

"You know," he said in a *Blues & Soul* interview, "I knew how people in the ghetto would relate to words like 'Instead of treated we get tricked' and 'Instead of kisses we get kicked'... It's like when we watch movies we're always rooting for the villain or the underdog because that's who we feel we are. It's us against society. And, to me, the way the kids in the chorus are singing 'It's a hard knock life' is more like they're rejoicing about it. Like they're too strong to let it bring them down."[1]

With Jay-Z laying down a list of project hard knocks over the top – murder scenes and prison cells, guns and gang invasions, stripping mothers and murderous foes, all encased in his relief at getting rap skills, getting rich and getting out – 'Hard Knock Life (Ghetto Anthem)' flew from Broadway to Brooklyn and landed like a buzz-bomb. Only problem was, The 45 King couldn't get copyright clearance for the sample. The musical *Annie* had a clean-cut reputation built over 20 years since its 1977 Broadway opening and cemented by the 1982 movie adaptation, and the copyright holders – composer Charles Strouse and lyricist Martin Charnin – were loathe to sully their ultimate family-friendly musical by association with the drugs and violence prevalent in rap. So Jay-Z invented a small part of a past to win them over. He wrote them a letter directly to tell them that, as a schoolchild, he'd won an essay-writing competition in seventh grade with the prize of seeing the musical on Broadway. He'd been so moved by the story, he wrote, that he could see a direct connection between the orphans of the tale and the fatherless, disenfranchised, hopeless children out in Marcy. His sociological point that those kids trapped in ghetto crack culture were the new *Annie* generation was astute, and his argument that the *Annie* story was universally applicable was convincing; only the essay competition was invented, to tug at the heartstrings of the heartstring tuggers. And it worked. Copyright approved.

"If the request had been sent without the song, I don't think I would've done it," Charnin told *Vibe* magazine, admitting they'd been paid between $25,000 and $50,000 for the initial use of the song, plus a royalty cut. "Saying you want to make a 'ghetto anthem' is unspecific. It had to be demonstrated instead of just talked about... [But] here was a serious rap artist with a point to make. The fact that [Annie and Jay-Z] lived parallel lives that met was exciting."[2]

As an increasingly wealthy and famous rapper, Jay had been struggling to recreate the punch and passion of *Reasonable Doubt* from the perspective of his new, far more comfortable life, far from the pains and paranoias of hustling. He was concerned, after the mild roastings afforded to ... *Vol. 1*, that he'd never regain his debut's street-wisdom credibility. So he leapt on this fresh connection to his origins, this shiny slab of street truth. He was so pleased that permission had been granted for the sample that he decided to dedicate his entire third album to the concept, the link between popular commercialism and the trials of growing up and living in the Brooklyn projects. He'd call the album *Vol. 2... Hard Knock Life*.

Unlike the rush of *Reasonable Doubt* and the stress of ... *Vol. 1*, *Vol. 2...* was a joy to record, flowing out of the studio in under a month. "With this album I was really in a zone," Jay said. "I was like [Michael] Jordan that night when he hit nine threes and he walked off the court like 'I'm HOT! I can't MISS right now!'... With my guests, I felt like a conductor directing a concerto... Every time I went to the studio, it was one big party – and I think that just translated to the music."[3]

Before landing the 'Hard Knock...' killer blow on the rap world, though, Jay had a battle of the sexes to oversee...

Buildings and cars exploded. Heroes made death-defying plunges from rooftops or collapsing walkways. Kung fu partners defied gravity to simultaneously kick opponents in the face. On screens behind the bar where Chris Penn from *Reservoir Dogs* was clownishly flinging vodka bottles around like a trainee Tom Cruise in *Cocktail*, the blockbuster action blazed on, clips from the movie *Rush Hour* on whose soundtrack the song was a key cut – another movie studio who'd cottoned on to the cult street cred of Jay-Z and wanted to carve off a slice for their film. But in the bar, where the satin-clad dancers bounced and jolted, nobody cared about those big-budget stunts and pyrotechnics. They had their own big-budget rumble going down.

"Can I get a 'fuck you' to the bitches from all of my niggas who don't love hoes, they get no dough," deadpanned Jay-Z, knowing his boy Ja Rule would have his back. "Can I get a 'WHOOP WHOOP!' to these niggas from all of my bitches who don't got love for niggas without dubs," replied Amil from the Major Coins act Jay had signed to Roc-A-Fella, surrounded by her defiant dancing girlfriends, leading the feminist fightback against men with inadequate wheel rims. And thus was played out the age-old hip-hop argument – the men who detest women who want their money and the women who demand they give it to them. There was a minor level of added sophistication to 'Can I Get A…', the sparkling modernist Irv Gotti and Lil Rob production featuring Amil and Ja Rule, as Jay questioned whether a girl would still be interested in him if he was poor or talentless and Amil replied that lack of money equals a lack of ambition, and ambition is what turned her on. Ambition and designer labels. It was a lyric that left no winners: the women seemed shallow, demanding and mercenary, and the men seemed cruel, heartless and manipulative, particularly Ja Rule, who claimed he'll leave a conquest a hundred dollars even if they don't want it, just to "make 'em feel slutted". As great as it sounded, 'Can I Get A…' was sexual loathing you could dance to.

As such, it was a major US hit. With Jay's chorus line censored to "Can I get a 'what what'," arguably improving the song's attitude and mainstream appeal immeasurably, 'Can I Get A…' was a radio smash, crystallising the war of the sexes in a way which an increasingly marginalised and sexualised popular culture could embrace. Club dancefloors across the States rocked to the 'WHOOP WHOOP!' chant and the track hit number 19 in the *Billboard* chart in August 1998, rocketing Jay-Z into the hip-hop stratosphere. Just in time for 'Hard Knock Life (Ghetto Anthem)' to start eating up the radio, and for the album *Vol. 2... Hard Knock Life* to smash apart the charts.

From its introduction, however, you'd have thought Jay had already retired[*], given up the hip-hop ghost, handed on the baton and resigned to the grave. Over a pulsing heartbeat, a dejected Pain In Da Ass recited an elegy to Jay-Z, apologising to Biggie for failing him and naming Memphis Bleek as his successor: "Bleek's gonna be a good rapper/New improved Jay-Z/I quit, I'm retiring/Ain't enough money in this game to keep me around/Sorry Big, I tried." His catchphrase of "Okay, I'm reloaded!" gave way to a Bleek solo slot[†] on 'Hand It Down', as if taking on Jay-Z's mantle, with Jigga nowhere to be heard. But this real-life enactment of 'Coming Of Age', with Bleek seeming to step up to run the whole operation, was obviously a smokescreen, a taunt; after Bleek's rap about low-level hustling and his lust for the newest Jordans, 'Hard Knock Life (Ghetto Anthem)' crashed in and Jay announced his comeback as emphatically as possible. "I stretched the game out/X'd your name out/Put Jigga on top and drop albums non-stop."

The comeback was justified by 'If I Should Die', the first of three Swizz Beatz productions on the album that, alongside Timbaland's inspired tracks, would seamlessly make the crossover to the pop mainstream that Bad Boy had attempted so clunkily on ... *Vol. 1*. Swizz and Timbaland's main evolution for Jay-Z's world was to take the emphasis off soul samples – no samples at all were credited for their tracks, suggesting entirely original beats. It was a shift that would further frustrate fans of *Reasonable Doubt*, prompting AllMusic's Steve Birchmeier to mourn ...*Doubt* as being from "a foregone era when samples fuelled the beats and turntablism supplied the hooks, [which] sets *Reasonable Doubt* apart from Jay-Z's later work." But it would be pivotal in making *Vol. 2...* the most coherent and successful album of Jay's 'Lifetime' trilogy, and in

---

[*] His initial two-album agreement with Def Jam was completed with *Vol. 2...* after all.

[†] Helmed by DJ Premier from a sample of The Four Tops' 'Are You Man Enough' to give Bleek added *Reasonable Doubt* kudos as the new Jay-Z.

catapulting him, at 28 years of age, into a whole new league of modern hip-hop. A league he'd ultimately end up owning.

Lyrically, 'If I Should Die' also continued the reflective tone of 'You Must Love Me', an angle that would add emotion and resonance to Jay-Z's albums from now on. It had Jay facing death with a grin, remembering his high school sexual encounters, his best battles and his duets with Mary J. Blige, his shoot-outs and evaded arrests, and deciding he'd had a decent enough ride. It was a rap will and testament in the tradition of Biggie and Tupac's foretellings of their own deaths, given an intense, nervy edge by Swizz's insistent strings, synth and bulbous beat, with urgent verses from Wais and Half Dead recalling their own triumphs and regrets. It would eventually unveil its fair share of shallow braggadocio but from its opening salvo *Vol. 2...* was shaping up to be a far more mature and thoughtful record lyrically than its predecessor, steeped in significances – social, political and personal.

And, amid the familiar roll-call of guns, money, jewels, girls, beefs and high-level hustling that were dashed across Stevie J's jittery and breathy 'Ride Or Die', more secrets were exposed. "I probably make more money off your album than you," Jay lets on to the "wack rap niggas... that get fucked for they publishing": "I'm Platinum a million times nigga, check the credits/S. Carter, ghost writer." It was the first on-record admission that Jay had been writing rhymes for other rappers undercover, a common practice in hip-hop but one that comes with blushes for the rappers throwing out other people's rhymes. Though Jay would be contractually tight-lipped about who he wrote for, telling *Vibe* magazine "I get paid a lot of money to not tell you who I write for," Dr. Dre would openly use him as a ghost writer for the following year's 'Still D.R.E.' single, of which Jay is particularly proud. "My greatest moment ever is as a ghost writer," Jay-Z would tell me some years later. "[Dre] is perceived as the greatest producer in hip-hop so no one looks at it any kind of way because he's not a rapper by trade. He's an entertainer, he's really a great producer. So whether it's Dre or Puff for that matter, no one really cares."

Another of his proudest moments was next up on *Vol. 2....* With 'Nigga What, Nigga Who – Originator 99', two sets of innovation were asserted. In the lyric, buried beneath smuggling scenes, rabid gunplay and graphic sex with betrayable women, Jay and Big Jaz (formerly Jaz-O) reminded a hip-hop world starting to embrace speed-rapping that they did it first on 'The Originators' way back in 1990, delivered in a staggeringly fast example of the style. And musically 'Nigga What…' was a wonder, Timbaland creating the perfect amalgam of thundercloud strings, electro blips and click-cracking percussion that felt to Jay like a glimpse of his stylistic future.

Those thunderclouds thickened for Swizz's second contribution, 'Money, Cash, Hoes', and out of its dense cinematic fog prowled DMX, hinting at mad dogs, mutilated corpses and cannibalism, growling and barking like a werewolf in heat. Jay had made great leaps by presenting himself as the melodic, soul-tinged and approachable face of gangsta rap, but this was his first grab at the demonic rap dollar, bursting with horror flick orchestration, DMX's chart-topping snarls, murder talk and a synthesiser sweep like *The Munsters* gone psycho. 'Money, Cash, Hoes' was a concerted effort for Jay-Z to be taken seriously by the burgeoning murder rap fraternity and bring some underground grime to *Vol. 2…*, if only to offset the *Annie* sample that might potentially see him labelled as a novelty rap sell-out. The R&B pop glints of …*Vol. 1* seemed a lifetime away from here.

The envelope pushed, familiarity was called for. 'A Week Ago' and 'Coming Of Age (Da Sequel)' revisited Jay's knack for the hustling narrative song, and his manner of continuing their stories from album to album. In 'A Week Ago' he was a dealer shopped to the police by a partner turned snitch who'd been caught in a raid. In the space of a week Jay's ex-friend had gone from breaking his bread and swearing his blood oaths to ratting him out and ruining his street rep for life. "Your son gotta grow up like 'this is my dad?'/The labeling of a snitch is a lifetime scar/You'll always be in jail nigga, just minus the bars." Over a reformed Isley Brothers soul beat, Jay and Too Short dissect criminal loyalty and the tight-lipped honour of the game with an abrasive reality, and laying out the minutiae of such a specific corner of the hustling mentality just added credibility to a backstory that was increasingly being probed and prodded under the sceptical microscope of the music press.

A similar ode to loyalty, the brilliantly tense 'Coming Of Age (Da Sequel)', picked up the story of Jay's recruitment of Memphis Bleek as his hustling apprentice on *Reasonable Doubt*. You'd imagine Jay wrote it as a lesson to Bleek to know his place, after failing to show up for sessions on ... *Vol. 1*. Now Jay's character had moved out to the suburbs while Bleek had taken over the city running, coping with the life-threatening situations, the fear and the stress while surrounded by people telling him the kingpin had gotten lazy, old, prime for replacement. So Bleek had his sights set on Jay's position at the top, and the two faced each other down in the street, weighing each other up, each pondering his own internal monologue. With one of Swizz Beatz's most action-packed, explosive and panic-stricken backings stirring the sense of impending conflict and Bleek hurling out desperate rhymes about having earned his place at the top, it was a riveting scene, pinpointing every detail of that moment on the streets that could shift a partnership from brotherhood to deadly enemies. Jay, sensing Bleek's restlessness and dissatisfaction and paying him a visit "'fore he decide to get cute", spotted a "fake smile" and considered killing him there and then; Bleek, his thinking muddied by dope, realised Jay was on to him and had no choice but to reassert his faithfulness. Their tightness was emphasised by the way they swapped lines and finished each other's rhymes – in the end the tension dissolved and the conflict was averted. They were brothers again – for now – and we, as listeners, had been granted an intimate four minutes inside the head of a very humanised gangster, the perfect soundtrack if ever Spike Jonze decided to make a film called Being John Gotti.

Following such an insightful tour de force, 'Can I Get A...' acted as bounce-along pop relief before Timbaland's smooth flowing 'Paper Chase' gave us another high-definition snapshot of the game, and one where the sexes are slightly more united. Here, Foxy Brown played one of the girls Jay would use to start up new hustling operations in small towns for him, opening the track with a Herculean bout of swearing that repeated "bitch" 11 times in the first 40 seconds, as if she'd stepped straight out of a Tarantino title sequence. Then Jay, the Clyde to her Bonnie, rode into town to round up the local hoods, scare them into compliance, recruit the most willing and pliable and take over. The devotion and riches Jay's character lavished on Foxy's in the final verse of 'Paper Chase', in contrast to the withdrawal of funds from Amil in 'Can I Get A…', was indicative of Jay's approach to the gender divide at this point – it reflected his stance towards hustling culture in general, i.e. he had contempt for those women who wanted to gain from or control him and loyalty and luxury goods for those helping him prosper.

As the album drew to a close, there was space for one more tug of the collective musical conscience. The wah-wah guitar and pimp-rolling bassline from 'Theme From *Shaft*' are as universally recognisable (in their way) as any *Annie* tune, and their sampling on 'Reservoir Dogs', a posse cut featuring Beanie Sigel, Sauce Money and Sheek Louch, Styles P and Jadakiss from The LOX*, gave the track a cool, cultish air, as if the six rappers were rolling into action like the Mr Whites and Mr Pinks of the movie the track was named after. Full of gangbanging rage and arrogance, the verses writhed with oily gangsterisms – robberies, jail time, shoot-outs, expanding drug empires, flooding blocks with ecstasy and cocaine – and the image was built of a gang on the rampage, each character more vicious, deadly and talented than the last. But Jay-Z ruled the posse, bringing up the rear with a stellar spurt of rhymes on the word "pop" which proved him the don of these '… Dogs'. He was so caught up in the drive of it, he ran out of beat; if the themes were formulaic, the performance was a rush.

It was no surprise that, following its initial release on September 29, 1998, *Vol. 2…* was soon re-released with the sparkling radio hits 'It's Alright' and 'Money Ain't A Thang' added to the end†; previously, 'I'm Like That' was a weak ending to a forceful record. A loping Kid Capri production with a mildly catchy chorus, it retrod Jay's hustling, sex and retribution themes with no particular insight or impact, a shadow of 'You Must Love Me'. Its only notable line was Jay's promise of more to come: "I recycle my life/I shall return." That, and the revelation "I only bone divas".

---

* A Bad Boy group close to Jay's heart after their moving tribute to Biggie 'We'll All Love Big Poppa'.

† A 'clean' version of the album was also released, editing out all offensive words.

An inauspicious close to an impressive album, an album which succeeded in advancing and modernising Jay's sound for a chart and radio audience while focusing his ability to both hone in on the complex nuances, details and emotions of underworld ghetto life and expand out to take in a much broader sociopolitical picture. Though at times its themes verged on self-parody, gangsta cliché or testosterone egotism, at others it was deep and reflective, and any record that could make a Broadway show tune sound like cutting-edge political rhetoric had to be granted some small shard of genius.

The critics wavered – "A periodically good album," claimed *NME*; a "hard-hitting, lyrically intense opus," said Soren Baker in the *Los Angeles Times*; "before, Jay-Z wasn't trying to play by the rules of the mainstream, but here he's trying to co-opt them," argued AllMusic's Stephen Thomas Erlewine. Jay's fans were more emphatic in their opinion of *Vol. 2...* though. The record sold 300,000 copies in its first week, flew straight to number one on the *Billboard* Hot 100 and perched there triumphantly for five weeks, a record for a rap album, kept aloft by the October 27 release and number 15 US chart placing of the single 'Hard Knock Life (Ghetto Anthem)', with its heart-warming and conscience-tugging video of project children swaying, preening and singing along with its globe-straddling chorus sentiment.*

Before it was done, *Vol. 2...* would have sold 5 million copies, gone five times Platinum, garnered two Grammy nominations and become the biggest album of Jay-Z's career, past or future, earning him between $15 million and $20 million in the process. It would also start a run of consecutive number one albums for Jay that would eventually see him outstrip Elvis Presley as the solo artist with the most US chart-topping albums. But, for the time being, as he was thrust into the highest levels of hip-hop fame, fortune and success, mobbed at Labor Day football games and demanded by every TV and radio station on the globe, Jay began to recognise his wider cultural appeal.

---

* The single was an even bigger hit in Europe, where it reached the Top 10 in six countries and number two in the UK.

"Primarily I see myself as so much more than a rapper," he said. "I wanted to represent and tell the story of everybody who's been through what I've been through, or knows somebody that has. I also wanted to speak about our lifestyle to people who – though they may live in, say, the suburbs and not be part of that world – still want to know about it and understand it."[4]

Noting that his album topped a *Billboard* Top Four ahead of the southern psychedelia of OutKast, the lounge raps of A Tribe Called Quest and Lauryn Hill's soulful classicism, Jay could see he was suddenly at the forefront of a watershed diversion in hip-hop, a relaxing of rap's reliance on violence, rage and gang and drug culture references to allow for subtler and more inventive tones. And Jay was right there at the edgiest end of rap's new acceptable face. As 1998 ended and his initial two-album contract with Def Jam was fulfilled, though, his sights were more firmly set on expanding his business than on consolidating his rap achievements. He and Dash felt the label they were building was more than just a collection of hip-hop acts, and that they were initiating a cultural shift or, as Dash would put it in the 2000 documentary *Backstage*, "when niggas think of Roc-A-Fella it's not just Jay-Z they think about, it's not just me they think about, they think of the whole movement and what we represent."

Hence, Roc-A-Fella had big and elaborate plans for 1999 that reached far beyond a rundown office near Wall Street. Having discovered a rich seam of talent in Philadelphia, signed many of them and brought them to NYC to form what entertainment lawyer Bernie Resnick would call "a factory" in the style of a hip-hop Andy Warhol, over 1999 Roc-A-Fella planned to release albums by DJ Clue, Memphis Bleek, Beanie Sigel*, Amil, Rell and Diamonds In Da Rough. They were also looking to ink deals with M.O.P., N.O.R.E. and Irv Gotti's Murder Inc., and Jay had been put on to a hot young emerging producer out of Chicago State University by the name of Kanye West, who he was hoping to bring through into his regular team of producers. What's more, Jay and Dash were already casting, largely from their Roc-A-Fella roster

---

* Sigel's debut album *The Truth* would sell 1 million on its release in 2000.

and close friends and family, another movie script about three Harlem hustlers which they hoped to go into production, directed by Abbott and starring themselves. There was the creation of a production wing called Roc-A-Bloc to put into place, overseen by Ski*, and there was Jay's first major national arena tour booked to support *Vol. 2...*

And then there was a possible move into the rag trade. Plans were afoot for a Roc-A-Fella clothing line, focusing on baggy threads. Grand plans, carefully plotted. But little did Jay-Z know, the bigger his bubble would get in 1999, the nearer his closest relationships would come to bursting point.

---

* The Roc-A-Bloc project wouldn't last long, dissolved when Ski moved out of NYC to take a break from the music business in 1999.

Chapter Seven

Hunted

"I don't think we set out to make history, it just happened."
— Jay-Z, *Backstage* documentary

Rappers getting lap dances from half-naked girls in backstage corridors, or blow jobs in bathrooms. Hotels swamped with screaming fans and rampaging crews. Copious blunts smoked from weed bags as thick as mail sacks. More girls cavorting naked in rigging trailers. High-stakes cee-lo games in dressing rooms, $1,500 a throw. Tour buses rocking with violent rows and splitter vans thumping with triumphant gang chants. Signing sessions turning into all-out mobbings. Method Man and Redman flying over the crowd on wires. Puffy, Chuck D and Busta Rhymes loitering backstage chewing fat with the basketball-shirted stars of the tour – Ja Rule, Amil, Memphis Bleek, Beanie Sigel, DJ Clue and, if they could make it past the security dog and 'keep out' notices on his dressing room door, DMX. Champagne flowing like tap water, cigars puffed like JR, and every city they hit, those wide-open arenas of wild, screaming crowds of air-pumping hip-hoppers, tens of thousands strong.

The voices of the rappers on the bill[*] summed it up. "A world hip-

---

[*] As narrated over the opening titles of the *Backstage* documentary film of the tour.

hop concert"; "being on this tour is the right place at the right time"; "a great day for hip-hop"; "it'll bring hip-hop to the next level"; "cats like Garth Brookes, now they know our name". From out front, the Hard Knock Life tour of 1999 – all two-and-a-half months and 54 dates of it – looked like the biggest, most revolutionary and most successful rap tour ever conceived. And from out back, it felt like the wildest block party ever to hit the road.

For Jay-Z, travelling slightly outside the chaos on a bus with a ban on drink or drugs on board, this landmark hip-hop event he'd created was a celebratory jaunt. Freestyling every chance he got – with DMX in his dressing room, to casual hangers-on in his own bunker or to backstage rooms rammed with whooping party-goers – he watched the tour mayhem ricochet around him with a sly chuckle and a knowing nod. Offstage he could be found play-boxing with Pain In Da Ass or acting the ringleader of the grand-a-go dice games. Onstage he was nothing short of a hero of hip-hop, blasting rap into the arenas with all the showmanship he'd learned from his own more modest tours and from wing-manning Big Daddy Kane.

His introductory film was a boiler suit-clad chase scene through underground tunnels resembling a prison escape, with Jay-Z finally reaching a ladder he climbed up just as the real Jay rose through a manhole cover in the stage, swathed in smoke. To a snippet of a new tune called 'Jigga My Nigga' he'd pull off his boiler suit and bust into 'A Million And One Questions' to a roar that ripped off every roof. Later, after a "fuck you"-free 'Can I Get A...' divided the sexes with a sassy Amil rousing the female fightback and a topless Ja Rule swooning them into surrender, Jay would race around the arena to make a surprise appearance on a small stage at the back of the huge halls, opening 'Money, Cash, Hoes' from there before security raced him through the crowd to join DMX on the main stage again. And his most dramatic piece of showmanship came at the end of the show, when he'd stop 'Hard Knock Life' at the line "flow infinitely like the memory of my nigga Biggie", drop in a few of Biggie's rhymes and play a video of his friend being interviewed on the arena screens. Then, with a tribute to both Biggie and Tupac, he'd leap straight back into 'Hard Knock Life' as if he'd never missed a beat. Consummate.

A celebratory riot of a tour, from the opening night at the Charlotte Coliseum in North Carolina on February 27, when Jay-Z sold all 19,200 tickets (more than any black artist had achieved in the venue's history), to the final show in the Miami Arena on May 7 where the entire cast joined Jay onstage for the encore, thanking everyone who'd come to see "a tour they said could never happen". But along the way, one voice repeatedly rang discordant.

"You're the president of a company, right? So that means you're smart, right? So don't sit there and play dumb. If everybody on the tour has a Def Jam jacket on, what would be the general perception?"[1]

In a tiled bathroom, mid-hairshave and on camera, Damon Dash was bawling out a Def Jam representative for presenting each of the tour's acts with a Def Jam jacket with the rapper's name embroidered on it. The Def Jam guy was on the defensive, blaming a "mistake", but Dash just yelled louder. "Those little 'mistakes' you make are making it so that it looks like it's your tour!"[2]

You can understand Dash's anger. He was a man so dedicated to his business he'd had the name of Roc-A-Fella tattooed on his arm alongside those of his son and mother, and he'd put his ass on the line for this tour and for the future of rap. Initially promoters had approached Jay-Z to tour alongside an R&B group in order to soften the rough edges for the arena audience, but Dash had rejected these advances and, imagining a future where Jay could play U2-style stadium tours across the globe to a wide and disparate audience, had instead come up with his own fresh vision of a touring rap circus of major and rising players, a joint tour of Roc-A-Fella and Ruff Ryders acts. The whole concept had met with derision from promoters and industry figures claiming it'd never work; rap shows in the late Nineties were regularly being cancelled by police order due to rumours of gang violence and gunfire, riot police lined up outside many of the venues, and tour manager Ron Byrd was warned off working on the tour as people thought such a huge collection of volatile acts would disintegrate inside a week.

But Dash sold out arenas across the States, kept the whole thing on track and pulled in $18 million in the process.* The Hard Knock Life tour didn't only prove hip-hop to be a viable – nay essential – arena-level concern, it also helped destroy the image of rap shows (and rap culture) as dangerous, thug-filled disturbances of the peace. It's no wonder Dash was adamant that Roc-A-Fella would get the credit for the success of such a risky, rap-advancing event.

Similarly, Dash was forefront in trying to get the Hard Knock Life tour album made. There was a plan to record an album featuring all of the acts on the tour while on the road, each act being ushered onto DJ Clue's tour bus to rap over the beats Clue was intending to produce along the way. When the plan looked set to fail due to Clue's unwillingness to produce tracks so quickly and the rappers' lackadaisical attitude to the project, it was Dash who'd try to rouse and rile them into recording, pointing out that they needed to keep up the momentum of their success or it could all end tomorrow. In the end the album would never come to be, but not for want of Dash trying.

But, while Dash was often to be found chilling out at after-parties and in dressing rooms, conducting sprint races down corridors, taking part in the backstage paintball bouts or even allowing himself to be jokingly 'kidnapped' by DMX's crew to be ransomed back to Jay-Z for $4, his aggressive management style, in close quarters, was beginning to grate on Jay. The shock is clear on Jay's face in the scene in the documentary from the tour, *Backstage*, where Dash's row with Roc-A-Fella's party organiser ends in play-fighting with a vicious undercurrent.

It would be some years before the differences between Jay-Z and Dash would become unmanageable though, and in the meantime Dash's forthright attitude was solid in keeping the Jay-Z juggernaut rolling and the fresh income streams flowing. He'd bought a Mercedes-Benz E-class 320 and pasted a Roc-A-Fella logo onto the hood to drive around NYC as a promotional vehicle, giving out CDs, stickers and posters. And he'd decided that Jay should start getting paid for name-dropping

---

* The only date that didn't make a profit for the tour was in Denver; the Columbine shootings had occurred nearby, so the decision was made to donate all proceeds from the show to a relevant charity.

brands in his rhymes, brands that would then see their sales and profits soar as a result of the free advertising as part of Roc-A-Fella's luxury rap aesthetic. He set up a meeting with the Iceberg clothing company, whom Jay had named in song and worn in videos and whose income as a result (at least in Roc-A-Fella's eyes) had tripled. Roc-A-Fella went in demanding Iceberg pay them millions to set up their own strand of the label and allow Roc-A-Fella use of their private jets; Iceberg offered them free clothes and no more, uncertain they wanted to milk the hip-hop association at all. As with those early record label meetings, Dash left furious but determined. If nobody would pay them to promote their clothes, they'd simply have to start promoting their own.

Three old black sewing machines were purchased and installed in a back corner of Roc-A-Fella's already cramped John Street office. There, employees would hand-stitch Roc-A-Fella branded T-shirts themselves, taking three weeks per shirt since none of them knew how to sew. Eventually, Dash sought the advice of Russell Simmons, who'd launched his own Phat Farm clothing range to great success, and Simmons put him in touch with clothing experts Alex Bize and Norton Cher, who guided Roc-A-Fella through their first serious range of clothes – jeans, sweatshirts, oversized and kids' clothes, shoes and a cologne called 9IX.

Via licensing deals with manufacturers and cross-promoting the new line in Jay-Z's songs, the newly founded Rocawear clothing line would grow from those three sewing machines to turning over $80 million inside 18 months.

Dash was also pivotal in helping keep Jay's street reputation immaculate as he threatened to be glossed clean by the mainstream in 1999. When the 41st Grammy Awards rolled around on February 24, the Hard Knock Life tour was yet to get underway, but despite nominations for Best Rap Album, Best Rap Solo Performance for '… (Ghetto Anthem)' and Best Rap Performance By A Duo Or Group, Jay-Z and Dash were not in attendance. They'd decided to boycott the ceremony in protest at DMX receiving no nominations and knowing that none of the rap award presentations would receive airtime on the national TV broadcast. Jay and Dash saw this as a blanking of hip-hop by the musical establishment at a time when the genre was truly breaking through and gaining a strong foothold in the mainstream, and they refused to bow and scrape to such a hegemony, to be complicit in the sidelining and suppression of rap, to craft their own pop culture camouflage. By not turning up to accept his Grammy for Best Rap Album for *Vol. 2...* Jay-Z kept one righteous and subversive foot firmly in the musical underground.

The fact that the awards were held one day after the release of Jay-Z's darkest and most murderous single yet only added to his bleak modernist mystique. 'Money, Cash, Hoes (Remix)', with its gritty urban video laced with scenes of police raids and gun battles from the Mark Wahlberg and Chow Yun-Fat movie *The Corruptor* that it soundtracked, hit number 19 despite the remix stripping off most of DMX's contribution in favour of two new verses from Memphis and Beanie. The contrast with the cuddly rap realism of 'Hard Knock Life (Ghetto Anthem)' couldn't have been starker.

And, by the end of 1999, Jay-Z's magnanimous gangsta image would be all but destroyed, in the glint of a blade...

"I don't want everyone to think that everything is 'Bounce Bounce' or 'Can I Get A...' or 'Hard Knock Life'... I have my dark days also."
        – Jay-Z, *Fox 5 News*

"A top rap star is busted. Jay-Z turned himself in tonight and the cops started working on his rap sheet accusing him of a stabbing at a trendy party... he had a confrontation with record producer Lance Rivera... Jay-Z and his crew surrounded the 33-year-old Rivera and his 29-year-old brother Corey. Witnesses say that Jay-Z allegedly plunged a knife into Rivera's stomach and smashed a bottle over his brother's head before running out of the club..."
        – *Fox 5 News*, December 10, 1999

Early hours, December 10, Jay-Z sat in his suite at the Trump Hotel, NYC, watching his life unravel on CNN. The news reports rolled in full of scandal and rumour – a stabbing at the Kit Kat Club in Times Square where Q-Tip was holding a high-class party to celebrate the launch of his debut album *Amplified*, a major rap name fleeing the scene, whispers of a warrant. The sinking dread made him a kid again, hiding out overnight from the guilt of shooting his brother. But this time, he felt, with the media deluge and the public baying for a hip-hop scapegoat to demonise, he wouldn't get off so easy.

Slowly, as the fug of the night's events began to clear, he replayed over and over the causes, the actions, the consequences.

Man, it looked bad.

Until November 1999, *Vol. 3… The Life And Times Of S. Carter* had been perfectly protected. The only hint of new Jay-Z material all year had come in the shape of two non-album single releases. In June, the slow synth single 'Jigga My Nigga' featuring Amil – a leisurely, assured slab of gat-blazing self-aggrandisement sounding not unlike Gary Numan's 'Cars' for added populist effect – had become a number 28 hit in the *Billboard* chart, prominantly featured on the Ruff Ryders compilation album *Ryde Or Die Vol. 1*. In October, a pop-clicking love song to diamonds called 'Girl's Best Friend' was released in promotion of the diamond heist movie *Blue Streak*, a box office smash.* Those two tunes, though, would only make his fourth album as bonus tracks hidden after the album's official close. The album itself was locked tight.

Meanwhile, in September, Jay surprised his hardcore fans by releasing a duet with Mariah Carey called 'Heartbreaker'. His guest verse on the ultra-pop lead single from Mariah's seventh album *Rainbow* was the voice of a cutesy put-upon boyfriend trying to deal with a demanding and suspicious partner, i.e. Carey. For a man who'd refused to tour with an R&B act and gone to great lengths with the *Streets Is Watching* film and tracks like 'Money, Cash, Hoes' to counterpoint his poppier

---

* With a video of Jay rapping inside a gigantic diamond surrounded by glistening dancers, 'Girl's Best Friend' made number 52 in the US and was included on the soundtrack for *Blue Streak*. Both singles were Swizz Beatz tracks.

elements with hard-hitting gangsta grit, this sweet, kiddie-friendly collaboration was a shock, but a fantastic profile-raiser for Jay. If he was going to widen his appeal, de-threaten rap for the mainstream and straddle the pop and hip-hop divide, then there was no better opportunity than answering Carey's offer – Carey had had 13 US number ones and this lead album track was unlikely to come with any bad charm attached.

Sure enough, 'Heartbreaker' gave Jay his first taste of life atop the *Billboard* Hot 100 singles chart[*], and also added to his high-end reputation. Because he was contractually banned from appearing in a music video for a fortnight after shooting the clip for 'Girl's Best Friend', Jay-Z couldn't appear in the 'Heartbreaker' video, and the animation used to replace him tipped the cost of the already costly video over $2.5 million, one of the most expensive ever made. The impression was, Jay didn't get out of bed for less than $3 mill.

So he'd stoked his audience's hunger for new tracks, hit the top of singles charts worldwide, asserted his seven-figure credentials, inked a new deal with Def Jam and recorded a fourth album he was sure would place him as the undisputed king of hip-hop. The timer was set for the explosion: this bomb would drop on December 28.

Then, at the worst possible moment – just as the release of 'Nigga What, Nigga Who (Originator 99)'[†] closed the book on *Vol. 2...* in time for the fuse of *Vol. 3...* to be lit – word reached Roc-A-Fella that *Vol. 3...* was already on the streets. People were playing it from passing cars, selling fake copies on street corners. A month upfront, the album had been bootlegged. It hadn't been a huge issue on previous Jay-Z albums and they'd always lowered their expectations by around 100,000 sales every time to allow for pirated copies. But this leak was a torrent of tapes onto the streets.

Jay and Dash were furious, going back to the album to change the track

---

[*] As well as the singles charts of Canada, New Zealand and Spain.
[†] With a radio edit changing 'Nigga' to 'Jigga' in the title.

listing in order to foil the bootleggers* and descending on the Def Jam offices demanding answers. Though none were officially forthcoming, one name kept cropping up. Lance 'Un' Rivera, the producer of a track called 'Dope Man' from the album alongside DJ Clue, Darrell Branch and Ken Ifill. Lance would know more, the whispers went.

It was pure chance that Jay-Z and the Roc-A-Fella crew caught up with Rivera at the Kit Kat Club on December 9. Having come from an exclusive playback party for the album at the Irving Plaza, where Jay had performed a selection of tracks from the record, Jay spotted Rivera from across the Kit Kat and, still fuming, went over to have the matter out with him. He had no plan of violence, just a firm discussion, but he was shocked at Rivera's response. Rivera was casual, brash and unrepentant†, brushing off Jay's accusations and leaving the rapper stunned.

Jay-Z retreated to the bar, wracked with tension, anger and confusion. From deep within, something primal rose, a core rush of rage and retribution. A black-out descended.

The rest, we can only piece together.

Witnesses at the party reported that Jay-Z and his entourage encircled Rivera and his brother in the VIP area, that Jay-Z was heard to say "Lance, you broke my heart," and then stabbed Rivera in the stomach with a concealed five-inch blade, possibly while other members of Jay-Z's group provided a distraction and possibly with a follow-up stab to the back. Rivera's injuries thankfully were not fatal. When the case came to trial by grand jury, Jay-Z would plead not guilty and his defence would try to ascertain with witness reports and the club's CCTV footage that he was nowhere nearby at the time of the attack. It would be two

---

* The UK and Europe version of the album had already been manufactured so could not be changed; they have the original track listing including 'Hova Interlude' and 'Is That Yo Bitch' featuring Missy Elliott and Twista. On the US release, those tracks were replaced by 'Watch Me' and 'There's Been A Murder' respectively and 'Anything' was removed as the 16th and final track and added later on the album as a hidden bonus track after 'Jigga My Nigga' and 'Girl's Best Friend'.

† Indeed, it's unclear whether Rivera was ever behind any bootlegging of the album at all.

years and many hearings before any conclusion would be reached. In his autobiography, however, Jay expresses regret that the attack had happened, cited a loss of control and vowed never to put himself and his dependants in such jeopardy again.

In the Trump Hotel suite in the early hours of December 10, Jay-Z sat with his entertainment lawyer Michael Guido who was teaching him to play a high-stakes gambling card game called guts, in which the player must make decisions fast and instinctively, but those decisions are often proved wrong. It was a lesson Jay was about to learn the very hard way – he was facing a maximum of 17 years in jail. By the morning he had an attorney in the shape of major legal figure Murray Richman, who'd not only represented DMX in the past but also the mob boss John Gotti – even in such serious trouble Jay-Z didn't pass up the chance to play on his *Scarface* image.

Jay voluntarily turned himself in for questioning that day and after several hours in custody was released on $50,000 bail. A press conference was organised to try to quell the rising press suppositions that the assault was part of another rap war in the style of Biggie and Tupac, or that the whole thing had been a marketing stunt set up to enhance Jay-Z's gangster image on the eve of the release of his new album – it was, after all, only five days before the lead single from *Vol. 3…* would hit the shelves. A suspicion not helped by Jay wearing a Rocawear bubble coat as prominently as possible.

"It was just a bar fight," Jay would claim to the *Guardian*'s Simon Hattenstone many years later. "I'm not going to blame it only on success, but there's a bar fight every night and it's not on the front page of the paper and nobody's being offered seven years. The guy wasn't hurt – he took an aspirin and went home. I'm a hunted man. But it was a wake-up call for me. I've got to move more careful, I've got to watch my temper, everything has to change."[3]

So a gory shadow hung over the launch of *Vol. 3…* and its lead single 'Do It Again (Put Ya Hands Up)', released on December 14 and featuring Beanie and Amil. The lead-in for this club-based anthem was unfortunate, an announcement over a tinny doom rock backing from Jay demanding everyone go to the dancefloor and that "all the bustas, we're giving you five seconds to get close to an exit/It's about to get real ugly in here." Jay's verse about the millions he'd made and the styles that'd been stolen from him was ironically offset by Beanie Sigel's verse including the line: "If a nigga wanna draw then the blood it can drip in the club." Even the video was eerily reminiscent of the Kit Kat incident, with scenes of police attending a disturbance at a rammed club venue. But Rockwilder's beat was a mellow shuffle adorned with tremulous Indian-esque strings, a tune to pacify the furore, and Jay-Z's rhymes were less aggressive and more obsessed with seducing and discarding willing girls than settling any scores. It was, if anything, a calming before the album's storm.

As the final instalment in a three-part album autobiography, *Vol. 3... The Life And Times Of S. Carter* was purposefully glamorous, epic, ostentatious, showy, boastful and gunning for haters. After all, if the first two volumes were intended to describe Jay's transition from poverty-stricken child of the projects to street hustler to drug kingpin to rapper, and to chart his gradual ascendancy to the peak of New York hip-hop, then this record was to portray him at the pinnacle of 20th century rap music, reflecting the state of mind of an artist looking out at life and music from the very top. The 'ballin'' lifestyle of flagrantly flaunted wealth and designer goods that he'd slipped into from a sense of broken spirit and deadness inside. The torrents of money, the deluge of girls and the emptiness they both brought with them. The plethora of other rappers intent on speaking ill of him, hoping to knock him off his pedestal so they could scale it themselves. The hordes of hands, open or disguised, grasping at his money, his business, his fame. The endless demands on his time, his talent, his endorsement, his name. And, above all, the hustler within him that hated he'd gone straight.

On its December 28 release, neatly pinpointed to ensure a number one album in the January release lull, *Vol. 3...* needed to show that life wasn't all gilded at the top.

Sonically, the album took in a far wider array of styles than any previous Jay-Z record. Rock riffs, Arabian chimes, choral music, cinematic orchestration and progressive electronica now merged with the funk, soul, disco, pop and hip-hop snap-beats as Swizz Beatz, Timbaland, Clue, Gotti and Premier stretched their musical imaginations to create a ground-breaking rap stew from which Jay could drink deep. Just take the introductory track 'Hova Song (Intro)', a reiteration of Jay-Z's God MC persona as Jay-Hova ("Hova the God... Mike Jordan of rap") that welcomed the excited listener to the album over celestial choirs, filthy guitar squeals and Pain In Da Ass mulling meaningfully over what Biggie would say about honour, friendship and the rules of the streets. It sounded like a 1950s Hollywood vision of heaven and its Busby Berkeley grandeur was a mere hint of the glories to come.

Premier's 'So Ghetto' opened with a brief bout of jazz rock before giving way to a chiming piano loop sampled from Ennio Morricone's 'Sporco Ma Distinto' that was redolent of an archaic prohibition-era criminality or the UK ska of Madness and The Specials. A captivating and inspired backing for Jay's lyric tracing his hedonistic sex'n'party lifestyle, his murderous tendencies and his inability to let the gun-wielding gangsta life go despite his rap success: "We tote guns to the Grammys, pop bottles on the White House lawn/Guess I'm just the same old Shawn... thug nigga to the end." It was a song designed to assert Jay's faithfulness to his Brooklyn roots, but as he mocked radio stations for having to play him despite his offensive language, and manipulative magazines for putting him on their covers while calling his lyrics shallow, in the end Jay-Z was the victim. Thanks to the rough-edged reputation he insisted on maintaining, he seemed to get only the ghetto girls.

The sizzling 'Do It Again (Put Ya Hands Up)' gave way to an even more experimental track, DJ Clue's 'Dope Man'. That it was co-produced by Rivera was particularly ironic, since it was swathed in faked news reports covering the song's fictional trial of Jay-Z, nicknamed The Dope Man, charged with distributing "raw" raps that were as addictive as drugs to the world's youth since 1996. The prosecution presented evidence including "exhibit A: *Reasonable*

Doubt" and "a lethal dose called *Volume 2*" and tried to drag Roc-A-Fella collaborators down with him, even implicating Irv Gotti's Murder Inc. in the scandal. A comic reflection of Jay's feeling that the rap superstar is constantly under scrutiny, hounded or on trial simply for being successful, it had all the import of a cinematic courtroom drama thanks to imposing strings and tolling bells and even ended on a suitably dramatic climax. Jay-Z gave a stirring testimony on how the state contains and suppresses the poor, kills their ambitions and dreams and then expects them not to rebel into crime. Referencing death row inmate Mumia Abu-Jamal, a Black Panther member who was (and remains) the subject of controversy over his guilt and the fairness of his trial, it was a rousing indictment of the justice system itself and The Dope Man inevitably walked free, a new subculture icon. A result the real Jay-Z could only pray for in 1999.

If the appearance of Mariah Carey paying Jay back for 'Heartbreaker' on the next track, 'Things That U Do', smacked of a sell-out far deeper than any Jay-Z had been accused of before, Swizz Beatz's track was the collaboration's saving grace. Inspired by traditional Japanese Shinto music it featured flutes and koto and Carey taking a subdued, velvety approach to the R&B chorus; the kind of experimental beat-making that would echo through the decades to inspire the 21st century inventions in R&B and pop that today drive Beyoncé tracks such as 'Run The World (Girls)' and 'Single Ladies (Put A Ring On It)'. Fittingly, Jay-Z's creative rap took a more spiritual angle on the origins of his "God-given" flow and dictionary-defying pronunciations, contemplating a higher power stopping him from being "lost in the system", killed in car crashes or landed in jail – "I know I must be part of some grand mission." From a position of safety and success, this was Jay-Z's prayer of thanks to that angel that perched on his Lexus hood along all those cold hustling highways.

'It's Hot (Some Like It Hot)' announced Timbaland's arrival on *Vol. 3...* with the sort of portentous synthesised strings that would usually accompany the arrival of a ring to Mordor or an *X Factor* judge to their podium. They quickly moved aside to make way for a playful beat built from handclaps and decorated with elastic bass, surf guitar, backwards synth hisses, percussive "pop-pop"s peppering a whip-cracking Jay-Z rap and a couple of witty one-liners. Mentioning that he's had a string of hits like Michael Jackson elicited a Jacko "ee-heee!" in the background, and then there was the dig at a new Columbia Records signing that Jay had been hearing a lot of hype about: "I'm about a dollar, what the fuck is 50 Cents?"

While Jay-Z's dense rhyme on 'It's Hot…' descended from a tongue-twisting first verse that proved his mastery of the art towards a finale full of sex, bank jobs, kidnappings and gunfire that exposed the paucity of his themes on *Vol. 3…*, the music's brilliance never showed any sign of dulling. Timbaland was also behind the futuristic Prodigy warps of 'Snoopy Track' that Jay-Z and Juvenile* used to toast the walk-on extras of "black culture", from the pole dancers to the gangbangers, Gucci girls, dope smokers, groupies and baby-mamas, with an "eat a dick" reserved for "the haters". And then came 'S. Carter', Jay-Z's catchiest song since 'Hard Knock Life (Ghetto Anthem)' and his first contribution from producers Russell Howard, Sean Francis and Chauncey Mahan. An obvious single that never was, this tune of joyful boasts and vicious death threats was a skipping pop hit with nods to the dancehall reggae tradition[†], synthetic strings and a purposefully out-of-tune chorus from Amil that was all the more melodic for its intentional flatness. For all its R-rated images of torture chambers and rough sex, Jay's "no, no, no" hook was as cuddly as a nursery rhyme and a brilliantly blatant lurch for the crossover.

More electro-rock riffs adorned 'Pop 4 Roc', with Amil, Beanie Sigel and Memphis Bleek taking turns to etch their names on the Roc-A-Fella wall of fame – Bleek as the apprentice coming good, Amil the label's own diva glamourpuss ("Diana Ross of the ROC" as Jay calls her) and Beanie the late-arriving rap natural come to keep the Roc-A-Fella flame burning. "I'm the reason why Jay feel comfortable retiring" he raps, sparking a million more rumours that this would be Jay-Z's

---

* A member of Hot Boys who'd had a solo hit in 1999 with the ass-obsessed single 'Back That Thang Up'.

† And specifically 'Heads High' by Mr Vegas.

last album. The track acted as a 'coming soon' advert for a 2000 album that Jay intended to release showcasing tracks by the various acts on Roc-A-Fella. He planned to call it 'Roc La Familia' to stress the label's family bond, although by the time it hit the streets it would be a rather different beast.

Sadly, US buyers were denied 'Hova Interlude', the reprise of 'Hova Song' that Jay-Z had intended to break up the album at this point, a rhyme that briefly reminded the listener of his wealth, his sex appeal, his need for guns and his standing as a deity, "Hova the God", with Bleek and Sigel as his "disciples". Instead, it was replaced with the unremarkable 'Watch Me' featuring Dr. Dre barking a chorus of pure baller narcissism and Jay laying out a convincing argument for spending your money while you can, since sex could kill and the police had it in for him. "Save for what? Ball 'til your days is up" he insisted, the devil turned financial advisor, his diamonds lighting up the night wherever he goes, every bar bought out and the same sexual conquest never conquered twice. The sociopolitical conscience of 'Dope Man' and the spiritual soul of 'Things That U Do' seemed a long way behind us by now. And Hova would only get nastier before he was through.

Even Jay-Z himself now regrets the lyric of 'Big Pimpin'', his collaboration with southern hip-hoppers UGK inspired by the king pimp Pretty Tony in the film *The Mack*. "Some [lyrics] become really profound when you see them in writing," he told *The Wall Street Journal* later. "Not 'Big Pimpin'. That's the exception. It was like, I can't believe I said that. And kept saying it. What kind of animal would say this sort of thing?"[4] His autobiography claims the arrogance and bullishness towards women on 'Big Pimpin'' was down to the song being written at the height of his wild partying lifestyle and the selfishness that came from being so suddenly rich and in demand, the groupies making him feel as manipulative and superficial as a pimp and suspicious of girls who might be after him just for his lucrative pre-nup. In the song, the main character's knowledge that his drug stash could see him sent down for life just makes him want to accelerate towards oblivion. Even so, it was a brutal sentiment: he'd never fall for a woman, just use them when the urge took him, any "fuss" from them and he's gone. "Heart cold as assassins/I got no passion" he rapped, out to devour all the pleasure he could with no thought for the feelings of others. You almost felt sorry for him.

Musically, though, 'Big Pimpin'' was a revelation, a busting of boundaries, Timbaland on fire. Adding scratches and wails to a sample from Egyptian composer Baligh Hamdi that Timbaland discovered on a belly-dancing compilation from the Middle East, its Arabian sounds gave *Vol. 3...* a whole new dimension, a global breadth. It was pioneering rap stuff: this one track opened up not just Jay-Z's music but hip-hop as a whole to a world of new influences and possibilities, and it's not inconceivable to claim it as the source of M.I.A.'s world rhythms. If Jay-Z was the snake, Timbaland was the charmer.[*]

Next, the UK fans got the nifty speed-rap cinematics of 'Is That Yo Bitch' featuring Missy Elliott and Twista, an expansion on 'Big Pimpin'' to the point where Jay-Z's character was now openly sleeping with a friend's errant wife, doing the dirty on his friends as much as their girls. The US, meanwhile, got gunshots, sirens, an Alana Davis soul sample[†] and a less vital tune but a more intriguing lyric in 'There's Been A Murder', the first of three songs that would link the bragging and balling of *Vol. 3...* back to Jay-Z's Marcy roots. Here he imagines the metaphorical slaughter of his rapping persona and a return to Shawn Carter the hustler, the rap retirement he'd promised on album one since "my life is like a see-saw". It was a chance, among the general high-rolling glitz of *Vol. 3...*, to revisit the meanings and motivations of hustling in an even more microscoped manner, to talk about minutiae like the lack of tears that hardened and loveless hustlers shed when their friends die, pouring liquor on the pavement with a prayer in their honour instead. And it ended on a dolorous note, Jay-Z recognising that no matter how big he got in rap, the weight of his drug trade past and the deep thoughts it provoked would always weigh him down,

---

[*] 'Big Pimpin' would eventually be ranked among the Top 500 songs of all time by *Rolling Stone* magazine in 2010.

[†] From a track called 'Murder'.

spiritually and emotionally. And yet he seemed to look back at that time as having a sense of freedom and youthful vigour, "playing cops and robbers, like shots can't stop us/Flipping a bird to the choppers… reckless abandon." Even teenage years spent dodging death and jail and freezing on street corners weren't immune from the nostalgic glow of Saturn's return*; Jay-Z had just turned 30.

'Come And Get Me' brought that story right up to date, with enemies from Jay-Z's past plotting to kidnap him or rob him of his rapping riches despite his pleas that he'd worked wonders for Marcy's reputation without selling out his projects roots, arguing that "I ain't crossover, I brought the suburbs to the hood/Made 'em relate to your struggle." A damning indictment of the ungratefulness and back-stabbing nature of rap and projects culture, and it cut Jay deep: "I represent y'all every time I spit a verse/And that's the shit that hurts." So even at the peak of the rap game he was, the song claimed, still carrying weapons and hiding guns around his apartment, prepared to kill to protect what he'd earned. It was a claim the police would take a little too seriously over the coming months; Jay-Z's paranoia that the cops were gunning for him would soon be proved right.

Timbaland's track, built around a sample from Bullet's hitman-themed 'The Contract Man', mirrored the gangsta swagger of the words but still managed to smash boundaries and shatter expectations – the track included an abstract central section of avant-garde Tibetan flutes and bells, backwards whooshes, irregular drumbeats and birdsong, the kind of psychedelic outburst that exemplified Jay-Z and Timbaland's revolutionary and experimental rap ambitions. What Radiohead were doing to rock, in their own little way, Timbaland and Jay-Z were doing, right here, to hip-hop. For a minute then, Jay-Z had his own 'Revolution 9'.

With shimmering beats and scything guitar squeals, 'NYMP' provided a closing overview of street life at the end of the 20th century, compiling

---

* Saturn's return is the state of reflection upon life around the age of 29, reflected in Saturn's returning to the same point in its orbit around the sun as it occupied on the day one was born, marking a shift from youth to adulthood.

all its dangers from the cops, the kidnappers, the shooters and fiends and death itself. That Jay-Z ended his three-part autobiography with him back hustling and blazing violence on the streets reflected his feeling that the Marcy street punk would always be at the core of him, but from his lofty position of success he could deliver a wider perspective on the "battle" of life on the "mean streets". He rapped of the spectral wails of "tortured souls" in prisons and how showing weakness could be fatal in the ghetto, but also turned from micro to macro, referenced the JFK shooting, implicating government and politics in the human tragedies he describes. "It's all political now, I think big when I spit at you now," he rhymed, echoing the social commentaries of 'Dope Man' and 'Hard Knock Life (Ghetto Anthem)'.

But it soon reverted to the personal. For an album flinging its brashness, cash, sex, invulnerability and talent in your face so relentlessly *Vol. 3...* ends with the knowledge that life and success always come edged with defeat. 'NYMP' closed with an admission that fame, money and fear had broken his spirit in the end, a glimmer of humanity and weakness and almost a confession of the hidden pain driving the album's wild excesses. Most human of all, it was followed by a final coda of 'Hova Song (Outro)', a closing message of hope that pictured a young Shawn Carter rapping at the rain on his window, unaware of the glories he'd achieve, the obstacles he'd overcome, the father he'd lose. *Vol. 3...* was a spectacular musical step forward and a hard-hitting lyrical exploration of the cruelties and extravagances that go on inside fame's bubble, but the autobiography ended with a touching moment, the superstar Jay-Z reaching out to a Marcy child so nearly lost.

Some reviewers relished their slatings of *Vol. 3...*, declaring Jay-Z's talent dried up and his best rhymes long since spat. But overall it received widespread acclaim, with many reviews recognising the album's modern and ground-breaking sonic originality and diversity and trumpeting Jay-Z as the greatest MC in hip-hop. As the Millennium broke, *Vol. 3...* became the first *Billboard* number one album of the 21st century, selling 462,000 copies in its opening week, one-third more than *Vol. 2...*, bootlegging or no bootlegging. The fact that the album shipped 2 million copies within a month but stalled at 3 million sales rather than the 5 million *Vol. 2…* achieved*, though, may have been down to a botched run of promotional singles.

The Mariah Carey collaboration 'Things That U Do' was slated as the next single to be released from the album on February 15, 2000, but it received little promotion and no CD version, keeping it from the charts. Why? Because Roc-A-Fella had what they thought was a far bigger bomb to drop only a fortnight later. Since 'Hard Knock Life (Ghetto Anthem)' had done so well by sampling a Broadway show and relating it to modern ghetto society, they thought, why couldn't they do it again? So producer Sam Sneed had gained permission to sample another hit show, *Oliver!*, taking the chorus from Lionel Bart's classic 'I'd Do Anything' showtune and beefing it up with hip-hop snaps and crackles. Jay-Z added a rhyme of huge hood heart, taking the sentiment of the line "I'd do anything for you" to mean the dedication and reliability Jay owed to his crew members and family. Verse one was an oath of faith to his Roc-A-Fella compadres, naming Gotti, Dash, Burke and Ja Rule. Verse two was a dedication and thanks to his mother for all the wisdom and care she'd imparted and the ambitions she'd instilled, and apologies for the pain he'd caused her. And finally, verse three was full of love and advice for his young nephews, telling them he'll always be there for them, even willing to replace their own father if he fails them. And Jay-Z's adoration of his nephews was always strong, leaving him devastated only a few years later.

A catchy famous melody, a universal and heart-warming lyric with little violence or cussing to put off the Broadway crowds, a video of Jay-Z paying his respects around the Marcy projects, and most Jay-Z fans wouldn't have the track already since it had appeared on Beanie Sigel's album *The Truth* instead of *Vol. 3…*. Gold dust, right? Money in the bank. How could it not be a smash, the new '… (Ghetto Anthem)'? Yet 'Anything' flopped, failing to chart just like its predecessor.† You might argue that a reason for this disaster was that there might have been a nugget of insincerity to the song's brothers-forever sentiment – Jay-

---

* It would eventually be certified as Triple Platinum with 3 million sales a year later.
† The single did, however, hit the Top 20 in the UK.

Z's mentor Jaz-O, for example, was nowhere to be found on *Vol. 3…* and wouldn't make an appearance on any subsequent Jay-Z album. But a more likely reason for the single's failure was that the moving lyric clashed with the cynical concept. After recording an album so pioneering and full of ideas, this shameless retread of '… (Ghetto Anthem)' seemed painfully transparent and formulaic. Jay-Z's public now expected better of him.

Dazed by his high-flying lifestyle, dazzled by his Platinum discs and diamond wrists and now shocked by these two almighty flops, Jay-Z might have been forgiven for thinking his bubble had burst with the first popped corks of the Millennium, that he was always meant to be no more than a 20th century rapper and his hip-hop number had been called, the backlash begun. Facing a court trial and possible prison sentence for stabbing Rivera too, it was a stressful and uncertain few months for Jay.

But 'Big Pimpin'' changed all that. Determined not to suffer a third embarrassment in a row, to ensure they'd make it onto MTV's *Making The Video* show Roc-A-Fella threw a million dollars at its promo clip, filmed by Hype Williams among the oily Satans and beaded rump-pumpers of the Trinidad Carnival and on the obligatory huge yacht full of models in Miami. Jay even added an extra verse of drug dealing snippets to the track, as if to remind us of his delinquent past after the squeaky clean 'Anything'. It worked – 'Big Pimpin'' hit number 18, *Vol.3…*'s biggest hit single. The blip was almost instantly buried.

The 'Lifetime' trilogy was complete, though, and it had seen Jay-Z rise from respected speed-rapper finding his feet in the pop world to innovative hip-hop frontiersman, consummate arena rapper, undisputed King Of New York and hard-partying, girl-gorging, ice-flashing God MC. So where did he go from here?

He needed a new beginning, a new phase, a new team. He needed to strip hip-hop back to the bare bones.

And set out a brand new master plan.

Chapter Eight

Goading God's Son

"You see me with a bodyguard that means police is watchin'/And I only use his waist to keep my Glock in/But when shit goes down you know who's doin' the poppin'/And if you don't know, guess who's doin' the droppin'/S dot again"

— Jay-Z, 'Streets Is Talking', 2000

The sirens didn't surprise him. The screech of cop wheels at his Chevy door were no shock. His paranoia was just being justified. The NYPD really were trailing him, staking him out, gathering intelligence, tensed to swoop. Hell, he knew there was at least one specific, dedicated officer paid full-time to keep on his tail, sitting outside every club he hit, every bar he cruised by. He'd got to know the guy, shared jokes with him.

So when the undercover police van crunched to a halt in front of his brand new Chevrolet Suburban as it drove him away from Club Exit in Hell's Kitchen on the West Side of Manhattan at 3 a.m. on April 13, 2001 having spent 20 minutes inside to perform 'Can I Get A...' with Ja Rule, it was no more than he'd been expecting. He'd been stirring up police attention, not just with lyrics openly claiming to always have guns close to hand and prepared to kill anyone coming to take him down, or by recording a song called 'Guilty Until Proven Innocent' with R Kelly – himself recently the subject of misdemeanour charges including breaking noise ordinance in his car. There'd been further questions of criminality raised by a scene in the film *Backstage** in which Jay-Z was seen to push a woman in the face backstage. Some viewers found the scene upsetting and aggressive, accusing Jay of beating the woman on screen, but Jay-Z responded saying the woman in question was long-term Roc-A-Fella associate Chaka Pilgrim, that the incident was part of friendly horseplay and the move was "playful". Indeed, Jay's uncaring playboy image was mellowing somewhat, since he was being linked in the press to rising *Kids* actress Rosario Dawson.

Still, the authorities may well have been further riled by Jay speaking out in *Vibe* magazine in December 2000 – against his lawyers' advice – about the delays to his court hearing over the Rivera stabbing. With no court date set for his trial a full year after the incident, he felt he was being made an example because of his celebrity status, the police dragging out the publicity far longer than necessary. Now he finally had a hearing set for the following Monday, who wouldn't expect the Feds to descend, looking for anything to ramp up the charges?

Bemused, he glared out at a pack of black and whites squealing up, blues flashing, sirens howling. It was no surprise to be hauled out of the SUV, rammed up against the side of the car and searched. And certainly no shock that the cops had found the gun they were looking for, tucked in the waistband of Jay-Z's bodyguard Hamzah Hewitt, a loaded semi-automatic Glock handgun, just like 'Streets Is Talking' said. The sideswipe, after Hewitt had showed the officers that the gun was his and legally licensed, was for the confused cop searching him to radio in the words "I got Jay-Z" and for Jay to be arrested along with Hewitt and the car's two other occupants, music exec Tyran Smith and limo company owner Romero Chalmers, and charged with third-degree criminal possession of a weapon.

---

* A behind-the-scenes documentary of the Hard Knock Life tour produced by Dash and released by Roc-A-Fella via Dimension Films in September 2000 as a further push for Dash's movie-producing ambitions.

A simple check might have cleared up the situation right there; instead, Jay and his crew were taken to the precinct and paraded before the photographers waiting on the street on their way into the building. If Jay was suspicious then that the police, in targeting him for arrest, had motives of publicity, justification of resources and a quelling of a perceived public outrage at the image, lyrics and behaviour of rap acts, they were bolstered by what he saw in the charge room. On one wall, a chart of rappers that a new division for 2001 known as the Gang Intelligence Unit were singling out for capture. It was worse than even Jay-Z had suspected: the NYPD had its very own Rap Squad.

"It would be ignorant for us to ignore the fact that there have been violent incidents where the only common denominator is the music industry," said police spokesperson Sgt Brian Burke of the surveillance of hip-hop artists begun in the wake of the Biggie and Tupac murders and a more recent shooting incident at Club New York for which Sean Combs and Shyne were facing trial at the time. "In an effort to ensure the safety of individuals in the music industry as well as other additional victims, we've initiated this effort… We monitor clubs and nightlife to prevent future acts of violence and to prevent persons from the music industry from becoming targets or victims," he said. "It's not just hip-hop; it's the entire music industry."

Though Jay-Z felt his arrest was part of a set-up sting following months of surveillance*, and though Hewitt's licence proved the gun was being carried legally, the charges were pressed, the process possibly complicated by the fact that bodyguard Hewitt had been arrested in November 2000 for possession of a different handgun while backstage at a Jay-Z gig in Boston. Jay had no worries in this case: having entered a plea of not guilty and posted $10,000 bail at his arraignment, he stood on the steps of Manhattan Criminal Court, pointed the swarm of press microphones towards his mother and said: "That's my mom. She can

---

* Police counteracted this claim by stating that the arrests weren't conducted by the Gang Intelligence Unit themselves but by the more general Street Crime Unit, although they admitted they had been "keeping tabs" on Jay-Z.

go anywhere in the world and hold her head up because her son is 100 per cent innocent."

The snappers snapped, the tappers tapped, the police got their press deluge – a tide of coverage infinitely greater than the non-reporting of the charges being quietly dropped later that year, overshadowed by the more salacious story of the assault trial later that year. But if Jay-Z felt justifiably victimised, he wasn't going to be beaten. Because he knew that only hours before his arrest he'd been in Manhattan's Baseline recording studio working a track called 'Izzo (H.O.V.A.)'. Masterfully melding a clinically catchy pop chant chorus with a sample of one of the best-loved tunes in Motown history – The Jackson 5's 'I Want You Back' – re-jigged until it's a warm, nostalgic niggle in the back of the song, it would go on to be his biggest chart hit yet and the cornerstone of an album so seminal it would set a new benchmark for 21st century hip-hop.

And now the song would gain a message for the prosecutors too. "Cops wanna knock me, DA wanna box me in/But somehow I beat them charges like Rocky…"

The foundations for *The Blueprint* were laid a full year before its conception. Back in July 2000, Jay-Z was hunting for a new concept, a new direction or trilogy to get his teeth into. He'd followed the raging success of 'Big Pimpin'' with a one-off movie tie-in single 'Hey Papi' from the second film in Eddie Murphy's Nutty Professor franchise, *Nutty Professor II: The Klumps*. With Memphis Bleek on his wing and Timbaland providing the horn-heavy funk rock beat, Jay's rhyme seemed designed to repair some of the damage 'Big Pimpin'' may have done to the loverman side of his persona, acting as a slightly more gallant counterpoint. Six months after *Vol. 3…* and Jay was claiming he was a reformed character "off that playa shit", that his days of stealing other guys' girls then kicking girls out at dawn and refusing to pay their cab fares or room service bills were over. Now he was ideal boyfriend material – "You can stay all night/We can go bowling, it ain't like before… I was so immature." He clearly wasn't so over the glitzy lifestyle though, since the big-budget Hype Williams video catapulted the concept of 'balling' into whole new stratospheres, set in a mansion the size of a small island, featuring Jay-Z and Dash rolling around a CGI private jet and even including a cameo from Pamela Anderson. And self-promotion hadn't dropped off the agenda either. The video was the first filmed appearance of the Roc-A-Fella sign, the thumb and forefingers joined in a diamond, a gesture that denoted one's affiliation to the Roc as proudly as the devil horns marked you for metal.

In the meantime, the abandoned plan for a Roc-A-Fella umbrella album – the album that never got made on the Hard Knock Life tour – was revived. It was to be called *The Dynasty: Roc la Familia*, and it would feature tracks from the majority of the Roc-A-Fella stable with Jay-Z as guest rapper to tie the whole thing together. It'd even have a shot of Jay giving the Roc-A-Fella sign on the album cover, the ultimate branding.

Looking for a change of tone and approach from his 'Lifetime' trilogy to mark the record out from his solo work, Jay-Z decided not to call on Timbaland and Swizz Beatz for the project – now major names thanks to their work on Jay-Z's biggest hits – but instead try out a clutch of new, emerging production talents. Just Blaze was a producer who'd worked on other Roc-A-Fella albums by Beanie Sigel and Amil from an early stage, helping craft the label's distinctive edgy soul sound full of drama and feeling, but Jay had never used his beats himself before now and wanted to try him out more extensively. Similarly, along with rising talents like Bink! and Rick Rock, he'd heard promising things from a couple of kids called Pharrell Williams and Chad Hugo, going by the name The Neptunes, who'd impressed him with their work with Mase, N.O.R.E., Kelis and Ol' Dirty Bastard. And how could he forget that other cocky young hopeful looking for his big break, one Kanye West?

Little did Jay-Z know this showcase side project would change the course of his career forever.

As the beats rolled in, slinky and soulful, and the verses went down hotter than ever, it was clear some acts were going to be stamping their mark on the Roc-A-Fella identity far more than others. Most notably Amil, Beanie, Memphis and Jay-Z himself. Between them they ran away with the album, and Jay-Z eventually decided, to aid its profile and sales, that it should be released as a solo album heavily featuring these three acts plus a few big name spots thrown in for extra stardust.

The first regal wave from the balcony of *The Dynasty...* came in October 2000, when The Neptunes' 'I Just Wanna Love U (Give It 2 Me)' cannonballed the airwaves. A huge hit, number 11 on the *Billboard* Hot 100 and Jay's first number one on the hip-hop/R&B chart, it twisted Rick James' funk legend 'Give It To Me Baby' into a dancefloor pop'n'grind with a Prince guitar swagger and Pharrell himself filling in the chorus lines. Coasting on the boudoir vibe, Jay-Z lays out to the song's grasping cluster of models his regular romantic deal: a little designer luxury in return for a lot of high-quality sex. Contrary to the title, love's the last thing on his mind.*

For a glorified compilation project on which he often sounded like a bit-player, *The Dynasty...* itself had enough meat and magic to stand proud among Jay-Z's canon thus far. Musically it was fearless, opening boldly with a Just Blaze 'Intro' of sparkling hair rock, soul singer wails and a vivid portrait of the artist as a hungry, fatherless but ambitious young punk on the street with Malcolm X's "by any means necessary" quote ringing in his ears. Then came a welcoming toast to the Roc, a musical credit sequence called 'Change The Game' introducing the main players – Jay-Z, Beanie and Bleek – and their killer flows over a bouncing bass throb and robotic hook. There would follow frivolous moments: the funk strut of 'I Just Wanna Love U...', the witty satires of Beastie Boys' shout-rap style on 'Stick 2 The Script', and the elastic cartoon basslines being popularised by a fresh and offensive white rapper from Detroit called Eminem on 'Parking Lot Pimpin'' and 'Squeeze 1st'. There would be trademark coke-and-guns anthems ('Squeeze 1st', 'You, Me, Him And Her') and boasts of bounty ('Parking Lot Pimpin'' was a catalogue of expensive cars and the action they earn). But, crucially, there would also be moments of deep anguish and emotion, intense soul-searching, blazing defiance and

---

* The single came with a video boasting another mansion full of half-naked models, but with a comedy twist – Jay-Z mimed the hook line, his first, albeit faked, attempt at singing on one of his tracks.

bursts of enlightenment. *The Dynasty…* sounded like Jay-Z waking up from the wild, self-centred party of *Vol. 3…* and reconnecting with his heart and soul, maturing past the playboy. It was a record for tackling his troubles head on.

His impending assault case? That was raged over twice. 'Streets Is Talking' matched the Seventies perp paranoia of 'Streets Is Watching' but now as well as eyes on him Jay was hearing whispers of his guilt everywhere, rumours about his life twisting, stretching and contorting all across town – did he do it, is his career finished, is he about to have a love child? Without rhyming anything that might affect his defence, he sets some records straight, suggesting the "plaintiff" had taken advantage of him, that he'd tried to be as calm and reasonable as possible but had been pushed too far, and that he now kept his gun in his bodyguard's belt since the cops were watching him. He was unrepentant though, and similarly brash in Rockwilder's 'Guilty Until Proven Innocent', almost a sequel to 'Dope Man' but this time a comment on the presumptions of guilt that the press and public had instantly leapt to, long before his case came to trial. Making a sidelong admission that the incident was sparked by bootlegging – "anxiously the public can't wait/Niggaz had to have it before its release date" – he unravelled his thoughts around the case. His refusal to have his work stolen; the stress, shame, bad-mouthing and intrusion inflicted on him and his mother by the press and police; the expensive lawyers he'd hired to secure his acquittal; the opportunists who wanted to rinse him for every cent by claiming he attacked them; and his determination not to stay incarcerated for long.

As an artist inclined to rap directly about his life, this was a stark and defiant insight into the mentality of the dock that bordered on a musical pre-trial testimony, but it also exposed the wider issue that, for the accused celebrity those months and years between arrest and verdict are one long, continuous trial by public opinion, from cuffs to courtroom. But one deceptive aspect of these tunes was Jay-Z's reference in 'Streets Is Talking' to the absent father he'd still had no contact with – "I ain't mad at you dad/Holla at your lad." Deceptive because the most anguished moments on *The Dynasty…* sprang from the loss of family.

All vinyl crackles, mournful piano and a chorus sung by a desolate child, 'Where Have You Been' was a heartfelt, brutal and moving ballad – cut where Beanie Sigel wept and raged over his abusive father and Jay-Z filled the grooves with fury at his own dad, admonishing him for the poverty in which he left his family and taunting him with the money he missed out on. And 'This Can't Be Life' was rawer still. Built by Kanye over a Dr. Dre sample from 'Xplosive'*, it was intended to be a hard-hitting exploration of life's hardest knocks. Jay-Z's verse spoke about his girlfriend's miscarriage, his family's split, his risks of death and arrest and his fears of a failed career in a West Coast-dominated rap scene, but it was the dark and desperate verse from another big name guest rapper, Scarface, that probed deepest. While waiting to record his verse, Scarface received a phone call with the news that one of his friend's sons had died. Discarding the verse about his own troubles that he'd originally intended to put on the track, Scarface wrote a tribute to his friend's tragedy on the spot. Over Kanye's slick soul beat, it made for a devastating five-and-a-half minutes.

Jay-Z's attitude towards relationships in song took a further twist on *The Dynasty...* too. While 'Get Your Mind Right Mami' was an ultra-manipulative pimp tune (featuring Snoop Dogg) about glamorising, training up and beating a girl until she's fit to sell, Blaze's ghostly theremin creeper 'Soon You'll Understand'† saw Jay considering the tricky situation of having a good friend's young sister hitting on him, a girl he'd known from a child, driven to college, bought jewellery for and become close friends with. He was scared of upsetting his friend and the mother who thought of him as one of her own; he begged the girl to forget about him, but by verse two they've started a family and he's inevitably cheating. His thinking behind wanting to break off the relationship was complex, based on love and respect for the girl and their young family and his inability to be the devoted family man,

---

* Jay-Z's autobiography also credits a tune by Harold Melvin & The Blue Notes as sampled on the track.

† A song even more eerily reminiscent of that year's Eminem hit 'Stan' than 'Wishing On A Star', with its thunderstorm noises and slasher movie vibe.

but wracked with the knowledge he too is about to become one of the errant fathers he criticised so strongly elsewhere on the album. It's no wonder the final verse was another open letter of apology to his mother – in this fictionalised story Jay-Z was coming to reason out and understand his father's departure, and even acknowledge a little of the runner in himself.

It wasn't all heartbreak and despair, of course. 'The R.O.C.' was an effervescent mobster bob, all bubble noises and fingerclicks. And Bink!'s brassy soul barnstormer '1-900-Hustler'* was a fun new angle on the hustler rhyme Jay-Z had made his own. It imagined a Hustlers' Hotline manned by Jay-Z, Bleek and another Roc-A-Fella rapper, Freeway, dishing out advice to other hustlers trying to break into new territories, protecting their block or making some money until their hip-hop deal comes through. The advice is to play it tight and aggressive: start small, infiltrate, get big by quiet methods but be willing to take down anyone who opposes you, don't throw away all your money on gambling and hookers and never talk about your deals on the telephone.

And that Hustling For Dummies rounded off a multifaceted album that seamlessly melded light-hearted frivolity with dark desperation, deep emotion and deadpan inhumanity. An inclusive, label-encompassing concept from the start, it also seemed to embrace Jay-Z's entire career to date, the new clutch of producers harking back to the soul shuffles of *Reasonable Doubt* while also continuing the pioneering pop work of the 'Lifetime' trilogy. *The Dynasty...* would ultimately prove to be an intermediary album between major phases in Jay-Z's career but it would not be forgotten nor go unloved. Even the critics who found the record 'hard work' still praised the innovative rhythms, cadences, shifts and breaks in Jay-Z's rapping technique, not least *The Village Voice*'s Kelefa Sanneh, who claimed "his albums evoke a fantasy of total control: mind over matter, mind over mouth... the syllables just pour out confident, conversational

---

* Based around a sample of 'Ain't Gonna Happen' by Ten Wheel Drive & Genya Ravan.

– as if he'd have us believe that his every thought is an exquisite couplet," and praised his "propensity for polysyllabic rhyme by repeating words and sounds so that each line bleeds into the next".

The public were equally bewitched. Jay-Z's third number one album on both the *Billboard* Hot 100 and hip-hop/R&B chart, selling even faster than *Vol. 3...*, racking up 557,000 sales in its first week and going on to sell 2.3 million. The implication was clear – if the police and Middle America were trying to bring Jay-Z down in the wake of his arrest, his fanbase had only grown more obsessive. Only nine months into the new Millennium and Jay-Z had already released an album that would become the 20th best-selling hip-hop record of the coming decade.

Two more singles would keep *The Dynasty...* building well into 2001, although neither set the charts on fire. In January 'Change The Game' peaked at number 86 despite a hilarious video in which Jay-Z, Bleek and Sigel had found themselves working as rim fitters in the only motorcycle mechanic's workshop staffed almost entirely by models with the urge to randomly get topless. And in March, 'Guilty Until Proven Innocent' did a little better on the back of a video that dramatised Jay's coming trial and all the newscast froth that would whirlpool around it, with Jay and R Kelly delivering their indictments on mass media 'justice' from the witness box.* The modest chart performance of 'Guilty...' was soon forgotten amidst the heavy rotation and five weeks at number one achieved by R Kelly's tropical R&B hit 'Fiesta (Remix)' in May, which featured Jay-Z spitting a guns-and-girls rhyme and driving micro-cars around Caribbean dirt roads in the video.

And anyway, if it was notoriety that Jay-Z was courting as the summer of 2001 approached, he was about to hit the jackpot.

---

* The video caused enough of a stir to warrant the release of a *Making Of Guilty Until Proven Innocent* documentary disc that June, which went behind the scenes on director Paul Hunter's shoot.

The roar died down. The faces in the front row turned from amazed to confused to disappointed. The curtain at the back of the stage resolutely refused to move.

And so began what Jay-Z would come to describe as the longest 90 seconds of his life.

There is, after all, no bigger dread than introducing onstage one of the biggest stars in music history only for that superstar not to come onstage.

"I know Michael Jackson better come out from behind that muthafuckin' curtain," he said into the mic as the panic rose and the crowd got restless. Some of them started laughing, others were merely baffled at the bizarre pause in Jay-Z's otherwise faultless headline set at the Hot 97 Summer Jam 2001 in the Nassau Coliseum in Long Island. After a dazzle of hip-hop luminaries including OutKast, Jadakiss, Nelly, Ja Rule, Eve, R Kelly and Destiny's Child had taken the stage – all rapturously received apart from Destiny's Child, who were booed throughout their set – Jay-Z romped through his show with energy and panache from the opening onstage rush of an army of rappers for his section of Mya's 'Best Of Me Remix'* to a Missy Elliott appearance for 'Is That Yo Bitch', now cunningly retitled 'Is That Yo Chick' to appease the censors. But the highlight of his show, the grand introduction to his new, Jackson 5-sampling single 'Izzo (H.O.V.A.)' which was tearing up the airwaves ahead of its June 22 release, was rapidly turning into one of the biggest disasters of his onstage career.

"You want me to go back and get him myself? Okay, I'ma go get him."

A few seconds later, drenched in relief, Jay-Z returned to the stage with a frail and dazed-looking Michael Jackson on his arm, posing for photos and allowing Jacko a brief word on the mic: "I love you all." Then Jackson was swept offstage as the cart-wheeling loop of 'I Want You Back' struck up in the belly of 'Izzo...' and Jay-Z's set closed triumphant.

---

* A guest slot he'd recorded early in 2000.

The real notoriety, however, came earlier in the set. Jay-Z had an album's worth of material ready to record the following month of July, arguably the best of his career so far, and he used the Summer Jam to showcase some of it. One particular rhyme, the second verse of a bulbous and bluesy Kanye West track called 'Takeover'*, raised eyebrows since it was Jay's first all-out dive into the tradition of the diss song. Besides asserting that it was Roc-A-Fella who were "running this rap shit" on the East Coast, he took a potshot at Nas with the line "Ask Nas, he don't want it with Hov, no", but mainly he piled into Prodigy from Queens duo Mobb Deep: "I don't care if you Mobb Deep, I hold triggers to crews/You little fuck, I got money stacks bigger than you/ When I was pushing weight back in eighty-eight/You was a ballerina, I got your pictures, I seen ya." To prove his point, at that moment up on the Coliseum's JumboTron flashed several pictures of Prodigy as a child dancer, dressed as Michael Jackson and pulling some classic Jacko dance moves. The deathly threats of the rest of the verse cut through the laughter with ominous echoes of Biggie and Tupac.

A low blow, but not unprovoked. Aside from the disagreements over use of Nas samples in Jay-Z's songs and Nas failing to turn up for Jay's recording sessions, the roots of this beef were convoluted and stirred up unnecessarily by the bit-players. As far back as 1999 Prodigy had taken umbrage at several lines he perceived to be attacks on himself and his close associate Nas in the lyrics of Jay-Z and Memphis Bleek, particularly the line "your lifestyle's written" in Bleek's 'My Mind Right', which Prodigy convinced Nas was a reference to his second album's title *It Was Written*.

Though Nas had already taken a sideswipe at Jay-Z in his track 'We Will Survive' from his 1999 third album *I Am...*† he was reluctant to engage in direct lyrical conflict with Bleek or Jay-Z over such a minor

---

* Built around a sample from The Doors' 'Five To One'.

† In a verse directed at the deceased Biggie Smalls, Nas rapped: "It used to be fun, making records to see your response/But now competition is none, now that you're gone/And these niggas is wrong using your name in vain/And they claim to be New York's king?"

slight, but Prodigy stoked the fire. In interviews Prodigy also pointed to a perceived diss against his beef with Snoop Dogg and Death Row in 'Money, Cash, Hoes'*, the shift in image from speedboats to basketball jerseys for Jay-Z's video for 'Where I'm From', which he thought was a direct mocking of himself and Nas, and a line in that song that he felt was an attack: "I'm from a place where you and your man's hung in every verse in ya rhyme."

"I was like 'Nas, what we need to do is go at these niggas'," he told Planet Ill website, "because number one, his lil' man is trying to shit on you; talking about your life is written and all this shit… I was like these niggas is going at us subliminally and I was like fuck that, we need to go at those nigga [sic]. Let's make a song about them, son. And he was like nah nah that nigga ain't nobody to be doing that son… I'm like aight cool. 'Cause in my mind, I'mma address it on my own anyway. I don't give a fuck what this nigga do. I love you Nas but I'mma handle this 'cause you buggin."[1]

Prodigy's anger at the Roc-A-Fella posse was heightened further when he heard Jay-Z, Freeway, Beanie Sigel and Young Gunz freestyling on Flexmaster Flex's show on Hot 97, alongside a new guy they introduced as H Moneybags. When Prodigy heard it he was in the studio with a friend of his who rapped under the name of E Moneybags and claimed to have gone to high school with Jay-Z. The pair phoned the station to accuse Jay and his new guy of stealing E's stage name. Down the Hot 97 phone line, the beef heated up.

Jay-Z's diss of Prodigy in 'Takeover' and his showing the photos of Prodigy dancing were a direct response to the ire Prodigy had been casting at him via interviews and phone calls, but the Summer Jam show just got Prodigy angrier. He claimed the photos were from a pre-teen age when he would help out at his grandmother's tap-dance school. "[Jay-Z] puts it up on the screen and changes the date," he said, "and… he says in a rhyme 'You was a ballerina, I got the pictures I seen you'… So the people that wasn't at that show, automatically

---

* The line: "it's like New York's been soft/Ever since Snoop came through and crushed the buildings/I'm trying to restore the feelings."

they going to be like, 'Jay-Z had a picture of P with a tutu on!' 'Cause that's the way he put it out there, you know what I'm saying? But that's not even the reality of it. So the nigga's lying... 'Wow, this nigga's a fake phony ass nigga right here, man.' Aight you made people laugh, aight that's funny... Back to reality, the laughs is over... now what? You going at me? Are you crazy, son? Do you know how personal I am? I will fucking make a personal vendetta for the rest of my life to make sure I will expose you, let people know what's real and what's not."[2]

Prodigy himself would respond on two tracks of Mobb Deep's next album *Infamy* that winter, calling Jay-Z "a female-ass nigga, the homo rapper, H to the you-know" in 'Crawlin'' and stating "your retaliation was weak, baby pictures". Nas' response, though, would be far quicker coming. Within weeks of the Summer Jam show, while Jay-Z was busy breezing through the recording of his sixth album, *The Blueprint*, in just two weeks (and writing the lyrics, reportedly, in one weekend at Baseline, laying down nine tracks in 48 hours – "I work in spurts" he'd say[3]), Nas appeared on a radio show freestyling over the beat to Eric B. & Rakim's 'Paid In Full' – itself possibly a dig at Jay-Z not having gained permission for Nas samples. On the freestyle, originally untitled but later to be named 'Stillmatic', 'Stillmatic Freestyle' or 'H To The Omo', Nas was brutal in his dissing of Jay-Z, calling him out as a pretend hustler rapping "fake coke rhymes/And those times, they never took place, you liar/'Un' was your first court case, you had no priors/You master fabricated stories of streets." He didn't stop there – Nas abused Rocawear ("your wack clothes line"), the Roc-A-Fella crew ("Rip the Freeway, shoot through Memphis... remove the fake king of New York") and insinuated that Jay-Z had stolen both his style and his hooks from Nas while simultaneously mocking the lyrics of Jay's latest track 'Izzo (H.O.V.A.)' – "For shizzle you phony, the rapping version of Sisqo/And that's for certain, you clone me." He was sly in his jibes at Jay-Z's sexuality, referencing "all you hip-hop queers" rather than accusing Jay directly of being gay (for now), but forthright in his tackling of the sampling issue. "I count off when you sample my voice..."

Immediately upon hearing Nas' freestyle, his revenge reflex triggered once again, Jay-Z went back to 'Takeover' and added a far more vitriolic third verse. This was all-out warfare. First target, Nas' career. He'd stopped having hit records, the verse mocked, his initial spark of talent, hype and respect was burned out, he was only releasing one great album every decade, even his own bodyguard now rapped better than him. Next, Jay-Z flipped back Nas' accusations that he was a fake hustler and gay, calling Nas "the fag model from Karl Kani/Esco ads" and a "fake thug" who'd never seen a TEC-9 gun until Jay-Z himself had shown Nas one while on tour with Main Source's Large Professor. Jay even hinted at having some dirt on Nas, claiming that "you know who did you know what with you know who" and warning him not to end up as "the next contestant on that Summer Jam screen". Finally, in one of his greatest lines, Jay replied to Nas' dig at Jay for sampling him by stating that, financially, "you ain't got a corn nigga, you was getting fucked/And I know who I paid God, Serchlite Publishing," and dropping one of the suavest disses in hip-hop history. "Yeah I sampled your voice, you was using it wrong/You made it a hot line, I made it a hot song."

Roc-A-Fella's A&R man Lenny 'S' Santiago recalls the session. "Everybody in there was obviously super-biased. Biggest Jay fans and supporters in the world. We were 100 per cent gung-ho, gassing Jay to do it."[4] Gimel 'Young Guru' Keaton, the Roc-A-Fella engineer working with Kanye West to produce the track, remembers Jay's calmness about the whole recording. "It wasn't this super-angry vibe. I've never seen Jay super-angry, or he doesn't show it, it's always the poker face."[5] Jay himself is brief and sanguine about his motives behind the new verses. "I only could take so much," he said.[6]

Whatever the motivations behind the developing beef – and Jay-Z would later play it down as, to some degree on his part at least, a publicity ploy to replace Tupac and Biggie as the most fiery and infamous beef in hip-hop – it would do both parties a great deal of good. Nas' profile was indeed slipping by 2001 and the attention helped to reassert him as one of hip-hop's pivotal figures, critically if not in sales terms. And for Jay-Z, on one hand feeling persecuted by rivals and society at large and on the other riding high on his biggest chart hit yet with the number eight success of the self-celebratory hustler's history 'Izzo (H.O.V.A.)', it allowed him to further court mainstream crossover audiences while maintaining his dangerous street edge.

And heaven knows it wasn't the most portentous diss Jay received in 2001. That came from Damon Dash, questioning his Roc-A-Fella partner's business abilities in *The New Yorker* magazine on the eve of the launch of the first Roc-A-Fella alcohol brand, Armadale vodka.* The Nas feud would propel Roc-A-Fella higher; such differences with Dash would ultimately rip them apart.

---

* A venture launched alongside Scottish vodka makers William Grant & Sons so that Roc-A-Fella acts could plug their own vodka in their rhymes rather than give free advertising to other companies.

Chapter Nine

Setting The Blueprint

It shook New York City. The reverberations were felt across Manhattan, across the country, across the globe, and for a decade to come. Two airplanes shrieking against metal 99 floors above ground, plunging the 21st century into war, grief and unfathomable fear.

Unboxed quietly onto the shelves of the Downtown megastores with a far more subdued boom than it deserved on that devastating morning of September 11, 2001, *The Blueprint* emerged into a much darker world than that in which it had been made.

And it, too, redefined the times.

Unroll *The Blueprint* bit by bit, pin it as it came, study its details and nuances as they gradually become visible, and over the course of the build-up to its release the whole thing looked a colourful but indecipherable splurge. The first glimpse, in the shape of the video for 'Izzo (H.O.V.A.)' promised a glamorous cornucopia of special guests and cameos. The presidential parade staged in Jay-Z's honour is applauded on TV screens by the likes of Nelly, Eve, Kanye West, OutKast and Destiny's Child, a sign of the growing closeness between Jay-Z and a certain R&B singer. For all the celebrity endorsements in the video though, the album came with only one guest appearance listed – hip-hop's latest soaraway sensation Eminem appeared on the track 'Renegade'.*

And the tunes, at first, seemed incongruous. 'Izzo…' was a bright pop banger of a first single but the album's opening track, 'The Ruler's Back'†, though it shared 'Izzo…''s proud self-aggrandisement and defiant cockiness in the face of his criminal charges‡ and bail costs, oozed a reformed soul glory, horns jubilantly blazing and strings spiralling in from the ether. Its lines attempting to place Jay-Z alongside Malcolm X, Martin Luther King and Rosa Parks as a righteous black culture freedom fighter were at odds with the fact that he was facing arguably justified charges for violent assault. Plus, it gave way to the fuzzed-up, spite-spewing and furious blues rock of 'Takeover', fired in from the other end of the classic black culture spectrum.

Close up then, confusion. But glide a dozen steps back, take in the whole fresco, soak it in from a distance, and *The Blueprint* seems less like a sketchy design for some grand but unrealised scheme and more like the finished masterpiece. It was an album that took hip-hop's focus back to sampling, a 'lost' practice that had made *Reasonable Doubt* so cohesive and celebrated. But *The Blueprint*'s innovation was to combine it with the modernist edge, populist nous and technological trickery that Jay-Z and his various producers had picked up on their journey through the 'Lifetime' trilogy and *The Dynasty*…. So sped-up soul samples mingled seamlessly with pop hooks, studio cuts and glitch beats

---

* What's more, the Jay-Z single released a fortnight before the album wasn't even on it. This was '20 Bag Shorty' from a compilation album *The Projects Presents: Balhers Forever*, a sultry but unexceptional soul parp featuring Baltimore rappers Frody and Gotti that received little promotion, no chart action and a video lacking Jay's usual budget and class – half a dozen bikini models on a very small boat draped around a couple of rappers waving clearly fake bundles of cash, neither of whom was Jay-Z. Jay's name was writ large on the sleeve, but this was some serious imaginary player shit.

† A Bink! production designed around samples from Jackie Moore's 'If'. Trivia spot: when Bink! came to mix the completed track the disc was corrupted, forcing him to go back to the studio where he'd worked on it and desperately hunt through stacks of records to find the Jackie Moore disc and sample it again in time to recreate the ruined track for *The Blueprint*.

‡ "I'm too sexy for jail like I'm Right Said Fred."

147

gleaned from cutting-edge electronica and trip-hop. The result was Jay-Z's first unified, complete piece of work, a record that sat alongside the best classic soul and Motown rather than smothering them in rhyme, technique and gangsta rhetoric. It was a blueprint not just for the dramatic, gritty soul sound of future Roc-A-Fella records but for the next decade of hip-hop.

It was also the most personal and revealing album yet from an act already renowned for splaying open his life and history, his fears, flashiness and furies on record. If 'Takeover' was an obvious fresh wound being prised open, 'Izzo...' was deceptive in its pop sheen. Beneath lurked one of Jay-Z's most precise and detailed visions of his drug trade days yet. It examined three separate stages of his life and career in the lyric – first as the coke syndicate boss of a town, then as a rapper taking over the music business using the same strategies and finally bringing it back to the beginning, in sharp focus: a spotlight on his Marcy street corner, the crack capsules in his palm and his lookouts keeping watch, selling crack and then telling his listeners his experiences not as guidance into a life of crime but as a moralistic warning. "Niggas acting like I sold you crack/Like I told you sell drugs; no, Hov did that/So hopefully you won't have to go through that," he rapped, a rare moment of warmth and care between rapper and listener.

Ironically, in recording 'Izzo...' Jay-Z's legal lookouts let him down. Thinking the chorus too repetitive, Jay leapt on Tone's (from Trackmasters) advice to put a female voice on the hook. The extra lilt added immeasurably to the slickness of the chorus, but the girl in question was angry her contribution wasn't credited (since 'featuring' credits were only given to name artists) or sufficiently recompensed. "The best and worst mistake we ever made," Jay would later claim. "I got sued messing with Tone on 'Izzo...' because he had a girl with him who we put under the hook. She said she created that hook."

When Young Guru questioned the credibility of using such a well-known tune as 'I Want You Back' on the song, Jay-Z laid out the thinking to him. "This had become the key to his success," Guru told *XXL* magazine. "He was just like 'Guru, I could rap forever and please you... these are the songs that keep the registers ringing'."[1] Indeed,

Jay-Z was lucky to end up with the track, since the beat almost ended up as a Cam'ron song. "Our system really was on some new-age Motown," Atlantic A&R chief Gee Roberson explains. "We treated it no differently than when Berry Gordy used to have his producers cook up the beat, and then he gives it to his writers, and the best song wins."[2]

Blaze's 'Girls, Girls, Girls' was just as deceptive. A gorgeous, loping swoon of vintage boudoir soul* it was ostensibly a catalogue of the ladies Jay-Z had ensconced all over the globe. Spanish homebodies, black princesses, French romantics, Native American gold-diggers, students, models, stewardesses, drug mules and hypochondriacs – girls of every hue, in every city. Giving a brief summation of each character and relationship, it was Jay's homage and pastiche of the soul loverman tradition of Barry White and Tom Brock, whose wail of "ooooh baby" repeats behind Q-Tip, Biz Markie and Slick Rick's guest vocals in the chorus. But the tone of the track is revealing; the wit, warmth and even the hint of courtship and romance in the offer of "I would love to date ya" marked a turning point in Jay-Z's attitude towards women and relationships. Although the song was all about promiscuity and unfaithfulness, the more approachable, playful and humane attitude towards these girls he professed to "love" and "adore" seemed to sit better with his burgeoning cool-but-cuddly crossover image. Better that, certainly, than the abusive, manipulative and dismissive "bitch" magnet he portrayed himself as on *Vol. 3...*

Jay-Z had originally wanted Tone from Trackmasters to oversee the production of the entire album, impressed by the way he worked beats in the same way rappers worked their rhymes. Tone was an unreliable studio presence, though, and missed out on the glory of being *The Blueprint*'s mastermind – "He was supposed to oversee *The Blueprint*," Jay would say, "he missed the whole opportunity. I would kill myself."[3] Trackmasters' one production credit on the record, though, came on 'Jigga That Nigga', a token R&B pop interlude complete with girl-group vocals from unknowns Stephanie Miller and Michelle Mills and a

---

* From samples of Tom Brock's 'There's Nothing In This World That Can Stop Me From Loving You'; Blaze originally considered giving it to Ghostface Killah.

rhyme about impressing one of those 'Girls, Girls, Girls' into bed with his fancy cars, clothes, rims, bracelets and panoramic apartments. There was a comedy twist to this traditional tale of the high-rolling player, though – when he wasn't about to "slay bed or sofa" where the "sex is explosive", he was stoned to the point of immobility. Unlike the track itself, according to Jay. "It kept you awake," he said. "It was one of those joints that was out of place, but out of place in a good way."[4]

After that mid-album shake-awake, *The Blueprint* immediately got back to business. 'U Don't Know' was a pivotal song for both the album and hip-hop. Its seminal opening is now as instantly recognisable as any of the mainstream hits Jay-Z had assimilated into his raps before, thanks to its combination of strident strings and vocal sample of Bobby Byrd's 'I'm Not To Blame', both sped up to a reedy, silvery gleam. It was a sound that would be repeated by Just Blaze and Kanye West in their own tracks and imitated throughout urban music from that point on, forming the background bedrock of rap, R&B and grime-pop across the globe. And it was a sound that arrived out of healthy but fierce competition in the studio.

"I had two rooms in Baseline," Jay-Z remembers. "It was a big room… that I'd record in. Then it would be a small room that Just would be in doing beats. What happened was, Just would peep his head in and hear what me and Kanye was doing and would just go back mad… It was like a heavyweight slugfest. For three days they was just knocking each other out. And I remember him playing that joint, and I was like 'Oh my God'."[5]

Since they were recording so quickly, Blaze himself was never completely happy with the beat, throwing himself at it numerous times before feeling he'd got it right, although he would claim that was the tune that cemented his and Jay's working relationship for good. But Jay-Z's rhyme was as forceful and blazing as the beat demanded, and his biggest bragging tune yet. Throwing us back into those meanest of streets, he reminded us first of the guns, drugs, violence and narc cop shakedowns of his days in Marcy with a stream of breathless and brilliant rhymes that didn't so much flow as geyser-gush. Then he laid out just how far he'd come from those deadly beginnings. He claimed a starting fortune of $900,000 from his hustling alone, but that's nothing. "Could make 40 off a brick, but one rhyme could beat that", he estimated, counting off his escalating bank balance – "One million, 2 million, 3 million, 4/In just five years 40 million more/You are now looking at the 40 million boy." And the rap reckoned Rocawear had done even better for him. This deadly spreadsheet put its income at $80 million. Musically and mathematically, 'U Don't Know' was as bold as hustler rap had ever been.

The classics kept coming. Timbaland's only contribution to the album, 'Hola' Hovito', was a traditional Jay-Z story of dodging cops, stealing girls and humiliating hip-hop rivals, but swathed in Latino block party jubilance, as if imagining Jay-Z cruising through Little Havana, top down. Jay had his regular Latino and Caribbean friends and associates – Juan Perez from the Dominican Republic, for example – so the swing into favela chic with Jay-Z greeted like a brother from a different ghetto by the Mexican and Latino community was totally natural. And over Miami-Mex trumpets, reggae squonks and choirs of chanting Latin Americans, Jay-Z delivers some of his wisest and most revealing words. The lines "Push perrico if I need to, for the rule of evil/Was born in the belly, that's the way the streets breed you," for instance, suggested that a life immersed in poverty and surrounded by crime breeds an inherent wickedness virtually from birth, a deeper and more damning tack than his previous stance that the threat of death or arrest as a hopeless hood youth makes a life of crime and violence little more dangerous than an honest path. Like the rhyme said, "My food for thought so hot it give you dudes ulcers."

If these immaculate upbeat confections weren't impressive enough, *The Blueprint*'s legend was sealed by a trio of sublime, emotion-drenched tracks shifting the tempo gradually slower and the mood ever closer to heartbroken. 'Heart Of The City (Ain't No Love)' was the brassiest of the bunch, Kanye twisting Bobby 'Blue' Bland's strutting soul masterpiece 'Ain't No Love In The Heart Of The City' into a dusty demon of funky strings and flirting flutes, backed with Bland's inimitable chorus croon. Referencing Biggie's 'Mo Money, Mo Problems', Jay's rhyme despaired over the lack of love and respect between competitors in the rap scene and the jealousy and hatred his success had inspired in his rivals when all he was trying to do was make a few million and sleep with more than a few drugged-up women at a time. "Every day I wake up, somebody got a problem with Hov'… young fucks spitting at me/ Young rappers getting at me," he rapped before delivering the perfect patronising put-down, "sensitive thugs, you all need hugs."

It was a rhyme that came like a bullet from a hurt heart. Young Guru recalls sitting in the studio listening to the beat for 30 minutes, then seeing the video for 'Fiesta' come on a TV screen. Jay tapped his shoulder, told him he was ready. He'd hit the booth, spat three verses and was back at the mixing desk before the 'Fiesta' video was over. "That's how fast he recorded that song."[6]

The ironic thing about the proud soul pulse of Kanye's 'Never Change'* was that, of course, Jay-Z had changed dramatically. Here was a song about "still fucking with crime, 'cause crime pays" sung by a man purporting to have left his criminal ways far behind him. But the lyric was about something more fundamental: an exhortation to stay true to yourself and your roots, an admission that the resourceful, determined and street-honourable hustler of his youth would never truly leave him.

The song included a detailed dissection of the time he lost his entire stash in his arrest at Trenton High School and then struggled and laboured to make up his loss – or a situation much like it, since the song mentions losing "92 bricks", much more than he could've had on his person that day – a memory of his hardest hustling experiences and an example of the ground-in grit and tenacity that were the backbone of his character even now, as a Multi-Platinum rap artist. He was still the same guy, still hustling, still making crime work for him, but now in the arena of A-list music. When he rapped about being "knee deep in coke… we flood streets with dope" it was as much a metaphor for the drug references swamping his lyrics and the narcotic-level rhymes he drowns the nation in as a literal statement of hustling prowess.

His exposé of his "92 bricks" story was too much for Def Jam's A&R chief Tyran 'Ty Ty' Smith, who argued vehemently that the line should

---

* Created using a sample from 'Common Man' by David Ruffin.

be cut for legal reasons. But for the listener, the hardest thing to take was the tragedy inherent in the autobiographical closing verse on Jay's boyhood – that a child so young "my big sis still playing wit Barbie" should need to be taught all the lessons of street survival. The guns, the surveillance, the accumulation of dead presidents by any means necessary.

It's amazing to think that a track as smooth and fluid as 'Song Cry' was formed by utter artful butchery. Blaze chopped out virtually every note heard on the finished track, making 70 cuts to the sample from Bobby Glenn's 'Sounds Like A Love Song' in all. In the hands of a master, the result was as flawless as keyhole surgery. Maudlin pianos and passionate sepia soul singers draped a soundtrack as sad and glamorous as a diva's divorce. What better backing for Jay-Z's most intricate and emotion-fuelled relationship rap to date. With a sudden gush of honest humanity, as if completely bursting the gangsta shield and player posturing of his previous albums and of 'Girls, Girls, Girls', here Jay-Z's womanising ways finally catch up with him. Married but absent for months on end, playing around out of town, the girl who'd seen him from poorer to richer had had enough, started cheating herself, demanding a separation. Suddenly Jay-Z feels remorse for the way he's treated this girl, ends up lonely and heartbroken, admits to real-life emotions, real-life hurt and loss. "You don't just throw away what we had, just like that... I'll mourn forever/Shit, I gotta live with the fact I did you wrong forever."

Stripped of sneer and cockiness, this was by far Jay-Z's most raw romantic revelation yet, and a major turning point in his image. He'd been pioneering in rapping about his most painful emotions and experiences before, but never had we seen him so vulnerable, sensitive and broken. Unlike the vast majority of hip-hop love songs, he allowed the girl in the lyric – a combination of events from three separate but real-life relationships of Jay's, amalgamated into one girl – to cheat on him, he let himself lose and be damaged by it, rather than always being the guy who got the girl. "Jay challenged himself on how to end the song," said Roc-A-Fella A&R director Lenny Santiago. "He didn't want it to be typical. Jay felt that wasn't real in life. So... he let the girl cheat on him, and he was actually hurt. He definitely took a minute to just be vulnerable. We were all sitting there, and I could see it in his eyes."[7]

If 'All I Need'* was a recovery, a reassurance, a traditional Jay-Z slice of baller soul, it was a necessary correction of the album's balance before 'Renegade'. By mid-2001 Eminem was on a stratospheric ascent to the very peak of hip-hop fame and success[†] thanks to his unique melodic tongue-twister raps combining family-friendly Saturday morning *Munsters*-theme sounds with the most brutal and violent imagery, witty and confrontational asides, vicious attacks on mainstream personalities, bouts of maniacal anger and anguished autobiography. His success was accelerated by the initial novelty of his white trailer-trash background, a whole new kind of ghetto upbringing that an America addicted to *The Jerry Springer Show* could instantly connect with. On a project with as wide a cultural and stylistic remit as *The Blueprint*, Jay felt Eminem would fit perfectly. A collaboration between the two would be a dual power punch of hip-hop aristocracy and next generation zeitgeist that worked well for them both. Eminem would gain respect from a scene that until then saw him as something of a token white rapper, a puppet pop act of Dr. Dre. And Jay-Z – and hip-hop as a whole – would take a huge step towards wider cultural acceptance by gleaning some of Marshall Mathers' mainstream crossover potential. Everybody won.

The call went out, the only major guest request of the whole project. "Jay just called me and asked if I would make something for us to be on for his album," Eminem said. "It was an honour… 'Renegade' just felt right for [Jay] to be on. It's an open, sparse beat made for spitting, and I knew he would sound great on it."[8]

Jay-Z's team had a beat prepared for Eminem, but Marshall had his own ideas, a track he'd built by reworking 'Renegades' by Michigan duo Bad Meets Evil, who'd appeared on a song named after them on Eminem's *The Slim Shady LP* in 1999. Eminem recorded his verses and the hook and sent it to Jay, the last track to be completed on the album.

---

* Produced by Bink! from a sample of Natalie Cole's 'I Can't Break Away'.
† His second album *The Marshall Mathers LP* had sold 1.76 million copies in its first week in May 2000 and had won the 2001 Grammy for Best Rap Album.

Jay was stunned by Eminem's howl of defiance in the face of the public outrage and debate he'd raised, this forceful stand against the politicians and "fucking do-gooders" scapegoating him, calling him a hate-monger and filth-flinger. Rather than the rapping itself he bugged off the passion and theme, couldn't wait to add the verses he'd already written, gripped by the idea of using the track to tackle people's perceptions of himself and explore his own idea of being a renegade, an underground figure out to expose an alternative society the world wants to ignore. His targets were the critics who misrepresented him as "foolish" and belittled the pain and truth in his words – words that he knew people in the projects clung to as a lifeline and guide rope through their own perilous path – by awarding them stars – "how you rate music that thugs with nothing relate to it?" He'd use the track to assert his achievements in waking up pop culture to the generations of human tragedy squirming beneath its nose, beneath the breadline, beyond acceptable zip codes. The voice of the buried, brushed-away world.

"Jay's whole thing of being a renegade was... to say 'even though I'm in rap and you view rap as this, we're intelligent, thinking people'," said Young Guru. "Jay's expression is 'I'm gonna be a renegade to pop culture, and culture in general, from the underclass perspective, the inner-city, black perspective. You put us in this position of not respecting us, and we're supposed to be forgotten about, the sons of slaves... We're renegades because we don't believe in that. So we're gonna do what we wanna do, dress how we wanna dress and start our own companies.'"[9]

The track was a moody piece full of stalker strings and pulsing organs; monkish electro lit up by Eminem's impossibly tight rhymes and hysterical yowl of "renegade!" at the chorus. It made for a rousing and righteous finale for a practically flawless album, the most sonically cohesive and melodically consistent of Jay-Z's career, after which he could only roll the credits. The credits, in fact, for his entire life thus far. 'Momma Loves Me' was a catalogue of thanks to all the people and neighbourhoods who'd ever supported and believed in him. A first verse dedicated to his family and close friends, full of childhood details about being fed and dressed by his brother and sisters and even a nod to how much he missed his father; a second to the hustling partners and early rap mentors, producers and Roc-A-Fella cohorts; a third to his crew of Bleek and Beanie and the nephews and niece he adored like his own kids. With Al Green's 'Free At Last' looping sweetly behind, 'Momma Loves Me' was as personal and reflective an album-closer as 'You Must Love Me' and 'Regrets' and read like an acceptance speech for the Grammy *The Blueprint* deserved but never won.

Two tracks lurked hidden past a short silence at the end of *The Blueprint*. 'Breathe Easy (Lyrical Exercise)' was just that, a test to see how far he could stretch the metaphor of rap as sport. With heavy breathing as a rhythm section and Just Blaze's sonorous piano twists from a Stanley Clarke track* building up a tense sweat, Jay opened with a one-two of cocksure swipes like Ali riling an opponent – "I'm the all-time heavyweight champion of flow-ers/I'm leading the league in at least six statistical categories right now/Best flow, most consistent, realest stories, most charisma…" Then the bell, and he launched into round after round of sport and exercise similes for rap or hustling: interviews were spring training, drugs were weights, cocaine was taught to "stretch" and gun-dodging rivals to squat. It was a masterful lesson in punning and wordplay from a man whose talent was "rap on steroids".

The final hidden track was 'Girls, Girls, Girls (Part 2)', a Kanye reworking of the earlier track, this time over samples from The Persuaders' bubbly pop sparkler 'Trying Girls Out' and featuring uncredited vocals from Michael Jackson. Like a cheeky final wink, Jay-Z leafed further into his little black book to bombard us with sexual double entendres concerning a student girl he was giving "in-house tutoring" while "moving through her student body union" and a suspicious wannabe actress wary of his busy schedule, before finally detailing what he was after in his perfect woman. Any size, height or skin tone would do so long as she had a sizable behind, was fun but faithful, an extravagant dresser, an accomplished cook and was as comfortable cooking cocaine into crack as negotiating discounts on first-class airline seats. Quite a

---

* 'Got To Find My Own Place'.

lady. Yet, within a year, Jay-Z would be eating the song's opening words: "I'm not a one girl's guy…"

★★★

They actually watched the hysteria building. Right there, in their own studio, in front of their faces. Friends and colleagues would drop by to hear the finished album, leave dumbstruck and then turn up again a day or so later with five friends, insisting they hear it too. Eventually they could barely move in there for whooping, excited hangers-on.

"The listening sessions was getting bigger and bigger between us," Jay recalls. "People was coming back with their friends and shit, like, 'Yo, you gotta hear this shit'. And it was so much energy in the studio that I was like, 'Oh, this is special. This gon' be really serious.'"[10]

When the promo CDs hit the desks of the press, the wildfire turned to conflagration. The effortless combination of mainstream appeal and urban edge hit a critical nerve. Reviews were almost universally gushing – garnering an esteemed five mic review in *The Source*, a perfect XXL from *XXL* and a maximum five discs and Album Of The Year in *Vibe*, *The Blueprint*'s critical plaudits would eventually stretch to high placings in Albums Of The Decade lists in *Rolling Stone*, *Billboard*, *Paste*, *Rhapsody* and *Entertainment Weekly*. Kanye and Blaze were hailed as production geniuses. Retrospectives over the years would declare it Jay-Z's best work since *Reasonable Doubt* and a benchmark in modern hip-hop, spawning a generation of soul-centric sampling imitators. Despite America's shock at the 9/11 attacks, 427,000 sales in week one sent it hurtling to number one, his fourth in as many years. By the end of the month, it'd topped 1 million.*

There's one thing the press loves more than a classic album to fawn over, and that's a very public celebrity fight. Gossip-mongers leapt on 'Takeover' and the rising Jay-Z vs Nas feud, and, as Jay set out on a short tour of small venues to promote the album† and released 'Girls,

---

* The album is currently Double Platinum, selling over 2 million copies in the US alone since 2001.

† The first two dates rescheduled in the wake of 9/11.

Girls, Girls'* alongside a fittingly fittie-filled video featuring cameos from Tamala Jones, Carmen Electra, Paula Jai Parker and Amil as some of the girlfriends whose flaws Jay wearily dissects, the press stoked the beef to boiling point. And both rappers rose to the bait.

Nas bit back. December 18 saw the release of his fifth album, *Stillmatic*, on which, going against his previously aloof attitude towards the feud, he laid into Jay-Z with gusto. Its second song, the same slot as 'Takeover' held on *The Blueprint*, was called 'Ether', and it had a pungent waft of retaliation. Opening with a sample of Tupac's voice chopped and screwed from his track 'Fuck Friendz' so that he was saying "fuck Jay-Z", the disses rang like gat-fire. "I keep my eyes on Judas with 'Hawaiian Sophie' fame"; "this Gay-Z and Cock-A-Fella Records wanted beef"; "you got nerve to say that you better than Big/Dick sucking lips, why not you let the late great veteran live?" Nas claimed to be hurt and betrayed by this rapper he'd felt proud to see develop into fame and success – "what's sad is I love you 'cause you're my brother" – but still digs deeper into the wounds he'd just opened. "You traded your soul for riches," he accused, "you seem to be only concerned with dissing women/Were you abused as a child, scared to smile, they called you ugly?" Recalling a time he took a young Jay in when he was "getting chased through your building, calling my crib", he states that the Jay he met wasn't the high-level hustler he likes to portray himself – "no TECs, no cash, no cars, no jail bars Jigga, no pies, no case... you a fan, a phony, a fake, a pussy." Making further allusions to homosexuality in the Roc-A-Fella crew ("I rock hoes, you rock fellas... you a dick-riding faggot") and mocking "Eminem murdered you on your own shit," he alleged a Jay-Z affair with Foxy Brown, that he was the fall guy in the Lance Rivera stabbing and, finally, that he was constantly ripping off Biggie: "how much of Biggie's rhymes is gonna come out your fat lips?"

'Ether' was a vitriolic bullet-spray of bile every bit as primed and pointed as 'Takeover', and for Prodigy it was his cue to step aside.

---

* A number 17 *Billboard* Hot 100 hit.

"Then it became a Nas/Jay-Z thing," he told *XXL*. "When he dropped 'Ether' I was like I'mma fall back anyway. I could have never made a song like that song, wow!"[11]

Rebounding off the ropes, Jay-Z jabbed back instantly, deep below the belt. A matter of days after the release of 'Ether' on *Stillmatic* he made public 'Supa Ugly', a freestyle over Nas' 'Got Ur Self A…' that declared "the gloves is off" and swung out hard. Declaring himself unbruised by Nas' attacks, he criticised his opponent for adopting an underworld identity – "This nigga never sold aspirin/How you Escobar?" – and then dished up the dirt that 'Takeover' had threatened, by the potload. After a cutting sample from Dr. Dre's 'Bad Intentions' of the line "all I really know is that your ho wants to be with me", verse three insinuated that Jay had slept with Carmen Bryan, who had mothered Nas' child Destiny, as had someone called AI, taken to refer to basketball player Allen Iverson whom Bryan graphically admits to also sleeping with in her autobiography *It's No Secret*. Jay claims his trysts with Bryan even happened in Nas' own Bentley, and hit back at his gay jibes with a grisly detail: "You was kissing my dick when you was kissing that bitch."

When Gloria Carter heard the track on the radio she was disgusted at her son and called him to insist he apologised to Nas and his family for his vicious slights. Eventually, in *Rolling Stone*, he would – with the caveat that he'd mentioned his relationship with Carmen as a fair rebuke to Nas claiming he was gay. But the rivalry raged on. In a radio interview on Power 105, Nas lambasted rappers who he thought were puppets of the music industry, name-checking Nelly, Cam'ron*, N.O.R.E. and, of course, Jay-Z.

For the media, all of this was pure gold, a real-life clash of the hip-hop titans. Radio station Hot 97 sponsored a phone-in poll to determine whether listeners thought 'Ether' or 'Supa Ugly' was the better track –

---

* This complicated matters further as a Nas vs Cam'ron side-beef developed with Cam'ron disparaging Nas' mother and Nas making reference to rumours of Cam'ron having AIDS on his 2002 track 'Zone Out'.

'Ether' won – and MTV canvassed DJs, moguls and rappers to determine who was winning the Nas vs Jay-Z battle. Funkmaster Flex and DJ Kay Slay sided with Nas as "wearing the street battle crown" and having "the last hottest record going at his nemesis... until Jay-Z does a record better than 'Ether' it will remain that way."[12]

Damon Dash resented that the feud was being played out on radio. "I don't consider it a loss," he said. "It was a freestyle against a song. I feel if we're gonna battle we should keep it in the street. Don't put it on radio. It commercialises it. Then you have too many people judging it... 'Super Ugly' was just a freestyle that was meant for mix-tapes, but it got put on such a bigger venue, it was considered a song." Nonetheless, he hinted at further Jay-Z strikes to come. "If anybody knows Jay-Z, they know what he's gonna do. He'll never leave any questions unanswered."[13]

At the time Jay-Z stayed tight-lipped, concentrating on playing promotional gigs for *The Blueprint* and throwing himself into recording its follow-up, sessions for which began that December, within two months of *The Blueprint*'s almighty splash. But his stance on the feud was clear from comments he made to MTV earlier that year. "Nas is definitely going to bring out the best of me. He's gonna put me at the top of my game. I hope I do the same for him. It's like playing basketball with a guy. It's just verbal sparring – no one's fighting, it's just records."[14]

The slugs swung, the profiles rose, the street menace edge was retained, the sales rocketed. The Nas versus Jay-Z feud was a masterstroke in public relations for both acts and for Jay-Z, intentionally or not, it had a further bonus. It was a publicity sleight of hand distracting the media's gaze when, that October, he'd appeared before a court and told the judge "I stabbed Lance Rivera," pleading guilty to a misdemeanour assault charge, a charge bargained in return for a sentence of three years' probation. Though he'd go on to settle a civil suit with Rivera over the assault for somewhere between $500,000 and $1 million, he was glad to put the case behind him and keen to avoid the press hysteria and DA tub-thumping that had attended the trial of Puff Daddy the year before. By verbally attacking Nas, ironically Jay had avoided becoming the media and government's latest high-profile scapegoat over a real-life assault.

Around the same time, Damon Dash was quietly shifted a little out of the Roc-A-Fella picture. Though he was still to be spotted skanking archfully away alongside Jay-Z in every video, he was in the grip of personal issues, reeling emotionally over the death of his singer girlfriend Aaliyah in an airplane crash on the way back from shooting a video in the Bahamas in August, a tragic twist to the tradition of the tropical promo clip. Whether this disaster distracted Dash from his business affairs for a time is unknown, but gradually over 2000 and 2001 Dash was eased out as Jay-Z's main business partner and advisor in favour of a marketing expert called Steve Stoute. Stoute's cross-brand approach to the Jay-Z business was clear from the start – it was him who had convinced the rapper to name-check Motorola on *The Dynasty...*'s 'I Just Wanna Love U (Give It To Me)'. And his vision of expanding Jay's income streams in every direction would instantly be put into effect.

For Jay-Z Incorporated, it was time to start the serious selling.

The acoustic live album. The *Greatest Hits*. The second feature film. The high-profile collaboration album. And all the while holding regular writing and recording sessions for the next album proper. Most artists, finding themselves with a massive critical and commercial hit of the stature of *The Blueprint* on their hands, would take years to carefully formulate a follow-up, taking great care not to disappoint the high expectations of their fans and critics, not to stamp out the growing fire at its peak.

Not Jay-Z. As 2001 bled into 2002 there was a tsunami of Jay-Z product flooding the shelves. On December 18, 2001, the same day of release as Nas' *Stillmatic* and the feud explosion, Roc-A-Fella put out *Jay-Z: Unplugged*, a live recording of an *MTV Unplugged 2.0* show from November 18 where Jay performed stripped-down versions of six tracks from *The Blueprint* interspersed with a selection of older hits that suited the more laid-back instrumentation of his backing band for the occasion, The Roots.* "Welcome to my poetry reading" Jay-Z joked as he led The Roots through an intimate, funky, string-laden set of liquid grooves and organic recreations of his soul samples†, his hits draped in velvet.

January 18, two days after the release of the single 'Jigga That Nigga'‡, Dash held the premiere for Roc-A-Fella Films' second picture, *State Property*, a drug trade crime drama directed by Abdul Malik Abbott and produced by Dash and Phyllis Cedar. Once again, their casting net hadn't been flung too far outside the Roc-A-Fella offices – the film, based on the story of the JBM gang in Philadelphia in the Eighties and Nineties, starred Beanie Sigel as a drug crew leader (imaginatively called Beans) out to take over the city and conquer the existing major crime syndicate, whose heads were played by Jay-Z and Dash (playing Untouchable J and Dame, respectively) in cameo roles. Though it inevitably came with a home-made feel, it would ultimately take over $10 million at the box office worldwide and spawn a sequel in 2005.

March 11 saw the release of Jay-Z's first singles compilation *Chapter One: Greatest Hits*, a retrospective 18-tracker bringing together his biggest singles from the first three albums only, the more recent tracks being saved, presumably, for a planned *Chapter Two*…. Including noteworthy remixes of tracks such as 'I Know What Girls Like', 'Wishing On A Star', 'Can't Knock The Hustle' and 'Ain't No Nigga', it provided new fans with a hook-heavy (if edge and emotion-lite) summary of his early career, and gave fresh royalty sops to discarded production partners like Ski and Big Jaz.

And only two weeks later, an entirely new album. Announced at a press conference at the upmarket Waldorf-Astoria hotel in January and hyped as a generation-defining meeting of meteoric talents, *The*

---

* 'Big Pimpin'', 'Ain't No Nigga', 'Can't Knock The Hustle', 'Jigga What, Jigga Who', 'Can I Get A…', 'Hard Knock Life (Ghetto Anthem)' and 'I Just Wanna Love U (Give It To Me)' – the album hit number 20 and would sell 600,000.

† Right down to a backing vocalist singing all of the vocal samples, including the *Annie* chorus from 'Hard Knock Life…'.

‡ A minor hit at number 66.

Best Of Both Worlds was Jay-Z's first full-album collaboration with R Kelly, recorded largely apart during separate sessions in New York and Chicago between October 2001 and January 2002 with Poke & Tone dominating the desk, Kelly dominating the chorus warbling and Jay dominating the verse rhymes. The title encapsulated the concept with the simplicity of those tacky pop compilation series – to deliver an immaculate combination of hip-hop and R&B from each genre's biggest players in the hope of bridging a cultural and gender divide in the market, to hook more girls into rap and lure more boys into R&B. It was an experiment in melding rough and slick, thug and loverman, diamond and ice.

In urban music terms, this was massive news, the sure-fire biggest seller of the year, Album Of The Century stuff. Thirty million albums sold between them, 10 Platinum discs, numerous number ones; expectations were sky-high for an album that would see the pair push each other to dizzying creative heights. "When you get two people like this coming together, it sends a signal out," said Jay-Z at the conference. "It's bigger than music. It's like Martin and Malcolm coming together."

Unfortunately, that star-studded press conference – Puffy and Russell Simmons both turned up to show support – was as pumped-up as the project would ever get. And not just because demand for the record was so great that there was rampant bootlegging weeks upfront of the release, forcing the release date forward a week.

On February 3, a videotape from an anonymous source arrived at a desk at the *Chicago Sun-Times*. On the tape was footage of a man having sex with and urinating on what the package claimed was a 14-year-old girl. The man in the tape, it said, was R Kelly.

The outrage was widespread, the video went as viral on illegal file-sharing networks as the primitive internet of 2002 would allow. Kelly vehemently denied it was him on the tape, but it was too late, the golden coupling of Kelly and Jay-Z now seemed tarnished. Def Jam pulled the plug on all videos and promotion for the album and Jay-Z refused to do any interviews, photos or promotion with Kelly and delayed plans to announce a tour in support of the record until the issue was cleared up. His caution was astute: that June, still protesting his innocence, Kelly

would be indicted on 21 counts of child pornography, with witnesses coming forward to claim that the girl in the video was indeed a minor.*
All plans for the Best Of Both Worlds tour of 2002 were canned; the record was a dead duck.

When it finally – and somewhat shamefully – shuffled into the stores, *The Best Of Both Worlds* proved as lame as its push. The record cheapened Jay-Z, not by enveloping him in the R Kelly scandal but by diminishing his burgeoning reputation as a ground-breaking artist by association with Kelly's bland and formulaic mainstream mimics of Michael Jackson. His lyrical barbs and gritty themes were necessarily reined in and he seemed confined and at odds with Kelly's ultra-smooth vocals. It sounded less a coming together of genres, more a compromise between them.

It started impressively – the title track found Jay hyping up the album as a world-quaking meeting of titanic talents, mourning Aaliyah and taking further pops at Nas ("I eat 'Ether' and breathe acid, weak bastards"), a suitably bold and aggressive opening. 'The Streets' was a rare and enjoyable chance to hear Jay-Z bristling out a classic tale of an abandoned teenager lost to guns and gang crime on a pure R&B song. The pedestrian bedroom soul of 'Take You Home With Me A.K.A. Body' featured some of Jay's most poetic descriptions of rough ghetto sex to date – "this ain't R&B smooth, I ain't a R&B dude" he rapped over a very R&B backing – and 'It Ain't Personal' outlined a firm friendship breaking apart over money with a hint of grace and sadness. But for all Trackmasters' best attempts to imbue some hip-hop crackle and Arabian enigma, the record soon descended into insipid R&B-by-numbers and trite sexual score-sheeting on tracks like 'Pussy', 'Naked' and 'Somebody's Girl': post-argument sex, sex with other guys' girlfriends, sex with girls with hypnotic genitals. Even – disastrously, considering – sex with underage girls, although this was in a verse of 'Pussy' rapped by Devin The Dude, in which he claims to have slept

---

* Kelly's case would take six years to come to trial, by which time the charges were reduced to 14 counts. Kelly was acquitted of all charges after a three-week trial in 2008.

with an 11-year-old when he was seven. Only the Seventies-tinged 'Honey', with Jay rolling out his best howl-smattered rhymes on the record, showed any imagination when it came to relationships, Jay and Kelly caught between their love of a girl and their previous marriage to making drug money on street corners.

Though Jay-Z brought a certain streetwise punch to the project and exhibited his ever-gymnastic flow at every turn, little of *The Blueprint*'s artful charm was present. Jay seemed very much a distant and dislocated guest on Kelly's turf, and Kelly's attempts to imitate his ghetto rhetoric and badass language in his crystal R&B croon – and fuel a beef with Sisqo, as if R&B could be as malevolent as rap – sounded laughably contrived and incongruous.

Despite scathing reviews, bootlegging, a promotional black-out and a seedy tabloid scandal in the wings, the album reached number two with sales of 285,000 in week one, but soon sank from the charts and the memory of all but the most avid fans. Three weeks later, as if to remind the world how sublime and powerful his raps could be, and to wipe *The Best Of Both Worlds* clean from the public's tainted psyche, Jay-Z put out 'Song Cry' and earned himself another Grammy nomination.

'Song Cry''s video pictured this sensitive thug pulling up at his old house in June 2002, thinking back to moving in there with a woman 10 years earlier, and watching that decade-long relationship disintegrate. Though viewers may have linked the image to Jay's split with Rosario Dawson in 2002, little did they know he was right then in the first throes of a new relationship that would become one of the most secretive, powerful, solid and admired in music history.

And, for a bond so private, it was a courtship played out entirely in the camera lens.

Chapter Ten

Crazy In Love

The Aston Martin getaway car. The deserted mansion hideout. The bundles of cash zipped in a Louis Vuitton holdall. The trappings of the A-list criminal partnership on the lam. With speeding convoys of black-tinted FBI cruisers on your tail, it's tough staying under the radar when you're turning heads everywhere you go, making a dash for the Mexican border while keeping up your demanding standards of high-end designer luxury.

No problem for this modern-day Bonnie and Clyde, though. They effortlessly stayed one step ahead of the body-armoured Feds with a few low-rent tricks. Ducking into skuzzy motels, a tarp over the Lexus, bejewelled pumps on dusty staircases, counting cash in a cheap room but always vacating via the fire escape before the cops kick in the door. Making out in phone booths beside huge murals of dedication to Tupac while the Feds squeal by, unaware that would be the natural place for the hip-hop fugitive to hole up. Trading your sports car for a truck at a gas station and sending the poor schmucks on up the freeway into the waiting arms of the FBI roadblock.

They made a scandalous couple, the glamorous, squeaky-clean pop star dragged into the hip-hop hustler's world of casual criminality. But the romantic movie vision of life on the run wasn't the big story. That came in the chorus. The point when Jay-Z draped his arm around Beyoncé's shoulder and muttered: "All I need in this life of sin is me and my girlfriend." And Beyoncé trilled back, catching his eye, "Down to ride 'til the very end, it's me and my boyfriend."

Pandemonium.

Sure, there were whole reams of artistic licence to be read into '03 Bonnie & Clyde' and its video of two lovers outwitting the small army of cops on their trail. Jay-Z had often made reference to criminal couples in his raps, a fascination that had taken in name-dropping Mickey and Mallory from *Natural Born Killers* and even acting out a bank robbery in rhyme with Foxy Brown as his sidekick on 'Bonnie And Clyde (Part 2)' on Foxy's 1999 album *Chyna Doll*.* This new flamenco-flecked version was said to be inspired by the 1967 film *Bonnie And Clyde*, so this could easily be Jay-Z fulfilling his own lovers-on-the-run filmic fantasy. But the song wasn't about partners in crime in the traditional sense. It was about how unbeatable two major stars could be if they became both romantic and musical partners, and how perfectly their characters complemented each other. Jay-Z suggested openly that they were music's newest power couple with an intimate home life: "the new Bobby and Whitney, only time she doesn't speak is during *Sex And The City*, she gets Carrie fever." Even the samples seemed blatant – the beat from Tupac's 'Me And My Girlfriend', lyrical lines lifted from Prince's 'If I Was Your Girlfriend'.† Neither party was admitting to an affair publicly but the song and video seemed like an announcement of their attachment as loud and proud as the flashing of any million-dollar eternity ring.

Gossip columns had been buzzing for some years over a possible involvement between Beyoncé and Jay-Z. They'd performed together at the Summer Jam in 2001 and Destiny's Child had made a surprising cameo in the video for 'Izzy (H.O.V.A.)', suggesting an unusual cross-genre connection that raised eyebrows. Certainly, the couple knew

---

* Of which many critics claimed '03 Bonnie & Clyde' was essentially a remake.

† The tune also included an interpolation of 'Pastime Paradise' by Stevie Wonder and lyrics from Mariah Carey's 'How Much'.

each other from the urban celebrity circuit, but even as late as early 2002 Beyoncé was claiming in interviews to be dating but not meeting the right men, and was romantically linked by the press to both Eminem and Pharrell Williams. As a middle-class church girl raised Methodist in Houston and rising to fame through talent shows, she seemed an unlikely starlet to be meddling with rappers with rough reputations, but a psychologist might point out the classic signs – the strict taskmaster father who trained Destiny's Child through rigorous and demanding rehearsals, and her shy wallflower youth dating nice religious boys. In both rebelling and searching for familiarity and security, a promiscuous poet on probation like Jay-Z ticked a lot of boxes. On his part, as a man whom Jaz-O believed didn't feel attractive and depended on his fortune to attract women, Jay-Z must have been over the moon to have met, as 'Money Ain't A Thang' had predicted, the R&B chick who fit the bill.

It's unsure how pre-designed the relationship was on Jay-Z's part: if there were previous hints, flirts or encounters, if inviting Beyoncé to guest on his next record early in 2002 was the prelude to an overture, if one had already been made or if, as he attested at the time, he just wanted the best singer in the country on his album. But it's certain that, from day one, he wanted only the very best for her. "He had told me a week before that he needed a joint for him and Beyoncé," Kanye West told MTV at the time. "I remember he called [and] said, 'We got this joint, it has to be the best beat you ever made. Just picture if you got my first single – Hov and Beyoncé – how big you would be then.'"[1]

Perhaps it was a mischievous cupid impulse, or a premonition, that drew Kanye to pick out Tupac's 'Me And My Girlfriend' but he thought the beat perfect for them. Whatever, it leapt out of Shakur's *The Don Killuminati: The Seven Day Theory* album as the perfect joint vehicle. He programmed the beats, had the bass and guitars played live by a guy named E Dog that he and Blaze used up at Baseline, and delivered it to Jay within a week. Perhaps letting on how much he was obsessed with the visual aspect of the collaboration, Jay-Z devised the video plotline before he'd even written the lyric. "I brought it to Hov that night," Kanye recalls, "he heard it, he thought of the video treatment before he thought of the rap. He just knew it was gonna be the one."[2]

'03 Bonnie & Clyde' turned out to be a triumph, a far more credible and cohesive crossover of rap and R&B than *The Best Of Both Worlds*. And the suggestive nature of the chorus clearly spilt over into the real world. The pair began dating around the time of the recording. The media got wind quickly; by July, three months before the single's street date, photos had appeared in the press of the couple embracing and Beyoncé was admitting in *Newsweek* that something romantic might be afoot. Under the auspices of being "good friends", she disclosed, "It's hard to trust people but I'm hopeful." And if Beyoncé was being cautious in light of such loverman boastings as 'Girls, Girls, Girls', Jay-Z was also reluctant to let himself go completely. The weight of his father's absconding still hung heavy.

Hitting the stores on October 10, '03 Bonnie & Clyde' was the rap-pop smash that *The Best Of Both Worlds* had been meant to produce. It hit number four in the US *Billboard* chart – Jay-Z's second Top 10 and Beyoncé's first solo hit – and stormed the upper echelons of charts worldwide, hitting number one in Switzerland, number two in Australia and the UK and going Top 10 across Europe and Canada. A joint appearance performing the song on *Saturday Night Live* on November 2 stoked the record beyond boiling point. Music's new magic couple had arrived.

No sooner were they established, than someone tried to knock them down. Having already narrowly dodged some edge-of-the-seat copyright issues over the track when Shakur's mother withheld permission to use the samples until the day before the single's release, a further storm brewed when R&B singer Toni Braxton released a statement claiming that Jay-Z had only had the idea of sampling Tupac's 'Me And My Girlfriend' after hearing, through Kevin Liles at Def Jam, a pre-release version of a track on Braxton's 2002 album *More Than A Woman* called 'Me & My Boyfriend', recorded in the summer of 2002 and also sampling Shakur's track. "Jay-Z and Beyoncé are messing with my money," Braxton stated in a phone-in interview with a New York radio station. "They're trying to steal my mojo."[3]

All players on the Roc-A-Fella side of the dispute claimed coincidence. "I had no idea about Toni Braxton's [song]," said Kanye. "She can't act like ain't nobody ever heard 'Me And My Girlfriend' before. People hear the song all the time."[4]

"It's an ill coincidence," Dash added. "I know he didn't intentionally make the same record she made. I don't think he even heard it."[5]

Jay himself, claiming Liles had never played him the track and it'd had "zero" influence on his record, was philosophical about the new feud. "I wouldn't want to take it from her," he told MTV. "I don't even think like that. My first thought would be, 'Maybe I could call her up, maybe I could get on that record.' The most obvious [explanation] is it's neither one of our records. It's not like you made an original idea. She's not in hip-hop, but it happens in hip-hop often. We go to sample the same thing and my record came out first. I'm sorry. What can I do?"[6]

The suggestion that he was taking cues from pop singers must've felt pretty laughable to Jay-Z. By this point he felt way ahead of the game, way out on top, unrivalled, a lonely pioneer at the forefront of rap music who was starting to become disillusioned with his peers. 'Hovi Baby', the single released in November 2002 as an introduction to his eighth studio album* laid it out plain. In one of his most imperious lyrics yet he portrayed himself as a titanic giant of hip-hop, a rapper and executive with the entire world of rap standing on his shoulders to see higher or trying to bring him down in David versus Goliath-style battles. Over Just Blaze-produced soap opera dramatics, impassioned synths forever building to crescendos, he rapped: "I'm so far ahead of my time I'm about to start another life… ain't no living person can test him/Only two resting in heaven can be mentioned in the same breath as him." It suggested he'd eventually be forced to crush his niggling detractors and unveiled the next stage in his blueprint for modern hip-hop. "How they propose to deal with my perfect present/When I unwrap *The Gift & The Curse* in one session?"

---

* Without a video, as it was the soundtrack to a Reebok TV ad campaign, more evidence of Jay-Z's new ultra-commercialist business approach. Perhaps as a result of the lack of a promo clip for stations to show, the record failed to hit the *Billboard* Hot 100.

A curse, a gift, an offering to be feared. The magnum opus was upon us…

★★★

After the acclaim, so often the indulgence. An act who finds one of their albums declared a benchmark, a seminal classic of its genre lauded for its concise perfection and wild flashes of genius and inspiration, will often convince themselves they can do no musical wrong, produce no filler. Given carte blanche to record and release whatever they'd like by their yes-men labels who will bow to public opinion that they're dealing with an artist of untaintable genius, the act will indulge themselves under the semblance of treating their fans to an overwhelming banquet of their music and follow it with a double album full of experiments, linking concepts and a wide spectrum of styles as proof that the act in question can transcend boundaries. The Beatles' *The Beatles*. The Smashing Pumpkins' *Mellon Collie And The Infinite Sadness*. Fleetwood Mac's *Tusk*. The Who's *Tommy*.

And now *The Blueprint²: The Gift & The Curse*.*

Recorded over almost eight months between December 2001 and August 2002, in stark contrast to the fortnight it took to produce its predecessor, it was 25 songs over 110 minutes†, swamped in guests (again unlike *The Blueprint*) and promising a brazen leap of creativity, a sprawling splurge of styles and scope. Split into two CDs, the 50-minute *The Gift* consisted largely of more lively club-friendly tracks with a leaning towards the pop and lounge end of Jay-Z's canon, while the hour-long *The Curse* delved into his more sombre and dangerous depths. Its success would not just solidify Jay-Z's standing as an artist operating at the peak of his genre but also bring credibility to hip-hop as a form just as worthy and capable of grand statements and major artistic endeavour as any before it. Like Public Enemy's *Fear Of A Black Planet* and The Wu-Tang Clan's *Wu-Tang Forever*, *The Blueprint²: The Gift & The Curse* was hip-hop taking its seat at the high table of music culture.

---

* Released November 12, 2002.

† Picked from a total of 40 written for the record.

It would also, for a man teetering uncertainly on the brink of true love, mark a small but perceptible shift in attitude and perspective. The promiscuity would be toned down, turned on its head or excused, the romance ramped up, his reputation as a shallow playboy/baller/hustler character contested, his thoughtful depths explored further. His image shifted an inch, from the damaged and dangerous millionaire gangsta with a soft centre to the lovable rogue with a machete-sharp edge.

Fittingly for a grandiose project out to beat rock at its own pomp-swathed game, it opened with blasts of stadium guitars worthy of the doomiest arena goths, and a voice from beyond the grave. This was Kanye's magnificent 'A Dream': ominous orchestras, crashing chords, guitars that might have been played by The Crow, Faith Evans warbling wonderfully and Notorious B.I.G. – an entire verse sampled wholesale from his track 'Juicy'* – making his second guest appearance on a Jay-Z track, in spirit at least. In this '… Dream' Jay-Z was visited by the spirit of Biggie who told him he was killed because of jealousy of his fame and success, and advised Jay to "remind yourself nobody built like you, you designed yourself… just keep doing your thing". It was Jay claiming the blessing of the hip-hop gods, the perfect introduction to his bravest album yet.

'Hovi Baby' was the first sign of experimentation, with its relentless attack of dislocated, dizzying synth chords sounding like a space-age cop theme gone psychotic. Then 'The Watcher 2' crept in with the threat and hush of a housebreaker, Dr. Dre producing a remake of his own 'The Watcher' from 2001's *The Chronic* with its stalker horns, plucked strings, Bond theme spy guitar and Dre himself whispering the title with a salivating sense of stealth and ill intent. If anybody should be afraid of it, it was Jay-Z's haters, since his half-whispered verse puts them in their place for disrespecting a rapper far more experienced and successful than themselves. "I was doing this shit when you was shitting Pampers, you got a few little bitches you think you're Hugh Hefner, you just

---

* With one minor alteration: the line "blow up like the World Trade", which was a reference to the 1993 bombing of the World Trade Center when Biggie wrote the verse, was blanked out for the last two words in the wake of 9/11.

ridiculous… I gave life to the game, it's only right I got the right to be king." And, as if to prove his standing, he lined up alongside Dr. Dre and Rakim[*] on the track, all legends bringing their A game, but watching their backs.

'03 Bonnie & Clyde' ushered in the album's first seductive segment, its flamenco crime romance giving way to 'Excuse Me Miss', a Neptunes production[†] that warped boudoir soul strings into an alluring futuristic swirl while Pharrell Williams provided falsetto coos and gasps intended to seduce a girl in a club. But this isn't just another casual Jay-Z conquest like all those playa-at-the-party rhymes before; his relationship mindset was creeping into his lyrics. He talks about "trust", needing a "missus" and a "partner", the chorus entreats the girl to "have my baby". There's an overturning of his playboy reputation, a fresh shunning of groupies, commitment at hand. A few text messages and he's ready to settle down – "either she the one or I'm caught in the *Matrix.*" By the end he's giving her "keys and security codes", giving her a "f'real, f'serious role". After the hints at a serious relationship to be gleaned from '03 Bonnie & Clyde', this could well have been a message that he'd changed – or would happily change, if he could learn to trust that the right woman would stay – his philandering ways.

Cue the afro-electro blares and tribal percussion of Timbaland's 'What They Gonna Do', a club pop banger with a world music edge and a deep jungle-tinged coda that was the most synthetic and modernist Jay-Z tune since *Vol. 3*… It launched *The Gift*'s party period with Jay taking his rhyming to extremes, a whole final verse of lines on the same rhyme scheme, all ending with the word "flow" yet all with witty and pertinent boasts and arguments – "In some places they say this, I am God with the flow/Like my office, but they're biased, too involved with the flow." Then *The Gift* flipped back to the scintillating soul samples of *The Blueprint* and *Reasonable Doubt* for 'All Around The World', a jubilant

[*] And Dre associate Truth Hurts, who brassily chewed out the chorus hook.
[†] From samples of Luther Vandross' 'Take You Out' and Biggie's 'Big Poppa'.

jive produced by No I.D.* that sampled George Clinton, Ed Hawkins, Digital Underground and Jay-Z's own 'Brooklyn's Finest'. A celebratory cut, it had Jay-Z globetrotting from southern France to Japan, London to St Barts, partying, pulling girls and attaining superstar status in every territory but never forgetting his roots. It was always New York he returns to to find the inspiration for his music and rhymes, and his mother who got the around-the-world ticket. If there was any deeper meaning beneath all this frequent-flyer flaunting, it was subliminal: "pool look like a hundred Beyoncés" he says of a particularly glamorous party, before incongruously adding "a couple fiancées" as either a sop to the gossip columns or inadvertent wishful thinking.

If 'All Around The World' gained a feminine flounce from the R&B acrobatics of guest singer LaToiya Williams, the boyband bounce of the next track, 'Poppin' Tags'† – despite its theme of designer shopping – was dominated by the all-male cast of Jay, Twista, Killer Mike and Big Boi from OutKast competing for an all-new speed-flow title. They were all winners. Twista fired out lines of haute couture high living with the crackle of pistols, Killer Mike turned the track from shopping spree to killing spree in a verse on gangsta style and Big Boi's thick southern drawl made his breakneck verse about the woes of the cash running out all the more superhuman. It was competitive company for Jay, whose verse was a sputter-fire catalogue of his designer lifestyle that made his second name-drop of Armadale vodka, a brand the US distribution of which Roc-A-Fella had taken over earlier in 2002. Here was another arm of the Jay-Z empire sprouting; just as he'd taken to advertising his own Rocawear range in his rhymes instead of making other clothing lines richer, no longer would Jay-Z promote a brand of clear spirit that he wasn't making money from himself. It was quite enough that he was still giving Cristal so much rap culture kudos.

---

* A new name in Jay-Z's production circle but a regular at Cam'ron's desk and the man who'd introduced Kanye West to production, mentoring him in his earliest sessions and pointing Roc-A-Fella's A&R man Kyambo 'Hip Hop' Joshua in West's direction.

† A Kanye West production sampling The Marvelettes' 'After All'.

Jay-Z's verse in 'Poppin' Tags' had him unrepentantly back on the party scene, scooping up cars full of girls to be seen to on a "first come, first served basis", but when it came to the album's first all-out sex song, once again there were hints of a change of heart for this one-time heartless dog. Over a suitable Neptunes R&B backing that sounded like a further attempt to break the mainstream market, 'Fuck All Night' found Jay-Z initially up to his old tricks of sleeping with other people's very willing girlfriends, but come verse two the situation is flipped, Jay's the one with feelings for a "mami" who won't leave her man for him. Suddenly there's a depth and narrative to what might previously have been a simple, selfish one-way exchange: "lately I've been having the strangest feelings/Your boy young Hov catching feelings/And it's messing up my dealings." As in 'Soon You'll Understand', this was a more mature Jay-Z coming to realise the consequences of his promiscuous ways, and finding real emotion stabbing at him through his shield of blind animalistic sex.

The electro-Indian pop of Timbaland's 'The Bounce', like a Bollywood populated by androids, was even more of a head-flip. Taunting not just copycat rappers but even Al Qaeda with the critical and commercial success of *The Blueprint* in the first few lines – "couldn't even be stopped by Bin Laden/So September 11 marks the era forever/Of a revolutionary Jay Guevero/Now it's a whole museum of Hov MCers/Everybody duping the flow" – come the second verse Jay seemed to let on he wasn't all he appeared on record. He mocked those who only listened to his shallower, more money, guns and sex-fixated singles and thought they were an accurate representation of his character, claiming that since he was so focused on business by now he'd not been partying as hard and so not letting on how much more refined he'd become: "In real life I'm much more distinguished." But, crucially to his critics, he implied that he kept rapping about those popular topics simply to "keep the registers ringing", an admission that verged on mocking his own fans and which would add fuel to the fire of those doubting the truth and extent of Jay-Z's colourful history and wildest brags.

His eye for a rising talent wasn't in question here, though. 'The

Bounce' was the first recorded collaboration between Jay-Z and Kanye West, with Kanye taking the final verse to promote himself as a rap star, innovator and sex symbol and stamp his ownership on 'Takeover' in a growling double-tracked snarl. It was a low-key introduction to a major rap star of the future, but boy did Kanye sound hungry for it.

The Gift closed with a track that's been so many singers' swansong. A sample of Paul Anka crooning Frank Sinatra's evergreen funeral classic 'My Way' introduced what would usually be the final track on most artists' albums, 'I Did It My Way', a hip-hop take on a track so often used as a summary of a lifetime's achievements and hardships and a celebration of individuality. Produced by a new pairing to Jay-Z's records, Jimmy Kendrix and Big Chuck, it was a perfect theme for Jay-Z to tackle and rework, and from the shocked comments about people waiting five days at a Japanese airport to see him arrive "like I'm a Beatle or something" over the opening sample, it was suitably proud and defiant. A brief précis of his childhood, hustling years, near-fatal shooting and rap rise quickly gave way to a sociopolitical comment on the shunning of the moneyed black man by the richer end of society. As a home-grown multimillionaire in a white man's business world, of course, Jay-Z expected no favours and instead lauded his self-made credentials, painting himself and the Roc-A-Fella team as a hip-hop Rat Pack, a "Rap Pack". With Jay as Sinatra, obviously.

What was curious was that having established his right to respect and respectability, he'd use his second verse to launch a similar tirade against a justice system trying to demonise and hound rappers for publicity while simultaneously confessing to the Lance Rivera stabbing. His point was that the furore far outweighed the crime: the lyric played down the incident as a "scratch" from which Rivera "went home without an aspirin" and claimed the two were now friends again, but that didn't excuse his actions. Here was a man admitting to a public act of violence while complaining about being publicly punished for it. A sour end to a solid disc.

From the first ominous church chords, *The Curse* was clearly the Hyde to *The Gift*'s Jekyll. Darker, more intense, angry, reflective, political and bristling with issues. The sonorous and sinister 'Diamond

Is Forever' expanded on 'I Did It My Way''s argument that ghetto kids would never be accepted into rich enclaves no matter how successful they became, admonishing residents of a high-rent apartment block for saying someone like Jay-Z was "a menace, he could never be a tenant", unable to see past his history, race and background to the sassy businessman and street poet beneath. It was a pinpoint condemnation of the protectionism, separatism and barely suppressed racism that infested society's upper echelons, a bulwark against such rocketing social mobility as Jay-Z's, the haves barricading themselves against anyone who should, in their eyes, traditionally have not. This was Jay-Z cast as a battering ram at the gates of the class system.

'Guns & Roses' was rather less fervent, being Jay-Z's half-baked attempt to break into AOR blues rock territory by collaborating with Lenny Kravitz. The plodding Heavy D production was hobbled further by Jay's confused lyrics about the fickle nature of fate (poor New York kids end up ruling the town; hot basketball players die young) and the opposing sides of life's coin: "in order to experience joy you need pain/Every time a baby is born, somebody slain." Added to lines about police harassment, dating models, becoming a clothing magnate and asserting his rock credentials by mentioning hanging out with Bono, they smothered the central message – to never lose hope that a hard life might turn around – in cliché and vague quack wisdoms. It was one of the album's least successful tracks and, followed by Just Blaze's invigorated but unnecessary remix of 'U Don't Know' from *The Blueprint* that was essentially a filler showcase for the impressive spitting skills of Lil' Fame and Billy Danze from M.O.P. (soon to sign to Roc-A-Fella)*, it suggested *The Blueprint²: The Gift & The Curse* might be running short of ideas, stretching itself into holes.

The moving and thought-provoking 'Meet The Parents' arrested the decline, an unsettling Just Blaze production built from original rock guitar riffs, doomy bass, oppressive strings and portentous pianos. Here Jay-Z unravelled one of his most riveting and disturbing stories. At the funeral of a close friend and crew-mate, a kid just like Jay killed in

---

* Plus a classic Jay-Z verse of murder and money.

a gun battle, he pictured the sobbing figure of the boy's mother Isis, wrecked with regret and blaming herself that his father had left them and she'd failed to raise him with the nous to protect himself ("damn near impossible, only men can raise men"). Isis' grief sends her spiralling into drug dependency, smoking crack and angel dust to alleviate the pain, lost in romantic reminiscence of her courtship with the boy's brutish and violent father Mike.

Mike was a street-fighter and biker who'd so thrilled her with his youthful fire that she'd turned down the security of a life in the country with a homely guy called Shy to rampage through the city with this untamed outlaw. But Mike rejected responsibility as much as the law – when Isis had his baby he saw the child only once before denying the boy was his and leaving. Then, the fatal twist: having never seen his son grow up or contacted Isis since leaving, when a 32-year-old Mike started a street fight with a 15-year-old kid many years later, he was angered by the familiarity in the boy's face. As Mike pulled out his snub-nosed .38, the boy was taken aback, "there was something in this man's face he knew he'd seen before/It's like looking in the mirror seeing himself more mature." Mike's shooting of his own son was a bold metaphor for a wider ghetto malaise, that absent fathers leave their sons to grow unguided into lives of crime, jeopardy and death, essentially killing them by their lack of care. But as a parable in itself, awash with deep sentiment and detail – the ritualistic pouring of Hennessy brandy on the pavement to honour the death of a crew member, the sighs of "him already? Such a good kid" at the funeral, the final freezing of the son staring into his lost father's eyes – 'Meet The Parents' was arguably Jay-Z's finest street tragedy. A mini hip-hop *Hamlet*.

The slinky smurf-soul of 'Some How Some Way'* focused in closer on those abandoned children scrimping and dealing to afford the latest sneakers, the latest Rocawear, the latest Glocks. Beanie Sigel painted a stressed-out picture of projects poverty – kids sleeping four to a

---

* The third Blaze track in a row, featuring sped-up samples from Jermaine Jackson's 'Castles Of Sand'.

bed, surviving on fried wings and cereal, fighting each other for every dollar, the mere thought of it all drove him to dope. Scarface lent his impassioned sobs to a verse about the stresses of hustling. But Jay's verse was the starkest, a catalogue of the various ways people get out of the ghetto, via basketball, rap, endless blue collar drudgery, dealing or death. But he ended by positing himself as a hope and inspiration – "look man, a tree grows in Brooklyn" – and wished he could lift the entire world of the projects into his sphere, "take us all on this magic carpet ride through the sky". It was a touching gnash of injustice that, no matter how rich and famous he got, there were parts of the world, parts lodged deep in his past and his soul, that he could never change.

Against this backdrop of a universal ghetto struggle, 'Some People Hate' sounded all the more hurt that the very people from his neighbourhood that Jay was representing, opening the door to rap music for and wishing a better life in his rhymes, were still so jealous and hateful towards him. With Kanye helium-twisting Brian & Brenda Russell's 'Word Called Love' into the tripwire-tense string backing, Jay despaired at the lack of respect for the work he'd done, "the penalty of leadership", and indulged the "chip on my shoulder the size of the Golden Nugget". But he emerged defiant, the hip-hop Muhammad Ali: "I'm back, stronger than ever, surprise surprise."

'Some People Hate' named no names; 'Blueprint²' wasn't so coy. Jay wasn't about to let the Nas feud die just yet, not when he was on the back foot jibe-wise and the hype was high. So, with the odd comedy imitation of Mike Myers' spoof spy Austin Powers' catchphrase "Oh behave!" bringing a touch of levity to the assault, Jay weighed back in to the mêlée. His first targets were rappers and producers dissing him in magazine articles, old associates complaining they weren't getting enough of his money or the support he once gave them. This was possibly a slight against Jaz-O, who'd been upset at Jay-Z since their relationship started deteriorating after Jaz refused to sign to Roc-A-Fella early on because of his mistrust of Dash and Burke, and who was rumoured to be behind some of the information Nas used against Jay in 'Ether'. Indeed, Jay had allegedly already recorded a track for an underground mix-tape released by DJ Kay 'The Drama King' Slay called 'Fuck Jaz-O AKA Jaz

Ho'* and went on later in 'Blueprint²' to state "I'ma let karma catch up with Jaz-O."† But Jaz wasn't Jay's primary mark.

With apologies to actress Rosie Pérez, who'd gone on record as considering Jay's rhymes about Carmen Bryan in 'Supa Ugly' as a low strike, and claiming "my momma can't save you this time", Jay re-sparked his feud with Nas, first by mocking him for falling into his "booby trap… just to see how the dude react", and then criticising him for his lack of charity (as opposed to Jay's claims here that he funded project gift schemes and gave a percentage of every ticket to 9/11 charities from all gigs around *The Blueprint*) and for the indecipherable poetry of his lyrics: "'cause you don't understand him, it don't mean he nice/It just means you don't understand all the bullshit that he write." Proclaiming himself the victor of the beef and by far the bigger rapper, Jay said that Nas should be thanking him for resurrecting his career with the battle, and finally declared all-out war. The viciousness and personal revelations had abated a little, but this clash was far from burned out.‡

'Blueprint²' was the album's nostalgia-sample number in the vein of 'Hard Knock Life (Ghetto Anthem)', 'Wishing On A Star' and 'Izzo (H.O.V.A.)', only this time turning to the spaghetti western soundtracks of Ennio Morricone for its inspiration, culling its tumbling pianos, orchestral rumbles, funeral chimes and Wild West arias from 'The Ecstasy Of Gold' from *The Good, The Bad And The Ugly*. And 'Nigga Please' – a classic Jay-Z boast track directed at lower-level rappers in tour buses rather than jets, with no groupies or necklaces with their logo encrusted in diamonds – was the Latino track akin to a stripped-down 'Hola' Hovito', given a more minimalist synthesiser click and crunch by The Neptunes and a James Brown-style coda by Pharrell himself, pulling out his best Soul Godfather vocal moves. By the time Timbaland pulled out his second android Bollywood number of the album with '2 Many

---

* Although there is little trace of this track.

† Jaz would retaliate on another DJ Kay Slay mix-tape, with a cut called 'It's Ova', and later with a diss track against Jay-Z called 'Friends Betrayed'.

‡ In retaliation, Nas' *God's Son* album contained a track called 'Last Real Nigga Alive', attacking Jay for forcing him into this feud while he was tending to his dying mother.

Hoes', *The Curse* was beginning to sound like it was circling old ground, despite the scandal-inducing lyric in which Jay-Z sees off a bothersome fan interrupting him when he's trying to score in a club.

So 'As One' came as a relief, its pumped-up disco sizzle* recalling 'Izzo (H.O.V.A.)' and the mic being passed at speed between Jay-Z, Beanie, Bleek, Freeway, Young Gunz, Peedi Peedi, Sparks and Rell to stake their claim to hip-hop mastery in a few lines each, like a Roc-A-Fella karaoke session. As blipverts for record label rosters go, it was a doozie, and brightened *The Curse* in time for its mournful close.

While Jay-Z had commented numerous times in his lyrics about social issues, police harassment and the politics of crime and poverty, he'd never yet made reference to his rising political interest. 'A Ballad For The Fallen Soldier' placed a tentative toe into that territory, without going so far as to condemn George W. Bush's invasion of Afghanistan in 2001. Instead, Jay used the song to draw similarities between a soldier going to war and a hustler fighting for his own survival on the block, but the details he drew out were honed to highlight the agony and heartbreak of modern warfare. The dislocation from family, the in-fighting, the isolation cells, the threat from chemical weapons (crack in Jay-Z's world) and terrorists (the police). The mentality of hustling and soldiering, Jay asserted, is identical – to protect and provide for your family and to be ready to die for your comrades and your honour. But the implication was that no one should ever have to resort to either.

Like *Vol. 3...* and *The Blueprint*, *The Blueprint²: The Gift & The Curse* featured bonus tracks at the end of the album, although this time they were listed on the sleeve: 'Show You How', 'Bitches & Sisters' and 'What They Gonna Do Part II'. On previous albums the bonus tracks were the place Jay would hide away reworked tunes, lyrical experiments and odd singles that didn't fit the album's flow. These tracks truly added to *The Blueprint²: The Gift & The Curse*'s artistic clout. 'Show You How' was Blaze's avant garde rap piece of swirling synthetics without a chorus hook; Jay rhymes his advice on how to become as rich as him – kidnap, selling crack, stealing from dealers – around a single repeated line: "I'll

---

* Concocted by Just Blaze from a sample of Earth, Wind & Fire's 'Fantasy'.

show you how to do this, son." 'Bitches & Sisters' worked on a similar structure, only this time the Kim Weston strings and Jay's rap revolved around a yell of "bitch!" culled from N.W.A.'s 'A Bitch Iz A Bitch'.

Having defended himself against accusations of misogyny on 'Blueprint^2', this was Jay's attempt to clear up his views on women by differentiating between those he considered 'sisters' and those he dismissed as 'bitches'. By the song's reckoning, a 'sister' works hard, supports her man, drives, cooks and looks after children and gives slow sex. A 'bitch', on the other hand, holds a guy back, lies, irritates, demands rides and fucks with a fury. Not that 'Bitches & Sisters' ruled out sleeping with them, of course.

The album finished with 'What They Gonna Do Part II', the same rhyme from 'What They Gonna Do' put in the hands of a new production name, Darrell 'Digga' Branch, to work into a fascinating musical development for Jay; a whoop, tin-pot percussion and a monotone throb like a wire rope spinning, an added hypnotic tension to an already breathless track. It rounded off a solid and impressive stab at the double-album masterpiece: a broad expanse of music that was patchier than *The Blueprint*, less bullish with its stylistic boundaries, less bright of melody and sharp of focus and less experimental than the project had initially suggested. Nonetheless, a double album with this much consistency and adventure is rare. *The Blueprint^2: The Gift & The Curse* was a formidable achievement lashed with bitebacks, politics, social comment, high-class living, low-class childhoods and even a glimmer of romance. It hit number one, of course – Jay-Z's fifth in a row now – shifting half a million units the first week on its way to 3 million in total.

Though 'Guns & Roses' would become a radio hit, only one further official single would be released from *The Blueprint^2: The Gift & The Curse*, the number eight smash 'Excuse Me Miss'* with its mega-budget, product-saturated video in which Jay-Z imagines all of the private jet trips, helicopter rides, expensive cars and diamond jewellery he'd happily lavish on a girl he sees in an elevator. The project would finally be wrapped up with a single disc version of the record called

---

* Released February 4, 2003.

The Blueprint 2.1 on April 8, 2003, an edited-down version for those fans put off by the original album's grand scale. And to lure in the completists too, three new tracks would be added as hidden bonus songs. Two of them would be released as a single to promote the condensed album.* The lead track would be 'La-La-La (Excuse Me Miss Again)', a sequel to the original also produced by The Neptunes that eschewed the slick modernist R&B of the first instalment for a skuzzy street-raga twist with a dark electro-goth chorus and a more aggressive lyric dripping drugs, violence, wealth and a lyrical sickness no medical prescription or voodoo witch doctor could cure. Its flip would be a Swizz Beatz track called 'Stop', an urgent flurry of spiking synths, horn blares, clicks, whoops and gasps over which Jay spat word of his own legend in the projects, taking in a sweet personal memory of catching his mother planting his presents under the tree one Christmas and culminating in news of another legend to come. "*The Black Album* on the way...*"

As if that snippet wasn't bait enough for his avid faithful, his remix of 'Beware Of The Boys'† by Panjabi MC that was the final new track on *The Blueprint 2.1* proved even more thrilling. On a visit to London early in 2003 Jay had heard Panjabi's 'Mundian To Bach Ke' in a club, a scintillating combination of Bollywood tumbi strums, Jamaican bashment and the famous theme from David Hasselhoff's Eighties talking-car series *Knight Rider*. As someone dabbling in Indian styles on his albums already, Jay adored it. The very next day he hunted down Panjabi MC's people and asked if he could do a remix, and rammed his verses with his most overtly political rhetoric yet. His anti-war stance was howled even louder as he gave lyrical nods to the protests around the world against the recently launched war in Iraq and stated "only love kills war, when will they learn?" Then he likened Osama Bin Laden to Ronald Reagan "in their indifference to the destruction each of them brought to the city I lived in".[7] Bold statements marking out a political

---

* As well as the soundtrack album to the movie *Bad Boys II*, on which 'La-La-La...' also appeared.
† The English translation of the track's original title.

183

stance that many of his detractors might have been surprised by – anti-violence, left-leaning, pacifist, referencing drugs as a blight on society.

'Beware Of The Boys' was a stark sign of Jay-Z wanting to stretch what he was capable of in hip-hop, but with his ultimate musical statement completed in the shape of ... *The Gift & The Curse,* his disillusionment with rap deepened. He'd released an album every year since 1996, produced at least two major hip-hop classics, had seven Platinum albums, sold 18 million records; his many comparisons between himself and basketball player Michael Jordan were becoming all the more pertinent. Like Jordan with his sport, Jay-Z was starting to believe he'd done everything there was to do in hip-hop, said everything he wanted to say. He found the whole genre "corny" and lacking any competition to force him to push himself; despite the likes of OutKast making albums that radically re-imagined hip-hop, Jay considered rap a dead force. Plus, the threats and dangers inherent in rapping, even at the highest level, were still too similar to those on the streets, a point which would be pressed home to him when he hit the studio to record 'Moment Of Clarity' for his next studio album with Eminem, and Em showed up wearing a bullet-proof vest.

Meanwhile, other interests were distracting him – his new relationship, his dissolving partnership with Dash, personal family issues, and his various businesses which now included two clothing lines, a brand of vodka and others in the pipeline. A bar in New York had been mentioned, a range of personalised sneakers, a basketball team all of his own.

He'd hinted at it with virtually every album he'd made, but this time his mind was set.

One more album and God MC was done with rap.

Chapter Eleven

Blackout

The bars glistened with stacks of the finest champagnes. The half-naked hostesses glistened with gold body paint. The screens on every wall glistened with big games in progress. The basketball jerseys, baseballs and priceless memorabilia in the glass cabinets lining every wall glistened with sporting legend. And the guest list glistened like none other that night. Jay-Z and Beyoncé, Chloë Sevigny, 50 Cent, Kanye, OutKast, Pharrell, Missy Elliott and Miss USA mingled with NBA stars and New York's sporting elite.

June 18, 2003, and the opening of the 40/40 Club on West 25th Street, NYC – Jay-Z's first high-end sports bar, where the discerning hip-hop basketball addict could hang with the players and talk tactics late into the night* – was about to glisten with rap legend too.

Taking to a mic in a white tux and black tie, a gold-frocked Beyoncé at his side, Jay-Z addressed his guests, thanked them for coming to this historic launch, and made an even more memorable announcement. He

---

* The club, opened with business partners Desiree Gonzalez and Juan Pérez, was named after another exclusive club, that of baseball players who've hit 40 home runs and stolen 40 bases in one season.

would be releasing his eighth album, *The Black Album*, at his traditional point in early winter. And it would be his last.

The biggest rap star on the planet was announcing his retirement.

Jay-Z didn't describe it himself as a retirement, he saw it more as a long break, but when the press picked up on the concept he didn't deny it, it was a move he'd consider. It had been a busy year for Jay, full of upheaval mixed with security, success tinged with sadnesses, and he needed a major change in his life.

His Roc-A-Fella output over 2003 had helped him cement his decision. At the start of the year Roc-A-Fella Films had released their fourth Dash-produced movie, this time with Dash himself taking the director's chair alongside cinematographer and camera operator David V Daniel. Beanie Sigel again took the starring role in a crime film, *Paper Soldiers*, but this time the movie was a comedy caper following the misadventures of a crew of small-time house-breakers who ill-advisedly break into the house of Jay-Z, playing himself.

The experience would be Jay-Z's last in front of the cinema camera, realising that the falseness of acting clashed with his openness of character. "I think I'd be a horrible actor," he told me some years later. "I think I'd get in the way. There's certain things that I won't do. I'm not gonna fake fight with someone. In order to be a great actor you have to step aside to let the character come in. Until I can officially do that then I can only play myself in a movie for 10 seconds. Jay-Z as himself."

If Jay was feeling a lure away from the spotlight after *Paper Soldiers*, the intense press attention focused on his burgeoning relationship with Beyoncé like a magnified sunray was also making him yearn for a greater level of privacy. In March 2003 the gossip columns ran stories that the pair were on the rocks, claiming that Jay had been seen with another woman at a nightclub.

Preferring to play out their relationship on record rather than on tattle sheet, they responded with the most brilliant denial imaginable. On May 20 Beyoncé released her debut solo single 'Crazy In Love', a horn-blasted funk-pop masterpiece about being utterly consumed by her feelings for a man. To press the solidity of their relationship

home, Jay-Z rapped a verse on the song*, Beyoncé draped around him
in a scrap of a dress reflecting the flames from a burning car. As much
for the feisty declaration of devotion as for the incredible horn hook,
the song was one of the smashes of the decade. Number one on the
Billboard chart on radio plays alone, staying put for eight full weeks and
selling over 5 million copies worldwide, two Grammy wins, voted the
best single of the decade by both *NME* and VH1, the second-biggest-
selling single since 2000.† Beyoncé spoke in interviews about how she
found Jay intelligent, charming, devoted, a gentleman growing in her
parents' affections. The sentiment in the song and video, she cooed, was
palpable. Suddenly, America had its new sweethearts.‡

Sport proved another distraction from his music during 2003.
While revelling in developing plans for the sport-themed 40/40 Club,
an offer came for Jay-Z to lead a basketball team in the Entertainers
Basketball Classic tournament at Holcombe Rucker Playground,
an annual amateur basketball contest where teams made up of
entertainment industry figures and the occasional pro would battle it
out in an arena usually reserved for breakdancers and graffiti punks.
Between sessions for his new album and flying back from the couple
of dates each week he was playing alongside 50 Cent on the Rock
The Mic tour to support …*The Gift & The Curse* that summer, Jay
used the contest as a chance to promote the new S. Carter sneaker
he'd developed with Reebok. A $150 shoe released in April 2003,
it came packaged with a 24-track CD mix-tape of fresh freestyles,
remixes of old tracks, skits featuring Mariah Carey and Russell
Simmons, and an archive interview with Notorious B.I.G. The mix-
tape was a cult hit, blasted from every car in every hood, a badge of
identity that fit as snug to black youth as the shoe itself, particularly
the opening freestyle, 'Young, Gifted And Black', in which Jay spat

---

* Written on the spot in the studio during a 3 a.m. visit while Beyoncé was recording
her debut album *Dangerously In Love*.
† Beaten only by 'Hips Don't Lie' by Shakira.
‡ When Beyoncé's debut album *Dangerously In Love* emerged, Jay was on there too,
rapping about how even thugs can have soft centres on the track 'That's How You
Like It'.

proudly of being "America's worst nightmare… young, black and holding my nuts" and laid out the stark differences between tough ghetto survival and cosy middle-class security.* Thanks, no doubt, to the new Jay-Z music included, the sneaker sold faster than any in Reebok's history, 10,000 units whisked from the shelves in its first hour of sale.

Jay's EBC team trumpeted the shoe; pulling in every favour he had in the sporting world he recruited major players to his team, including LeBron James, Jamal Crawford and rising star Sebastian Telfair. They would arrive at the park in a tour bus plastered with ads for the S. Carter sneaker, Jay-Z leading them out to the court to the sound of his own songs and Beyoncé, Puffy and other big music names chilling on the bus, causing a whirlwind of excitement and pandemonium as it ferried the celebrities to the court and then whisked them away after every game to the 40/40 Club for post-game celebrations. Jay even commissioned a film of his team's inevitable march to victory from graffiti legend Fred 'Fab Five' Brathwaite to be turned into an advert for the shoe, and started the S. Carter Academy for the basketball players involved, Reebok as their sponsor and the Roc-A-Fella diamond sign as their signal of membership. Jay's team of star ringers stormed through to the final, but when a power cut postponed the match to a date that clashed with Jay-Z and Beyoncé's first holiday together to Europe, he forfeited and scrapped the planned film. The project had fulfilled its purpose anyway – Jay-Z was now seen as a major patron of sports and all half a million units of the sneaker had sold out.

Managing his basketball team had given Jay a taste for team ownership. Later that year, at a birthday bash in the 40/40, NBA's Jason Kidd would make the light-hearted suggestion that Jay was rich enough to buy the New Jersey Nets, a team he played for that was enjoying a rare run of success in the NBA leagues. Jay didn't get the joke; within weeks he'd met with real estate developer Bruce Ratner to talk over Ratner's plans to move the Nets to a massive new arena complex in an upper middle-

---

* A lyric that exposed a little of Jay's own prejudices, believing that all middle-class kids needn't worry about losing their jobs as their parents are uniformly wealthy.

class area of Brooklyn, and how Jay's investment and local celebrity in the borough might help smooth through the plans and appease the opposing residents.

In all these deals and contracts, so many zeroes, each one adding to the allure of big business, alongside the corporate corner-office respectability. Jay-Z long hoped to take on more management roles in music, and was finding greater challenges now in the business side of his career. Roc-A-Fella seemed increasingly on the edge, though – his relationship with Dash had suffered further when Dash had sacked various label employees while Jay was away in the Mediterranean and promoted his close friend Cameron 'Cam'ron' Giles to the position of vice president, all without Jay's knowledge. Jay immediately reversed Dash's staff changes on his return, but an ocean liner could now be sailed through the rift between them; Dash, until now a constant presence at Jay's side in virtually all of his videos, was nowhere to be seen at Holcombe over the summer of 2003, preferring to hang with the Beckhams.

What's more, there were whispers and rustlings from the Def Jam boardroom. There'd been talk of bringing Jay into the executive level of Universal or Def Jam for some time, but as his working partnership with Dash dissolved, the latest Roc-A-Fella/Def Jam deal was reaching its end and rap was no longer inspiring him, he began planning to make it happen in earnest. On his trip to the South of France just prior to the opening of the 40/40 Club, he'd met with Jimmy Iovine, CEO of Interscope Records, and U2's Bono to talk over possible executive positions, and on his return he met with Universal CEO Doug Morris to discuss which seat he might fill. His skills as a great spotter of fresh talent and his history of building a huge label from nothing made him prime executive material.

So, business, sport, love and the decline of rap all contributed to Jay-Z's decision to 'retire'. But one event of 2003, perhaps most of all, brought it home to him that one distinct chapter of his life was winding up, and another opening.

Adnis Reeves was finally about to holla at his son.

It was his mother Gloria who told Jay-Z his father was dying. News had reached her that Adnis was terminally ill, with a bare few months to live, and she advised her son that now, if ever, was the time to make his peace with the old man.

In October 2009, Jay spoke frankly with Oprah Winfrey in her own *O* magazine about this wrenching emotional reconnection – of the first arranged meeting that Adnis didn't show for, and the eventual calm and mature reconciliation:

Jay-Z: *Reconnecting with my father changed me more than anything. Because it allowed me to let people in... I always had that wall up. And whenever someone got close to me, I would shut down... My mom set up a meeting... I had a conversation with her in my kitchen. I was saying, 'You know, ma, I've really been trying to look inward, and maybe I'm just not meant to fall in love like other people do'... I guess from that point, she figured out what was wrong with me, and she planned a meeting between me and my father... I told her he wouldn't come – and the first time, he didn't. At that point, I was really done, but mom pushed for another meeting, because she's just a beautiful soul... [The second time] he showed up. And I gave him the real conversation. I told him how I felt the day he left. He was saying stuff like 'Man, you knew where I was.' I'm like, 'I was a kid! Do you realise how wrong you were? It was your responsibility to see me.' He finally accepted that... [He'd been] at his mom's house 10 minutes away from me. That was the sad part.*

Oprah: *Was there any explanation he could have offered that would have satisfied you?*

Jay-Z: *Yes – and that's why we were able to mend our relationship... He was broken. He had a bad liver, and he knew that if he continued drinking, it would kill him. But he didn't stop.*

Oprah: *Did you instantly make peace with him during that conversation?*

Jay-Z: *Pretty much. I felt lighter.*

Oprah: *Did it open the door for you to have a life with love in it?*

Jay-Z: *Absolutely.*[1]

Jay also spoke to *GQ* magazine about what was said at the meeting. "[I talked about] what it did to me," he recalled, "what it meant, asked him why. There was no real answer. There was nothing he could say, because there's no excuse for that. There really isn't. So there was nothing he could say to satisfy me, except to hear me out. And it was up to me to forgive and let it go."[2]

And so Jay-Z forgave his father, the dying man wrecked with tears at what he'd done. Jay bought him an apartment and was furnishing it for him when the old man passed away a few short months after their reconciliation. Though he had difficulty grieving – staying dry-eyed at his funeral, more confused than upset – his final meeting with Adnis and his father's death had a huge impact on Jay-Z, not only in opening up his emotional attachments, making him less withdrawn and wary of people and helping him commit fully to his relationship with Beyoncé as well as his Roc-A-Fella protégés and business partners, but also on an artistic level. He vowed to rap about his father before he retired, and to make his last album an autobiographical tribute to his life and family. To that end, on his mother's birthday, he bought her a fine meal and took her to his regular recording base at Baseline studios, where he asked her to tell stories about his life onto the tape, the two of them sitting face to face over the microphone. Her words would adorn his most raw and personal song to date, his swansong, 'December 4th', named after his birth date.

And, as if in tribute to the passing of his father and his rap career, the album would come cloaked in the colours of mourning.

But would sound like a resurrection.

"Shawn Carter was born December 4th, weighing in at 10 pounds 8 ounces. He was the last of my four children, the only one that didn't give me any pain when I gave birth to him. And that's how I knew he was a special child…"

No cover art, he said. No promotion, no adverts, no fanfare. Jay-Z intended *The Black Album* to drift across popular culture like a ghost. It wouldn't – the ads and promo and fanfare were inevitable for a release this monumental, although early magazine ads were stark, listing the producers of each track by number, with no titles. But to this day *The Black Album* – a reprise of the style of *The Blueprint* with its focus on vintage soul samples and distinct lack of guests – is a record shrouded in mystery, import and gravity.

Its haunting introduction set the scene for Jay-Z's final bow. A faraway voice roiling "all things must come to an end, it's an inevitable part of the cycle of existence" over Sixties sci-fi Moogs and blaxploitation soul[*], talking of trees growing in Brooklyn and new lives beginning. Then that fanfare; a crescendo of sped-up strings, horns and timpani introducing Gloria Carter and her tales of Jay-Z's birth, his shy childhood, his bike trick, his loss of confidence after his father left, his early raps. This was 'December 4th'[†], the potted autobiography that introduced the album as a 'story so far'.

Announcing, in the opening line of the album, his departure from rap at the end of this record and slyly acknowledging that to disappear is the best way to gain respect[‡], Jay retold his story from his conception "under the sycamore tree, which makes me a more sicker MC" and the painless birth that augured later pain he'd inflict upon his mother, right up to leaving the hustling game for rap, tired of the stress of all the droughts, ghouls, cop swoops, kidnapping and revenge mutilations. Inbetween, touching details. His need to fit in by wearing the right clothes as a kid, the teachers that couldn't get through to him after Adnis absconded, the name-checks of DeHaven and a guy named Spanish José

---

[*] Actually a Just Blaze production culled from a sample of synth pioneer Hugo Montenegro's 1969 cover of Tommy Roe's 'Dizzy'.

[†] Just Blaze again, skilfully remodelling The Chi-Lites' 'That's How Long'.

[‡] "They say 'they never really miss you 'til you're dead and gone'/So on that note I'm leaving after this song" – a line which had critics immediately doubting the retirement would be permanent, or even particularly long.

for introducing him to dealing, the genesis of his consumerist obsessions with status symbols: the right car, the right sneaker, the right diamond necklace to attract the right kind of girl. And there was the pop at Jaz-O, more grist to their beef: the money he'd give to his mother to pay the bills was clearly from drugs rather than the gigs he'd claim, since "nobody paid Jaz' wack ass".

Over Stalinist atmospherics and an emphatic Philly blare reminiscent of 'U Don't Know'*, 'What More Can I Say' brought the story right up to date. As if throwing his hands up at having no more to add to his life's narrative, Jay-Z declared the record as his final statement to "finish my business up", and reiterated his rise from "moving wet off the step"† to the private jets, champagne and being quoted in magazines as being worth "half a billi". Yet even at his bowing out he wasn't satisfied. He was still frustrated at the rappers stealing his style, taking digs at him or doubting his industry-wide talent ("I'm not a biter, I'm a writer/ For myself and others") or his backstory – the line "no I ain't got shot up a whole bunch of times" is a response to the street credibility his then-touring partner 50 Cent was claiming from having been shot nine times. He couldn't believe he wasn't the most respected rapper of all time, considering his achievements – "I supposed to be number one on everybody's list," he snapped: "We'll see what happens when I no longer exist." Before throwing down his mic at the end of the tune with a despairing "fuck this, man", he promised an even more spectacular show to come, on the business side of music: "I'm not through with it, in fact I'm just previewing it/This ain't the show, I'm just EQing it."

The Black Album had its 'Encore' early. Envisioning the finale of a Vegas crooner's show, all glittering backdrop and standing ovations, Jay thanked the roaring crowd over variety show brass‡, noted that this "victory lap" was the perfect time to leave his crowd wanting more

---

* The atmospherics were actually sampled from the movie *Gladiator* by production team The Buchanans and linked to sections of 'Something For Nothing' by Seventies Philly sound originators MFSB.

† Slang for dealing drugs.

‡ Which Kanye sampled from John Holt's 'I Will'.

since "Jay's status appears to be at an all-time high/Perfect time to say goodbye," but also hinted that he may well be back if the appreciation and demand become strong enough. "When I come back like Jordan," he said, referencing Michael Jordan's return from retirement in basketball, and, acknowledging the taped applause on the track, he advised "that's how you get me back". No wonder few reviewers took the retirement too seriously; on this evidence it was more a cry for reverence and respect than a heartfelt adieu.

From an autobiographical farewell album following in the wake of a hugely successful single playing on the solid romance of Jay and Beyoncé, 'Change Clothes' was an unusual choice for its first single. A slick, catchy but unremarkable R&B Neptunes production harking back to Jay's playboy persona, it hit number 10 on the back of a fashionista-themed video featuring Naomi Campbell, Jessica White, Jade Cole, Liliana Domínguez and a host of other supermodels parading a catwalk beneath the admiring gaze of Pharrell, who supplied the tripping soul hook. Lightweight as lint from a designer gown, it seemed brushed off the album immediately by 'Dirt Off Your Shoulder', a track destined to finally make dandruff cool. Among Timbaland's greatest productions, it was a menacing slab of afrotronica, all filthy tribal drumbeats and synth hooks crackling like warfare. For Jay, the action of dusting off his shoulders was a statement of an immaculate career brushed clean of petty haters and rivals, a life gone "from grams to Grammys" and culminating in selling out Madison Square Garden "in a day" for his farewell show. For his fans, the track was a hint of the hip-hop wonders that might never get written, and the shoulder brush became a dismissive taunt to someone they considered troublesome or worthless and a new sign of devotion to the Jay-Z clique, alongside the Roc-A-Fella diamond. When the song was released as a single the following March and hit number five, the video* full of street-smart characters casually brushing their troubles from their shoulders embedded the move in popular rap culture; one day a future president would use it.

---

* Which strangely included a night-vision dance routine segment set to a verse of 'Public Service Announcement (Interlude)' in place of verse three.

In case there was any suspicion that the love of a good R&B starlet might have dulled Jay-Z's violent edge, 9th Wonder produced 'Threat', the story of a gangsta* fresh from a three-year jail stretch taking murderous revenge on those who put him behind bars. A sinister reshaping of R Kelly's 'A Woman's Threat', 'Threat' had a fascinating lyric, one of Jay-Z's most accomplished and poetic. As a comment on the rising tide of celebrity obsession, Jay dotted the song with celebrity pop culture references. Letting the whole world see him put an enemy in his coffin was likened to David Blaine sitting in a clear plastic box in London for 40 days. His hell-for-leather revenge rampage was conducted with the recklessness of Halle Berry's various driving accidents. His bullet to a rival's head would change their face as completely as Nicholas Cage's character Castor Troy in *Face/Off*, and having discharged, his guns would sweep into his armpit holster with the smooth skill of Jet-Li's nunchuks. With Jay also name-dropping Christina Aguilera, millionaire magnate Warren Buffett and even returning to his Rat Pack simile to liken himself to Frank Sinatra, the song's gossipy tilt clashed rather brilliantly with the poetic violence of the imagery – his gun sings to his victim, joined by a second gun for a "duet, and you wet" – and the most politically charged line, admonishing the then-president for his war-hungry attitude: "I George Bush the button." Like the music, the lyric to 'Threat' was a masterful balancing act of light and dark.

Another such master returned for 'Moment Of Clarity', Eminem producing a cinematic orchestral track onto which Jay-Z laid another highly personal and honest slice of autobiography. It was partly a career retrospective and exposé, linking his album titles together to trace his journey, admitting to dumbing down his raps to appeal to a wider audience and explaining that he was always an outsider in the music industry as the music industry hadn't made him. But the song's real heart is in Jay's recounting of his meeting with his father, in the physical similarities he noticed between them, in his acknowledgement that drugs

---

* The lyric smacks of third-person fiction here, despite the introduction relating the sentiment to Jay personally by talking about how he'd spent nine albums telling his enemies "stop fuckin' with me".

had torn his family apart from every direction, and in his admission to smirking through Adnis' funeral, not knowing what other emotion he should be feeling. The line "When pop died, didn't cry, didn't know him that well" is among the most heartbreaking in modern music.

And the next track on *The Black Album* was one of modern music's most thrilling. It was fitting that Mike D from the Beastie Boys turned up for the recording of '99 Problems' at Rick Rubin's house, since, of all Jay-Z's songs up to this point, it was the one that most brilliantly captured their electrified rap/rock crossover crunch. It was a complex production: legendary Def Jam founder and rap and rock producer Rick Rubin* pieced it together from a wide array of samples from Mountain, Wilson Pickett, Billy Squier and Slick Rick, while Jay lifted the chorus and hook wholesale from Ice-T's own '99 Problems'. Recording in Rubin's home studio decorated with magic books and bizarre Tibetan nick-nacks – at one point during the session a bison wandered in from outside to have a sniff around – Jay was heard to say, leaving the vocal booth after recording his lyric, "that might be something special".

What emerged were fiery hard rock guitar chords and Caribbean percussion, an intense and confrontational benchmark in rap-rock to rival Rubin's other seminal productions for the Beastie Boys on 'Fight For Your Right To Party' and 'No Sleep 'Til Brooklyn'. And the lyric was memorable too, Jay using the track in the mischievous tradition of rap to spin accusations of misogyny against him to his own ends. The pivotal line "I got 99 problems but a bitch ain't one", he claims, was never once used to refer to a woman in the song (and certainly not Beyoncé, since he knew many would speculate the song was referring to the end of Jay's relationship issues); he flipped the meaning with each verse to outwit and provoke his critics in order to flush them out as not listening to his raps properly.†

---

* The man who virtually invented rap-rock by producing 'Walk This Way' for Run-D.M.C. and Aerosmith in 1986.

† In his autobiography *Decoded*, Jay happily admits to being proud that his rhymes are often misunderstood, since it mirrors the treatment doled out to black youths in America.

So in a first verse attacking radio and press for using him to sell ad space, not playing his records or misrepresenting him as sexist, over-flashy and stupid (while simultaneously laying a trap for them to misrepresent him further), the "bitch" referred to the spiteful critics. In the second verse, a fictionalised retelling of the time in 1994 when Jay was stopped by a cop on the highway with a large stash of drugs hidden in a secret compartment in the roof, the "bitch" was the sniffer dog the cop called for in place of a warrant to search the car, but which arrived just after the cop had let Jay go – he passed the dog unit speeding the other way up the highway. And in the final verse the line changed to "being a bitch ain't one", a reference to his refusal to be a "bitch" to the justice system and police as the result of an enemy informing on him. There are plain-to-spot clues to the song's intention – the shock line "a nigga like myself had to strong arm a ho" is swiftly followed by the rejoinder "not a ho in the sense of having a pussy, but a pussy having no goddamn sense".

Yet '99 Problems' would, sure enough, provoke accusations of sexism, albeit ones drowned out by the acclaim: a Grammy for Best Rap Performance, the number two slot on *Rolling Stone*'s list of Best Songs Of The '00s, a number 30 hit in May 2004, all capped by a stylishly rough black-and-white video of Jay-Z cruising various Brooklyn neighbourhoods in a Lexus GS300 with a heavily bearded and fur-coated Rick Rubin by his side in place of Beyoncé and a cameo appearance by Vincent Gallo. The scenes Jay ducked through were fraught with symbolism and dark meaning – Bronx prisoners, funeral directors, praying rabbis, motorcycle stunt teams, Marcy breakdancers. But the final shots of Jay being gunned down in the street were the most controversial. MTV policy disallowed videos featuring violence to be shown in full on the channel, but director Mark Romanek and Jay-Z canvassed hard for them to show the clip uncut, but with an introduction explaining why the network felt the video should be seen without cuts, and also from Jay-Z to pinpoint why the shooting was so pivotal. It was, he explained, a literal enactment of the demise of Jay-Z the rapper and the rebirth of Shawn Carter the businessman.

The clip, the best he ever made according to the rapper himself, won three MVPA Awards and four MTV Video Music Awards*, and '99 Problems' was *The Black Album*'s highlight and centrepiece. After which came another interlude to get our breath back. The last track on the album to be finished (Just Blaze almost missed the deadline Jay-Z set to get the album out on Black Friday since he was busy working on video-game soundtracks), 'Public Service Announcement (Interlude)' was a laid-back piano funk piece with an Armageddon mood[†] describing hustling experiences in rap terminology and vice versa, and how Jay was still the same old dealer and diamond-coveter inside since none of us really change our core being: "I'm 10 years removed, still the vibe is in my veins/I got a hustler spirit... you can try to change but that's just the top layer." Besides the humorous asides – his history of selling crack, for instance, means that "even back then you can call me CEO of the R-O-C" – and the sly mention of Beyoncé ("got the hottest chick in the game wearing my chain"), Jay was pleased to discover new ways to stoke his own ego in song, to expose the guilt he felt at continuing hustling when it became all about materialism rather than survival, and to examine both the acclaim and danger of that life, a rush he was still desperate for a decade later.

But the line that Jay was proudest of was "I'm like Che Guevara with bling on, I'm complex". It was inspired by a journalist who, just the day before Blaze delivered the track, criticised him for wearing both a diamond and platinum chain and a Che T-shirt, claiming that the two were morally incompatible. But, reading up on Che in the wake of the article and reflecting on the struggles both men had gone through – one political, the other economic – Jay felt differently. "Che was coming from the perspective, 'We deserve these rights; we are ready to lead'," he wrote in his autobiography. "We were coming from the perspective, 'We need some kind of opportunity; we are ready to die'."

---

* Although the Humane Society of the United States publicly denounced its portrayal of dog fighting.
† Built around Little Boy Blues' 'Seed Of Love' and featuring Blaze himself delivering the opening address.

Heavy, high-minded stuff, after which came some slightly lighter relief. 'Justify My Thug' was the album's delve into populist samples, with Madonna's huge hit 'Justify My Love' used as a hook[*] for a ponderous electro march around which Jay could do exactly that, justify the rules and reasoning behind his youthful thuggishness. As if writing a code of conduct for the streets, Jay set down the commandments of thug life: thou shalt not rat, thou shalt not run, thou shalt not pay another to do anything you wouldn't do yourself, thou shalt have too much pride to beg, thou shalt exact revenge but not when you're in the wrong, thou shalt improve your situation at whatever cost. And above all, thou shalt choose "death before dishonour". Rarely has Jay-Z so succinctly described the honour among thugs.

These were themes repeated over the next few tracks. Revenge consumed 'Lucifer', a discussion with God drenched in religious imagery over the Satan inside Jay that emerged from a clash of grief and the need for retribution. As reggae standard 'Chase The Devil' by Max Romeo[†] slinked by on one of Kanye's most accomplished funk-reggae grooves, Jay imagined himself heading to LA to take revenge on Biggie's killers, driven by "dark forces" and "a righteous cause for sinning"[‡], as if on a "holy war". Having dispatched them "with the holy water spray from the Heckler Koch automatic", he then turned to the killer of Biggie's brother Bobalob, dreaming of holding a nine millimetre pistol to their forehead and demanding an explanation. But Jay recognised the evil within him and knew such thoughts were the work of the devils of grief, loss and confusion broiling inside. He asked God's forgiveness for his vengeful thoughts, and the central lines found him wrestling this Lucifer himself: "I gotta get these devils out my life… they won't be happy 'til somebody dies/Man I gotta get my soul right/Before I'm locked up for my whole life."

---

[*] Alongside vocals from Run-D.M.C.'s 'Rock Box', pieced together by Will Smith and Talib Kweli producer DJ Quik.

[†] A track widely sampled in rap and electronica, most notably on The Qemists and Dreadzone and The Prodigy's huge smash 'Out Of Space'.

[‡] A *Pulp Fiction* reference.

And then 'Allure' concerned the pulse-quickening thrill of the criminal life and the riches it can bring, how it too can consume a man. A Neptunes production draped in their trademark soul grace and orchestral lushness (plus a few catchy gunshots), here Jay was caught in a cycle, not just of family and poverty – the track suggested his elder brother was dealing before he was – but of an emotional and psychological attachment to crime and its rewards: "I'm living proof that crime do pay." The more he swore off money, drugs and women, knowing "how this movie ends", the more he's lured back by the excitement, the ritual of crack production and the risk involved in smuggling. It's not just Jay suffering from the 'allure' either; he rapped about women always drawn to bad guys who use them as drug mules, risk their lives for profit, and then turn out to be married when the girl meets his wife at his funeral. Admitting his addiction to the dealing life was so extreme he was ultimately prepared to kill for a car "when the doors lift from the floor and the tops come off", Jay set the high of criminality as greater than that from any drug, and far more addictive – "the game is a light bulb with eleventy million volts and I'm just a moth". The song's key cry of "oh no!" was a heartfelt despair.

The 'final' song of Jay-Z's recorded career was intended to bring the whole thing full circle. Introduced with a snippet of an interview with Biggie to honour his biggest friend and influence, Jay closed his rap book by taking advice from it, "treat everything like it's your first project". So, speed-rapping like his *Reasonable Doubt* days and swathed in a haze of psychedelic desert guitars*, Jay finished *The Black Album* with 'My 1st Song', a look at how he still had the same hunger as when he started in 1992, how this diamond-studded last song was just as fresh and driven as his project-trapped first. Tracing once more his ascent from the worthless bottom of society to its priceless peak and declaring it his second split after his first retirement from hustling, Jay signed off with a long farewell, sending out shouts to everyone who'd helped him along the way, dropping affectionate reminiscences about their time together

---

* Taken by producers Aqua and Joe '3H' Weinberger from a Seventies Chilean psych-funk band Los Ángeles Negros.

on Jay-Z's rocket ride to stardom. Dash's bad handwriting scribbling out the huge sums for their early videos. Original Flavor's accountancy problems. Kareen's dog pissing on a guy called Rudy's leg during the St Thomas video shoot for 'Ain't No Nigga'. Clark Kent, Ta-Ta, Emory, Bobalob, Biggie, nephews, cousins, his mom – everybody got their line in the closing credits of Jay-Z: Rap Star.

And *The Black Album* was a fitting swansong. As focused and creative as *The Blueprint* and with a similar classic bearing, it was a milestone record that saw Jay stepping out of hip-hop at the very peak of his powers. It came wrapped in the original spirit of rap – the enigma, proud autobiography and menace combined with a sense of social altruism and wisdom. The album would also be released as an a cappella version with only Jay's vocals included, a gesture of giving something back, allowing other producers and artists to use the raps as they saw fit. And several did, inventively. DJ and producer Kev Brown remixed many of the album's tracks for *The Brown Album* within a week. Other producers mashed Jay's vocals into Prince songs to make *The Purple Album*, Weezer hits to produce *The Black And Blue Album*, and songs by grunge slackers Pavement to make *The Slack Album*. But the most successful was *The Grey Album* by the then-unknown producer Danger Mouse, who'd go on to form Gnarls Barkley with Cee-Lo Green and Broken Bells with James Mercer of The Shins, largely off the back of the acclaim from that record. An incredible artistic achievement, it crossed *The Black Album* with The Beatles' self-titled double album widely known as 'The White Album', mashing '99 Problems' into the proto-metal 'Helter Skelter' and 'Change Clothes' into the harpsichord and cello rouser 'Piggies', and so on. It was a stunning concoction made all the more edgy by the fact that Danger Mouse had no permission to use The Beatles' music and found himself the subject of a 'cease and desist' order from EMI. But not before the album had hit 100,000 digital downloads and pushed sales of *The Black Album* over 3 million.

In 2009, Jay-Z told me of his thoughts on *The Grey Album*. "I thought it was fantastic. I was very happy to see that because I wanted everyone to know that this is the way of the world, this is how kids listen to music, you want to understand this, this is what it is now. I really believe hip-hop has done so much to improve racial relations. Racism is taught in the home, you can't teach racism in the home if your kid loves Jay-Z. It's hard to say 'that guy is beneath you' – no, that guy is a hero! Now people are listening to the same music, going to the same clubs. There were black clubs and white clubs before, now people go to a club."

As he closed the door on rap, Jay stopped for one last beef, too. In the spirit of hip-hop competition, when the album had to be shifted forward a fortnight to November 14 to combat bootlegging, it then clashed with the release date of the debut album from 50 Cent's crew G Unit. 50 Cent was to be heard on radio in the lead-up to the releases throwing down the gauntlet to Jay-Z that his album would outsell *The Black Album*, a fair bet after the 6 million sales his debut *Get Rich Or Die Tryin'* had racked up by that point. Against his label's advice, Jay didn't back away from the challenge and in the end, inevitably, *The Black Album* triumphed in the charts. Almost half a million first week sales, a number one chart, widespread critical acclaim and a Grammy nomination which Jay would ironically lose to Kanye West's debut solo album *The College Dropout*, another Roc-A-Fella release. G Unit never had a hope.*

For Jay-Z, the most satisfying part of the contest wasn't beating G Unit, but landing a number one spot ahead of Tupac's soundtrack to the documentary *Resurrection*. At last, his chance to battle a true legend. And win.

★★★

"I knew saying goodbye was the right thing to do but this goodbye began like a long kiss."
                                                        – Jay-Z, *Fade To Black*, 2004

"Ladies and gentlemen, tonight we've come to Madison Square Garden, New York City, to hear a legendary superstar. From Marcy projects, Bed-Stuy, Brooklyn, New York, presenting the one, the only, undisputed, undefeated heavyweight champion of the world of hip-hop, he is… Jay-Z!"
                                        – boxing announcer Michael Buffer,
                                Madison Square Garden, November 25, 2003

---

* *The Black Album* would eventually become Jay-Z's best-selling album of the 2000s.

The roar at the lights going down lasted almost as long as it took to sell out the place.* His name in the brightest of lights, his dream of selling out Madison Square Garden come true†, security so tight his own bodyguard couldn't get in the venue and with hints of an onstage Beyoncé collaboration dropped on radio in the lead-up to the show, anticipation was at fever pitch for star and audience alike as Michael Buffer stepped up to a spotlit mic and introduced the main attraction like a heavyweight Broadway rumble, a huge Roc-A-Fella shirt rising above the crowd as he barked.

Then the trumpet fanfare of the outgoing King Of New York blared, the backing band The Roots kicked into 'What More Can I Say', and Jay stepped out of the flurry of the labyrinthine backstage warren – so many photos to have taken, well-wishers to hug, details to iron out – and onto the stage in a jacket adorned with swords and eagles on the sleeves and back, alongside the motto 'Death Before Dishonor'. "I said it all, done it all," he declared as the backing screens pumped images of huge speakers pounding with sound, and Jay-Z's farewell show leapt from the blocks, promising spectacle, the greatest last show on earth.

All proceeds going to charity, Jay-Z was determined his Madison Square Garden show would stretch the possibilities of what hip-hop acts could do in an arena, lift rap to a new level. So the night was as star-studded as a hip-hop Oscars. Jay brought out Questlove and a gaggle of rappers before introducing himself: "Myself, I go by a couple of names. Sometimes they call me Jigga, sometimes they call me Jigga-Man, sometimes they call me HOV, but tonight I'll be… 'H-to the Izzo'…" Bleek hit the stage for 'Nigga What, Nigga Who?', the pair leading one side of the arena each through the chorus and timing each other's speed raps on their ice-encrusted wristwatches. Missy Elliott and Twista joined him for 'Is That Yo Chick?'; Foxy Brown narrowly avoided a

---

* Jay-Z's farewell concert sold out in four minutes, according to Kanye in the *Fade To Black* documentary about the event.

† The Madison Square Garden gig was the last of a short run of equally huge gigs across the US.

wardrobe malfunction during her energised guest spots on 'Where I'm From' and 'Ain't No Nigga'; Pharrell added sizzling soul wails to 'I Just Wanna Love U'; Mary J. Blige recreated her immaculate vocals for 'Can't Knock The Hustle' and 'Song Cry', which segued into Biggie's 'Me And My Bitch' and LL Cool J's 'I Need Love'; R Kelly emerged in a storm of mirrorballs to join Jay on 'The Best Of Both Worlds', both decked out in puffy white ski gear for added sparkle.

But one collaboration really lifted the roof: Jay announced "history in the making", the arena erupted and Beyoncé flounced from the wings to the majestic horn blast of a spectacular 'Crazy In Love'. A whirlwind of sexually charged choreography during the verses and draped around Jay-Z like a diamante lizard queen during his rap, the crowd went so wild for his girlfriend that Jay left her onstage to play two more numbers with Ghostface Killah while he went off for a costume change.

A roaring rap gala of a night, but the show was still at its best when Jay was in the spotlight. Leading the crazed crowd in a floor-wide bounce for 'Big Pimpin''. Uniting them in the passionate sing-a-long ghetto struggle of 'Hard Knock Life…' Playing the gangsta clown in a white fedora and pimp suit for 'Dead Presidents II'. And driving Madison Square Garden to tears when he took the music down to pay tribute to rappers lost to the battle – Lisa 'Left Eye' Lopez, Tupac and, of course, Biggie, his and Tupac's mothers both present and watching on.

The biggest tears, though, were saved for the final curtain call. Surrounded by the entire cast, Jay-Z threw his personalised Nets jersey into the crowd during an emotional 'Encore' and then got the entire arena to hold up lighters and phones as firework fountains exploded at the close of a moving 'December 4th', the crowd saluting him off the world's stage with chants of "HO-VA! HO-VA!" more fitting for a returning Roman emperor. The dressing room champagne was well deserved that night – not only had Jay-Z left rap in the most noble way imaginable, he'd also taken hip-hop to a new peak of arena spectacular as he went, stamping down one more barrier between rap and the stadium league. No longer could the rap show consist of groups of men in baggy shorts shouting over a DJ; Jay-Z was forcing them to take a look at his level of production and performance and compete at the highest levels of arena entertainment.

And with that, Jay-Z was gone, leaving rap a lot stronger, more popular and more ambitious than he'd found it.

It wouldn't be too long, however, before he'd be back to save it once more.

Chapter Twelve

The Boardroom Years

The year 2004 was one of consolidation for Jay-Z, of rounding off rap, of unfinished business. The singles from *The Black Album* trickled out throughout the early part of the year, wrapping up the campaign – 'Dirt Off Your Shoulder' in March and '99 Problems' marking his final explosive exit that April. The Madison Square Garden show was celebrated with the documentary *Fade To Black* late in 2004, featuring chunks from the gig interspersed with behind-the-scenes footage of the final album being recorded – Jay and Bleek discussing modern rappers' reluctance to rap about hustling or violence and how Jay-Z believed the public had got rappers "afraid to be themself"; Kanye cooking up "genius" on 'Lucifer'; Jay's mother recording her parts for 'December 4th'; scenes of listening to endless beats and samples, hunting down inspiration's spark. In voice-over, Jay-Z played hip-hop's elder statesman, full of grace and wisdom. "A wise man once told me luck isn't some mystical energy randomly dancing around the universe bestowing people with satisfaction and joy – you create your own luck," he said, and later, "I knew saying goodbye was the right thing to do but this goodbye began like a long kiss."[1]

A 15-track compilation album *Bring It On: The Best Of Jay-Z* attempted to bring together the forgotten greats from the first three albums of Jay's catalogue in chronological order; '22 Two's' instead of 'Can I Get A…', both 'Coming Of Age's rather than 'Big Pimpin'' or 'Izzo (H.O.V.A.)'. And beside hitting the Grammys in 2005 to pick up his award for Best Rap Solo Performance for '99 Problems', that should have been the last we ever heard of Jay-Z, rap superstar. His business empire was gradually expanding, with new stakes purchased in the Carol's Daughter range of hair and skin products, a favoured Beyoncé brand, and further involvement in a team of businessmen investing in the $2.5 billion proposals for a new Frank Gehry-designed stadium for the Nets in Brooklyn. By the spring of 2004 Jay-Z would own 1.5 per cent of the team in return for $1 million, be making high-level decisions as a part-owner, be using all his influence in sport to try to convince LeBron James and Shareef Abdur-Rahim to join the team[*], and be seen watching virtually every game from the sidelines, boosting the credibility of New York's basketball underdog team, Beyoncé at his side.

For around nine months in 2004, with *The Black Album* campaign winding to a close and no whisper of any new recordings, it looked like Jay-Z's retirement from music was for real.

Like that endless allure of the criminal life, however, something was calling Jay-Z back. There was, he'd decided, *Unfinished Business* to attend to. Having reconnected with R Kelly at the Madison Square Garden show, the topic of their scrapped joint tour had arisen again, as had talk of the plethora of leftover tracks from the *The Best Of Both Worlds* album that had never seen the light of day. Though their joint album had failed to live up to its billing, they decided that the project needed a more honourable climax, a sweeter end to a soured concept. Kelly's rapid bounce back from the allegations of child pornography was another positive omen. His post-scandal album *Chocolate Factory* had gone Platinum in three weeks. In popularity terms, R Kelly was no longer damaged goods.

So, on August 19, 2004, the Best Of Both Worlds tour was finally announced, 40 cities over two months from September to November,

---

[*] Shareef agreed to the move from the Trailblazers but a knee injury put paid to the transfer.

forecasted profit around $30 million. A snappy fiesta-flamenco beach-bar track called 'Big Chips' produced by Poke & Tone and Alexander Mosley was chosen as the only single from the album that would be the fulcrum of the tour – *Unfinished Business*, a collection of spare tracks from the sessions for *The Best Of Both Worlds*. Dominated by a very horny Kelly, who was permanently priapic throughout the song, 'Big Chips' seemed like a dispatch from R&B history with its brazen horn blasts, its Latino guitar plucks, its coconut-rattling Caribbean beach temperament and the reassuring flow of Jay doling out Vegas seduction techniques – basically, throw money at the girls and high-value chips at the roulette table – like Beyoncé never happened. Yet it boded well for the duo's second instalment, being too crisp and minimalist to verge on R&B cheese.* On the record Kelly certainly seemed optimistic about the forthcoming album – "In the first week I predict a million sold," he crooned, silkily.

It was a misplaced optimism. The Best Of Both Worlds tour was a disaster from day one.

Playing major arenas, winding across the country and spiking once more through Madison Square Garden on its way, it was a slickly planned show, another step up for Jay-Z in terms of arena spectacle. As the lights dimmed, a news report of two police chases flashed across the screens, separate streams of squad cars in high-speed pursuit of two tour buses, heading direct for the arena. In a squeal of smoke and destruction they both crash through a fake wall onto the stage, Jay-Z and R Kelly arriving for the gig in unflustered criminal style, emerging from their respective buses in matching white suits unruffled by the chase.

From there it was a tag-team affair – the pair opened with a run of songs from *The Best Of Both Worlds*, including the title track, 'Shake Ya Body', 'Take You Home With Me A.K.A. Body' and 'Somebody's Girl', then Jay would leave the stage for Kelly to play a few of his own numbers, returning with a Roc-A-Fella rap crew in tow for his own short segment around 15 minutes later. Kelly would let loose his smooth

---

* 'Big Chips' made minor waves on its release, hitting number 39.

soul balladry, Jay would bang out his most hardcore hip-hop hits. Over three hours the pair alternated many brief solo segments before a joint encore of 'Fiesta (Remix)', 'Big Chips' and 'Hell Yeah'. A fast-paced night full of chances to change costume, make showy entrances and bold exits, create memorable set pieces. Jay-Z would rise from a reclining chair to bolt into '99 Problems', biting on a fat cigar; Kelly would open a section by projecting an open, handwritten letter dissing former friends being scrawled onto the stage-wide banks of screens. It would be a real crossover 'Event'.

According to court papers filed the following year by Jay-Z, the Best Of Both Worlds tour was doomed from rehearsals onward. Or, that is, the lack of rehearsals. Jay claimed that, having missed days of essential technical and choreography planning and rehearsal booked at the Northern Illinois University Convocation Center prior to the tour, Kelly eventually turned up with just three days to go, only to waste one precious rehearsal day playing basketball in the arena. Neglecting vital discussions with the technical and lighting crew, Kelly then spent much of the rest of the pre-production time working on a tongue-in-cheek skit he had planned for the opening night that he knew would bring the house down.

Unfortunately, on the opening night, September 29, at the Allstate Arena in Rosemont, Illinois, it brought the house down on top of him.

A 'comedy' text message advert seeking a new girlfriend bleeped across the screens, listing the attributes Kelly was seeking in a girl, including "she MUST be down with everything" and with the final condition "she's got to be at least… 19 years old". Then the lights rose on Kelly in a mock-up of a jail cell, writhing sexily with two dancers. The taste was bad, perceived as joking about his arrest and criminal case, the reception worse. The *Chicago Tribune* called Kelly's skit a "major error" beneath the headline 'R Kelly, Jay-Z Show Feels More Like Collision Than Collaboration'. MSN reported that critics deemed the prank "inappropriate and callous". For the second show at Rosemont the skit was dropped.

But the crowd became agitated anyway. Refusing to leave his tour bus until some new pre-programmed vocals arrived for the show, R

Kelly was two hours late onstage, leaving the authorities considering deploying riot police to quell the increasingly violent and unruly crowd, in case the gig was cancelled. Kelly, annoyed at issues with his new vocals, then left the venue before the final joint set, leaving a furious Jay-Z to round off with 'Fiesta' alone at 1 a.m. The third show in Cincinnati was cancelled as the tour couldn't make it to town in time following the previous night's delays, an added frustration for Jay as he was planning to use the Ohio shows as a chance to encourage his fans to register to vote in the upcoming presidential elections through his own Voice Your Choice programme, in the hope of drumming up a youth vote to oust George W. Bush.*

Kelly would later blame such diva behaviour – behaviour which became increasingly regular as the tour wound on – on technical problems (i.e. the lights not being pointed at him enough) and his own perfectionism. Jay would blame Kelly being under-rehearsed and unprepared for the tour, his constant time-consuming alterations to his set and his jealousy of the reception Hov was receiving, which fed into his insecurities and egomania, all riled up by an army of sycophantic yes-men he kept around him. Whoever was right, almost every night the tour hit trouble. In Memphis, Jay-Z left the FedEx Forum venue early citing an emergency, only to be later seen at Usher's birthday party. Shows in Hartford and Milwaukee were cancelled, others ran hours late, often due to 'technical issues'. In Columbus Jay-Z called a meeting with Kelly to raise his issues over Kelly's timekeeping, attitude and performances; in Baltimore, 90 minutes late for showtime again, Kelly exploded in anger at criticisms of his sets, throwing anything to hand and having to be barricaded in from leaving the venue in his tour bus, a weeping wreck. In St Louis, Kelly halted his set midway through the night to run to the lighting desk, assault the lighting director, smash a computer, leave the stage and the arena and instead reportedly spend the rest of the night at a nearby McDonald's restaurant serving bemused customers at the drive-through window.

---

* Two further Ohio dates did go ahead, with the Voice Your Choice stalls in action.

Though both Jay and Kelly denied any falling out with each other during interviews throughout the tour, on the rarer and rarer occasions they were seen onstage together reviewers noted tension and discomfort rather than brotherly camaraderie.

At Madison Square Garden, October 29, those tensions went Krakatoa.

A call was placed to Kelly before the gig, the first of three sold-out nights in NYC; a warning, a threat. R Kelly took it very seriously indeed. During the opening joint set he looked distracted, disturbed, scouring the crowd. His first solo set went according to plan but when he came back for his second, dressed in the black and white vest of his *12 Play* album, he was visibly distraught. He took the mic, deadly serious. His voice cracking, he thanked his fans for their support, claimed he'd intended to send security out with this message and that this was the hardest thing he'd ever had to do. "Two people are waving guns at me," he told the crowd. "I can't do no show like that… this shit is over." He left the stage in tears, telling the promoter and security what he thought he'd seen. In the first set, a man in the third row opening his jacket with a threatening gesture to show him what he thought was a gun. In his solo slot, a second man in the bleachers, same thing. "Dude opened up his coat – I can't say dude had a gun, I don't know what I saw," Kelly told radio show Hot 97 later that night. "I wasn't going to take any chances when I saw what I saw. I'm not crazy."

Security stormed the arena, searched the men in question, turned up nothing. Meanwhile an infuriated Jay-Z had taken to the stage with his Roc-A-Fella crew, yelling "Fuck that! I got this shit myself New York! Give me my old skool shit. I got hits!" With Memphis Bleek and Foxy Brown at his side, he ran through his next scheduled solo slot of 'Ain't No Nigga', 'Where I'm From', 'Heart Of The City (Ain't No Love)' and 'Encore'. With the crowd screaming "HOVA!" to the hero saving the show, he then told the arena: "I got some good news and bad news. R Kelly is not coming back. If y'all waiting to see him, go home. The good news is I got a lot of records, and I got y'all."

It took Jay only a few minutes' break to put together a galaxy of a

211

gala. "I got it together," he said on his return to the stage, "I found a couple of people." And the stars kept flowing. Ja Rule emerged for 'Can I Get A...'. Usher, there just as a fan that night, hit the stage for 'Caught Up' and his own 'Throwback' and 'Confessions' hits. Memphis, T.I., Young Gunz and Freeway all piled on for a finale of *The Dynasty*... tunes. "I don't need that nigga," he said of R Kelly, hugging Mary J. Blige as she left the stage after a stirring 'Song Cry'. New York rapturously agreed.

The stealing of the show would have riled R Kelly to distraction, if he hadn't already been in hospital by then. When security and the promoter had returned to tell him the men he pointed out were unarmed, Kelly had tried to return to the stage for his next allotted solo set, crowded with bodyguards. Pushed over the edge by his behaviour, however, one member of Jay-Z's entourage had had enough. Without Jay-Z's knowledge, as Kelly walked to the stage his old childhood friend Tyran 'Ty-Ty' Smith stepped up to him and pepper-sprayed him in the face, refusing to let Kelly ruin any more of Jay-Z's show. Kelly was rushed to St Vincent's Catholic Medical Center to be treated, but his stinging eyes were the least of the fall-out from Madison Square Garden.

Early morning after the gig, Jay appeared on Hot 97 to talk over the events. He admitted his assurances that there'd been no problems between him and Kelly on the tour had been untrue and that the 'technical difficulties' cited for the cancellations and late runnings were false excuses. Painting his tourmate as a pampered egotist, he told the station's Angie Martinez, "he has problems with the love people give me... he's insecure with himself." This followed a comment to MTV the previous day, when Jay had admitted: "It's very frustrating to cancel shows because I wanna see every single person. I don't want somebody to be holding their ticket for 29 days and on the 30th day it gets cancelled." When Martinez asked him about Kelly's claims to have seen men holding guns, Jay scoffed. "That's Madison Square Garden. You cannot get a gun in Madison Square Garden. Does he know where he's at?"[2]

Having heard the interview, Kelly himself went to Hot 97 to put across his own side of the story, describing his threatening phone call, his belief there were gunmen in the audience and being pepper-sprayed. He denied being insecure or jealous of Jay-Z's crowd response, cited perfectionism for pulling or delaying shows, and reassured his fans he'd be at the venue for Saturday's show ready and willing to perform. But Jay-Z had other ideas. A statement was released on October 30 telling fans and press that R Kelly would no longer be performing on the entire tour, and that the remaining gigs would be billed as 'Jay-Z and Special Guests'. "The fans deserve better than this," read Kelly's own statement in response. "I'd like the show to go on. It's really disappointing that Jay-Z and the promoter don't."

The show did go on, in New York at least, without Kelly. On Saturday October 30, Jay played with a plethora of star guests including P. Diddy, Mariah Carey and Method Man. On Monday, Pharrell joined him onstage. The rest of the tour was scrapped.

Next stop, the courts. On November 1, the day after he was kicked off the tour, R Kelly sued Jay-Z, his Marcy Projects production company and the tour's promoters, Atlantic Worldwide, seeking $75 million damages for breach of contract. In his suit, Kelly placed the blame for the tour's failure at the door of Jay-Z and his production crew, stating that Jay-Z's lighting technicians had been causing problems during his sets from the very beginning. "During the first Chicago show, critical lighting cues were missed, forcing R Kelly to stay up all night in order to completely reprogramme the staging of the show himself. As a result, he got to the second Chicago show two-and-a-half hours late, forcing cancellation of R Kelly's performance in Cincinnati on October 1 due to the logistical impossibility of traveling and setting up on time. The technical problems persisted, leading R Kelly and his staff to suspect that Jay-Z's lighting director was sabotaging R Kelly's performances." The document also claimed that the uneven split of revenue from the tour – Kelly was getting 60 per cent to Jay-Z's 40 per cent of the take – was the reason Jay had plotted to have him banned from the tour, insinuating that Jay might even have been behind the events at Madison Square Garden.

For his part, Ty-Ty was charged with third-degree assault on November 12 and would eventually plead guilty to disorderly conduct and receive no jail term.* And Jay-Z? He would first respond to Kelly's suit in rhyme, recording a remix of Snoop Dogg's 'Drop It Like It's Hot' in the aftermath of the tour: "All the money it made/I'm like forget the law I'm not 'fr-iz-aid/it J-iz-ay homie you got pl-iz-ayed/Take it like a man, the flow ran you off the st-iz-age... Wastin' ya time tryin' to sue S./Tell ya lawyer take that civil case and drop it like it's hot."

Then, in January 2005, he counter-sued, blaming Kelly for unprofessional and erratic behaviour and unacceptable demands, missing deadlines and rehearsals and causing gigs to be delayed or cancelled. His suit referred to the tour as "a nightmarish odyssey" and Kelly as delivering "mediocre" performances, displaying "unsafe and unpredictable behaviour" such as crying fits, holding up shows by hiding in his tour bus for hours and being desperate for money due to his "precarious financial and legal circumstances". Jay's case was thrown out by a judge who sided with Kelly's lawyers that this had little bearing on the breach of contract suit. Kelly was under contract to perform, he was willing to, and he'd been denied the opportunity.

If only *Unfinished Business* the album had been half as tense, deranged and unpredictable as its tour. Released on October 26, at the planned midpoint of the tour, it proved to be a dreary, nondescript clanger. Largely recorded during sessions for *The Best Of Both Worlds*, there were some new tracks produced for the album, most notably the track that opened the album, 'The Return', and its remix that closed the record. Despite its comedy skit opening in which producer Tone played an ancient warrior's messenger boy bringing news of the return of *The Best Of Both Worlds*, it was a brazen, insanely catchy party track, but in retrospect this album highlight was rendered laughable by Kelly's rhymes claiming the tour would traverse the world, a globe-smashing success. And other than a dizzying turn from Twista on 'Mo Money' and a strident appearance from Foxy Brown on 'Stop', the album was one-dimensional, formulaic and thin, a glorified R Kelly solo album on

---

* Ty-Ty would be the subject of another R Kelly lawsuit against Jay-Z in November 2005, when Kelly would try to sue Jay claiming that Ty-Ty was 'paid' for his part in the night's events with a job as Def Jam's VP of A&R.

which minimalist identikit R&B tracks about meeting girls at clubs – sometimes set to limp Latino guitars – merged anonymously into each other and Jay-Z seemed a distant, disconnected presence. He only truly came to life to own the taut and brassy 'Don't Let Me Die', largely because it was the album's major foray away from tired seduction routines into more political ground. With Kelly whimpering like a wounded marine, the pair got inside the heads of soldiers at war, once again from the joint perspective of the war they experienced on the projects streets, both fighters praying that wouldn't be their last night on earth, both seeing Uncle Sam staring back at them from the mirror. A rare moment of depth in the shallowest of shagging records.

Kelly's prediction on 'Big Chips' of the album selling half a million in week one was grossly optimistic. The record made number one for a week, but on the back of 215,000 sales. Like *The Best Of Both Worlds* before it, it slipped quickly and inauspiciously into the murk of musical history.

The relatively poor sales of the album and the fiasco around the tour didn't put Jay-Z off collaborating with other acts. Earlier in 2004 he'd been approached by the MTV show *Ultimate Mash-Ups* with an unignorable offer. The series was to feature acts combining their songs to make mash-ups and then performing them live on the show, a concept that fascinated Jay after hearing what the likes of Danger Mouse had managed to do with *The Black Album*. The station gave Jay free choice across the music spectrum of who he'd like to collaborate with, an offer Jay saw as another opportunity to break down more musical barriers and invade a hugely lucrative youth genre that more narrow-minded rappers might have thought was out of bounds for hip-hop.

He contacted Mike Shinoda of the leading emo rock group Linkin Park – as it so happened, an email that Mike had been waiting for his whole life. As a huge Jay-Z fan, he'd already been mashing up *Reasonable Doubt* songs with hard rock anthems by the likes of Smashing Pumpkins and Nine Inch Nails for some time, an activity Jay had perhaps caught wind of. Jay suggested they work on tracks together; Mike had three songs from the a cappella version of *The Black Album* mashed into

Linkin Park tracks ready before he even emailed back. Jay loved what he heard so much he texted his manager two simple words: "Oh shit". The pair agreed to take the project beyond the simple studio merging of two songs that the MTV show required. They'd get together and work on six tunes, re-recording vocals, raps and instrumentation sections for them to make sure the vibe fit the tempo. "Jay and I realised it's better to re-perform the rap vocals if you're gonna do it to a new beat," Shinoda explained, "because the vibe changes and you have to deliver your verse a little differently."[3] They'd make the 20-minute, six-track album – so short it was considered an EP on its release – a real event. Mike was so stoked he even used his 2004 Grammy acceptance speech to announce the record.

As a pioneering artist who by now seemed more at home overturning expectations than playing it safe, Jay seemed far more suited to the innovative rap-rock Linkin Park experiment than the R&B-by-numbers R Kelly project. And *Collision Course* felt far more like a cohesive meeting of major talents too. Linkin Park singer Chester Bennington recorded his own version of Jay-Z's spoken introduction to 'Izzo (H.O.V.A.)' for its mash-up with their 'In The End'. The grungy wartronica of 'Dirt Off Your Shoulder' melded electrically with the gnarled Linkin synth metal of 'Lying From You'. Bennington's original lyrics from his hit 'Papercuts' fit onto the warped Arabia of 'Big Pimpin'' as though they were born for the song. 'Jigga What' smashed headlong into Linkin's 'Faint'; '99 Problems' was sandwiched between equally strident chunks of 'Points Of Authority' and 'One Step Closer', again with Bennington recreating Jay's rhymes and the policeman's part in the second verse as Jay laughed along.

"There was no ego at all working with Jay," Mike told MTV. "If I asked him to perform something a certain way or put a vocal line here or there, he was happy to do it. He's really easy to work with."[4]

"You bring what you do to the table, I bring what I do to the table," Jay-Z told the band during the sessions, outlining his central philosophy. "It's uncompromising. You're not trying to be me and I'm not trying to be you. There's fusion and whatever happens happens. I love that."[5]

Finished over four enthused days, *Collision Course* was fun, creative and incendiary – the crowd at the MTV filming at the Roxy Theatre, West Hollywood that July lost their tiny minds.*

As did the entire country. Registered as an EP†, it was only the second ever to reach number one when it hit the stores on November 30, selling 300,000 copies in week one and almost 2 million in the US and 5 million across the globe by the end of the decade. The inspired amalgam of Linkin Park's stirring nu metal ballad 'Numb' and Jay-Z's 'Encore' – a favourite during the initial recording sessions – energised every radio it touched, making number 20 and staying on the *Billboard* chart for a full six months. The song earned Jay-Z another Grammy; come the following year's ceremony, Linkin Park and Jay-Z could be seen performing it together, all clad in tailored suits, Jay-Z's covering a T-shirt of John Lennon. A hint, it turned out. Halfway through the song the guitars dropped out for Jay to rap his second verse over a lilting, familiar piano refrain. Bennington began singing along to it: "Yesterday, all my troubles seemed so far away…" Then another white-suited figure appeared to take up the tune, Sir Paul McCartney, acknowledging and honouring his own new-found hip-hop credibility via *The Grey Album*. Here was a legendary breaching of cultures, on global TV, Jay-Z at its fulcrum. Danger Mouse must have been stunned at the history he'd created.

Besides an ongoing friendship and working partnership with Shinoda – by the Grammys Jay was already working as executive producer helping to track-list Shinoda's solo album under the Fort Minor moniker, *The Rising Tied* – *Collision Course* also gave Jay a rare and crucial benefit for a black rapper; credibility among the predominantly white teenage skate-rock audience. *Collision Course*, more than any record before, cued up

---

* Linkin Park hand-picked the fans who were given tickets to the gig based on an internet poll they conducted asking them: "Which other artists do you listen to?" Those who said Jay-Z won tickets. The show aired on November 10.

† With a second DVD consisting of a *Making Of…* mini-documentary and footage from the Roxy performance.

Jay-Z's straddling of all music culture. He was, increasingly, cool in every scene.

With all this touring and chart activity throughout 2004, onlookers might have been forgiven for thinking Jay-Z's retirement was something of a smokescreen, a publicity stunt. In fact, the slow-turning cogs of business were holding up his shift to the corporate. But as the end of 2004 approached, the serious executive offers started to mass. The main players at the four major labels were playing musical chairs, shifting between companies and positions. At the end of the game, the seat left free was the president of Def Jam. It wasn't the only offer Jay-Z received – Warner Brothers gave him the opportunity of heading up all of their labels for a vast salary. But Jay-Z plumped for the lesser-paying Def Jam position at a mere $8–$10 million for three years because, having bought out the remaining stake in Roc-A-Fella earlier in 2004 for $10 million, Def Jam owned the rights to Jay-Z's precious master recordings, worth incredible sums. Part of the presidency contract was that after 10 years in the job, those rights would revert to him as one of the biggest bonus pay-offs in the world. And Jay wasn't a man to turn down an un–turn–downable offer.

"I try to pay attention to the signs around me," he later told me, "and all the signs pointed to that being what I should be doing next… all the signs pointed to that. I'd just been offered the head of Def Jam, I guess this was the next level of my life. It just shows that artists can ascend to the executive ranks and not just go away or be 'where are they now?' specials. I've always been an entrepreneur, I have my own companies, I just thought it was time to show artists a different ending."

Before the move was announced, Jay had some emotional business to tie up. His move to Def Jam would mean the dissolution of the original Roc-A-Fella collective – indeed, as Def Jam president, Jay-Z was effectively the boss of Roc-A-Fella now. The relationship between Dash and Jay had been cracking for some years, disagreements over staffing issues, promotions and the direction in which to take the company. By 2004 their business relationship extended little past having screaming matches in their offices and then having to schedule in 'fixing meetings' to try to heal the rift, only for another to break open at the next row. Now it was crunch time.

Over dinner that winter Jay-Z sat down with Dash and Burke to deliver the news and, aware of the understandable feelings of anger and betrayal they might feel, he came up with a package he hoped might sugar their bitterness. He told them he would give Dash and Burke complete control over Roc-A-Fella in return for the master tapes of *Reasonable Doubt*, the record they still owned jointly.

It wasn't enough. With Dash and Burke turning down Jay-Z's sop in favour of simply selling up their remaining Roc-A-Fella interests, the meeting ended acrimoniously. Within a few weeks Dash set about launching his own label under the Universal umbrella called Damon Dash Music Group, out in a wing of the company that wasn't under Jay-Z's control. His frustration that Jay-Z, as the face and front of Roc-A-Fella, had gained the acclaim, credit and huge industry salary from the label's success rather than him, having worked alongside Jay from the very beginning, led him to demand a higher role in Universal than they were prepared to give him, and plans for the label broke down. Dash took to the press, criticising Jay openly for his pattern of taking on mentors and partners for as long as they were of use to him, then discarding them out of hand – Jaz-O, his early production team, now Dash. Jay and Dash were clearly a partnership that no longer functioned, and within 18 months Jay had bought Dash out of their final business connection, Rocawear, for $22 million. When they next ran into each other in an elevator, they exchanged nods and little more.

The Roc-A-Fella era was over, a decade that had changed hip-hop to its very core, opened doors that had seemed welded shut to rap, turned an exploding genre into a constant, blinding cultural glare.

Now Jay-Z set his mind to doing the same with the entire music industry.

On his arrival, things at Def Jam didn't seem so rosy. The label was stagnant and struggling to retain its former sales glories. Its staff were disillusioned and workmanlike, lacking the passion for music and salesmanship that had driven Jay-Z to the top. Co-founders Rick Rubin and Russell Simmons had long since departed, along with key acts such as the Beastie Boys and Public Enemy, leaving the label full of a burnt-out old guard going through the music industry motions with no thrill or enthusiasm for the music they were discovering and releasing. The place was a dead-eyed production line. And it was Jay-Z's formidable task to turn the business around, return Def Jam to the dynamic, frontier hip-hop label of its roots.

Jay's first instinct was to quit, but he was no quitter. Instead, he vowed to rouse the label out of its torpor by any means necessary. His first move was to inspire his staff with a two-day trip to the Tribeca Grand hotel where he gave the most inspirational speech he could muster and then played his staff a recording of the original Def Jam sales pitch from 1984, a thunderous and passionate declaration of the label's *raison d'être* and manifesto, a stirring reminder of what Def Jam was all about. He conducted a Q&A to find out why his staff members were working in music and what excited them about it. Back at the offices, he made himself an accessible boss, friendly and complimentary to everyone from intern to executive, oozing pleasantness and productivity. He threw himself into the intricacies of deals, studying every cranny of the business. It was as though he'd spent the previous 10 years cramming management courses rather than rapping his heart out.

His first signings, though, did little to improve the label's prospects. Turning instinctively back to his close circle of crew and associates, he inked deals with Young Gunz, Foxy Brown and Memphis Bleek, only to find their albums for the label underperforming despite his best promotional efforts. He fared better, critically at least, with The Roots, his backing band for the *Unplugged* and Madison Square Garden farewell show. Having convinced Jimmy Iovine, the head of their previous label, Interscope, to let them free of their contract to sign to Def Jam – and the band themselves turning down higher-money offers out of their trust and respect for Jay and the integrity of his working practices – Jay took a deep personal interest in their debut Def Jam release, *Game Theory*, keen for the band to stay true to their art and not try to appeal to the mass market by adopting traditional rap themes, as many critics of the move expected when the band fell under Jay-Z's control. When they found they had only 24 hours to clear a sample of a song by alternative rock act Radiohead with Radiohead's lawyers demanding $700,000 for the clip, Jay put in a call and had Thom Yorke on the phone within an hour granting permission with honour.

Summer 2005 brought sunnier times. Kanye was signed to the label via his Roc-A-Fella deal and went Platinum with his hugely acclaimed and inventive Grammy-winning second album *Late Registration*, an album Jay helped to form by begging Kanye to hold back one of his biggest hits, 'Hey Mama', from his debut to put on the second. Young Jeezy had similar success. But perhaps the finest moment in Jay-Z's first year as head of Def Jam was when he turned away from his long-term associates and auditioned a new act in his office. A nervy, inexperienced 17-year-old Barbadian girl who trod warily through the doorway and introduced herself as Rihanna. Hearing her sing 'Pon De Replay' for him, he insisted on signing her that very night.

"Jay-Z said 'there's only two ways out. Out the door after you sign this deal, or through this window,'" she recalled in 2007. "And we were on the 29th floor. Very flattering."[6]

"She was a star, immediately," Jay-Z told me at our interview. "She never had an album or a record out before, she walked in the room and the room moved. It moved at that moment." His A&R sense, he explained, was all about not following bandwagons. "I go to a lot of shows, to a lot of early bands. I really like music so it's not really a job to me. I have a great team of talent-finders. I'm really drawn to stars. I'm not looking for the next anything. A lot of times a lot of A&Rs go wrong, they look for the next Rihanna. I'm not looking for the next anything, I'm looking for the newest thing."

Rihanna's 2005 debut album *Music Of The Sun* sold half a million in its first six months on the shelves, and within two years Rihanna would be making landmark pop records of the 21st century. Suddenly, Jay-Z was living up to his hit-maker reputation.

Outside the boardroom, Jay's personal business ventures were expanding. He bought a hefty share of the Spotted Pig, a gastropub in the West

Village with prestigious Michelin stars. He considered purchasing a stake in British football club Arsenal FC. During the play-off season in basketball, he broke his musical silence to release a special themed version of 'Takeover' based on the Nets' season and featuring Young Gunz, to promote the team and become its anthem for the year. High-end industrial designer Adrian Van Anz was tasked with designing Jay-Z his very own colour – Jay-Z blue, a reflective silver fish-tone with flecks of platinum – with the intention that a large array of products could be made in a 'special edition' of the colour, including, allegedly, a Jay-Z version of a top-of-the-range Chrysler jeep.* In terms of cross-promotion, Jay-Z wasn't just thinking outside the box, he was thinking outside geometry as a whole.

Not that his efforts were entirely self-serving. When his nephew Colleek Luckie graduated that year, Jay-Z bought him a brand new Chrysler as a celebration gift, only to be utterly devastated when Colleek died in an accident in the car only a few weeks later. When Hurricane Katrina hit Louisiana on August 29, Jay was one of many glued to the TV, horrified at the loss of life and livelihood unfolding on his screen and the inhumanity and apparent lack of concern shown by the country's leaders towards some of the poorest and most needful members of American society. Backing Kanye West's statement on a live TV telethon in aid of the emergency that "George Bush doesn't care about black people", an attitude he saw as echoing through generations, he donated $1 million via the Red Cross, as did P. Diddy.

Still, life in the back room was tough to get used to. The money was great, the respectability all he'd ever dreamed of, the feeling of blazing a trail from the poorest of backgrounds to the richest of career highs, of being an inspiration to millions, was hugely satisfying. But there was so little acclaim. So few awards, no applause, no spotlights, screams or ovations. So few visceral thrills. And, outside the office walls and trade journals, no one was talking about him any more, this figure who'd thrived on controversy and confrontation all his life.

---

* Plans for the jeep were apparently shelved when new management came in at Chrysler, less keen on associating the brand with an ex-hustler.

On vacation in 2005, he found himself rapping again, but from a deeper and more perceptive angle than ever before. The rhyme was called 'Beach Chair', inspired by the death of his nephew and his feelings of blame for the tragedy, and it addressed Jay-Z's baby girl who was not just unborn then but un-conceived. Exploring questions of faith and spirituality, he attempted to map out a fearless and hopeful life path for his child, free of the death terrors that had haunted him throughout his youth or the need to hanker after others' wealth, and free of having to pay for her father's many sins, but also driven by a similarly fervent ambition and self-belief. The lyric was almost ghetto Shakespeare in language and theme – "I barter my tomorrows against my yesterdays"; "no compass comes wit' this life, just eyes/So to map it out you must look inside" – and centred around his own death and rise to "an even higher plane", leaving his daughter the life skills and resources for a fulfilled and happy life.

Reciting 'Beach Chair' over and over to himself that summer of 2005, Jay-Z realised that he still had a lot to say in hip-hop. He couldn't stay silent forever, people had to hear it.

But rap was a battleground for him, full of enemies and saboteurs and minefields. If he was going to return, he'd have to do it with a landscape-levelling bang.

Chapter Thirteen

Return Of The King

War was scheduled to break out at around 9 p.m., October 27. Its hub and nerve centre, the annual Powerhouse concert for NYC's Power 105.1 station at Continental Airlines Arena, East Rutherford, New Jersey. The warlords gathered, huddled conspiratorially. The concert was entitled 'I Declare War', battle was imminent, lyrical blood would surely be shed. "I gotta put 'em in the choke hold, the Boston crab," Jay said to Ed Lover on Power 105.1 before the gig. "I gotta smash a couple of people. Everybody better make up and be my friend."[1] But who were they fighting? Was Jay-Z about to launch a thermonuclear attack on Nas? A hip-hop Scud against those attacking him in the press – Damon Dash, Jaz-O, 50 Cent, Cam'ron or The Game? Or would this be all-out ack-ack against the entire rap industry, gunning down every hater, biter and back-stabber who'd ever criticised what he'd referred to in lead-up interviews as "the Carter administration"?

Whatever, the crowds flocking to the CAA that night expected fireworks.

An hour late*, Jay-Z took to his new office – a huge onstage set designed to mimic the Oval Office, redolent of his new position as

---

* Reportedly due to the late arrival of several special guests for the show.

head of a record label, and his cultural standing. The speakers blared out Martin Luther King's 'I Have A Dream' speech as Jay spun into sight in an enormous leather swivel chair, his fist poised over a big red phone. "I don't think y'all muthafuckers ready tonight!" he yelled to the "HO-VA"-chanting throng, pointing out that since the arena was where the Nets played, "this is my house" and throwing himself into 'U Don't Know', 'What More Can I Say' and a track called 'Dear Summer' that had hit the airwaves with impact that summer. The song was culled from Memphis Bleek's album *534* but featured only Jay-Z freestyling, an almost nostalgic (and ironic, considering its considerable airplay) tribute to the time of year he'd usually have a new hit song commanding the radio playlists as a warm-up for his annual winter album. "Dear summer, I know you're gonna miss me/For we been together like Nike Airs and crisp tees… you know how I do, Summer/I drop heat when you bring the sun up," he rapped over a crackly Weldon Irvine sample, dragging a random fan out of the front row to act as his emergency hype man. It was a tug-of-war sort of rhyme, at once marking a toe-dip back into music and rapping to his "beloved" summer hit season about how "it's tugging at my heart but this time apart is needed from the public". It was also the only real sign of warfare being declared for the entire night – the lines about rappers who were making "subliminal records" that were obtusely taking shots at him were taken to refer to recent releases by The Game, and his response was defiant, offering an open duel. "I put a couple careers on hold, you could be the next kid… if you that hungry for fame muthafucker, c'mon/Say when, take 10 paces and spin."

But as Jay wished his ex-lover, the summer release schedule, a fond au revoir, hoping it'd be kind to his friends in his absence, the show slipped further towards a joyous unity rather than the drawing of battle lines. Freeway, Beanie Sigel, Sauce Money and The LOX all hit the stage for a rare revisit to 'Reservoir Dogs'. Kanye popped up through the stage floor for 'Drive Slow' and 'Gold Digger'. Teairra Mari, Ne-Yo, T.I., Young Jeezy, Bleek and Peedi Peedi all appeared to rap with Jay or perform their own tunes. As the surprise guests kept mounting up like the opposite of bodybags, peace and harmony abounded, conflict had left the building. The hawks in the audience grumbled.

Then, after two hours of Jay-Z's latest star parade, in the middle of 'Where I'm From', Jay came across the line "I'm from where niggas pull your card and argue all day about who's the best MC, Biggie, Jay-Z or Nas..." And the music cut out. The stunned crowd went wild, the whole arena got the shivers. "This was called 'I Declare War'," Jay-Z said into the mic. "It's bigger than 'I Declare War'. It's like the motherfucking president presents the United Nations. So you know what I did for hip-hop? I said 'Fuck that shit'. Let's go, Esco!"

A spotlight lit the top of the stage, where Nas stood in military garb, basking in 20,000 tumultuous roars. He stepped down onto the stage, hugged Jay, shook his hand in mock-presidential manner and made his peace-time address. "A lot of niggas is makin' money and still fuckin' mad at the world. We're saving the East Coast, with your help." And with that, the pair launched into 'Dead Presidents', Nas on the hook. Jay gave Nas his stage to perform 'The World Is Yours', 'It Ain't Hard To Tell' and 'N.Y. State Of Mind' before returning to rap Nas' 'They Shootin'' and 'Hate Me Now' together, with P. Diddy joining them onstage, flinging champagne foam across the front of the stage. "We all in this shit together," Jay said at the song's end. "Y'all just witnessed history. Everybody in this building is part of history. All that beef shit is wack. Let's get this money."

The money they went to get was presumably Nas' Def Jam signing fee – a major part of their reconciliation – and the closure of their feud came with Jay-Z signing Nas to his label, the two artistically combined at last. Jay would even go on to appear on 'Black Republicans' on Nas' first Def Jam album *Hip Hop Is Dead*, and the duo would appear together throughout 2006 on stage, TV and radio.

The big event concerts. The secretive guest appearances. The itch to write new tracks. Inexorably, Jay-Z was being sucked back out of the boardroom, into the spotlight. He approved another *Greatest Hits* for September 2006, comprising his bigger hits from *Reasonable Doubt* and his 'Lifetime' trilogy. He agreed to guest on two songs for Beyoncé's new album for 2006, *B'Day*. When the original guest T.I. was unable to make the recording of 'Upgrade U', Jay stepped in to rap on a song that provided insights into a relationship they were otherwise keeping strictly private, determined not to allow it to become a plaything of the press or burn up in the media glare. 'Upgrade U' was about Beyoncé smartening up her man with Cartier tie clips and Hermès briefcases, and adding value to his million-dollar deals just by accompanying him to the meetings. It was a fascinating exposé of the insider dealings of celebrity relationships and how they complement each partner's interests; how fame sells but famous couples sell fourfold. And it also uncovered new layers of wit and playfulness in their relationship, with Jay's opening lines tutting "how you gonna upgrade me? What's higher than number one?" and his main verse mocking the press for spreading marriage rumours and working so hard to spy on the couple relaxing on holiday. For her part, Beyoncé's lyrics were cheekily controlling, full of female empowerment, hinting that she's the one in charge right down to her uncanny impersonation of Jay-Z in the video, all thick gold chain and puffed pout.

"I love it," she told MTV, "because it's completely out of my character, or at least the character that people think I am. I was pretending to be Jay, and he was there, and I told him he had to leave, because I couldn't do it with him in the room – it was way too embarrassing. I think I did a pretty good job. I had the lip curl down!"[2]

The other number, 'Déjà Vu', was to be the first single from the record, mirroring her debut album's successful opening collaboration with Jay with 'Crazy In Love'. A number four hit, it was the first Beyoncé and Jay-Z duet that didn't ooze love-struck devotion – Beyoncé's character was obsessed with a former boyfriend and Jay-Z was verging on paranoia that he wasn't matching up to this godlike ex. The video made up for it, though, with Beyoncé choosing outfits, movements and poses reminiscent of a young Tina Turner, writhing around Jay so suggestively that 7,000 fans signed an online petition to have the video re-shot, partly because of its overt sexuality. At one point the more imaginative viewers deciphered Beyoncé grabbing Jay's belt while squirming down a wall as indicative of imminent oral sex.

Every chance of a sly guest spot, every possibility of an event gig, all were suddenly irresistible. In June 2006, at the venerated Radio City Music Hall in Manhattan, Jay-Z performed *Reasonable Doubt* in its entirety to celebrate its 10th anniversary, all 3,000 tickets snapped up inside two minutes. Before a 50-piece orchestra called The Hustla's Symphony and a backing band including Questlove from The Roots and the Illadelphonics, the seminal hip-hop classic rolled out in sumptuous splendour, with only a few notable alterations. Without Biggie to parry with, Jay rapped all of 'Brooklyn's Finest' by himself. Without the love of his former mentor, Jaz-O's verse was cut from 'Bring It On'. With Mary J. Blige deep in rehearsal for a world tour, Beyoncé emerged to sing her parts on 'Can't Knock The Hustle'. And a new verse appeared on '22 Two's', set to a sample from 'Can I Kick It?' by A Tribe Called Quest: 44 switches of the words 'for' and 'four'. The crowd – including Jadakiss, LeBron James, Chris Tucker and Alicia Keys – were so wowed that Jay felt this too needed a more public airing.

Another change to the album was noted. All references to Cristal champagne were changed to Dom Pérignon. This was due to the offence Jay had taken to comments made by Cristal MD Frédéric Rouzaud. When asked by *The Economist* how he felt about the numerous name-drops Cristal was receiving in hip-hop songs, he replied: "What can we do? We can't forbid people from buying it. I'm sure Dom Pérignon or Krug would be delighted to have their business." Considering this slight tantamount to racism, Jay issued his own statement: "It has come to my attention that the managing director of Cristal, Frédéric Rouzaud, views the 'hip-hop' culture as 'unwelcome attention'. I view his comments as racist and will no longer support any of his products through any of my various brands, including the 40/40 Club, nor in my personal life." Sure enough, Cristal was banned from Jay's 40/40 clubs, all reference to it exorcised from his lyrics, and he wouldn't have a sniff of it in his home. Instead, he began looking into more exclusive champagnes to promote.

Even his charity work during his retirement bled through into music. A trip to the poorer reaches of Africa during a previous world tour had highlighted to Jay the dreadful water plight on the continent. He saw how the simple installation of 'play pumps' in villages – merry-go-rounds that draw from the ground and store water as children play on them – could go far in alleviating the struggle of many villagers. Moved by their plight, back in the US in 2006 he arranged a meeting with Kofi Annan, the Secretary-General of the United Nations, to concoct plans for him to help instigate such a scheme, and with MTV to sponsor a documentary covering a proposed trip to Africa by Jay to help focus attention on the problem. Hence, on August 9, a press conference at the UN's New York hub announced a partnership between Jay-Z and the UN on the Water For Life programme. That October MTV would join Jay in Nigeria, Rwanda, South Africa and Algeria as he met the people struggling to access clean drinking water and looked into possible solutions. The documentary was called *Diary Of Jay-Z: Water For Life** and it was filmed on days off during Jay-Z's 2006 tour of Africa, playing gigs and festivals in Nigeria at a time when the US was warning its citizens against visiting the country.† The African jaunt was part of a world tour, named after the Water For Life project and dedicated to promoting the issue across the globe.

And if there was a world tour in 2006, naturally there had to be a new album to go alongside it.

The lure of the old ways had become too much. The call of the mic too loud. MTV was ranking him as the Number One Best MC Of All Time, *Time* magazine was declaring him and Beyoncé to be the most powerful couple in the world, but still, Jay-Z felt he had things to prove.

The retirement was over.

It was time to make the comeback of the century.

"You got this fantasy in your head about getting out of the life and setting the corporate world on its ear. What the fuck you gonna do except hustle?"
      – Pain In Da Ass, 'The Prelude', *Kingdom Come*

---

* Which aired in November.
† Jay also used the trip to shoot a Rocawear ad campaign in South Africa, holding lion cubs on a Madikwe game reserve for the cameras and playing with schoolchildren in Durban, all making the Roc sign for him as he walked into their classroom.

The trouble with superheroes is that eventually they turn rotten. Power, corruption, greed, misuse of their talents. Without a strong leader they eventually fracture, go rogue, stray from the righteous path. So Superman found when he returned from a self-imposed exile to find a new legion of renegade superhumans irradiating Kansas and killing millions when an ultra-violent attack on Captain Atom unleashes his inner nuclear energies. It took Superman to re-form the Justice League to bring these crazed anti-heroes to order, to remind them of their responsibilities, to show them once again how it should be done. It's all written in the Alex Ross and Mark Waid DC Comics mini-series *Kingdom Come*.

And so felt Jay-Z when he looked out at hip-hop in 2006. His own crew members were out there making records that bent the boundaries of what rap music could be, but for every Kanye there were a hundred pretenders treading old ground, dishonouring the genre, using rap wrong. When his engineer Young Guru, a huge comic book fanatic, told him the plot line of *Kingdom Come*, Jay had his concept and his title. Having killed off Jay-Z in the video for '99 Problems', Jay had planned his comeback album to be released under the name Shawn Carter, but here was a grander purpose. Jay-Z was flying back into town to save hip-hop from itself.

It was a slow salvation at first. "The first couple of weeks in the studio I was just sitting around and really doing nothing," he told the *Observer*, "and then one week everything just came rushing back. I guess it's like everything if you take a lay-off – like a basketball player. You've got to get match fit."[3]

His first instinct was to return to what he knew, in heroic style. The first single from his comeback album *Kingdom Come* was Just Blaze's 'Show Me What You Got'. A track built around a classic big band brass blaze sampled from Johnny Pate's soundtrack to *Shaft In Africa* and Public Enemy's 'Show 'Em Whatcha Got'*, it opened with Jay declaring "a state of emergency" and returning to save the day like "the Mike Jordan of recording" or a modern-day urban Bond. The video drove home

---

* As well as credits to 'Darkest Light' by Lafayette Afro Rock Band and 'Rump Shaker' by Wreckx-N-Effect.

the 007 connection – returning to the big-budget millionaire showiness of his early promos, Jay recreated several Bond scenes including a race around the Monaco Grand Prix course with celebrated racing driver Dale Earnhardt, Jr. in a Ferrari F430 Spider (a homage to *GoldenEye*), a motorboat race (from *The World Is Not Enough*), a huge model-strewn party in a Bond villain cave (akin to *You Only Live Twice*) and a high-roller poker game (*Casino Royale*). The substantial cost of the video – plus a reported $1 million fee – was fronted by Budweiser, for whom Jay also made an advertisement at the same time as his video, itself a tribute to *Never Say Never Again*.*

Brought forward by two weeks when it was leaked on the internet, the catchy and propulsive energy of 'Show Me What You Got' was a hit on radio at the start of October†, its metaphors of seduction and rap rejuvenation reflecting Jay's real excitement at being back in music – "get the fuck out the throne you clone, the king's back". Peaking at number eight on the *Billboard* chart, it seemed Jay's return was every bit as big news as he'd expected.

Kingdom Come arrived somewhat more leisurely. From that Pain In Da Ass opening quote, a nod to his 'Lifetime' trilogy past, the record bled into 'The Prelude', a laid-back pastoral piece of smooth strings, clarinet and slack bass‡ that raised the album's recurring theme. Just

---

* This wasn't the only commercial use of the video and song. Towards the end of the video, Jay-Z is seen to dismiss an offer of a bottle of Cristal from a waitress, instead ordering the $300 per bottle champagne Armand de Brignac, while also mentioning the brand's distinctive design in the lyric "gold bottles of that ace of spade". Sales of Cristal declined following Jay-Z's denouncement of the brand, and Armand de Brignac thrived in the wake of the video, selling out every bottle of its limited annual run each year. Financial journalist Zack O'Malley Greenburg, in his book *Empire State Of Mind*, alleges that Jay-Z may have brokered a deal whereby he profits by up to $4 million per year from the sales of Armand de Brignac without publicly acknowledging the connection. Certainly, cross-advertising wasn't unusual for Jay-Z at this point – an advert he filmed for Hewlett-Packard's new HP Pavilion notebook that year also plugged Rocawear and Jay's forthcoming world tour.
† Indeed, the leaked track was played so widely that the FBI launched an investigation into the source.
‡ A B-Money production sampling Mel & Tim's 'Keep The Faith'.

as *The Black Album* was obsessed with Jay-Z leaving the rap business, *Kingdom Come* was all about why he was returning. "The game's fucked up," he argued before going over his thinking from the previous few years: "forget this rap shit, I need a new hustle... the new improved Russell/I say that reluctantly 'cause I do struggle/As you see, I can't leave so I do love you." Stressing his realness, his pre-rap success and his longevity, it was an uncharacteristically low-key return that some critics would take to be an apologetic shuffle back into the limelight, as opposed to the brazen comeback they'd expected.*

The first third of the record felt like a consolidation parry rather than a knock-out roundhouse from the returning undisputed rap champion. With Just Blaze at the helm, the mid-period Jay-Z traditions of sped-up soul samples were deployed in formulaic fashion, particularly on the second track 'Oh My God', an almost painfully relentless loop of Genya Ravan's impassioned yelp from her cover of The Allman Brothers' 'Whipping Post' that sounded like 'U Don't Know' on a crystal meth comedown. For all its energy and dazzle it felt like old ground retrodden, with Jay-Z revisiting his hustling days again, a period he'd arguably exhausted in his first incarnation. Nonetheless, he did it with a breathless enthusiasm reminiscent of his earliest work and dropped in ultra-modern references to emo act My Chemical Romance (relating to his romance with the drug trade) and *Grand Theft Auto* alongside his trademark apologies to his mother for the shame his dealing brought upon the family. In bringing his story right up to date, though, there were fascinating

---

* 'The Prelude' wasn't originally the tune Jay had intended to open the album. In May 2005 he'd recorded a freestyle called 'Operation Corporate Takeover' full of artfully twisted corporate speak about his invasion of the world of big business, the respect he gained there mingling with anonymous industry moguls – who, his autobiography claimed, "quietly run the world" – and his intentions of remoulding the music industry in the spirit of hip-hop reinvention. By the time *Kingdom Come* came about, however, the rhyme seemed out of date and the intentions within it had proved impossible, even for him. The freestyle eventually ended up being released on a Green Lantern mix-tape in 2006 called *Presidential Invasion*.

details – boasts of selling out gigs from Seoul to Tanzania, his first recorded reference to Water For Life and a claim to have had lunch with Nelson Mandela and dinner with fashion designer Roberto Cavalli on the same day.

The title track of the album was more experimental, incorporating compelling modern electronica elements into Blaze's sample-weaving, this time a combination of the riff from Rick James' 'Super Freak' that MC Hammer had used for 'U Can't Touch This'* and the ominous synth slashes of '100 Guns' by Boogie Down Productions. It was the first sign of the more mature and sophisticated album Jay had planned to make, but also, with a teenage twist, put Jay in the Superman role from the *Kingdom Come* comic strip, admitting to having been "sick of rap" for a while, but tearing off his business suit to fly to the rescue of hip-hop when he was needed, dubbing himself "hip-hop's saviour". The superhero metaphors kept coming – he was Spider-Man "climbing the charts", a light-bringing Flash Gordon in the recording booth and a rap Batman who comes running whenever the ROC sign is flashed. A colourful rap cartoon strip come brightly to life.

After 'Show Me What You Got' rounded off Just Blaze's segment of Jay-Z's comeback album, essentially a reminder of where Jay was at when we'd last left him, Dr. Dre took control to steer his career down new paths, some of which were better paved than others. 'Lost One', for example, was a dislocated sort of tune, an awkward piano and strings ballad that failed to hang together† despite an intoxicating, velvet chorus hook from Chrisette Michele and a revealing, sensitive lyric about grief, loss and relationships shattered. Jay seemed regretful over the loss of old friends and partners – the first verse could be interpreted as an examination of the breakdown of his relationship with Dash and Burke, with Jay putting his friends before his business interests and his partners taking too much credit for having "made" him while not pulling their weight on the business front. But Jay was open about his own failings

---

* Jay-Z's song features one line of the famous MC Hammer chorus.
† Dr. Dre would later claim he'd studied piano theory in order to compose this tune; he was clearly in the early stages.

too, admitting that fame became an addiction for everyone involved, the "worst drug known to man, it's stronger than heroin", although Jay argues that he didn't suffer from its ego-bulging effects as much as others. In the end it's the disgruntled ex-associates he felt had lost out, musing "I guess we forgot what we came for".

The "one" that was lost in verse two was a girl, a workaholic girlfriend whose obsession with her job leads to a rift with her man. Which girl in particular is open to interpretation – since Jay talks of her being 23 years old at the time, the verse could refer to the long-term girlfriend from his hustling years, to Rosario Dawson who was 23 when they split in 2002, or even to early problems with Beyoncé, who was 25 at the time of the song's release (they'd been dating for three years by this point). But later references to the song's narrator being in the army suggests it might be an entirely fictitious section, unlike the undeniably autobiographical final verse, which dealt with the loss of his nephew Colleek, his feelings of guilt over the accident and how he chose to throw himself into the pain rather than shut it out. The song's final lines were both heartbreaking and redemptive at once – Colleek was about to become a father at the time of his death. Jay saw this as "the Lord's gift", as the boy's life "restarted" and a renewal of his own faith that had been shaken by the tragedy. He'd lost a nephew, but he was overjoyed to be waiting to meet his nephew's child. This was Jay-Z's rhyming at its most raw, confessional and moving.

Kanye's 'Do You Wanna Ride?' was a far more successful new-age ballad, a jungledelic psych-hop cut with an underworld edge of spy movie guitars, distorted beats and the inimitable vocal talents of John Legend to hand. The song itself was an open letter to Emory Jones, Jay-Z's cousin and a close friend through his childhood, who was then serving a 16-year jail term for cocaine trafficking, allegedly as the head of a coke ring in Maryland.* With Jay-Z speaking rather than rapping many of his lines to Emory and requesting a joint as though in

---

* It was also reported by The Smoking Gun website that Jones had been the boss of Jay and DeHaven Irby when the pair were low-level hustlers on the streets of New Jersey.

mockery of Jones' drug conviction, he added a new perspective to the sociopolitical aspects of projects life by spotlighting a different ending for those kids sitting on their buildings' steps admiring the cars, jewels and trappings of the hustlers in their neighbourhood. But Emory's story wasn't a morality tale or tragedy – Jay reassured him that "your spot is reserved", the high life would be waiting for him at the jailhouse gate and in the meantime he could experience success through his connection with Jay while keeping his spirit and mind free in the prison library. It was an idyllic picture Jay painted of Emory's life of luxury once he was out of jail, and he was true to his word, too. According to a letter published by The Smoking Gun website, in 2009 Jay would write to Judge Benson Legg to state that he was offering Jones a $50,000 job at Roc Apparel Group as an executive assistant, an offer which added to Legg's decision to cut over three years from Jones' sentence and release him in April 2010. Jay's Maybach car was waiting for Jones at the gates when he emerged. The multimillionaire rap star hadn't forgotten the honour of the streets.

Dre's West Coast lounge-soul bouncer '30 Something' kept the tempo relaxed to complete a chilled mid-section to the record, and found Jay maturing into his thirties, mocking the rappers in their twenties (and his own younger self) for their ridiculous clothes and showy attitude – the rims obsessions, the lack of taste and sophistication, the need to advertise their wealth. The wiser, richer baller, Jay argued, was subtler, more refined and even more quietly extravagant: "I don't buy out the bar, I buy the nightspot… we used to ball like that, now we own the ball team." Here was the next chapter of Jay-Z's boasting raps, discarding his youthful flash and becoming less confrontational. An important step in becoming part of the mainstream establishment, and taking hip-hop into the realms of respectability with him.

DJ Khalil was one half of LA rap team Self Scientific, and his track 'I Made It' returned the increasingly mid-tempo *Kingdom Come* to the party, albeit still during cocktail hour rather than the rave finale. In honour of his mother and her financial strife during his youth, this was a celebration of Jay-Z having made his fortune from their humble beginnings struggling to pay electricity bills and finding their joys in music: "I was happy with not having everything, long as Saturdays you had The Commodores playing." Then The Neptunes' 'Anything' upped the pace with an afro-funk R&B groove similar to Jay's work with R Kelly, but with Usher and Pharrell providing the honeyed chorus vocals and Jay playing the clubland love leopard to the highest level of cash-flinging extravagance, hissing to his pole-dancing target about the thousand-dollar bills he'll toss her and his liking for splaying cash on his bed – "ever had sex on a million?" Again, a well-worn formula was at play here, at odds with Jay's new taken-man image and his declaration that he'd returned to reinvigorate a tired rap scene. Where, critics would roar, was the innovation, the originality that would rescue a drowning genre?

It was in 'Hollywood'. A new producer and Beyoncé favourite Syience brought a blaze of pop dazzle to *Kingdom Come*, with Beyoncé herself as the glittering A-list chorus star. Jay's lyrics concerned the annoyances and the sometimes fatally addictive qualities of fame: from an opening section bemoaning paparazzi attention and the way fame distances you from old friends, Jay explored the gradual dependency the star develops on the attention, climaxing in a final verse referencing the deaths of James Dean, John Belushi, Janis Joplin, River Phoenix, Hendrix and Jim Morrison, examples of how fame is a drug that consumes you, and not necessarily something to wish for. He also paid tribute to the quandary of being a huge star with an even more famous partner. "When your girl is more famous than you then it's time to get all your windows tinted," he rapped, and also made mention of an unlikely new friendship that had developed at the top end of music – "when your friends is Chris and Gwyneth…"

Jay and Beyoncé had met Coldplay's Chris Martin and his actress wife Gwyneth Paltrow at a charity event around 2003 and had become close friends. Chris and Gwyneth would even appear onstage with Jay at the Royal Albert Hall on the Water For Life tour – the venerated venue's first ever hip-hop gig – to sing on 'Heart Of The City (Ain't No Love)' and Mary J. Blige's parts on 'Song Cry' respectively. "We visit each other's homes and really hang out," Jay told me. "[Chris is] a really great guy, a really great person and a brilliant musician and I respect his craft and how he approaches it. How he looks at it is exactly how he should be looking at it. He wants to be the best in the world but he's willing to put in the work. He really cares. I love his passion for what he does... He doesn't beat on his chest and say 'I'm the best'. In rap we have this bravado so we do it all the time; he lets the music speak and he's very humble."

Chris had even become so ingrained in Jay-Z's life by 2006 that he produced and performed an enthralling chorus loop of "I hear my angel sing" on the sinister, warped orchestral album-closer 'Beach Chair', the rhyme that had drawn Jay back into rap in the first place. It was yet another firm step by Jay-Z into mainstream acceptability – Coldplay were becoming one of the biggest alternative acts on the planet by this point – and the culmination of a darker, more intriguing final third of *Kingdom Come*.

Dre's claustrophobic electro-crunch on 'Trouble' soundtracked Jay hitting back at the "little niggaz" sniping at him since he'd become CEO at Def Jam*, a theme continued on Swizz Beatz' ominous, cinematic and riveting 'Dig A Hole'. And Dre's real spark of genius on the album, 'Minority Report', was the darkest of the batch. Swathed in spectral pianos, rainfall, samples of Pavarotti's opera and Ne-Yo's funereal soul warbles, an audibly upset Jay-Z vented his disgust and despair at the horrors of Hurricane Katrina and George W. Bush's response to the emergency, interspersed with news report sound clips telling of deaths in convention centres, shortages of drinking water and food drops, and Kanye's famous telethon comment.

Jay's stance was one of disbelief that such inhumanity could occur in a supposedly civilised country, pinpointing the news helicopters that would hover above the desperate families to get footage rather than save their lives, and the President flying by without offering his spare seats to the people stranded on their roofs by the rising floodwaters. But amid his condemnation of a society that brushed off the tragedy because it affected largely poor black communities, there was also guilt; that his

---

* It's uncertain who Jay was responding to here, since only LL Cool J had publicly been unhappy with his handling on Def Jam since Jay had taken over the presidency.

million-dollar donation was a "band aid" over a major wound, handed to ineffectual organisations in order for Jay to feel he had done his part and, like the rest of the country, forget about the problem once the news helicopters swooped towards a fresher story. Combined with the intense personal revelations of 'Beach Chair' it made for a hard-hitting close to the album, lightened a touch by the bonus inclusion of the live take of '22 Two's' from the *Reasonable Doubt* live show, which included the virtuoso verse rhyming 44 fors/fours.

Despite a Grammy nomination for Best Rap Album, the reception was mixed. The Jay-Z faithful welcomed him back enthusiastically, lavishing the record with relieved praise, but several critics gave the record a mild mauling for not being the sort of startling reinvention or game-changing record that would have necessitated Jay's comeback. *Entertainment Weekly* stated: "Four duds out of 14 tracks isn't a fireable offense. But shouldn't the corner-office mogul demand more of his top earner?" While crediting Jay for being "a grown-up rapper trying to make a grown-up album", *The New York Times'* Kelefa Sanneh noted its discomfort and called the record "halfway successful". As time wore on it was this vague sense of anticlimax that shrouded the album, a response Jay-Z himself put down to the ludicrously high expectations placed upon him. "I thought *Kingdom Come* was experimental and sophisticated," he told the *Guardian* in 2007. "But people hold me to a different standard."[4]

As far as the American public were concerned, *Kingdom Come* was quite epochal enough. Released on November 21[*], the record hit number one, selling a massive 680,000 copies in its first week, Jay-Z's highest first-week sales ever,[†] and these figures would have a far wider impact on music culture than Jay-Z could possibly have imagined. Just as he'd pioneered so many streams of hip-hop from speed-rapping to arena spectacle, his bigger-than-ever comeback would inspire an industry-

---

[*] In the UK copies were clad in a red jewel CD case and accompanied by a bonus disc of songs from the *Reasonable Doubt* gig.

[†] The record would go on to sell 2 million units, mostly within its first three weeks of release.

wide tendency towards reformations. Following Jay-Z's formula, as soon as a major act would see their audience or cultural significance wain, they would split up and reform as little as three or four years later, only to be heaped with renewed respect and appreciation and offered far bigger and more lucrative festival slots than they would otherwise have commanded. Within five years the festival circuit would be swamped with reformed headline acts and, in an industry where income from record sales was plummeting, Jay-Z would have started a whole new comeback culture in music.

The singles from *Kingdom Come* fared worse than these initial sales augured, though. On his birthday, while Jay and Beyoncé were partying with 20 friends in the Caribbean, 'Lost One' was released into the number 58 slot along with a video that was as much an advert for the new $8 million Maybach Exelero as a music promo. Both '30 Something' and 'Hollywood' would fail to make the *Billboard* chart, ironically out-done by the unreleased title track, which made number 98 on digital sales alone. In addition, a video was filmed for MTV of 'Minority Report', featuring footage of New Orleans post-Katrina to remind people of the devastation, wreckage and ruined lives.

For such an explosive comeback, the album's aftershock was remarkably short. But, like Jordan, Jay-Z was just warming up. Finding his feet again, settling back into his A-game.

A shot of cinematic inspiration and he'd once more be running the block.

Chapter Fourteen

Godfather Of America

In a courtroom holding cell, over coffee in cheap paper cups, police detective Richie Roberts faced down captured multimillionaire drug-ring boss Frank Lucas, laying out the links in the chain that was about to drag Lucas down. The crooked business affairs, the police bribery, the line of mothers stretching around the block to testify that their sons had OD'd on Lucas' cheap, high-quality heroin he'd called Blue Magic.

"You damaged a lot of lives, Frank," Richie said, "I got the Mezanos crime family, remember them? You put them out of business... Apart from the fact that they hate you personally, they hate what you represent."

Lucas blanks his face. "I don't represent nothing but Frank Lucas."

"You sure?" Richie snaps back. "Black businessman like you? You represent progress. The kind of progress that's gonna see them lose a lot of money. With you out of the way, everything can return to normal."

As Lucas' coffee cup went flying from the table into the wall and

the crime lord raved and ranted about what was "normal" in his life
– police brutality and murder – a lot of bells were being rung in
the private NYC screening room where Jay-Z was watching Ridley
Scott's movie *American Gangster*, summer 2007. The soundtrack was
classic soul, the themes money, drugs and the social ascension of
the racial underdog by any means necessary; Denzel Washington's
portrayal of Seventies drug lord Lucas seemed intrinsically linked
to Jay-Z's own story. Lucas had risen from a humble background
to the peak of respectability and success by dint of searching out
a cheap pure source of heroin in Vietnam and then importing
and distributing it with the utmost decency, fairness and moments
of cold-blooded violence. Then, at his peak, Russell Crowe's
determined police officer had finally caught up with him, clamped
him in jail with an unshakeable case, and demanded his help in
fulfilling his own personal mission. To flush the police force clean
of corrupt cops.

For Jay-Z, himself a successful businessman feeling that the
establishment resented his rise and would destroy him if it could, it was
like watching a metaphor for his life playing out on the screen, and
one he felt compelled to respond to. He'd make an album that would
act as a companion piece and soundtrack to the film, in the hustler
style of *Reasonable Doubt*, he decided. His own version of a big-budget
Hollywood gangster movie.

"It's a New York City true story, you know," Jay told the *Charlie
Rose* show later that year. "So as soon as the movie came on, it was
like familiar… things I've seen growing up… It's one of those movies
where you champion the bad guy, because the bad guy, you know,
he don't seem like a bad guy, and the good guys are bad… I loved the
complexity of the human beings."[1]

American Gangster, the Jay-Z album, would cap one of Jay's most
successful years to date. In January 2007 he'd launched his own car,
the Jay-Z Blue GMC Yukon that had been in development for two
years and was launched at a promo show hosted by Carmen Electra and
Christian Slater. In March, Jay sold his stake in Rocawear to the Iconix
Brand Group, bargaining himself $204 million for a company for which

he'd paid Dash only $22 million for his equal share just over two years earlier.* The zeros kept multiplying.

As did Jay's celebrity.† That same month, he appeared as guest rapper on another of the biggest pop hits of the decade, and one which would make his profile as huge as it could be without literally having the pop mega-hits himself. His opening rhyme on Rihanna's 'Umbrella', rewritten from the original lines he'd been given to link better with the theme of the song, might have seemed tokenistic and throwaway, a few brief references to saving money for a rainy day. Yet, it would become one of Jay's most famous, earning him another Grammy for Best Rap/ Sung Collaboration, and see him top the charts in countless countries – 10 weeks at number one in the UK, the longest run at the UK number one spot this century – and seven at the peak of the *Billboard* chart. At that point it was the biggest debut in iTunes history and it would go on to sell 6.6 million copies worldwide. And as not just her co-star but the man who'd signed her to Def Jam, if ever there was a sign that Jay-Z could follow whatever creative endeavour he wanted, it was this.

Plus, the naysayers were gathering voice. On DJ Kay Slay's show on Shade 45, one-time Brooklyn drug dealer and now Akon's tour manager Calvin Klein claimed that Jay had taken several of his rap stories from Klein's life, and that he had never been a serious dealer. Having recently finished a 13-year sentence for drug charges, Klein also called Jay out for not spreading the riches among or staying loyal to his original crew – Damon Dash, Jaz-O and Klein himself, who also said he'd taken the

---

* The deal included a bonus $35 million for Jay if the company met his projected sales figures and $5 million a year for him promoting and managing the brand. The money certainly would have eased concerns over a lawsuit brought against Jay later that year by Osama Admed Fahmy, the co-owner of the copyright on a song sampled on 'Big Pimpin''. Fahmy alleged that in producing the track Timbaland had illegally reproduced sections of his song's melody. Timbaland and Linkin Park were also named in the suit, Linkin Park being drawn in as the song had appeared on a mash-up on *Collision Course*.

† Not something he was particularly courting at the time; he and Beyoncé were trying to stay out of the spotlight despite regular appearances at Nets games and hitting Cannes for the film festival that summer.

weight of responsibility for joint attempted murder charges with Jay in 1989. For getting Jay off the hook, Klein said, Jay had promised to look after him on his release, but had never come through with money, work or support. In the wake of such claims, it was definitely time to reassert his story once again.

So Jay threw himself wholeheartedly into the *American Gangster* concept, working largely with Sean Combs for the first time since *In My Lifetime Vol. 1*. He had the film playing constantly on screens in the studio as the tracks were written, the raps recorded, and the whole cinematic piece was in the can within four weeks. Producer LV from The Hitmen explained the working process to MTV. "Jay would have the beats... He'd do the record, and he'd send it back to us. We'd fill in the blanks as far as making them full records. From having live horns, live strings, live drummers. This percussion dude, he was coming in with bottles, banging on bottles, just sprinkles of shit... Once we got the vocals back, we brought in all the extra candy... When I heard it with Jay's rhymes, I was just like, 'Jesus Christ! ... I gotta go in. I gotta show my ass.' Puff was hyped. He'd come in the studio and start bugging out, getting everybody hyped... Sometimes it'll take us three days to mix one record."[2]

Each song related to Jay's life and mirrored a scene in the film, placed chronologically to trace the similarities between Jay's story and that of the crime boss Frank Lucas, and the film's Seventies soul vibe re-sparked Jay's love of the sepia soul sounds of Marvin Gaye and Barry White that had made *Reasonable Doubt* slot so seamlessly alongside the classics. Hence, what emerged over those four soul-searching weeks was a record that took Jay back to his roots in so many ways, the return to form that so many had hoped for from *Kingdom Come* and the most honest album of Jay's revived rap career. Jay originally planned to record only nine tracks for *American Gangster*, but that it stretched to 15 was testament to a story that he couldn't stop telling.

Sampling Denzel Washington dialogue from the movie about how a man is owned by others unless he owns his own business – a central Jay-Z tenet – *American Gangster* opened with 'Intro', an atmospheric slice of Spanish Harlem, all dark flamenco guitar flurries, underworld synths, sampled strings, whip-crack beats and gunshots. Over this brooding backing* actors Idris Elba (of *Family Affairs*, *The Office: An American Workplace* and *The Wire*, in which he plays a business-minded drug kingpin) and Angel Wood defined some basic theories of "gangsterment" – "Gangsterment allows you to make up your own laws and create brand new worlds...", "Gangster mentality, an American way created by the white, mastered by the black, and absorbed by the fiends, taxed by the governmentality, charted by Forbes...", "To be a gangster swagger is not a must, it's a liability, a cliché, a bad suit, cut the bullshit..."

Then came Jay-Z's grand entrance on 'Pray'†: the religious overtones – Beyoncé recites a prayer in place of a hook and there's talk of incense and worship – reflecting Frank Lucas' arrest outside a church service in the film, and Jay's rhymes resembling a screenplay of his childhood. Against a taut backdrop of fearful gospel choirs, doomy guitar chords, dramatic strings and the looped roar of angry sampled spirits, Jay skilfully reintroduced himself as the "mind-state of a gangster from the Forties meet the vicious mind of Motown's Berry Gordy" and traced his part of a classic line of musicians linked to crime back to Sinatra hanging with the Genovese family. From there he recounts "the genesis of a nemesis" – his own youth – while making nods to the rise of the black businessman in New York. "The Harlem Renaissance birthed black businesses," he rapped, making a direct link from Lucas' Harlem drug ring to Roc-A-Fella, "this is the tale of lost innocences."

From there Jay recalls his father leaving to hunt down his uncle's killer, the syringes that would litter the projects and the dealers' BMWs pulling up to playgrounds. Then the teenage hustling life that "chose me", watching those same dealers from his childhood paying off police with "a treasure chest" of money the cops lugged out of their trunks, the mirror image of a scene in *American Gangster*

---

* Produced by Chris Flame along with Idris Elba.
† The first of a string of tracks on the album produced by Diddy with Sean C and LV, who concocted six of the first nine tracks.

in which detective Richie Roberts discovers an abandoned car with $1 million in cash in the trunk, intended to be picked up as a police bribe. When "the rules is blurred" by witnessing corrupt officers on the take, Jay argues, what's a poor boy to do, when "everything I've seen made me everything I am" and "anywhere there's oppression the drug profession flourishes like beverages refreshing"?* The answer, he concludes, is to be a man, get ahead however you can, and pray the Lord can forgive you.

'Pray' was an intoxicating opening highly redolent of Jay's *Reasonable Doubt* street-soul heyday, and the sweet falsetto coo of Marvin Gaye lilting through a sample of 'Soon I'll Be Loving You Again' cemented this magnificent mood at the opening of 'American Dreamin''. A slab of spectacular modern soul, it staged the next scene of Jay's story at the point when any hope of a college education and an honest life was discarded due to a permanent lack of funds, and the only way forward was to get themselves a pitch and follow their other, more realistic American dreams of growing up to be that hustler in the fancy car, "bagging snidd-ow the size of pillows". After all, those guys were being successful right before their eyes, and they sure didn't know anyone going to college.

The story traced Jay's hustling through his early amateurish attempts when he was struggling to find a source and having to wake up to the realities of the game. First, Jay claimed as if instructing a newcomer to the hustling business, you have to take yourself out of your environment, head to the root of the supply and convince men who may not speak English and who will kill you for breaking your word that you're reliable and trustworthy, you're not a cop and your money is "straight". Then you might just get a "consignment" to start up in a business of plotting partners and police stings, where Jay hoped "you could read they mind, you could see from behind". It was a scene lifted from Jay's own experience of finding his own supplier "where big coke is

---

* This, like the later mentions in the song to moving "coke like Pepsi" was a reference to Frank Lucas' claim that his heroin Blue Magic was a brand in just the same way as Pepsi or Coke.

processed", and from a scene in the film where Lucas travels to Bangkok to negotiate a supply of virtually pure heroin from the very plantation. And with it, as the song said, Lucas – like Jay - would "redefine the game as we know it, one dream at a time".

"HELLOOOOOO BROOOKLYYYYYYN!" yodelled a sample of the Beastie Boys* like a jubilant junk hawker as both Lucas and Jay launched themselves onto the New York streets in 'Hello Brooklyn 2.0', a bruising street buzz-bounce from the desk of producer Bigg D and half rapped by Lil Wayne in a breathy drawl akin to a Deep South version of Prince. In a virtual love letter to the borough that birthed, raised and schooled him, Jay pictured Brooklyn as a lover, baby-mama and daughter – "Hello Brooklyn, if we had a daughter, guess what I'm a call her, Brooklyn Carter," Jay rapped in an edgy stop-start cadence, little knowing how wrong he'd turn out to be. Cleverly using girls' names to represent extreme life shifts (Jay hoped Brooklyn wasn't jealous when he left for Virginia to set up his drug outfit there; when Lil Wayne felt the call from New York from his hometown of New Orleans he said "goodbye Katrina"), Jay explored his relationship with Marcy, considering her "bad influence" on him and the threats she had made against his life, but the love between them was too deep and strong to ever be broken. He ended by presenting her with a gift: "In a couple of years baby, I'm a bring you some Nets."

If 'Hello Brooklyn 2.0' was intended to point out the eternal bond between a man and the streets he came from, no matter how successful he becomes, 'No Hook' – Diddy's languid revisit to the funereal gloom of 'You Must Love Me' and 'Dope Man' – concerned a man's eternal bond to his street honour. More snippets of Denzel Washington as Frank Lucas introduced the track with a speech about the importance of "honesty, integrity, hard work, family, never forgetting where we came from" – a sign that Jay and Lucas shared the same strict moral compass throughout their criminality – before a wired Jay-Z broke in with a lyric about sticking to your principles and taking responsibility for your actions and decisions. The implication was clear: in a lawless

---

* From 'B-Boy Bouillabaisse'.

Taking it easy onstage at the *I Declare War* show at the Continental Airlines Arena in New Jersey on October 27, 2005, shortly before being joined onstage by Nas. SCOTT GRIES/GETTY IMAGES FOR UNIVERSAL MUSIC

H-to-the-Santo: Jay-Z delivers Christmas gifts to children in Bedford-Stuyvesant on December 25, 2005. SCOTT WINTROW/GETTY IMAGES

Taking questions alongside Russell Simmons in his role as President of Island Def Jam as they announce a partnership between Island Def Jam and the Russell Simmons Music Group, April 13, 2005. REX FEATURES

Performing 'Wonderwall' at Glastonbury, June 27, 2008. Guitar 'ironic'. RETNA PICTURES

Beyonce and Jay Z hang with Jay's brother Eric Carter, laughing off the youthful gunplay. JOHNNY NUNEZ/WIREIMAGE

Always aware of the best ways to cement his position amongst NYC icons, Jay poses in his Lennon t-shirt and his award for best rap collaboration at the 48th Grammy Awards, Los Angeles. ROBERT GALBRAITH/REUTERS/CORBIS

Jay-Z and his mother Gloria Carter at a Shawn Carter Foundation charity evening at Pier 54, NYC, September 29, 2011. JAMIE MCCARTHY/WIREIMAGE

Brushing up smart with Beyonce for an Alexander McQueen exhibition at the Metropolitan Museum Of Art, NYC, May 2, 2011. JUSTIN LANE/EPA/CORBIS

Jay-Z and Kanye West trade rhymes on the 'Home And Home' tour at Yankee Stadium in New York. Chad Batka/Corbis

Mogul mania: with Rick Rubin and Russell Simmons at the Def Jam 25th Year Private Dinner at The Spotted Pig, October 14, 2011.
JOHNNY NUNEZ/WIREIMAGE

Men of the Decade: Sean Combs, LA Reid, Kanye West & Jay Z at GQ Magazine's 50th Anniversary Party, NYC, September 18, 2007.
RD/Leon / Retna Digital. LEON/RETNA LTD./CORBIS

For Rocawear's 10th anniversary, Jay worked with Spike Lee for a new commercial for the brand - Brooklyn, New York, August 3, 2009.
WALIK GOSHORN /RETNA LTD./CORBIS

The sky's no limit: Jay-Z and Alicia Keys point out the sales graph of 'Empire State Of Mind' on the set of the video, Times Square, NYC, October 1, 2009. WALIK GOSHORN/RETNA LTD/CORBIS

Showing off his most successful signing, Rihanna, at the 52nd Grammy Awards, January 31, 2010, Los Angeles.
LESTER COHEN/WIREIMAGE

Bumping away the baby-bump – new parents Beyonce and Jay-Z celebrate a life less ordinary at a Nets game at Madison Square Garden on February 20, 2012. JAMES DEVANEY/WIREIMAGE

world, control your own business and adhere to your own strict rules or become utterly lost, utterly owned.

To which end, Jay created new guidelines for hip-hop in this very song. His outspoken refusal that the track would need a chorus hook – hence the title – emphasised the fact that this was a direct, almost private communication between rapper and listener, dislocated from all usual expectations of rap and "not for commercial usage", a message for his dedicated fans' ears only. So it felt like a true window on Jay's soul when he claimed to still feel like more of a hustler than a rapper ("don't compare me to other rappers, compare me to trappers/I'm more Frank Lucas than Ludacris") and he decries his old dealing partner DeHaven for, the lyric implies, not keeping his mouth shut in the police interview room: "fuck DeHaven for cavin', that's why we don't speak/Made men ain't supposed to make statements." His was a soul still bristling with age-old frustrations – rap rivals, critics and doubters of his veracity, traitorous ex-friends and anyone who has tried to take advantage of him or his wealth – and a deep-seated determination to look after his own. When the first verse dealt with memories of regaining then losing his father in a matter of weeks and the sad truth that the streets had been his real father, and the second went into his mother's worry that he might die from the dangers of dealing, these were tales he'd told before, but never with such a raw and confidential tone.

These two tracks were both dissections of the mentality and philosophy of the rising hustler, reflecting Lucas building his empire in the movie and Jay building his own in real life. 'Roc Boys (And The Winner Is...)' focused on the same characters at the very peak of their game. In the film this was portrayed by Lucas buying his family huge houses, taking ringside seats at Muhammad Ali fights and holding glamorous parties he'd ruin with bursts of his barely contained violence. In the song Jay imagined himself at a hustlers' award ceremony where the party is wild and the drinks are free, accepting the grand prize for his successes and thanking everyone who helped him achieve them. The rivals whose bullets missed him, the girls who transported his consignments, the cops who took bribes, the priests who oversaw his friends' funerals and, last but not least, his supplier and his customers.

Then, as Diddy recreated lush Seventies blaxploitation horns and crackles that Jay accurately described as "black superhero music"* and Beyoncé, Cassie and Kanye provided backing vocals, he went on to catalogue and celebrate his countless ill-gotten luxuries, from the paradise holiday resorts to the high-end shopping sprees, the flawless jewels and frictionless cars. Beneath the carefree extravagance, though, lurked a hint of menace akin to Lucas' own – no one should dare doubt the purity of his direct-from-the-source product, he suggested, or come anywhere near the "fortress" that produced it for fear of meeting "rare guns". Even at the height of success and celebration, as Jay's life and the film attested, the prime hustler had to keep both eyes firmly open.

Breezy, bright and brilliant, 'Roc Boys (And The Winner Is...)' would be declared the single of the year by *Rolling Stone* following its October 10 release, the critics no doubt a little starstruck by the cinematic Chris Robinson-directed video juxtaposing a young Jay-Z (played by teen actor Samgoma Edwards) putting together his first crew against scenes of Jay decades later as a crime kingpin popping endless bottles of Armand de Brignac in his own 40/40 Club with Nas, Diddy, Kanye, Mariah Carey, Irv Gotti and a glittering array of Roc-A-Fella alumni.† 'Sweet' continued the high-living theme, but with a creeping sense of paranoia and tension infiltrating Jay's dexterous rhyme and Diddy's elastic soul horn hooks. The party over, Jay was more reflective about his new position at the top of the crime game and, though he allows himself no shame, regrets or apologies for how he'd got there, he opened the lyric with the line "sweet, but still there's pain" and expressed deep-seated concerns that his cousin would follow in his perilous footsteps and that it might all end tomorrow: "One day you're up, next day you're down." Already, traces of storm cloud were gathering over Jay's "big boat" fantasy life.

'I Know', like the shots of the film interspersing scenes of dead junkies with Lucas' luxurious living, flipped the story to the addict's perspective.

---

* With the help of a sample from 'Make The Road By Walking' by the Menahan Street Band.

† The song was a minor US hit, reaching number 63.

With Pharrell providing the chorus – sung, like Jay's verses, as if the heroin itself were talking to its victim – Jay-Z looked into the nature of addiction, specifically to heroin, a drug he never sold himself. In a spirit of understanding rather than condemning the addict, in the first verse he likened addiction to an insatiable lust and the drug to a comforter – a method of numbing pain and sweetening dreams, a doctor in itself, a lover whose warmth is taken intravenously. Here, drug and dependant seemed in reasonable harmony, a mutually rewarding relationship despite the fevers the addict experiences without the drug. By verse two the power has shifted: the drug is in control, the addict more desperate, the heroin in shorter supply and its highs more fleeting and less intense. All attempts to get clean proved fruitless and the drug mocked the addict with her inevitable death – "Don't ever let 'em tell you that you'll never need me/My China White, 'til we D.O.A./Its Montego forever, baby, lets get away." Jay allowed his subject a happy ending, though, getting clean in the end and leaving the drug despairing that "your heart no longer pledge allegiance to me". A rare result, all told.

For such a harrowing but ultimately redemptive track, The Neptunes provided a deceptively upbeat and catchy track of afrobeats, lounge synths and Far Eastern tinklings. "I wanted to make something that sounded like *King Kong*," Pharrell explained to MTV. "[To] take people back to nostalgic drug dealing."[3] It certainly sounded like a seductive sedative.

Every movie must have a gratuitous sex scene, and Diddy's standard-issue bedroom groove 'Party Life', reeled out around a loop of Little Beaver's 'Get Into The Party Life' chorus, ticked the box as pointlessly and formulaically as most cinematic grinds. It was a distraction from the main action that even Jay seemed not to take seriously; he dropped awkward rhymes and let the tune roll out while he talked to his engineer Young Guru over the mic, so casual he considers letting the track run for seven minutes without rapping over it.

The album's movietone thrill ride got back on track with 'Ignorant Shit', a Just Blaze classic of strutting Smurf-soul (an accelerated sample of The Isley Brothers' 'Between The Sheets' gave the track its *Blueprint*-esque feel) on which Jay masterfully – and characteristically – twisted the entire concept of the record. As if stopping the movie mid-frame and introducing the director and cast, Jay announced "y'all hail me as the greatest writer of the 21st century… I'ma really confuse you on this one…" then brought up the house lights on hip-hop. Verse one was a regulation roll-call of rap themes and mores – half-naked girls, cops chasing gunshots, details of crack production, hints of private jets and gargantuan bankrolls. But come the chorus hook, Jay appeared to lift the lid on the whole 'sham' of hip-hop, taunting his listeners – "this is that ignorant shit you like/Nigga, fuck, shit, ass, bitch, trick plus ice… I'm only trying to give you what you want." Hip-hop was all smokescreen, he seemed to be saying, a scam with an easily recited lexicon that guaranteed success.

Verse two continued the whistle-blow, decrying all rappers as actors merely rolling out the sort of 'Ignorant Shit' about girls, drugs, guns and money that the public want to hear from them: "don't fear no rappers, they're all weirdos, De Niros in practice." Despite previous songs repeatedly attacking critics who'd doubted the truth of the history he'd claimed in his lyrics, on 'Ignorant Shit' he didn't disassociate himself from his own charges of fakery, but fudged the matter – "don't believe everything your earlobe captures/It's mostly backwards, unless it happens to be as accurate as me," he stated in one rhyme, then seemed to contradict himself a few lines later, rapping "believe half of what you see, none of what you hear even if it's spat by me". Having cast further doubt on the truth of all of his previous work and confounded his listener as to his own believability, Jay then piled into exaggerated examples of this form of rap acting, proclaiming himself a murderer and world leader that he clearly wasn't.

Confused? Casual listeners certainly were. But the final verse brought some clarity to Jay's thinking behind this controversial exposé of rap. Here he brought up Don Imus, a radio host who'd been lambasted for a racist comment he'd made on-air about a women's basketball team, describing some of the black players as "nappy-headed hos". His defence when later challenged on the comment was that the phrase had originated in hip-hop to demean women, and he was just repeating it for comic effect. Jay-Z found this outrageous, that a clearly offensive on-air comment was being used to denounce racism and sexism in rap, to sully hip-hop by association with Imus' words. 'Ignorant Shit', by openly admitting to some level of façade, poetic licence and exaggeration behind rap lyrics, was intended to point out that rappers weren't necessarily as dangerous, criminal, prejudiced and ignorant as some of the genre's lyrics might suggest.

How did this link to the film? Via 'Say Hello', the swoonful DJ Toomp reworking of Tom Brock's 'The Love We Share Is The Greatest Of Them All', which Jay used to emphasise the emotions, achievements, determination and fragilities behind the self-imposed hard-man image of the hustler, a side revealed in both Denzel Washington's portrayal of Frank Lucas and in Jay's many unflinchingly personal rhymes. "Out come the mask and the glove because we ain't feeling the love," he rapped, the cartoon image of the 'menace to society' made flesh and bone, not as merciless, cold and unfeeling a "bad guy" as the media would like to portray. It was the essence and point of Ridley Scott's film and Jay-Z's entire career; to expose and explore the humanity of the gangster.

The final reel of *American Gangster* was packed with drama. 'Success'* was a crash of intense and reedy Seventies funk organ, loping brass and percussion like crates of cash being thrown overboard, over which Jay ranted about the wastefulness of wealth and success: the expensive watches he never wore, the cars he never drove, the Trump Tower apartments he never stayed in. Then there were all of the chancers trying to extort a chunk of his money (a sure-fire way to get nothing but dead, he asserted), the jealous haters, the old friends he'd lost. "What do I think of success?" he snarled, "it sucks, too much stress... I had more fun when I was piss poor." Though Nas' final verse was traditionally boastful about his own success, Jay's was a lyric which went against so many of Jay-Z's raps about the extravagance and pleasure of high living, but it fit the scene, reflecting Lucas' innate dissatisfaction amid the empire he'd built. And setting them both up for their inevitable downfall.

---

* A Jermaine Dupri and No I.D. co-production sampling 'Funky Thing (Part 1)' by Larry Ellis & The Black Hammer.

There is a tiny part of ourselves, suggested 'Fallin'', that's so ashamed of success, that feels so undeserving of social ascendancy, that it wants to bring about our own decline. In Scott's film, Lucas paved the way for the collapse of his operation by wearing showy fur coats and expensive jewellery to a boxing bout, catching the eye of the detective studying photos of the rows of influential drug barons at the fight and wondering who this mysterious new face might be. And all this after Lucas himself, early in the film, warned the family members who worked for him distributing his product not to wear anything that might draw attention to their business and wealth.

In Jay's beautiful, lilting soul swoon of a tune – all tumbling strings and cartwheeling female vocals sampled by Jermaine Dupri and No I.D. from The Dramatics' 1973 classic 'Fell For You' – it was the greed of a hustler who becomes so addicted to the money, the trappings and the thrill of dealing that he stays in the game way past his original plan to shift just one brick then get out. "The irony of selling drugs is sort of like I'm using it/Guess it's two sides to what substance abuse is," he explained, and with this admission his downfall was ensured – "niggas never learn until they end up in the news clip". Jay's character made the same mistake as Lucas, showing off his wealth in front rows of fights and buying ever-bigger cars and TVs when "doing it this big will put you on the map". Before long he was under arrest, encouraged to launch hopeless appeals by greedy lawyers and finally locked away while a new generation of hustlers rose to take his place, inevitably doomed to follow the same rise and fall trajectory. Before long they too would be Frank Lucas, arrested on the church steps after Sunday service.

At the dramatic climax of the story, Jay took another step out of the frame, withdrew to take in an epilogue overview of the entire piece and his place within it. First, he focused on the root of all this evil. 'Blue Magic', named after the brand of heroin Lucas sold and packaged on its release in a replica of Lucas' blue paper baggies[*], was an inventive minimalist Neptunes production with a haunted-carnival horror-flick nuance

---

[*] As the lead single from *American Gangster*, 'Blue Magic' hit number 55 on its September 20 release.

emphasised by sampled snippets of Dr Frankenstein wailing "It's alive!", Pharrell's sinister chorus take on En Vogue's 'Hold On', a hint of a tune from the *Ghostbusters* theme and Jay-Z darkly declaring "blame Reagan for making me a monster, blame Oliver North and Iran-Contra/I ran contraband that they sponsored." Casting himself as an evil Barnum-style ringmaster – or certainly the master of his own drug ring – Jay described the processes of manufacturing crack and smuggling it into prisons as "treats" for his captured associates, all the while keeping his scene set in the Seventies and Eighties in keeping with the movie, peopling his rhymes with breakdancers and graffiti artists and tracing his story back to the era's CIA drug-smuggling scandals – "niggas wanna bring the Eighties back? That's okay with me, that's where they made me at."

'Blue Magic', though a fairly straightforward look at crack production, its political origins and the benefits of selling it, marked a shift in Jay-Z's lyrics towards a certain poetic and metaphorical surrealism, verging on the narcotic. As if the album were ending with a flashback dream sequence, he rapped of "fish scales in my veins like a Pisces" and imagined his stirring of the Pyrex crack pot "turning one into two like a Siamese twin". This approach bled into the album's closing title track, a kind of hip-hop 'My Way' in which Jay-Z summarised his hustling take on the American dream in a stream-of-consciousness flow over Just Blaze's celebratory soul swirl of Curtis Mayfield's 'Short Eyes'. Racing through references to his parents and Biggie, to cold winter nights on the streets, to Ibiza trips and faked paternity suits, it was a hyper-speed history all the more dizzying for its hallucinogenic merging of events, and of the concurrent characters of Jay-Z and Frank Lucas. What emerged from the maelstrom of images was a sense of struggle and achievement, of standing and honour in an underworld full of snakes, and the final verse almost paralleled Samuel Taylor Coleridge's 'Kubla Khan' in its self-portrayal of the poet as a demigod. Admitting "Muhammad Hovi" was "on the ropes" when Roc-A-Fella was breaking up but asserting that he was now "back in the go mode… throwing the diamond up", he declared that he wouldn't rest until "I hold the sky in my hand", at which point he could "disappear in the Bermuda Triangle", his name forever held in awe. For a cinematic album, a mythological ending.

So dedicated was Jay-Z to the concept of *American Gangster* as an aural movie that he asked iTunes to remove it as an album that could be purchased as individual tracks and sell it only as one continuous piece of music, a full-album download in one 'track'. "I made a movie in my mind," he'd later tell me, "and directors don't sell scenes of their movies, they sell entire movies, so I sold an entire movie."

In *Clash* magazine, he elaborated. "Maybe I am old fashioned, but a record is a piece of music from start to finish and that's what I set out to create... Even a record like *American Gangster* wasn't actually me looking to be the person in the film, it was my interpretation of the emotions I felt whilst watching it. I took emotions that related to my life from the movie scenes and talked about them in that way to make an album. It was a concept album, but not about the movie. It was influenced by the movie, so it was still me as me speaking and feeling, you know?"[4]

In his promotional interviews, Jay expanded on his reasons for wanting to recreate his life story in the image of Frank Lucas'. "That story – that real story – took place in Harlem, 20 minutes away from Brooklyn," he told Chris Salmon of the *Guardian*. "Stuff that people see in these neighbourhoods in one day, others will go their whole life and never see anything close to it. First time I saw someone get killed, I was nine years old... The person I'm describing in this album was a younger me going through the game. Right now, I'm a much more patient person. I'm not as reckless. When you grow up in these neighbourhoods and you don't have any hope, you feel you'll take a chance with your life to make the situation better. I don't have those thoughts any more."[5]

As satisfied as Jay-Z was with his bold artistic brushstrokes on *American Gangster*, the public was even more thrilled. This revival of his *Reasonable Doubt* era was exactly the record that both critics and fans had dreamed he'd come back from the wilderness to make. Though it wasn't such a runaway success as *Kingdom Come* in terms of sales, shifting 425,861 copies in its first week despite being leaked ahead of its release[*], it was

---

[*] An occurrence Jay-Z took in his stride, a calmer and more mature man now than the angry young kid of *Vol. 3*...

a critical hit, widely acclaimed as Jay-Z's true comeback album. "Jay sounds relaxed, no longer worried about impressing anyone," wrote *Rolling Stone*'s Rob Sheffield, while *The New York Times*' Kelefa Sanneh declared, "This is probably as close as the new Jay-Z will ever come to sounding like the old Jay-Z," and in *USA Today*, Edna Gundersen claimed the record found Jay-Z "establishing his status as hip-hop godfather". Mike Schiller of PopMatters put it best though: "What *American Gangster* truly gives us is Jay-Z through and through. Sure he's a gangster, but mostly he's a human being with loves and likes and pet peeves and needs and a natural predilection for camaraderie. It's superhero music in that Jay's supremacy is never questioned, but it's superhero music that insists on showing off more than just that hero's immense power."

An artistic triumph then, but also one with significances far beyond its retro filmic boundaries. On its way to 1 million sales on its release on November 6*, *American Gangster* became Jay-Z's 10th consecutive US number one album, equalling Elvis Presley's record for solo acts – only The Beatles had had more. It was a high water-mark for rap; finally, hip-hop could be ranked alongside the giants of rock'n'roll, legitimised by unignorable success. The fact that the short tour of small venues across the country where Jay would play only material from the new album all sold out within 60 seconds underlined Jay's A-list cultural standing.

Though Jay-Z's plan to shoot a mini-film for each track on the album never came to fruition, the record's videos, too, had impact. The clip for 'I Know' grabbed attention for its objective portrayal of the euphoria of the drug high, as four different girls blissed out across Manhattan to hallucinogenic visions of wall lights and skyscrapers, or the neon elation of the dancefloor. And the stylish Hype Williams promo for 'Blue Magic' was claimed by Harvard Professor Rawi E. Abdelal to be a "turning point in American pop culture's response to globalisation" by featuring stacks of euros in suitcases at a point when the dollar was

---

* As with *The Black Album*, *American Gangster* was also released as an a cappella album on Jay's 38th birthday, prompting remixers to make mash-up albums combining it with Led Zeppelin tracks, Bollywood classics or sound clips from *Godfather* movies.

in decline, highlighting the US's economic plight and its relation to a global economy to a populace for whom America was, until then, the world.

There was one further way in which *American Gangster* would go some way to changing the world. That winter, during an interview on the BET cable network, an influential Democrat senator with his eye on a very hot seat declared himself a fan of the record. And a bond was struck that would help make history.

Chapter Fifteen

World Leaders And Wedding Bells

"Having the President, on this campaign run, dust his shoulders off in front of the whole world," Jay-Z shook his head at me, dumbfounded. "It's like 'did he just do that? Does he have dandruff on his shoulder? Is that real?'"

It was real enough. At a press conference on April 17, 2008, under verbal attack from his Democratic presidential rival Hillary Clinton, who was using personal attacks he described as "textbook Washington" practices, Barack Obama lifted his hand to his shoulder and casually flicked off the dirt. When a spokesman confirmed Obama did have some Jay-Z records on his iPod, his youth support ballooned. Finally, here was a politician American youth culture could connect with, who didn't seem woefully out of touch, dismissive or afraid of hip-hop. Within two months, Obama was the selected Democrat candidate for the presidency. And Jay-Z would become one of his most vital unofficial cultural advisors.

Inevitably, given his growing status in business, Jay had begun to meet politicians. Bono had brought Bill Clinton to dinner with him at the Spotted Pig one night and, despite Clinton's 1992 denouncement of Sister Souljah for comments on the LA riots suggesting he wasn't particularly pro-rap, the pair got along a storm, Bill getting his picture taken with the restaurant staff, signing autographs and regaling Bono and Jay with tales from the White House in a back room for hours. But in the race between Barack Obama and Hillary Clinton for Democratic candidate in 2008, Jay saw hope in Obama, and quite a bit of himself. Obama was roughly his age – eight years his senior – and from the projects of Chicago, so, like Jay-Z, he was a figure of aspiration that a kid from the most unprivileged and downtrodden background can reach the pinnacles of modern society.

Where most politicians would distance themselves from such a controversial character, Obama saw the benefit in Jay-Z's support and advice, his connection with a segment of American society that rarely had its voice heard. At the start of his presidential campaign he called Jay and spoke for some hours about the issues concerning people in his culture and from his background. Jay expressed his disgust at Bush's dishonesty and his handling of the Katrina disaster; his support was pledged. Jay became an active Obama supporter, using his Heart Of The City tour that spring – 26 dates in arenas across America, co-headlined by Mary J. Blige, the most successful male/female urban music tour ever, grossing $34.2 million – to encourage his fans to vote. Onstage, when he reached the line "fuck Bush" in 'Blue Magic', he'd drop out of the song and leap into his Katrina anthem 'Minority Report', the stage backed with a huge image of Obama. The message, presumably, hit home.

Over the course of Obama's race for the White House, Jay performed regular voter-drive gigs across the country, funded by the Democratic Party but with Jay taking no fee himself. He became well acquainted with the man who would be king. "Every time I talk to Jay-Z, who is a brilliant talent and a good guy, I enjoy how he thinks," Obama told *Rolling Stone* magazine. "That's somebody who is going to start branching out and can help shape attitudes in a real positive way."[1]

Not that Jay was likely to branch off into politics himself. "I get that question now and it's really baffling to me from where my background is," he told me. "In political circles they like to pretend like they have this thing, these unrealistic rules and guidelines, you have to be perfect, you've never done anything, you can't say this. I think that's why Obama won, he became more of a real person. There's more perception, and I'm not into that. I'm gonna say a lot of inappropriate things and it's four years, a term is four years! Imagine how many bad things and politically incorrect things you say. Forget about it!"

Jay felt more able to pin his colours to Obama's mast since he was no longer a captain of industry. On Christmas Eve 2007 he'd announced his stepping down from the post of Def Jam president from the start of 2008, his statement reading: "I am pleased to have had the opportunity to build upon the Def Jam legacy. Now it's time for me to take on new challenges." After three years heading the label he'd become starkly aware of its limitations, throwing money at an outmoded model of simply selling records when profits were sliding off to other areas of the music market, and not using his tenacity in broadening the label's scope to take in clothing, headphones and other assorted paraphernalia. It was, he felt, a stubborn and immovable label full of people basking in long-dead glories and cemented in an old industry image, while he was looking to the future.

"People hear all this talk about problems in the industry, they think these guys are going broke," he told the *Observer*'s Alex Blimes. "They're not. It's just that they were making 6 billion a year and now they're making 1 billion. It's still a billion dollars... I'm more than happy. In the music business most people have one artist under their name that they live off of for the rest of their life. Like, 'Oh, he signed that person'. Twenty years later it's like, 'Yeah, what else?' I took an artist a year: Kanye, Ne-Yo and Rihanna. That's way past my quota."[2]

Instead, Jay focused on his own business expansion, launching new 40/40 clubs in Las Vegas* and Atlantic City and buying himself out

---

* The Vegas club stretched over 24,000 square feet, contained 84 plasma screens, had 24-carat gold lining in its floors and was opened at a VIP launch party attended by Jay, Beyoncé, Joe Jackson, Ne-Yo and LeBron James. Unfortunately, due to dwindling attendance, it was closed within a year.

of his Def Jam contract (with only one album remaining on it) for $5 million in order to get back his masters and explore other outlets to release his music, allegedly looking into deals with Apple and a joint label with Beyoncé. Instead, in April 2008 he signed a 10-year deal worth $150 million with Live Nation, very similar to one put together by the conglomerate entertainment company for Madonna the previous year. A 360 deal – i.e. Live Nation would take a percentage from every aspect of Jay-Z's income, including albums, live shows, merchandise and his cut of management deals – it gave Jay a $25 million advance for his recordings, the same for his live shows, $20 million for publishing and licensing rights, 775,000 shares in Live Nation plus $50 million to start up his own label he'd call Roc Nation.* Jay saw Roc Nation as the next generation of record labels; it wouldn't merely produce and sell records, it would have management wings, creative consultancy arms, publishing departments and look after artists, songwriters, producers and sound engineers. It would produce a line of headphones called Skullcandy, collaborate on merchandise with the New York Yankees and sign acts including Jermaine Cole, The Ting Tings, Mark Ronson and Wale, licensing the release of their music on an album-by-album basis through other major labels rather than distributing the records itself. Jay's first album for Roc Nation, for example, would come out via Atlantic, a record he was planning to complete a trilogy long since left unfinished.

The whole concept of Roc Nation spoke to Jay-Z's core philosophy. "It's an integration of all my interests," he told the *Observer*. "In hip-hop it's always been about the culture. It's not just music, it's fashion, it's business, it's lifestyle. I'm an entrepreneur. This allows me the freedom to do all those things without it being a fight."[3]

"It happened at a time when I was looking for a different approach to what the music business was going to look like in 10 years," he said to *The Wall Street Journal*. "There's a big variable on the equation. I was at the end of Def Jam and I was already preaching that idea to them.

---

* Alongside Roc Nation, Jay also launched StarRoc, a label in association with Norwegian production team Stargate.

[I said] why don't you give me a fund? Let me go out and acquire things. It would take the relief off of having to have a hit [song]. These things could help generate revenue while we found and developed great artists."[4]

His Roc Nation corner office was far swisher than the dive he'd started Roc-A-Fella in down on John Street: 1411 Broadway, 39th floor, the view panoramic, the Empire State practically his window-ledge ornament. A huge leather swivel chair before an imposing desk, on which he could spin to take in the Platinum discs and pictures on the wall – framed shots of Jimi Hendrix, Ray Charles, Muhammad Ali, Naomi Campbell, Cindy Crawford, Christy Turlington, members of his family, a downtime Beyoncé and himself meeting Prince Charles, hung in prime position over a scale model of the new Nets stadium. In pride of place, an original Warhol. It was an office resplendent in his wealth, standing and success. He could prosper here.

The deal with Roc Nation also allowed him to prosper in the live arena. It meant that Jay-Z went from earning up to $300,000 per gig to around $1 million, allowing him to put on bigger, more elaborate stage shows with full bands, brass orchestras and expensive sets that only the likes of Eminem had managed within hip-hop before. It was an important step in terms of rap's global profile – now the genre was as big as the huge rock tours not just in numbers but in spectacle.

And, beyond his own shows, Jay-Z's eyes were on an even greater crossover prize. The festival circuit.

"Records are covered," he told *The Wall Street Journal*. "We can make records in our sleep. Live Nation's specialty is touring. We came up with a plan to put together a touring schedule that would make this thing profitable. We really concentrated on building that profile. Playing Glastonbury, Coachella. There are certain posts I've always had on the bulletin board: Madison Square Garden, Yankee Stadium. Central Park is the next one. If we walked up to the Yankees cold, without Glastonbury, without Coachella, without those things under our portfolio, I don't know if Yankee Stadium gets done."[5]

First stop, the mystical vale of Avalonian hedonism that is Glastonbury. On February 2, 2008, organiser Michael Eavis, at the behest of his daughter Emily and with the intent to "break with tradition this time and put on something totally different", announced Glastonbury's first ever Pyramid Stage hip-hop headline act. "[Jay-Z] will appeal to the young people and under 25s," he said, "so that's a big pull for them. It's not like the traditional one we do, like Radiohead, Coldplay and Muse and Oasis." It was a major step up for rap, a barrier-crushing acceptance of the genre into the highest levels of musical culture – hip-hop had officially 'made it'. But as with all important emancipations throughout history, the reaction from the traditionalists was complete shock and denial. "I'm sorry, but Jay-Z?" said Oasis' Noel Gallagher to the BBC. "No chance. Glastonbury has a tradition of guitar music and even when they throw the odd curve ball in on a Sunday night you go 'Kylie Minogue?' I don't know about it. But I'm not having hip-hop at Glastonbury. It's wrong."

Noel at first seemed to have the festival-goers' backing: the event that usually sold out within hours saw slow sales for the first time in a decade. But Jay-Z was adamant that his booking was a progressive move by Glastonbury and music as a whole. "We don't play guitars, Noel," he said in an interview with *The Sun*'s Bizarre section, "but hip-hop has put in its work like any other form of music. This headline show is just a natural progression. Rap music is still evolving. From Afrika Bambaataa DJing in the Bronx and Run-D.M.C. going Platinum, to Jazzy Jeff & The Fresh Prince winning the first rap Grammy, I'm just next in the line. We have to respect each other's genre of music and move forward."

"There's an education process that needs to take place," he expanded in the *Observer*. "I'd like to sit him down, play him some really great poetic music, some incredible, well-produced hip-hop. He made a blanket statement. He hasn't heard every hip-hop record and I haven't heard every rock record so I can't make a blanket statement and say rock doesn't belong somewhere. I can't say that. I can say Noel Gallagher rips off The Beatles. I can say that. Because I've heard his music. But I can't say rock music rips off The Beatles. It's too general."[6]

"It felt like a chance to open the door for hip-hop again," he said in a later *Observer* interview. "It was almost like hip-hop had to prove itself yet again in that type of arena and performing there really brought it home."[7]

"That felt more like me progressing and knocking down a different barrier more than a thing with me and Noel," he told me. "I think it was more about [Glastonbury], we were arguing about that, not arguing with each other. He was 'I wanted it to be like I always saw it!' And I was like 'No, the world is changing.' It was really more a couple of people still trying to hold on to the tradition of what it has always been."

There was no such uproar when Jay announced a string of other European festival headline slots for the summer of 2008, including Denmark's Roskilde, Norway's Hove Festival and the O2 Festival in London's Hyde Park. But beneath the fuss and promotion of these huge shows, there was one event, possibly the biggest of Jay-Z's life, that was being kept very quiet indeed...

Silver candelabras unloaded onto the sidewalk from a truck. A white tent spotted on the roof of a Tribeca penthouse. Container box after container box carried inside, hiding away 50,000 orchids. Beyoncé's mother Tina Knowles spotted in Manhattan, as were the other members of Destiny's Child. It would have taken the most intrepid investigative reporter to have gained enough evidence that something major was afoot before it was too late, but plenty of press managed to follow the scent of matrimony from the rumours of a marriage licence being obtained at the village hall in upmarket Scarsdale, New York, to the reception being surreptitiously put together atop the couple's Manhattan apartment block.

Around 5.50 p.m. on April 4, 2008, Tina Knowles arrived at the Tribeca apartment, followed 20 minutes later by Beyoncé's father Mathew. At 6.30 p.m. Jay-Z's Maybach pulled up; an hour later Chris Martin and Gwyneth Paltrow were on the scene. Early evening, according to those in the know, Jay-Z and Beyoncé were wed in front of an invited audience of around 30 – Jay later told Oprah Winfrey that the couple had offended some people by their lack of an invite, but that those who really loved them would understand. The marriage entered public record on April 22. The closest America could get to a royal wedding was a strictly private affair.*

So it was as man and wife that Jay-Z and Beyoncé rode a tour bus to Shepton Mallet in Somerset that June – despite Glastonbury's legendary inclement conditions, they decided against the diva's approach of helicoptering in. Fresh from another hit with his guest spot on Lil Wayne's 'Mr Carter', Jay was in confident, playful mood and stunned by the size of the festival – "when you come over the hill and you see all those tents… that's when it stopped being [just] a concert," he told the *Observer*, "I was like, 'Wait a minute, this ain't a festival. This is a country! This is tent city.'"[8]

With BBC director Alan Yentob following him with a film crew to record this historic event for a documentary, Jay, Beyoncé and Bleek geared themselves up for the show in their backstage dressing room compound, deciding only an hour before showtime to mock Noel's comments by opening with a strummed attempt at the Oasis classic 'Wonderwall', designed to make the song sound lame and plodding in comparison to the hip-hop scream of '99 Problems' that would follow it. Watching other acts on the Pyramid Stage – the festival's main stage – from the side, Jay was staggered by the size of the crowd, 180,000 people stretching as far as he could see, the biggest crowd he'd ever witnessed, and it was chanting his name in huge rising crescendos in anticipation of his arrival. A delighted and relieved Emily Eavis would later claim she'd never seen the field so full and described Jay's triumphant, critic-defying set as "the most brilliant pop cultural crossover moment".[9]

Looking back on the rapturous reception and mass singalongs that greeted what he considered to be a career high point, he'd tell me, "I

---

* Far more private, it's asserted, than their first row as a married couple, which onlookers claim to have seen at the side of the stage at Jay-Z's show at the Hollywood Bowl a few weeks after the nuptuals, sparked by Jay jokingly stopping the DJ playing 'Crazy In Love'.

rank it as one of those moments like when I first got a Grammy. It's one of those moments for me. It felt like a cultural shift. It was a moment in time, it was a breaking down of barriers. And the people were ready for it, as we see as soon as I walked out, right? The people wanted it, the people was like 'No, we like Jay-Z and we like Noel, we like both of you guys'."

"Music should not be separated or segregated," he said to *Clash* magazine. "Live performance or anywhere. We live in the age of the iPod and people have everything on there all together; Kings of Leon next to Kanye West or Lil Wayne... There were these few people, a minority hanging on to this outdated idea of tradition. But the masses spoke the moment I walked out and the people were ready."[10]

After Glastonbury, nothing could be the same. The track '99 Problems' re-entered the UK charts four years after its initial release, on the back of its masterstroke opening at the festival. Jay headlined the Wireless Festival and the Milton Keynes Bowl, neither of them giving him quite the same buzz. He broke down similar barriers in the US, replacing the Beastie Boys as headliners at the predominantly rock-based All Points West Festival in New York, but it didn't seem such a pivotal moment. Jay-Z, and rap itself, had arrived; his new wife was about to publicly reveal her $5 million wedding ring designed by Lorraine Schwartz for the first time at New York's Fashion Rocks show that September; Obama would soon be on the phone again, encouraging him to play free voter-drive shows in the lead-up to the presidential election; and his philanthropic pursuits were in full flow too, playing the Africa Rising Festival in Nigeria to help highlight the plight of the continent.* He was happily married, culturally accepted, politically influential, immensely rich.† What more was there for Jay-Z to do?

---

* One faintly ludicrous rumour reported in the press from the Nigeria trip was that Jay had asked hotel staff to carve out of watermelon a replica of Beyoncé's breasts and deliver it to their room, using two cherries for the nipples.

† In January 2009 *Forbes* magazine placed Jay-Z and Beyoncé at the top of their list of high-earning couples, listing a combined income of $162 million between June 2007 and June 2008.

There was a trilogy to finish.

Heralded as early as January 2008 when DJ Clue yelled "off that *Blueprint 3* baby!" on a Timbaland track called 'I Ain't' released on a mix-tape (although that track didn't make the album), several times already Jay-Z had tried to start writing the third *Blueprint* album, but it was a project that had eluded him. Until, at his show at the Manchester MEN Arena on July 19, Kanye arrived for his onstage guest spot* with a CD of fully-synced new beats, a full album's worth he'd been stockpiling for Jay. "This is the new album," he said, counteracting Timbaland's claim to MTV that he would be producing all of Jay-Z's next album.† Jay loved the cockiness of Kanye's move.

"When it was the first *Blueprint*, he didn't have any opinion on anything," he said. "He didn't dare. He laid the beat and was just happy to have a beat on there. You know, now he's fucking Kanye West. We're going into the studio and having these tug of wars over the direction of a song, or how this should sound. Things like that. It was fantastic, I like it that he has the ego."[11]

Over the course of the following year, Jay and Kanye would bat the tracks back and forth, completing a full album by November 2008 but then going back to rework it, ditching many of the original CD's tracks and replacing them with even brighter and bolder numbers. One tune that didn't eventually make the cut was 'Jockin' Jay-Z', a track performed by the pair at the close of Kanye's own Madison Square Garden show on August 6 that relived some of the high points of Jay's year, how he "rock wit' Obama", his spat with Noel – "that bloke from Oasis said I couldn't play guitar/Somebody shoulda told 'em I'm a fuckin' rock star" he rapped before stealing a line from 'Wonderwall' – and the rock-style bonuses of his Glastonbury triumph: "180,000 screaming... it's too easy, I got ladies on shoulders showing me their chi-chis."

---

* Producer Mark Ronson also appeared onstage with Jay that night.
† Jay-Z and Timbaland had discussed this idea but no official decision had been made when Timbaland went public with the idea.

As his birthday rode around again – a limo ride around Paris with Beyoncé from L'Avenue restaurant to the Crazy Horse cabaret club – it was clear that the final *Blueprint* album would be no rushed job. Perfectionism was the key, and Jay would take the project very personally indeed…

Chapter Sixteen

Completing The Blueprint

Word went around the live room of Hampstead's AIR Studios like electric tumbleweed. "Hova's here," the hacks hissed, thrilled that this wouldn't be any ordinary album playback, the usual stale nibbles and three lukewarm lagers in a Soho hotel conference room, "he's going to play it to us personally…"

Sure enough, the 20 or so UK journalists selected by their editors to conduct interviews with Jay-Z about his new album *The Blueprint 3* over his few UK press days in August 2009 were ushered into the studio's control room where Jay-Z sat swinging his legs over the front of a platform before the mixing desk, his personal black iPod plugged into the studio's gigantic surround-sound system, twinkling with what appeared to be embedded diamonds. Over the course of an hour Jay chatted easily to the assembled writers while playing them songs from the album, each a barrelling blitz of hip-hop invention cut short by 30 seconds by Jay in case anyone had snuck in any secret recording equipment – with his albums leaking so regularly, and several songs from *The Blueprint 3* already leaked, Jay was taking no chances. Nonetheless, *The Blueprint 3* was clearly a dazzling step forward for Jay, a flurry of his peak rhymes set to sizzling modern beats, and one major standout tune that whooshed from the speakers, Jay's biggest hook ever: "In New York, concrete jungle where dreams are made…"

To have a major new album played to you by the artist themselves was a rare treat; Jay-Z's personal dedication to overseeing the promotion and publicity of his new album was endearing, and a little brave too, as was his jaunt out with Rihanna that evening to the Vendome club in Mayfair where he'd reportedly spend £7,000 on champagne and cocktails, and his desire to go jogging in Hyde Park at 3 a.m., a plan thwarted by his wary security men. Brave, considering that very month one Leon Desmond Barrett of Detroit had been arrested for allegedly being behind a string of death threats towards Jay-Z and Beyoncé between 2006 and 2009. "I'm getting ready to start killing some more people," he wrote on August 18, 2007. "Beyoncé, Jay-Z, Jerome Bettis and Tune-Up Man are the first four people I'm getting ready to kill."

The following day, sitting down to interview Jay in a Park Lane hotel suite, he seemed to this writer remarkably open and unassuming, as I questioned him over whether he'd always envisioned *The Blueprint* as a trilogy. "Yeah," he said, "I just never had a reason to do the third one before. I thought it was time to lay a blueprint for the next generation because everyone's making this type of music to fit onto radio because the sales are so bad, so everyone can't play around, understandably so. People are being concerned about their career so they're making songs to fit the format and I thought it was a great time to lay down the blueprint and be fearless and make music just because it sounds good. That's why I put out 'D.O.A.' first, because it was more of a challenge, a call to arms, like 'come on, let's go!' People took it as I was putting the younger generation down but I'm not, I'm really challenging them to make great music. I want them to be great, that's not a bad thing.

"I like to do things in threes, like I did the first trilogy, the 'Lifetime' series, and I always wanted to do the third [*Blueprint*] but I didn't have a reason until now. So I didn't do it. If you look at the first *Blueprint* it was a return to my roots, the soul samples and the music I grew up on, and the second one was a double album because it was all my influences, the music that I love, Lenny Kravitz on the rock and Jean Paul on the reggae and Faith Evans for R&B, it was all over the place. This one I guess is a bit of both, right, because we are becoming those icons that we looked up to growing up. So it's classic in that way and it also has a lot of my influences and the music I listen to now. I call it 'new classic'. It's not predicated on what's playing on the radio, it's just music for the sake of music, it sounds good. People emulate things that come out before them so there's so much [to emulate] now, so people go off in so many different directions. I want to get back to making music."

I pressed Jay on his latest bout of haters – his one-time collaborator Lil Wayne had recently claimed Jay was old and in the way. "First of all it's not up to me," Jay said, "it's up to the people. I wouldn't be in the way of the people who are like me. That's not what happens. Rakim was the greatest rapper of all time, he's somehow moved aside, not because he said 'okay, I'm stepping down guys'; it doesn't happen like that. The bigger you get the more haters you have. It's part of the process. People would rather root for the underdog."

He smirked, nodding. "Me too, I know the feeling."

Damn right he did. Having rooted for the cultural and political underdog that was Barack Obama throughout the presidential run in 2008, at the start of 2009 he was ecstatic to be invited to Washington to attend Obama's inauguration as America's 44th president, and to perform at various celebratory events. At the tiny, rammed and jumping Club Love on January 18 he hit the stage at a Young Jeezy after-party with two hefty security men flanking him and Beyoncé and Akon looking on to perform a new remix of Jeezy's 'My President Is Black', prefaced by Jeezy thanking "the guy who threw two shoes and Bush and the guys that helped him move his shit out". Jay's freshly penned verse on the epic cut featured a chunk of a poem about black emancipation that circulated on the internet in the wake of Obama's election – "Rosa Parks sat so Martin Luther could walk/Martin Luther walked so Barack Obama could run/Barack Obama ran so all our children could fly" – and threw this historic event back in the faces of anyone upset about having a black president by pointing out he was "half-white, so even if you've got a racist mind it's all right". Rounding off his lyric with an anti-Bush pun ("you can keep your puss, I don't want no more Bush/No more war, no more Iraq, no more lies…") and with his verse interrupted by wild jubilation at his most pertinent lines – "My president is black but his house is all white" – he posited his verse as a pointer to the potential of the black American following Obama's success, and left the cramped, overwhelmed stage to rabid howls and flapping stars'n'stripes from a crowd in unison with Jeezy's shout: "I'm so proud to be black right now I don't know what to say, nigga."

Two days later, Jay proudly took his seat to watch Obama's inauguration, waving George W. off in his helicopter out of the White House alongside Beyoncé, Sean Combs and Mary J. Blige. At Beyoncé's show at the Lincoln Memorial that day Jay was out among the audience, sharing the experience with the public and rejoicing in America's new chance for change. His faith in the US political system crushed by the Bush administration, he'd been ready to quit America for good if McCain/Palin had won, his best attempts to make a difference to a political hierarchy that controlled his and everyone else's lives thwarted, the anti-rap political lobby back in command, his culture frozen out once again. Instead, on January 21, he found himself in a tuxedo and black-framed glasses performing a free show for 4,000 of Barack's Obama For America campaign workers and volunteers at the exclusive Staff Ball, where he rapped the altered line "I got 99 problems but a Bush ain't one" and unveiled a new track produced especially for the occasion, 'History'.

Introducing it by asking the crowd to raise the Roc diamonds to celebrate how "you made history!", it was a lyric akin to a Greek lyric poem, with Jay rapping over a sumptuous soft-rock synth track with hints of 'The Star-Spangled Banner'.* Jay was the central

---

* The recorded version of 'History' featured Cee-Lo singing the stirring, patriotic chorus; it was a Kanye production sampling Veronique Sanson's 'Une Nuit Sur Ton Epaule'.

character representing America, involved with four women named Victory, Defeat, Success and Death: he was tied to Defeat while he hunted out her sister Victory in order to have a child with her called History. While waiting for History's time, he flirted with Death (by hustling) and Success (through rap) but found both shallow devotions compared with the lasting glory of finding Victory and leaving History as his legacy, speaking his name through generations. It was a crude metaphor for his part in Obama's triumph and the historic import of his win, sure, but great events sometimes call for broad, heroic statements, and 'History' unified political upheaval with popular culture like never before.

"I think he's restored hope around the world," he told me, referencing the celebrations that went on in Paris and London upon Obama's victory, "not just America, all around the world, which is all we can ask for. That's why we wake up in the morning, that's what pushed you and drives you. I've been moved and affected by it, absolutely."

"Obama represents so much hope for blacks and Latinos," Jay said to *Cigar Aficionado* magazine. "The hope he represents is bigger than any of the huge problems he could possibly correct. When you have positive role models, you can change your life for the better. The day Obama got elected, the gangsta became less relevant."

The year 2009 was one of celebrations for Jay-Z. In March, dazzling the crowd with a natty business suit and confetti cannons, he was one of a coterie of businessmen, NYC politicians and high-level industry figures who attended the ground-breaking ceremony for the Barclays Center, the new arena in Brooklyn for the Brooklyn Nets. The scheme had been a long time starting, hobbled by a recession that was costing it $35 million annually, harangued with lawsuits from a group called Develop – Don't Destroy Brooklyn and beset with rocketing construction costs hitting $1 billion. The team itself was on the back foot too, with attendance down to 1,000 per game and the team managing only 12 wins out of 80. But Jay had negotiated and canvassed hard in senior government for the scheme to go ahead, and the speech he made that day was full of local pride and colour, of bringing ambition and hope to the streets of Brooklyn. Plus, he had a plan in mind. His good friend

LeBron James was up for transfer, and Jay might just be the man to bring him to Brooklyn.*

In the meantime, *The Blueprint 3* was taking ever firmer shape. With fine-tuning being done on the album's track listing, Kanye – whose tracks were making up most of the album so took the role of main producer – suggested to Jay that they go to one of his favourite studios in Hawaii to record. It was partly to try to contain any leaks of material, partly to avoid the distractions of New York or LA and their perpetual hangers-on, and partly because the island had "a good vibe". Though sessions took place over 2008 and 2009 around the world, from studios in New York, Cleveland, Miami and LA to the Holy Chateau in Perth, Australia, the bulk of the album came together at Hawaii's Avex Honolulu Studios, where the very first track they recorded went down remarkably smooth, but would put a bomb under urban music, lay down a new law of rap. *The Blueprint 3* was already setting new standards, higher expectations, and his unwilling pupils out in the wider world of hip-hop were about to get a harsh lesson in anti-fakery.

The crisp but dislocated vocals. The unnatural, synthesised flickers between notes that could come from no human vocal chords. The hollow, plastic cheapness of the thing. It was fine when Cher had popularised the technique on her monster dancefloor hit 'Believe' in 1998, exposing a trade secret to innovative effect, but the use of this voice-correcting studio software had spread like a virus through music since, making divas out of donkeys and eliminating in the popular singer the need to be able to sing.

---

* In the end, he wasn't, though the efforts of the Nets to secure LeBron's signature that summer were extensive. Russian billionaire Mikhail Prokhorov – who bought 80 per cent of the Nets and 45 per cent of the stadium from Ratner in July 2009 for $200 million, so enamoured was he with the idea of working with Jay-Z – rented a huge billboard opposite Madison Square Garden when LeBron was playing there and posted a 225-foot picture of himself and Jay-Z on it with the slogan 'The Blueprint For Greatness' splashed across it but, despite giving the Nets the first meeting, LeBron eventually settled with Miami Heat.

The final straw for Jay-Z was a TV commercial for Wendy's new toffee coffee twisted frosty. A group of parched office workers transformed into a white-clad boyband, spinning on their hands and singing about the refreshing nature of the fast-food ice-based product in voices that were set to Auto-Tune extreme, undulating electronically to a comedy degree.

Watching at home, Jay felt a little ashamed and angry that it'd come to this. He'd seen Auto-Tune being used across urban music, in original and brilliant ways by a few visionary talents – indeed, he and Kanye had even tried their hand at using Auto-Tune themselves for one track – and in lazy, formulaic, chart-pleasing ways by many musical chancers who just wanted to get played on the radio. Gradually he'd come to see the technology as the enemy of hip-hop at its most fundamental level, the point and focus of which was to highlight and represent the humanity of the rapper's life and experiences. By robotising the songs, the rapper became distant, unreal. And Jay-Z in 2009 was all about the real.

"I don't have a problem with Auto-Tune," he told me that August, "I think it's really cool, but when 10 people use it, not 1,000. It's like 'C'mon, I heard that record already, I don't wanna hear the same thing'. I would have a problem with speed-rap if everyone was dibeddy-dibeddy-dibeddy, it would drive me insane. Too much of anything is bad. If I ate apple pie every day my teeth will rot, and I love apple pie. I like music, I wanna hear different kinds of music. Let's move past Auto-Tune, let 10 people use it, whoever does it really well and all the pretty girls, let them use it. The rest of you guys, the other 90 per cent, let's figure something else out."

So, on day one in Hawaii, for the sake of rap culture, Jay set about killing Auto-Tune. Opening with a splurge of atonal soprano saxophone and guitars and Jay's purposefully out-of-tune rendition of Steam's 1969 number one 'Na Na Hey Hey Kiss Him Goodbye' (made more famous in the UK by Bananarama in 1983) as if to wave goodbye to the machine, Jay and No I.D. launched into a gritty, grungy slab of garage-soul* that revelled in its rough edges, psychedelic jazz segments

---

* Using samples from 'In The Space' by Janko Nilovic and Dave Sucky, French film composers.

and unashamed air of unrefinement. This was 'D.O.A. (Death Of Auto-Tune)', a rallying call of realness. "I know we facin' a recession," Jay barked at other rappers, "but the music y'all makin' gonna make it the Great Depression," before going on to berate the modern rapper for his lack of aggression, obsession with chart placings and flamboyant styles. A track seething with an energised urgency to revitalise a rap scene slipping into chart-friendly complacency, it even stopped to have a swipe at the church of iTunes at which all modern music seemed to be worshipping. "'D.O.A. (Death Of Auto-Tune)' was my way of telling artists 'No, it's the other way around: you make music and iTunes come and get it, you don't make music for them,'" Jay told me.

Of course, having recorded it, they immediately wiped the album of any Auto-Tuning that might have crept on there, or else face the wrath of those rappers who were offended by Jay-Z's anti-Auto-Tune stance on the song's release as *The Blueprint 3*'s first single on June 5.* "Jay-Z, he has a lot of fans," said DJ Webstar in an interview for RealTalkNY.net, "he's done a lot for hip-hop. I'm a fan of Jay-Z. I was shocked when he did that. Mary J. and Drake just did a song with Auto-Tune. Drake and the whole Young Money just did Auto-Tune. If you take every song off the radio, what would you have? The biggest records of the year all had Auto-Tune – who are you to say people don't wanna hear it?"[1] Lil Wayne weighed in too, telling Radio One DJ Tim Westwood, "Stop it, stop it. No, there's no such thing as 'Death of Auto-Tune'. [Auto-Tune specialist rapper] T-Pain is my dude. He's been on everybody's single, and he had Auto-Tune on every single one of them. So, every song I do with him, he better have Auto-Tune on it. I love it. Keep your Auto-Tune popping. Auto-Tune ain't dead. You've got the whole game using that." And The Game responded on record, recording a track called 'I'm So Wavy (Death Of Hov)' that attacked Jay for being too old and out of touch with modern rap movements. On his first performance

---

* The date the song went to radio, played for the first time on Hot 97. As part of Jay-Z's new approach to the modern consumer music market, the song was only available to hear on radio and to download digitally on June 23 and no physical copies were made.

of the song at the Summer Jam at Giants Stadium that summer, T-Pain surprised Jay by turning up onstage to duet on 'Death Of Auto-Tune'.

Immune to backbiting and criticism from rival rappers by now, Jay pressed ahead with his revisionist rap concept. The video for 'D.O.A....' was one long metaphor for stripping away hip-hop artifice, featuring Jay rapping with a full rock band in a deserted warehouse between shots of exploding jewellery, fancy costumes and champagne bottles to signify rap gimmicks being blown apart. Whether the cameo appearances by Harvey Keitel playing cards and LeBron James playing basketball could be considered gimmicks is open to argument, but they certainly weren't blown up.

Though 'D.O.A. (Death Of Auto-Tune)' was only a modest hit, reaching number 24, it became one of Jay-Z's most highly respected singles, winning him another Grammy for Best Rap Solo Performance the following year, being ranked the song of the year by MTV and ramping up the hype for *The Blueprint 3* as a confrontational and experimental new challenge for Jay. Ironically, the next single upfront of *The Blueprint 3* would be exactly the sort of R&B chart warble that would so often utilise Auto-Tune, even though Rihanna's landmark vocal was entirely natural. 'Run This Town' was a brilliant Kanye and No I.D. joint* with a compulsive military bark-beat, gritty and urgent grunge guitar riffs and Rihanna's silky 'ay-ay' chorus melding seamlessly into what sounded like an ultra-modern radio smash, topped off with a spirited verse from Kanye added at the very last minute (which many critics applauded as being better than Jay's) about his own whirlwind success and the pitfalls it brings†, a sentiment reminiscent of Jay's 'Lifetime' era. Released shortly after Jay completed a five-date tour of the US with Ciara in July, it gave him his biggest *Billboard* hit so far, peaking at number two (and becoming his first UK number one as the lead artist), won two Grammys and was used as the intro song for the

---

* From a sample of a 1970s Greek band called The 4 Levels Of Existence, a track called 'Someday In Athens'.

† 'Run This Town' was the seventh single featuring Kanye West to sell over 2 million copies.

World Series, proof of its own theme – that Jay, Kanye, Rihanna and Roc Nation ran New York now, and that everyone should join their black-clad rap army.

Between the poker metaphors and general self-promotion of Jay-Z's rap, though, some found sinister references. The line "peace God... ain't nobody fresher/I'm in Maison, uh, Martin Margiela" was mis-heard by some to say "I'm in Mason", which they took as an admission by Jay that he'd joined the shadowy order of Freemasonry, an anonymous organisation which is said to include many high-ranking industry figures secretly influencing public affairs and arranging clandestine deals. While it's not unlikely that Jay-Z may have had dealings and associations with Freemasons in his many business affairs, this was no evidence of membership, instead Jay was referencing the high-class clothing line Maison Martin Margiela, a label he'd been photographed wearing. But once a rumour like this is sparked, there's an entire internet full of conspiracy theorists climbing over each other to find or fabricate further proof of it.

The video was a major source of 'evidence' of Jay's Masonic links and even a rumoured involvement with a secret but hugely influential 18th century group called the Illuminati, made popular by Dan Brown's mega-selling novel *The Da Vinci Code* but almost certainly nonexistent outside fiction in the modern day. Some, including Jaz-O, pointed to the masked and hooded outfits worn by Jay, Kanye and Rihanna in the song's video and the fact that they were surrounded by a subversive rebel mob in ancient stone vaults as representing rituals of an age-old secret cult and the idea of a Luciferian New World Order taking over society.[*] Others brought in the mysterious sculpture of white-painted instruments on the sleeve of the new album as representing an altar splashed with three blood-red slashes, a number important in Kabbalah; the fact that he wore a T-shirt bearing the line "do what thou wilt" in a trailer for

---

[*] A man holding a torch up to Rihanna at the start of the video, it's claimed, is a reference to occult practices of raising the Torch Of Illumination to Lucifer, a symbol repeated in such monuments as the Statue Of Liberty, which theorists argue is a gift from Freemason sects in France.

the 'Run This Town' video, the official motto of Aleister Crowley's Ordo Templi Orientis cult, with links to Freemasonry, Illuminati and Kabbalah; and designs on his Rocawear clothes resembling the head of the goat demon Baphomet, the ancient Egyptian Eye of Horus and the all-seeing eye symbol of Freemasonry. Director Anthony Mandler claimed the video, filmed in New York's Fort Totten Park rather than any mystical temple, reflected tribalism and rebellion in Brazil, the Middle East and Africa, bringing out the song's atmosphere of rising chaos, but to this day the rumours of Jay-Z being a member of various secret and occult groups – and that he'd happily and openly admit to it in his rhymes or hint at it at every opportunity from clothing design to baby name – persist.

All of this myth, hype and chatter highlighted how ardently anticipated the final instalment in the *Blueprint* trilogy was, ever since Jay had unveiled its title on the Shade 45 radio station in July. And the album itself didn't disappoint. Shifted forward three days to September 8 due to huge popular demand*, it was a worthy collection to take Jay into the history books – his 11th number one album†, beating Elvis to the record for the most solo number one albums in the US ever.

Where many previous Jay-Z albums opened with a spoken word intro or a brief prologue outlining where he was at in his life and career at that time, *The Blueprint 3* leapt straight into the experimental strangeness, challenging listeners from the off. Empire Of The Sun were a psychedelic synth-pop act from Australia, the latest outing from Luke Steele, frontman of The Sleepy Jackson on a more flamboyant sort of tip – he dressed for Empire Of The Sun like a futuristic chieftan priest, all neon wizard jackets and ice-king headdresses. An unusual collaborator for Jay-Z but *The Blueprint 3* was all about trying new directions, and Kanye's 'What We Talkin' About' was certainly unexplored territory

---

* The album had leaked in full on August 31, an event which Jay accepted with a far more sanguine approach than he had previously. "I may be the most bootlegged artist in history," he told MTV. "It's a preview. I'm excited for people to hear the album. I'm very proud of the work I've done, so enjoy it."[2]

† On the back of 467,000 first-week sales.

for Jay, delving into the highly on-trend indie synth-psych akin to MGMT while Steele delivered a falsetto gasp of a chorus that floated over the track like a gleaming spectre. In the lyric, Jay laid down a blueprint for his new rhyming direction – no more gossip and beefs*, he vowed to dedicate his words to what was real about life, its pain, shame and despair rather than anything as shallow as drug profits, gun crime or revenge – "ain't nothing cool about carrying a strap/'Bout worrying your moms or burying your best cat." He promised to press forward musically rather than recreating his past and not to help ghettoise rap by cordoning it off away from other music, having worked so hard to get the genre accepted by the world at large. And he gives us a reason for this fresh start, this line drawn under his previous work, these new outlooks and fresh rules. He saw Obama's election, which he allowed himself to take a small amount of credit for, as a chance for the culture to come together behind "the dream as predicted by Martin Luther" and move hip-hop on to a more universal level. Jay-Z, it seemed, had a dream…

His more magnanimous outlook carried over to the album's first boast rap, 'Thank You', a sumptuous old Vegas horn sway from Kanye sampling Marcos Valle's 'Ele E Ela' on which Jay, with huge dollops of tongue-in-cheek faux modesty, delivered an awards acceptance speech for his 11 number one albums, his ringside seats at Pacquiao fights and boxes at the opera. He even thanks the rival rappers he was going to try to kill off but who managed to demolish their own careers without him even trying, in a comedy final verse that imagined them not only flying planes into their careers, 9/11-style, but then racing to the site and breathing in the toxins to finish themselves off. And if this puffing of ego so early in the album seemed premature, Jay justified it by following it with two already huge hit songs – 'D.O.A. (Death Of Auto-Tune)' and 'Run This Town' – and one that would become bigger than anyone could possibly imagine.

---

* Although he did find space to have pops at Dash and Jaz-O, the latter for not signing his deal with Roc-A-Fella and thereby missing out on potentially huge sums.

'Empire State Of Mind' was, in terms of Jay-Z's career, an empire in itself. The album's only track from producers Al Shux, Janet Sewell-Ulepic and Angela Hunte, it was an instant hit from the opening tinkle of piano keys and luxuriant chords to Alicia Keys' soaring chorus in celebration of the Big Apple, exactly the sort of celebratory sentiment the city needed almost 10 years on from the World Trade Center attacks. It was a reclamation of New York's stunted pride, but its origins were half a world away. Writers and producers Hunte and Sewell-Ulepic, both Brooklynites, were feeling homesick on a holiday in London in February 2009, and decided to write a song in celebration of the city they missed. "We said to ourselves, we complain so much about New York – about the busy streets, about the crowds and the pushing, about the subway system – but I would trade that for anything right now," Hunte recalled. "Before we left the hotel that night, we knew we would write a song about our city."[3]

Reworking a sample of 'Love On A Two-Way Street' by The Moments, the pair pieced the track together as a traditional song with sung verses, and sent it to Roc Nation in the hope that Jay-Z might be interested in recording it. The song was rejected at first, but that summer the pair played the tune to EMI publisher Jon Platt at a barbecue, and Platt thought it would be perfect for Jay. While the song was being played, the vibrations from the speakers toppled over a figurine of Biggie Smalls that Hunte kept by her computer – it was an omen. "We all just looked at each other like, 'if Biggie approves, then send it to Jay'."[4] Platt played Jay the song the next day; Jay loved it so much he wrote his verses and recorded it that very evening around Hunte's original vocals on the chorus. Both Jay and Hunte, however, claim to have thought the chorus was made for Alicia Keys, considering her abilities on piano.* "I did try it a couple of times," Keys told MTV, "but it was more about capturing the kind of grand feeling of it."[5]

Knowing he'd got his hands on the 21st century anthem of New York, a track to rank alongside Sinatra's 'New York, New York', Jay-Z

---

* Mary J. Blige was Jay's first choice for the chorus, but after consideration he thought the choice would be too safe.

referenced Ol' Blue Eyes in his rhyme and flew across the city, verse by verse. Straining for the low notes, he traced his move from Brooklyn to Tribeca (now living "right next to De Niro") and his dealings from Harlem to his "stash spot" at 560 State Street. He name-checked neighbourhoods, boroughs and landmarks from the Statue Of Liberty to the dear departed World Trade Center as if taking a ticker-tape tour of his city and his history; then he slotted himself into the city's vibrant present, taking his old Bed-Stuy friends to Nets, Knicks and Yankees games. He gave the song breadth and beauty as wide as the city it was dedicated to, but at the core it was about the struggle and nobility of the people who lived there – "8 million stories out there and they're naked". He pinpointed a few: the dealers selling crack on the "melting pot" corners of the metropolis; a young model arriving in town, swept into the fashionista crowd, sucked dry and spat out. These were hints of tragedy amidst the glory of the "big city, street lights, all looking pretty/ No place in the world that can compare," Jay refusing to let this city-wide parade roll by without pointing out that some get pulled in and crushed beneath its wheels.

'Empire State Of Mind' was a show-stopper, but *The Blueprint 3* had much more still to say, much of it a conversation between Jay and those who wanted to see him fail. 'Real As It Gets' was the perfect follow-up to 'Empire…', its glorious orchestral sweeps and rampant horns* continuing the lush vibe and a hazy, rough-throated but elated rap from Young Jeezy spinning out classic hustling jargon. Jay's verse was one of honour, declaring himself a beacon of reality in a world of rap fakers, promising a jailed friend his own Lear jet ride on his release and claiming to be so far ahead of the rap game that all others could only follow in his wake.

The Blueprint 3 was sticking to its tenet of 'keeping it real', and 'On To The Next One' – produced by and featuring Swizz Beatz as the harsh, motoric voice demanding money on the chorus – upheld its promise to push the genre forward. Eschewing old soul samples for modern French dance music, Swizz twisted the electronic skipping song of 'D.A.N.C.E.'

---

* Put together by production team The Inkredibles.

by Justice into a pounding, ominous chant, like the marching of some futuristic child cult. In keeping with the imaginative backing, Jay's rap was all about progression and development, the shedding of old styles and the embracing of the new. Having got retro soul out of his sytem again on *American Gangster*, he told anyone wanting his old style to go listen to his old albums, while he got on with forging new paths for rap without repeating himself – "I move onward, the only direction/Can't be scared to fail, searching perfection… niggas don't be mad 'cause it's all about progression/Loiterers should be arrested." From cars to watches to holiday locations to sexual positions to champagne brands ("I used to drink Cristal, them fuckers racist/So I switched gold bottles onto that spade shit"), Jay pledged to keep trying new things, even throwing in a comedy burst of Auto-Tune in order to mock the method.

There was a thick seam of humour here, not only in the imagery of Jay tearing Jeeps apart to use as skateboards or putting major celebrities in unexpected settings – Oprah chilling on the steps of Marcy, Obama in his mobile contacts list, Michael Jackson at Summer Jam – but in the video for the song's December 15 single release too.* As if playing up to the internet rumours of his links to mystical and occult groups, he and director Sam Brown laced the stylish monochrome clip with images and references lifted from Satanism and the dark arts: a diamond-encrusted skull dripping blood, the skull of a ram representing Baphomet, a crucifix flanked by bullets, Colin Bailey of Drums Of Death with his face painted as his characteristic skeleton. Jay even appeared in a halo of lights. Either Jay was happily admitting to be a grand wizard of the Illuminati here, or he thought the association was funny, but kinda cool.

Timbaland's 'Off That' was equally modernist and ingenious. A splurge of sizzling space-age electronica akin to the most cutting-edge grime mixed with the contemporary techno-rock of bands such as Pendulum, it was all industrial crunches, glitched yelps, hissing piston beats, sped-up and rewound studio trickery and radar-tracking synths with Drake providing a robotic chorus hook celebrating the song's

---

* It hit number 37.

ahead-of-its-time nature – "Whatever you about to discover, we off that."

Unsurprisingly, Jay rapped up its creativity: "I may just let you borrow this/This the blueprint nigga, follow this/This is what tomorrow is," he rhymed, before revisiting the theme of progression from 'On To The Next One'. Between himself and Drake, they rapped, they were past concerning themselves with rims, chains, chasing fame, Cristal and racial opposition ("tell Rush Limbaugh to get off my balls/This is 2010, not 1864") and had no interest in hearing about the girls other rappers have slept with, the bulk drug deals they've made or the accoutrements that they have, and Jay used to have. Just as 'On To The Next One' had discarded Jay's old styles, now 'Off That' did away with his formulaic themes. This *Blueprint* was one of total reinvention.

'A Star Is Born' was certainly something the likes of which we'd never heard from Jay-Z before. Not just an anti-hate song, but an all-out celebration of an entire generation and history of rappers, paying respect to everyone from Mase and Kanye to Puff Daddy, 50 Cent, Eminem, Ludacris, OutKast, Drake, Snoop and Ja Rule for their successes in rap and making the Wu-Tang Clan sound like a basketball team of immense flow skill. Naturally Jay positioned himself as the king ruling over all of these rap princes, reminding us again of how far he'd come from the street corner, but as he handed over the final verse to rising hopeful J. Cole to ask "could I be a star?" over Kanye's masterful snapping percussion, looped howls and strident horns* there was a real sense of magnanimity, of Jay as the host and compère of all rap, geeing up the crowd to applaud the stars of his wide-reaching show. 'A Star Is Born' was one hell of a hip-hop curtain call.

'Venus Vs. Mars' took a different tack from Jay's previous relationship raps too, exploring, in a sinister hush, a dysfunctional relationship between two people with vastly opposing tastes and interests over a brooding Timbaland† creep of violin, synth squelch and woodstick

---

* Produced from a sample of 'Touch Me' by Mother Freedom Band, alongside No I.D. and Kenoe.

† With Jerome Harmon.

beats. Although they both finished with other partners to be together, at first the pair seemed incompatible: one liked Tupac, the other Biggie; one liked white wine, the other red; she drank Pepsi, he drank (and dealt) Coke; she was musical while he was criminal. Yet their opposites attracted, she was "the ying to my yang" and "the Bonnie to my Clyde", and the sex – judging by the passion in the chorus hook provided by an uncredited Beyoncé – sounded pretty harmonious. But in the end the girl turns out to be "a cheater" and leaves Jay broken and lifeless for a European guy, having gone crazy. There are hints throughout the first two verses that the girl in question in Beyoncé – she's a southern girl, she's advertised Pepsi and she sang on '03 Bonnie & Clyde' – but the song's conclusion suggests otherwise. Here was Jay taking his relationship experiences deep into the fictional realm, in order to unravel a battle of the sexes full of rich poetry and emotional tribulation. We were a million blessed miles from 'Can I Get A…' here.

Kanye's seething orchestral piece 'Already Home'* provided a backing for a more traditional overview of rap than 'A Star Is Born', biting back at his haters with the chorus help of Kanye's prodigy Kid Cudi. Attacking those rappers who considered him in the way, outdated and prime for a more permanent retirement, Jay-Z's answer, in keeping with the sentiment of 'On To The Next One' and 'Off That', was that he was in nobody's way since he was operating on a much higher level of rap than his rivals and critics, playing a different game, waving the chequered flag on a race they were still running. He existed in a rap stratosphere that others would need an oxygen supply to reach, inventing styles and opening doors for rappers only to find them merely copying him and then demanding he go home when, ironically, comfortable in his separate sphere far beyond their abilities, he was already home. Lacking spite and malice, it was a rhyme of supreme confidence and not a little wit – Jay took note of the introduction of high-occupancy vehicle lanes (or H.O.V. lanes) to claim he now had his own personal lane on rap's super-highway.

---

* The strings sampled from 'Mad Mad Ivy' by Gladstone Anderson & The Mudies All Stars and production credits for No I.D. and Jeff Bhasker as well as Kanye.

As a coda to 'Already Home', Kanye synthesised his own voice to create an electro-fied vocal melody swathed in traffic and surf sounds and ray gun 'pyew-pyews' for 'Hate' – one of *The Blueprint 3*'s least successful sonic mashes and the root of several critics' claims that the album had a weak and unfocused second half, but a fascinating twist on Jay's attitude to his haters nonetheless. While it opened with more assertions of Jay's realness in terms of his drug dealing days – likening stretching out his drugs to the yoga exercises favoured by Russell Simmons and Al Roker* – and bites about rappers who talked themselves up as Lear-flying millionaires but always seemed to be spotted in regular airports, it ended with an unusual but revealing admission. In stark contrast to his usual dismissive angle, Jay let on that he actually yearned for the approval of his enemies – "It hurts when you say I ain't the one, you haters/How do I gain your favour?... I need you to love me, I swear" – and that he loved his haters for giving him a sense of perspective, opposition and superiority, to justify his opinions of himself. Without rappers trying to drag him down, how else would he know he was on top?

Over more synthesised vocal hooks† and with Jay supplying background "aw"s that were his trademark on *The Blueprint 3* alongside the occasional croaked low note, Jay took another swipe at his opponents by reminding them of his immense status on 'Reminder'. Entreating his old sexual conquests and friends to speak up and confirm his history of womanising and dealing to those who doubted it, he went on to list again his statistical triumphs, his Double Platinum albums delivered year on year and his trumping of Elvis and The Rolling Stones in terms of number one albums. If anyone else could have survived the hustling game like Jay did, rapped so honestly about it and kept innovating in music while maintaining a huge business empire, only they, he argued, could criticise him.

---

* The fitness theme ran on into 'Reminder' with its talk of jogging memories and reciting track records.
† This time that of K. Briscoe, as set to sharp synth slices by Timbaland and Jerome Harmon.

The Blueprint 3 rolled on like a discussion between Jay and his critics, a more in-depth dissection of the relationship than Jay had ever attempted before. In 'So Ambitious' he followed up his need for challenge and opposition as a source of inspiration, as first described in 'Hate'. A classic Neptunes soul flounce* was given a serrated modernist techno-shiver while Pharrell crooned the song's key concept: "The motivation for me was them telling me what I could not be." From schoolteacher to naysaying uncles to the projects wisdom that said nobody ever made it big from roots like those, Jay listed everybody who'd ever told him he'd end up a deadbeat, drop-out or corpse and thanked them for giving him the drive and determination to so vastly exceed their expectations and escape the fatal fate of his birth and background. The song's inclusion itself was an act of bold ambition – keen to get it onto the record at the very last minute, Pharrell had sent it to Jay while the album was being mastered. Jay loved it so much he held up production on the record so they could squeeze the song on.

With the haters extensively answered and the *Blueprint* trilogy wrapped up, Jay ended with a happily ever after. 'Young Forever' was a vision of Jay living in an eternal hip-hop video where the sun was always shining, the yacht was always rammed with models and the champagne never stopped flowing through an endless youth, a picture of rap Valhalla. With the fluid chorus vocals of a British R&B singer who'd caught Jay's ear, Mr Hudson, harmonising perfectly with the soft rock ballad backing conjured by Kanye from a sample of Alphaville's pop hit 'Forever Young', it sounded at first like Jay taking his godlike supernatural fantasies even further – where 'So Ambitious' had pictured him growing wings and flying when backed up to the edge of failure's sheer drop, now he was claiming the gift of eternal youth. But on closer inspection the rhyme is steeped in knowledge of Jay's own mortality and the need for his legacy to survive him, it was his music that was keeping him and his listener young: "Just a picture perfect day that last a whole lifetime/And it never ends 'cause all we have to do is hit rewind." It was a fitting close to an album that consummately rebuffed

---

* Sampled from Minnie Riperton's 1979 swansong 'Memory Lane'.

all suggestion that Jay-Z was a spent force and saw him holding his own once more at the forefront of hip-hop, an elder statesman keeping two steps ahead of his pretenders.

Jay-Z marked *The Blueprint 3*'s release with a benefit show for families of the NYPD, Port Authority and Fire Department first responders to the 9/11 attacks – a Madison Square Garden show tagged Answer The Call that opened with the debut live performance of 'Empire State Of Mind' and climaxed with Jay announcing "make some noise for everybody that lost their lives so we could live ours" as images of the World Trade Center victims scrolled up skyscrapers on the stage-back screen to the tune of Alphaville's 'Forever Young'. A selfless gesture, but not one that could detract from *The Blueprint 3*'s inevitable rise towards Double Platinum status (it sold 1.9 million worldwide). But even Jay couldn't have suspected that it would be so vastly overshadowed by its biggest tune. During the Fall Tour in October and November that played to 800,000 fans in 18 cities in the US and seven Canadian stops, with Jay playing much of the new album between a smattering of career-wide hits and earning $25 million from the jaunt, 'Empire State Of Mind' was released as a single to a reception unprecedented even in a career as huge as Jay-Z's.

Accompanied by a Hype Williams video montage of idyllic NYC images and Alicia Keys seemingly playing a piano emblazoned with the Manhattan skyline slap bang in the middle of Times Square, the song raced to the number one spot and stayed there for five weeks – Jay's first ever US number one single as the lead artist, his very own 'Umbrella'.* It won him two Grammys, eight weeks on top of the airplay chart, multiple global Top 10 placings, 4 million sales in the US alone and spots singing a curse-free version of the tune with Alicia at the second game of the World Series and at the finale of the MTV Video Music Awards.† *The Village Voice* called it the song of the year; the Mayor called it the new Yankees anthem and had them play it again

---

* It was also the last US number one of the decade.
† The VMA performance was interrupted by Lil Mama wandering uninvited onto the stage, claiming later that she was overwhelmed by the emotion of the song.

at the Yankees' World Series victory celebrations at City Hall, with Jay swamped with hugs from the team's players as the final chord rang out.*
Jay wasn't wrong when he'd predicted he had the next New York tune to rival Sinatra's; 'Empire State Of Mind' had come to define, rouse and unite the modern NYC at the end of one of the toughest decades in its history.†

So emotive was the song and the performance of it that Keys herself felt she hadn't finished with the sentiment, she wanted to give it her own personal twist, more intimate and piano-led. Hence she recorded a sequel, 'Empire State Of Mind (Part II) Broken Down', featuring her own vocals where once Jay had rapped, a sweet soul summary of Jay's verses sticking largely to the same themes of pinpointing everyday New York street scenes and stories. It was a hit despite the removal of the new verse Jay had originally recorded for it, and the song lived on, gleaming like the Empire State itself.

For Jay-Z it was a personal anthem too. With every ounce of struggle and savvy he had made it in New York first, then he had made it everywhere. Now, at last, he was the undisputed King Of New York. Next, to be crowned King Of America.

---

* Jay's association with the Yankees would continue the following year with a range of co-branded 'S. Carter' jerseys.

† And its sentiment proved global – a Welsh spoof of the song called 'Newport (Ymerodraeth State of Mind)' became a viral hit on YouTube, clocking up 2.5 million views before being taken down at the insistence of the songwriters.

Chapter Seventeen

Ascending The Throne

A thousand soldiers at the door, his compound breached, his studio and instruments destroyed, he and his family beaten; the government setting out to crush the truth being surreptitiously exposed through music. As Jay-Z sat watching the tragedy of Nigerian afrobeat pioneer Fela Kuti's 1977 stand against the Nigerian government in the wake of his rebellious album *Zombie** play out on the stage of 37 Arts Theatre B at the climax of an off-Broadway production of new musical *Fela!*, he felt a similar association as he had towards Ridley Scott's *American Gangster*. He knew what it was to be suppressed and hounded by authority, to have his voice politically muffled and his music denigrated for its unwelcome messages. So he put his money, once more, where his soul was, putting up $1 million as producer alongside contributions from Will Smith and Jada Pinkett Smith to bring the production to Broadway. *Fela!* won 11 Tony Awards in 2010.

---

* The album, Kuti's 27th, was openly critical of the brutality of the Nigerian military dictatorship and hence a hit with the populous as a whole. The army responded by besieging Kuti's Kalakuta Republic commune, burning his studio and master tapes, torturing him and his wives and throwing his ageing mother from a window, the commanding officer then defecating on the dying woman's face.

That $1 million may have been a drop in Jay-Z's financial ocean at the time – *Newsweek* was ranking him as the fourth most influential new tycoon alongside Facebook's Mark Zuckerberg – but Jay's heart was leaning more and more towards magnanimity, strength in numbers. Virtually every project he's undertaken since *Fela!* has been a collaboration of sorts, as if winding his way towards his next cycle of solo works. In January 2010 his Mr Hudson duet on 'Young Forever' became the fifth single released from *The Blueprint 3*, accompanied by a black-and-white video of New York skaters, punks and kids in keeping with the stately clip for 'Empire State Of Mind', giving Jay-Z his 17th Top 10 US hit, a record equalled in rap only by Ludacris.

At the same time, while showing interest in buying a stake in UK football team Arsenal FC (he didn't invest in the end), Jay was captured by the tragedies of the January 2010 Haiti earthquake as strongly as he had been by the victims of Katrina. A text came through from Swizz Beatz asking if he wanted to contribute to a charity song to raise funds; the same text had gone out to Bono. Both agreed, and brought in U2's guitarist The Edge and Rihanna to record 'Stranded (Haiti Mon Amour)', a song for which Bono wrote the hook over the phone with Swizz. "The idea of the song is 'We're not gonna leave you stranded' and that's what the chorus is," Swizz explained to *Rolling Stone*. "So me and Bono started going back and forth with ideas, and he was like, 'You know, this word 'stranded' keeps standing out to me' and I asked him to sing it, and he put me on hold 'cause he's recording the ideas on a Dictaphone – so he did it there and then on the phone."[1] That night Bono and The Edge went into Swizz's studio to record the heartfelt Latino-tinged tune and Jay-Z and Rihanna sent in their contributions and the song was available on iTunes by January 23, a day after its debut performance in London on the Hope For Haiti Now global telethon and just 11 days after the 7.0 magnitude earthquake had hit, killing 316,000 people. The performance helped the telethon raise $61 million for the relief fund.

The summer of 2010 – as Jay toured Europe over 62 dates, including several more headline slots at rock-centric festivals such as Germany's Rock Am Ring – brought news of several more collaborations. Following

'Stranded...', Jay-Z would be the support act for the Australian and New Zealand leg of U2's 360° world tour that November and December, playing to hundreds of thousands of stadium rock fans in a further effort to extend his crossover audience.* Prior to that, he announced at a baseball game between the Detroit Tigers and the New York Yankees that May, he and Eminem would play joint shows at each of their hometown team's stadiums that September, each taking the headline slot in their own city. Essentially Jay-Z's first ever stadium gigs, the Home & Home tour, as these two dates were titled, sold out in one day, so an additional date was added in each venue – Comerica Park in Detroit and Yankee Stadium in New York. The shows were magical events, each act piling through two-hour sets packed with guest stars. Where Eminem surrounded himself with his D12 crew, 50 Cent, Drake and Dre, Jay opened with a clutch of numbers with Kanye (including their next single 'Monster'), recruited Beyoncé to add pop glamour to 'Young Forever', and even produced Chris Martin for a snippet of 'Heart Of The City (Ain't No Love)', a chunk of Coldplay's huge global smash 'Viva La Vida' and the piano refrain from Martin's 'Clocks', over which Jay rapped a verse from an unreleased cut called 'Most Kings' before a scrawled crown on the big screens. The king was finally home.

Then, in August, the most exciting news yet. His collaboration on the demonic single 'Monster' from Kanye's latest album *My Beautiful Dark Twisted Fantasy* – on which Jay spat a feral verse likening himself to a Godzilla and King Kong of rap, a hustler destroying whole towns and a killer of vampiric hip-hop pretenders sucking him dry† – wasn't to be the pair's last work together in the near future. Instead, they would be

---

* At the gigs, Jay would appear onstage with U2 during their politically charged hit 'Sunday Bloody Sunday'.

† Jay's line about raping and pillaging didn't help the track combat an outcry against the perceived misogyny and portrayal of violence against women in its Jake Nava-directed video, which included shots of women in lingerie hanging by the neck and Kanye manipulating two seemingly dead or unconscious women in a bed; the epitome of the modern male monster.

working on a joint EP entitled *Watch The Throne* from that November; five tracks recorded, initially, on the fly.

They were, after all, busy men. Kanye was still promoting his *My Beautiful Dark Twisted Fantasy* album, a record highly acclaimed for its experiments with prog, goth and rock styles and its epic, cathedral-like atmospheres. And Jay was hopping between cities, tentatively starting work with Q-Tip on the follow-up to *The Blueprint 3*, which he hoped to release in the spring of 2011 with one track featuring Odd Future member Frank Ocean; discussing his forthcoming memoir *Decoded* at the Miami Book Fair[*]; filming a HeadCount commercial to encourage younger people to vote in the midterm elections; and overseeing another compilation album, *Jay-Z: The Hits Collection, Volume One*, an elaborate package covering his 14 biggest hits to date. So inevitably, *Watch The Throne* came together piecemeal. Over the last few months of 2010, whenever breaks in Jay's or Kanye's schedule came up, they'd hop around the globe to a studio – Avex in Honolulu, Real World in Wiltshire, Electric Lady Studios in New York – to work on the latest cut, or record on portable studios set up in their luxurious hotel suites in Paris, Abu Dhabi, LA and the South of France. One lengthy session together in the private Barford Estate in Sydney, Australia, saw Russell Crowe turn up to the studio at Jay's invitation to hear himself name-dropped on one track and Seal and Bruno Mars contribute to 'Lift Off'.

From an outside perspective it sounded like an idyllic way to record, an album made virtually on a round-the-world holiday trip, arguably the most extravagant recording session ever.[†] But the early sessions were far from harmonious. Given the chance to develop their own idea of what the record should sound like apart from each other between sessions, on the occasions they did manage to be in the same room together they ended up clashing over the direction of the album in

---

[*] Compiled with the help of ghostwriter Dream Hampton.

[†] The choice of samples to mess around with wasn't the cheapest either – James Brown's most famous tunes, Otis Redding, Nina Simone and chunks of dialogue from Will Ferrell's *Blades Of Glory* movie.

heated arguments, so vehement that it would put Jay-Z off the idea of doing another collaboration project for some time. It became clear they would have to scale back their original vision of the enormous, dramatic sound they wanted for the record*, and equally clear that five tracks would never contain their plans or ambitions. *Watch The Throne* was shrinking sonically, but growing into a full album.

Barely half of the finished album would be made up of early material from their disparate sessions around the globe†, much of which was scrapped as too unwieldy and grandiose. But one telling track did see the light of day. 'H★A★M', an acronym for 'hard as a motherfucker', was a glimpse of the operatic grandeur the pair had originally envisioned for *Watch The Throne*. Opera singers warbled, orchestras crashed with Wagnerian might and Kanye and Jay stabbed out their rhymes like avenging theatrical demons, Kanye spilling out his interracial sexual conquests and Jay-Z reiterating how he'd done all the things the fakers were rapping about for real, things they would've died trying. The key image in Jay's verse, though, was his telling rap in general to "watch the throne, don't step on our robe" – the brazen bombast of 'H★A★M' was Jay and Kanye's self-coronation.

As the song hit number 23 on the back of digital downloads alone from its January 11 release, Jay and Kanye set to work completing the album via a completely different tack. Jay insisted they couldn't make the album in bits and pieces and that they could only form a cohesive piece if they set aside a proper amount of time to work on the record together – "If we were gonna do it, we were gonna do it together," he told a small press gathering at the album's first playback in July 2011, "no mailing it in." To which end, in January 2011, they hired a swathe of rooms at the Mercer Hotel and the Tribeca Grand in New York and installed recording equipment and their choice of producers and invited

---

* Jay would later claim the album went through "three iterations".
† From the Real World sessions they kept sections of 'Why I Love You', 'Illest Motherfucker Alive', 'H★A★M' and 'Murder To Excellence'; from Honolulu 'The Joy' and 'That's My Bitch' survived; from sessions at the five-star Le Meurice hotel in Paris they kept parts of 'Niggas In Paris' and 'New Day'; from the Sydney session only 'Lift Off' made the cut.

guest artists to come and record in this most salubrious of impromptu studios. The sessions became something of an artistic and celebrity free-for-all: producer 88-Keys happened by to say hi to his old friend Kanye, was asked if he had any beats with him and had produced 'No Church In The Wild' within days. Givenchy's creative director Riccardo Tisci (who'd been hired to design the album sleeve) and fashion designer Phoebe Philo stopped in to witness the focused but always light-hearted recording. The hotel shook to music from every room, a hive of producers, engineers and guest artists – Kid Cudi, Mr Hudson, Frank Ocean and Beyoncé.

Between sessions, Jay busied himself with family business. He flew Beyoncé to a villa in the Bahamas awash with white flowers and champagne ice buckets for a dream of a first wedding anniversary full of candlelit meals on the beach. He and Kanye turned up unexpectedly to rap at the sweet sixteen of Chaka Pilgrim's daughter. He also launched a new lifestyle website called Life + Times, personally overseeing content covering sports, music, technology and fashion, and it was here, on July 4, that the much anticipated *Watch The Throne* was first made available for pre-order in standard and deluxe editions.* The first two fans buying it won places at the Mercer Hotel press playback three days later, where, once again, Jay-Z personally played journalists the entire album from his MacBook, in the very rooms where it had been recorded.

The second slice of *Watch The Throne* to get an official release was among the highlights from the Mercer Hotel sessions, and a big hit at the press playback. On July 19, first on Funkmaster Flex's radio show and then via download, fans could hear a track called 'Otis', named after the instantly recognisable voice of Otis Redding that opened the song, blasting out his seminal 'Try A Little Tenderness' as Kanye looped him into a passionate jive and Jay said "sounds so soulful, don't you agree?" By positioning himself alongside Otis – and later on the

---

* The deluxe edition included four extra tracks – 'H★A★M', 'The Illest Motherfucker Alive', 'Primetime' and 'The Joy', including a sample of Curtis Mayfield's 'The Makings Of You'.

same track, James Brown* – Jay was making as bold a statement of his unrivalled cultural significance as he ever had, and the rap itself was just as brazen. Jay kicked off by claiming he'd invented the word 'swag' that the likes of Odd Future were throwing around, then both he and Kanye indulged in some classic boasting of their wealth and rap genius. Jay told of cruising the city with his $200,000 watch on display, threatening to kill anyone who disses Kanye† and escape in a private jet to buy asylum wherever he chose to land. His final verse had a more serious point to make, though, that drug dealing immigrants were building a network of businesses beneath the law and becoming very rich indeed – and he seemed to include himself under 'immigrants'.‡ There was honour and pride to be had in "driving Benzes with no benefits", he seemed to imply; these were people smashing a crooked and repressive system.

The video for 'Otis', directed by legendary promo maker Spike Jonze, found the pair in a frenzy of exuberant destruction. They cut apart a Maybach, ripping off doors and windows and filling it with models to race and skid around a huge industrial lot, spewing sparks and fire.§ With Kanye upping his rhyme skills as if to take on Jay – "Luxury rap, the Hermès of verses/Sophisticated ignorance, I write my curses in cursive" – the clip captured the sheer enjoyment of the entire *Watch The Throne* project, a sense of fun that shot the song to number 12, sold 440,000 copies and earned it a Grammy. Though Redding's yelps were the closest it had to a hook, critics raved, and anticipation for *Watch The Throne* shot off the scale.

Costing an estimated $2 million to make¶, *Watch The Throne* arrived wearing its expense on its golden, Riccardo Tisci-designed sleeve.

---

* 'Otis' sampled Brown's 'Don't Tell A Lie About Me And I Won't Tell The Truth About You', as well as 'Top Billin'' by Audio Two.

† And there were many people criticising Kanye after his interruption of Taylor Swift's acceptance speech at the 2009 MVA Awards to direct credit instead to Beyoncé's video, which he described as "one of the best videos of all time".

‡ A reference, perhaps, to the African American arriving in the US via the slave trade.

§ The car was eventually auctioned for the East African Drought Disaster charity.

¶ Everything about the album was extravagant – even the promotional T-shirts were designed by Givenchy and sold for $300 each.

Released via Roc-A-Fella, Roc Nation and Def Jam and previewed again at a star-thronged listening session for celebrities and industry on August 1 in the Earth And Space section of the American Museum Of Natural History – a reference, perhaps, to the album's celestial nature – it was bold, ambitious and grandiloquent enough to make you think their original, now curtailed plans for the album's sound must have been positively cataclysmic. The album thrived on the dynamic dissonance between the two: Jay the mature, loved-up family man with the dark past transformed into neat-suited respectability and clean-edged rap nous; Kanye the wild, narcotic sexual predator with the mouth he can't stop from running and a taste for sonic demonics. Continuing the intense electro-tribalism and synthetic rock moods of *My Beautiful Dark Twisted Fantasy*, it threw Jay-Z into the churning fires of Kanye's darkest imaginings. And he found he was a natural phoenix.

Like a claw hacked off 'Monster' but still writhing, 'No Church In The Wild' was a brilliantly brooding southern voodoo blues opening laced with James Brown yelps[*], sacrificial drums and a bridge from The-Dream ironically doused in Auto-Tune. Drawing from such southern gothic swamp rock as Tom Waits, Queens Of The Stone Age and Alabama 3, it energised the formula with death-ray synths and a smooth soul chorus from Frank Ocean – a singer Jay had plucked from new rap collective Odd Future after hearing his mix-tape *Nostalgia, Ultra* – that set the quasi-religious tone of the track, casting Jay-Z and Kanye as vampiric night preachers. Tracing a line of power full circle from the human being who's irrelevant to a mob, the mob that's irrelevant to a king, the king who's irrelevant to a god and the god who's irrelevant to a human being who doesn't believe in him, it posed the existential question of where faith, hope and survival lie in a godless world full of leaders who don't care about or listen to their own people. Though the chorus put the atheist in a position of peril, out in the wild with no church to take refuge in, it continued a line of arguably anti-religious

---

[*] Sampled from 'Don't Tell A Lie About Me And I Won't Tell The Truth About You' by producer 88-Keys, as were 'K-Scope' by Phil Manzanera and 'Sunshine Help Me' by Spooky Tooth.

thinking Jay began in 'Empire State Of Mind': "Jesus can't save you, life starts where the church ends." More grist, if they needed it, for the theorists hunting for evidence of Jay finding faith in secret occult organisations outside the church.

Jay's verse itself was steeped in biblical, ancient Greek and Roman imagery, surrounding a memory from his coke runs – his Rolls-Royce Corniche boasting "cocaine seats, all white like I got the whole thing bleached" – with hints of religious judgement and condemnation. It suggested a deep-seated religious interest, but seemed to overturn traditional ideas of faith since it was coming from a man who'd done many illegal things in his life, but often for what he saw as righteous reasons. If there were an all-knowing god, Jay was arguing, then he would know that some acts deemed wrong by society aren't nearly so black and white. The priests and popes damning him to hell for his crimes were described as liars and charlatans themselves, and Jay even went into Plato's *Euthyphro* dilemma to salvage some salvation, some hope that even a gangsta's prayer might get through to whatever omnipresent being might be listening. "Is Pious pious 'cause God loves pious?" he asked, referencing Socrates' philosophical question as to whether a person is innately good or if they are good because God loves them.[*] His answer was in the fact that he was asking such questions at all – in the end he dismisses and mocks religion by likening himself and Kanye to the Holy Ghost and Jesus respectively. Like The Beatles in 1966, they were at least as big, if not bigger, than the Holy Trinity.[†]

A roar of a lion, a brief haunted carnival interlude and we had 'Lift Off'. Built around an entire spacecraft ignition sequence, it was fittingly placed for a record about to go stratospheric – Beyoncé's brassiest vocals declaring "We're gonna take it to the moon, take it to the stars!" over

---

[*] Jay was exposed to the concept of Plato's *Euthyphro* during a Princeton seminar where he was a guest of lecturer Cornel West. The quiet master/vocal student relationship between Socrates and Plato led him to comment that he was Plato to Biggie's Socrates.

[†] In case Jay's philosophising here had confused fans of 'Girls, Girls, Girls', Kanye brought the track back from the heavens with his verse, which uses similar religious themes to talk about banging two chicks at once.

celebratory synth fanfares and torrents of synthetic drums, a number as shiny and spectacular as any glitterball spacesuit. A critic-dividing single released on August 23, it was the welcoming pageant for Jay and Kanye's arrival on their far-advanced new planet of rap, and it gave way to an ultra-slow sample of Baptist minister Reverend W.A. Donaldson's 1959 recording of 'Baptising Scene', an introduction to a perky churchy baller hit celebrating their European extravagances.

'Niggas In Paris' was exactly that, a clinked glass over the fact that a sure-fire jailbird like Jay was free and wealthy enough to party for six days straight with models and rap superstar collaborators in $20,000-a-night suites at Le Meurice, drenched in Armand de Brignac champagne and buried in tickets for exclusive fashion shows. As a wide-eyed hoorah at their own amazing lifestyles, Jay-Z and Kanye had fun with the track. Jay opened his rhyme with a cocked snook at the NBA fining him $50,000 for visiting the locker room of the Kentucky Wildcats that April*, a joke about the Nets' dreadful run that season and the line "this shit weird, we ain't even s'pose to be here… if you escaped what I escaped, you'd be in Paris getting fucked up too." Kanye took the opportunity to reference the marriage of Prince William and Kate Middleton that had Europe in its thrall that summer (joking that William should have married both of the Olsen twins instead), and Prince bringing Kim Kardashian onstage to dance, only to throw her off again when she refused. Before flooding the diamond-bright synths and demonic tribal drums with a final section of studio buzz, synthesised monk chants and bursts of static, he even stopped the track on the line "got my niggas in Paris and they're going gorillas" to lift the lid on hip-hop and mock the incomprehensibility of some rap lyrics with a sample from the Will Ferrell film *Blades Of Glory*. "I don't even know what that means!" said Jon Heder, to which an excited Ferrell replies, "No one knows what it means, but it's provocative. It gets the people going!"†

---

* As a minority owner, he was forbidden from mixing with college basketball players.

† The song's repeated line "that shit cray" was just such an example, prompting a storm of Twitter debate that it was actually a reference to the Kray Twins, famous London mobsters of the Sixties.

A big hit on its September 13 release – selling 2 million and hitting number five, making Jay-Z the rapper with the most Top 10 hits to his name in history – 'Niggas In Paris' became the fan favourite from *Watch The Throne*, so popular the pair played it three times at the first shows of the Watch The Throne tour and gradually increased the number of times they'd perform it, to a reported maximum of 11 times a night by the end of the 34-date US and Canada run in Vancouver.* Little could follow it live, but on record they pulled in a deluge of soul masters. First 'Otis', then James Brown, whose legendary vocals were sampled from three tracks† by The Neptunes to create the hook for the haunting, minimalist 'Gotta Have It', atop a ghost-story harpsichord, filthy synths and an airy female trill. Another single from the album that December, it was a random, confused bag lyrically. Kanye's verse shifted from complaints about being discredited by critics of his outspokenness over the Taylor Swift incident and his George W. Bush Katrina outburst to boasting of his private jets and huge club parties schmoozing radio executives in Miami, with Jay-Z interjecting more talk of expensive watches. Jay's own verse twisted incongruously from a scene where he kidnaps a family to force a debtor to pay him his money to a musing on the rise of black moneyed men in Maybachs, a regular theme on the album. What the track lacked in lyrical cohesion, though, it made up for with a rising tension and intensifying dexterity, Kanye and Jay passing lines like championship basketball players.

Jay's hatred of Auto-Tune was about to be rebuked in style. The chilling 'New Day' was built by guest producer RZA around a maudlin piano, a shuffling beat and a sample of Nina Simone singing 'Feeling Good' fed through the software from the highest setting to the lowest as the song progressed, becoming gradually less computerised, more human. It was a technique that reflected the theme of the song; Kanye and Jay directing their verses to their own unborn sons, who slowly became more fleshed out and real as they poured their wishes upon

---

* The tour continues in Europe in the summer of 2012.
† 'My Thang', 'Don't Tell A Lie About Me And I Won't Tell The Truth About You' and 'People Get Up And Drive Your Funky Soul'.

them. Kanye hoped his son wouldn't be hated, judged or pilloried as publicly as he had, or have his level of ego, lust, outspokenness and questionable views on race. This was all delivered with a tongue in his cheek as he took shots at his stripper ex-girlfriend Amber Rose and hoped his offspring would keep their mouth shut on sensitive issues even in times of national crisis, just to be liked more. Jay's verse was perhaps more pertinent as it's possible he knew when recording the track that he was soon to be a father. He apologised to his child for ruining their life with celebrity before it had even started, but promised to direct them onto their right path much quicker than the 26 years it had taken him, possibly by setting them up as a mogul in their own right. And, so as not to repeat the sins of his own father, Jay promised he'd always be there for them, "even if his mother tweaking". In an album full of ego, wealth and brag, 'New Day' was a moment of humility, selflessness and warmth.

If the more easily shocked listener had been offended by Jay-Z's perceived reference to Beyoncé as a "hot bitch in my home" in 'Otis', then 'That's My Bitch' was his more gallant appropriation of the various B-words. While Kanye used his verse to explore his relationship with Amber Rose, how she'd turn heads at A-list parties and became accustomed to the life of high art and big boats, Jay's was dedicated to celebrating his wife, and other black women in the spotlight. Continuing the album's themes of emancipation, he argued that more black and minority women should be accepted as great beauties to rank alongside the classics of art such as the Mona Lisa, name-checking Halle Berry, Penélope Cruz and Salma Hayek among others – "Marilyn Monroe, she's quite nice/But why are all the pretty icons always all white?" But obviously, he saved his biggest compliments for his wife. Not only was she "gangsta" in attitude, no gold-digger ("Told me keep my own money if we ever did split up") and would support him with more dedication than any of his male friends, but she was a work of art worthy of Picasso and a place in the Museum Of Modern Art. Set to a driving electro-jungle throb* and adorned with elated pop choruses

---

* Sampled from another James Brown track, 'Get Up, Get Into It, Get Involved', as well as The Incredible Bongo Band's 'Apache'.

from La Roux's Elly Jackson and Justin Vernon from Bon Iver, it felt like a dancefloor celebration of the female form, and Jay even seemed to be aware of the inappropriateness of likening Beyoncé to a dog in the closing line – "get ya own dog, you heard? That's my bitch" – as he mumbles the final "bitch" almost under his breath, as though hurting himself with the ill-fitting disrespect inherent in the word.

Having appreciated what he had, next he mourned what he'd lost. Over the insistent synth rock stabs of Swizz Beatz' 'Welcome To The Jungle'* and making regular references to the Guns'N'Roses song of the same name, Jay paid tribute to Biggie, Tupac, Pimp C† and Michael Jackson as well as to the childhood he lost selling crack, the family members he saw die and the loss of faith he felt as a result of the pain, the root cause perhaps of Jay's questioning of religion on 'No Church In The Wild'. As his rhyme went on it became increasingly desperate and despairing, arguably one of the most revealing raps of his career. Remembering the pain of losing Biggie and feeling tortured and in hiding like Michael Jackson, he internalises his feelings, unable to cry them out. He resorts to the fleeting highs of champagne and weed to get him through, but in the end he's alone with the mirror, when his celebrity and high connections don't count for anything: "Where the fuck is the press? Where the fuck is the Pres? Either they don't know or don't care, I'm fucking depressed." It was a glimpse of the grief and torment behind the money, glitz and glamour, and answer enough to anyone suggesting that half a billion in the bank ever made anyone completely happy, ever took anyone completely out of the jungle.

From the personal, once more to the political. "This is something like the Holocaust," Kanye rapped in deep distortion over a crazed hardcore dubstep sample of bunker-busting filth and fuzz from Fux Pavilion's 'I Can't Stop' at the opening of 'Who Gon Stop Me'‡, presumably referring to the widespread deaths of African Americans to

---

* Featuring Swizz himself on the chorus hook.
† The UGK rapper and guest on 'Big Pimpin'' who died in his sleep in 2007.
‡ A Top 50 US hit despite never being officially released as a single, on download figures alone.

crime, poverty and disease. Though the rest of his rhyme slipped back into rapping about haters, unfaithful exes, money, charges of racism and dodgy sex, there was an underlying truth that cut to the heart of *Watch The Throne* and hip-hop in general. Kanye was using this historical tragedy as a justification for his showy and excessive lifestyle, arguing that generations had died to get him where he was, and millions from his background still shared "common haters" (i.e. racist Middle America), so he and his culture had earned the right to flaunt it. Similarly, Jay's verse too honoured his own rise and how he was such a natural winner he could do it all again from scratch if necessary, building his fortune all over again from having one pot of crack to having his music played in the Museum Of Modern Art. Hence the visceral 'Who Gon Stop Me' acted as a daring introduction to a section of *Watch The Throne* with a wider social conscience than how many watches Jay owned and who Kanye was sleeping with, in which positions.

Next they tackled ghetto gun crime. Dedicating 'Murder To Excellence' to Danroy Henry, a college kid shot by police while allegedly unarmed in 2010, the track came in two parts: the first – 'Murder' – a pounding Swizz Beatz production of ominous piano, scuzzed beats and a noble and spirited children's choir*; and the second – 'Excellence' – put together by S1 from a similar choir sped-up to skipping poltergeists over chords oozing threat.† 'Murder' had Jay entreating ghetto kids to stop shooting each other since there were enough cops gunning for them from outside the projects already, trying to bring about a unity among black youth, rallying behind figures of hope and aspiration such as himself. His message is to put down the gun and pick up the mic or the spreadsheet.

"It's time for us to stop and redefine black power," Kanye added, looking for a shift in the black pride mentality away from the violence associated with groups trying to emulate the Black Panthers (of whom Kanye's father was a member) towards a more instinctive pride in their race, entrepreneurism and its associated extravagance. Noting the

---

* Sampled from Indiggo's 'La La La'.
† The track also samples Quincy Jones' 'Celie Shaves Mr/Scarification'.

ridiculous number of shootings between March 31 and April 2 of 2010 among black gangs in Chicago, he implied that there's no achievement in the poor and downtrodden fighting among themselves, besides further ghettoisation.* He went on to liken the self-culling of black youth to a "genocide" and paint moving portraits of the funerals of the victims, a regular occurrence considering, as Kanye points out, more men died in Chicago than died in the Iraq war in 2008. 'Murder' was stirring and emotive stuff, brought to a final note of unity by Jay hailing both Blood and Crip with their respective greeting and stating: "It's all black, I love us."

The more celebratory half of the song, 'Excellence', was the entire crux and point of the album: Kanye and Jay-Z leading that new black power charge by example, into the exclusive VIP clubs, the boardrooms and the highest levels of public influence. With more toasts to their style, sophistication and success, Kanye and Jay posited themselves as part of a "new black elite" alongside Obama, Oprah, Will Smith and very few others, the ultimate dream for all of those project kids hustling for sneakers, "the promised land of the OGs". The trouble was, there weren't enough black faces at high society events or hanging out with presidents just yet. "Only spot a few blacks the higher up I go," Jay complained, using a domino scorecard metaphor, "that ain't enough, we gonna need a million more," while Kanye joked "in the past if you picture events like a black tie/What's the last thing you expect to see? Black guys." Kanye rapped that this, and the low life expectancy of black men in the projects – hence Jay-Z's earlier line "And they say by 21 I was supposed to die/So I'm out here celebrating my post-demise" – were signs that the racist and genocidal American social system was working just as the white majority had designed it to. And *Watch The Throne*, with its metaphors of black ascendancy, royalty and religion, was all about shattering that tainted glass ceiling.

---

* Kanye references 'Lucifer' in the line "I'm from the murder capital where they murder for capital" in order to highlight the worrying gun death figures in his home city.

"I'm tryna lead a nation to leave to my little mans or my daughter," Jay rapped on the penultimate track, keen to readdress the racial imbalance in society, "the scales was lopsided, I'm just restoring order." If 'Murder' was the cause of the new black elite and 'Excellence' was its rallying cry, 'Made In America' was its inauguration speech. A lush chorus hook from Frank Ocean, set to inspire, thanked Martin Luther King and Malcolm X for opening the door for Jay and Kanye's rise and Kanye spat an autobiographical verse about his leaving college for rap against his mother's advice, craftily creating his early records alongside his production work and brushing off the mockery of *South Park** with success in the fashion world, but it was Jay's verse that stole the show. To a backing of industrial pings and delicate piano tinkles akin to a synthesised take on Springsteen's 'Philadelphia', Jay rewrote the Pledge Of Allegiance to suit his and Kanye's new leader state – an empire built on family, drugs and street honour – and this was its 'Star-Spangled Banner'.

Watch The Throne couldn't end on a slow fade-out like 'Made In America', of course, no matter how touching. It needed to go out in a blaze of bombastic glory, courtesy of 'Why I Love You'†, Mr Hudson's lusty sped-up bellow and a classic Kanye slab of plasticated hair rock. Ironically for the closing track on an album so confident and self-aggrandising, 'Why I Love You' was backward-looking and bitter, detailing the break-up of Roc-A-Fella and Jay's subsequent fall-out with Beanie Sigel.

Beanie had been jailed in 2004 for a year and a day on federal weapons charges, and was angry that, when a hearing came up to discuss his early release, Jay had been asked if he would be responsible for Sigel's whereabouts and refused; Beanie was led straight back to the cells. On his release in 2005 Jay was ensconsed as the president of Def Jam and keen for Sigel to stay with the now fractured Roc-A-Fella. The

---

* Kanye's ego was the target of an episode in which a cartoon Kanye believed he was personally the butt of a vague viral joke.

† Released as a single on the same day as 'Niggas In Paris' and built by Kanye around a sample from Cassius' 'I Love You So'.

shunned Sigel, however, obviously felt closer to Damon Dash in the split, claiming he never hung out with Jay when they weren't working and Jay hadn't tried to contact him while in prison, and opted to release his 2005 album *The B. Coming* with Damon Dash Music Group via Def Jam. Though Jay-Z guested on that album and Sigel would re-sign to Roc-A-Fella for his 2007 release *The Solution*, the rift between Jay and Beans deepened. Beanie was furious that Jay wouldn't release him from his Def Jam contract to pursue a bigger offer from 50 Cent's label G Unit*, especially now that Jay could sign the forms in a minute and was choosing, once again, to keep him locked up. Jay, in turn, was frustrated that Beanie would want to run off to join the opposition rather than follow Jay's example and build his own empire under the Def Jam umbrella.

Having finally managed to negotiate his way off Def Jam in 2009, Beanie's personal hurt started seeping out. In radio and TV interviews he started claiming that Jay-Z hadn't supported him enough. At a press conference for *The Blueprint 3* in October 2009, Jay responded by saying there was little more backing he could have given him, having financed Sigel's record deal, his own label and a clothing line, none of which had taken off to the stratospheric degree he'd have liked. The situation reached a head at a Philadelphia show on the Fall Tour, where Sigel was invited onstage by Jadakiss as part of his support slot for Jay-Z's set, and Sigel dropped a verse to *The Blueprint 3* and muttered "I run this town!" According to Sigel, he was later hauled from the front row of the show by police and thrown out of the building, at Jay-Z's behest.

Sigel claimed to have written an entire album's worth of rhymes about Jay and his Roc-A-Fella split, but only one track saw the light of day. In a spoken-word rant at the end of 'What You Talkin' Bout? (I Ain't Ya Average Cat)', recorded after the Philadelphia incident, Sigel explained his side of the original disagreement. "I went to the office and asked you, 'let me off of Roc-A-Fella because somebody (no name no blame) wanted me and wanted to give me some real money'. You

---

* It's unsurprising that Jay-Z wouldn't allow Beanie to sign to G Unit, since 50 Cent had dissed Jay-Z previously.

bounced that tennis ball around in your office for an hour and went back and forth with me and told me you ain't want to let me go. You even asked me if I wanted some money and I told you 'I don't want your money' but you were in a position to let me get my own money and you couldn't do that."

With Beanie claiming responsibility for bringing credibility to Roc-A-Fella and being a front-line soldier for the label in its various beefs with Nas or Jadakiss, the outburst became increasingly personal. "I got a knot in my chest that needs to get unloosened. When you got love for a muthafucka it don't go away that easy. Many people gonna walk in and out your life but only real friends leave footprints on your heart, dog. But I think yours is fading in the sand… The richest man ain't the one with his first dollar, dog; it's the one who still got his first friend."

'Why I Love You' was Jay-Z's response to Sigel, and his own take on the disintegration of Roc-A-Fella. It opened with an image of the throne burning, the empire crumbling and Jay left tormented and alone in his corner office, hated and hounded by the very people he'd spent his life fighting to build a business for, his most trusted associates wanting him dead. Having likened Kanye to Jesus at the start of the album, Jay now took the simile upon himself, picturing himself as the betrayed and crucified figurehead refusing to die for his old partners, but rising again "when Easter's over". He bemoaned Sigel's lack of loyalty and ambition – "I tried to teach niggas how to be kings, and all they ever wanted was to be soldiers" – said he'd had his heart "ripped out" by the betrayal and asserted the unbreachability of his new, smaller but more steadfast group of hip-hop hyper-stars: "the circle got smaller, the castle got bigger, the walls got taller". But for all his relating himself to tragic fallen godheads such as Jesus and Julius Caesar[*], for all his assertions that he'd brushed off Sigel's disses, covered his legal fees, been "a good king" and was now keeping firearms "under my pillow" for good measure, the emotional root of the song was of a frustrated brotherly love that still beat strong, hence Hudson's hook: "I love you so, but why I love you I'll never know."

---

[*] Another great leader assassinated by his closest circle.

Distorted, degraded and monstrous, 'Why I Love You' closed out *Watch The Throne* with a crescendo of strings, guitar squeals and battered emotion, a message that even the untouchables are human too. Not that you'd know it by the sales figures. This rallying cry for the new black elite fulfilled its own mission statement within one week of its August 8 release, debuting at number one on the iTunes store in 23 countries and selling a record 290,000 units on iTunes alone* (where it was released five days earlier than the physical album, to combat internet leaks), and scoring an inevitable *Billboard* number one hit on the back of 436,000 first-week physical sales. Publications of all styles and hues roared its praises, from cult to mainstream. Jay and Kanye – as well as rap itself – had reached the highest peaks of popular culture, outselling the behemoths of rock'n'roll, accepted and loved far beyond their niche beginnings or their exclusive rap audiences, dictating the vagaries of culture, fashion, music, changes in racial and social attitudes and – to a greater or lesser extent – politics. If modern, multicultural America could ever have a true People's King, it was Jay-Z.

And America was about to gain an heir to the ... *Throne*.

"Baby I paint the sky blue/My greatest creation was you, you: Glory"
           – Jay-Z, 'Glory', January 2012

The sky really was painted blue on January 7, 2012. The top of the Empire State Building shone a bright ultramarine as Blue Ivy Carter, weighing a healthy seven pounds, was born to a national outpouring of goodwill more suited to a new royal birth. Announced to the world five months earlier at the MTV Video Awards on August 28, 2011, the unsuspecting tot – the daughter Jay-Z had rapped to in 'Beach Chair' and mistaken for a boy on 'New Day' – was celebrated as if she were the nation's child, peering out beneath a thatch of black hair, from her

---

* Beating Coldplay's previous record, although Lil Wayne would crack Jay and Kanye's record by 10,000 less than a month later.

blankets, not yet conceiving what a charmed, extravagant, scrutinised and dissected life she was in for.

Even her birth was surrounded by scandal, rumour and widespread speculation. Whether Jay paid to change the colour of the Empire State in her honour or not was small fry compared with the stories from other expectant parents and 'insiders' at the Lennox Hill Hospital in New York. They'd paid $1.3 million to renovate the entire wing where Blue Ivy would be born, un-named staff suggested, including installing a bullet-proof door. Beyoncé had checked into a luxury birthing suite as Ingrid Jackson, rumour had it. Windows and bed curtains were blacked out and security was so tight other parents at the hospital were prevented from visiting their own newborns in intensive care, it was claimed. Beyoncé had a tearful reunion with her estranged father on her hospital bed, the story went. Jay had vowed never to use the word "bitch" in rhyme having seen his daughter's innocent face.*

And then there was the name. The conspiracists had a field day. Could Blue IV be a reference to Jay-Z's next album title – *The Blueprint IV*? Or was it an admission of Illuminati and Satanist connections, as any hugely famous couple embedded deep in secret occult societies and wanting to keep this fact firmly under wraps would obviously want to subliminally suggest in the naming of their first child? Did IVY stand for Illuminati's Very Youngest? Was BLUE an acronym for Born Living Under Evil? Was her name spelled backwards really the Latin phrase for Lucifer's Daughter?

No. There's no such Latin and Twitter mischief made the others up. But there was one comedy rumour that came true. "A new government report says that the nation must be on high alert for an upcoming barrage of terrible Jay-Z rap ballads about fatherhood," joked fake newsreaders on comedy news channel *The Onion* News Network. "The latest projections based on the Jigga man's career trajectory suggest we're heading for a disaster. He's already gone from ghetto anthems to Frank Sinatra-style ballads which seems to indicate we could be looking at unprecedented

---

* This one, and the story of their security preventing other parents seeing their new children, the couple have denied.

levels of cheesiness… from now on we can expect clichéd rhymes about trading liquor bottles for baby bottles, that sort of thing."

Though no one was heartless enough to label it 'terrible', a matter of days after Blue's birth the first of those "saccharine rhymes about the joys of fatherhood" hit the internet, free of charge. 'Glory' was a Pharrell gift, certainly saccharine but also deeply moving. With Pharrell contributing the preacherman soul wails of the title and backing gurgles performed by Blue Ivy herself, this sultry synth-soul lullaby was bedecked with trademark Jay revelations. That Blue was conceived in Paris the night before Beyoncé shot the cover for her latest album *4*.* That the couple had experienced "false alarms and false starts" in trying to have a baby, and that there had been a devastating previous miscarriage. But Jay's overwhelmed vocals as he described his joy at her arrival, how he'd lavish her with high-end styles from an early age and how she'd be "part two, a younger, smarter, faster me… a pinch of Hov, a whole glass of Be" could have defrosted the most satirical hearts at *The Onion* News Network.

While the new family settled back into their Manhattan apartment and toasted Blue's arrival with the press and photographers at the re-opening of the renovated New York 40/40 Club the following week, the Jigganaut rolls ever onwards. The Watch The Throne joint tour with Kanye – which broke all box-office records for a rap tour with almost $50 million taken on the US and Canada leg, and upped the game for rap show production by having the pair perform an integrated set of their classics on rising hydraulic cube screens at either end of the arena, swathed in bursts of laser and fireballs in what's been described as the most spectacular rap show ever staged – is scheduled to hit Europe in the summer of 2012, Jay and Kanye rising from stages across the continent to the operatic brimstone of 'H★A★M' to blast out epic sets of their biggest hits interspersed with every *Watch The Throne* track.

---

* A meaningful number for Beyoncé and her family, and perhaps a more realistic reason for giving her daughter the middle name Ivy.

Jay's political and social campaigning looks set to continue, since Rocawear, still under his management, was criticised by the Occupy Wall Street movement for printing T-shirts bearing their slogan without making any financial donation to the cause, forcing them to change the slogan slightly but not its message. "The 'Occupy All Streets' T-shirt was created in support of the Occupy Wall Street movement," Rocawear stated. "Rocawear strongly encourages all forms of constructive expression, whether it be artistic, political or social. 'Occupy All Streets' is our way of reminding people that there is change to be made everywhere, not just on Wall Street. At this time we have not made an official commitment to monetarily support the movement."

His business interests continue to expand, taking in a co-brand directing role with Budweiser Select, plans to grow the 40/40 franchise into 20 airports worldwide and an investment in a hotel venture called J Hotels, which has recently bought real estate in Chelsea, NYC, for $66 million with the aim of building a high-class hotel or an art gallery on the site. Though projects such as opening a slot machine casino at the Aqueduct Racetrack in New York have fallen through, Jay still approaches his businesses with an inspirational conviction. "Be fearless," he told me in 2009. "You have to not be afraid to fail. I've definitely failed. We had a thing called Wash-House in Rocawear which failed, a thing called Teen Tock which we're gonna start over again which failed the first time."

Then, of course, there will be a new solo album, for which three songs have already been recorded at the time of going to print, one featuring guest vocals from Frank Ocean once more. As he enters a new phase of his life – fatherhood, responsibility, a role model as much as a rapper – there's scope for a whole new era of Jay-Z rhymes and wisdom to develop over the next decade.

He's reminded us many times where he's come from, what he made of himself and how he got from there to here, but who is Jay-Z in 2012? He's the most successful rapper of all time. He's the President's friend and advisor. He's the guy who can appear on Oprah baking lemon pie during the day and discuss the cultural significance of rappers using the 'N' word over dinner. He's the underworld crime lord it's okay to love.

He's a man so rich he was once enjoying a meal in Capri, Italy, so much that he called a friend back in the States and flew them over to taste it with him. He's the crossover king who headlines rock music festivals, wants to work with Jack White and gets spotted at Coldplay, Muse and Grizzly Bear gigs. He's the rapper who's done so well from the art form that he now feels a responsibility to care for it and represent it positively, so that the next generation can save themselves with rhymes like he did. He's a cultural activist; a racial and musical frontiersman; an emancipator, philanthropist and insanely successful entrepreneur. He's a poet whose words have encompassed crude violence, brutal honesty, devastating revelation, borderline misogyny, immense ego and wealth, heart-wrenching autobiography, shameless bragging, intense street philosophy, deep social conscience, self-defence, fighting back, sorrow, love and mountains of grace and honour. All of it rapped in ever more inventive flows and cadences, and writhing with networks of complex and intelligent metaphors, double meanings, cross-references, deceptive wrong-footings and imagery so dense and dazzling you can take a course in it at NYU.

He's a new father who's worked tirelessly in fields lethal and illegal for 30 years, struggling and suffering so that his daughter will never have to.

He's the hopeless, lost and fatherless projects kid called Shawn, determined to beat the odds.

And who expects to top his first billion by 2015.

Notes

Chapter One: The School Of Hard Knocks

1 Oprah Winfrey interview, *O*, October 2009.
2 *Guardian*, Simon Hattenstone, November 20, 2010.
3 The World's Biggest Rap Star Reveals All, *Clash*, Adam Park, September 8, 2009.
4 *Decoded*, Jay-Z, 2010.
5 World's Biggest, *Clash*, Park, 2009.
6 Winfrey interview, *O*, 2009.
7 *Decoded*, Jay-Z, 2010.
8 Winfrey interview, *O*, 2009.
9 Ibid.
10 Ibid.
11 Men Of The Year issue, *GQ*, 2011.
12 *Decoded*, Jay-Z, 2010.
13 *Empire State Of Mind*, Zack O'Malley Greenburg, 2011.
14 DJ Clark Kent Tells All, *Complex Music*, Daniel Isenberg, November 11, 2011.

Chapter Two: The White Menace

1 World's Greatest, *Observer*, Alex Blimes, July 13, 2008.
2 The Cat Who Got The Cream, *Guardian*, Chris Salmon, November 9, 2007.

3   *Guardian*, Simon Hattenstone, November 20, 2010.
4   Ibid.
5   Oprah Winfrey interview, *O*, October 2009.
6   Ibid.
7   Jay-Z: The Life, *Vibe*, Dream Hampton, December 1998.
8   DJ Clark Kent Tells All, *Complex Music*, Daniel Isenberg, November 11, 2011.
9   Ibid.

Chapter Three: Roc The Block

1   Jay-Z: The Life, *Vibe*, Dream Hampton, December 1998.
2   Ibid.
3   Oprah Winfrey interview, *O*, October 2009.
4   *Vibe*, Hampton, 1998.
5   Winfrey interview, *O*, 2009.
6   Ibid.
7   *Vibe*, Hampton, 1998.
8   *Guardian*, Simon Hattenstone, November 20, 2010.
9   HipHopDX.com, October 14, 2010.
10   *Soul Culture*, June 25, 2011.
11   Return Of The 2000, Daily Mathematics, May 14, 2009.
12   Ibid.
13   Jay-Z: Rockin' On A Roc-A-Fella, Yahoo! Music, May 1, 1999.
14   *Blues & Soul*, Pete Lewis, December 1998.
15   *Guardian*, Hattenstone, 2010.

Chapter Four: Growing... Doubt

1   Jay-Z: Rockin' On A Roc-A-Fella, Yahoo! Music, May 1, 1999.
2   Ibid.
3   Ibid.
4   HitQuarters.com, May 23, 2005.
5   The Making Of Reasonable Doubt Told U So, *XXL*, August 2006.
6   Ibid.
7   Ibid.
8   Ibid.

9   Ibid.

10   Ibid.

11   Ibid.

12   Ibid.

13   Ibid.

14   Ibid.

15   Ibid.

16   HipHopDX.com, Sean Ryon, November 10, 2010.

17   *Blues & Soul*, Pete Lewis, December 1998.

Chapter Five: Streets Is Watching

1   *Contemporary Black Biography: Jay-Z*, Laura Hightower and Jennifer M.York, Gale, 2009.

2   TheBoombox.com, September 2, 2009.

3   Jay-Z:The Life, *Vibe*, Dream Hampton, December 1998.

4   In My Lifetime…Vol. 1 Review, *Vibe*, November 1997.

5   *Vibe*, Hampton, 1998.

6   TheBoombox.com, 2009.

7   *Guardian*, Simon Hattenstone, November 20, 2010.

Chapter Six: Annie Get Your Gun

1   *Blues & Soul*, Pete Lewis, December 1998.

2   *Vibe*, Jacob Ogles, November 1999.

3   *Blues & Soul*, Lewis, 1998.

4   Ibid.

Chapter Seven: Hunted

1   *Backstage* documentary, 2000.

2   Ibid.

3   *Guardian*, Simon Hattenstone, November 20, 2010.

4   *The Wall Street Journal*, John Jurgensen, October 21, 2010.

Chapter Eight: Goading God's Son

1   Prodigy: An Infamous Walk Down Memory Lane, PlanetIll.com, Ipoppedoff, January 26, 2010.

2   Ibid.

3   *The Making Of Collision Course* DVD, 2004.
4   *XXL*, Rob Markman, October 2009.
5   Ibid.
6   Ibid.

Chapter Nine: Setting The Blueprint
1   *XXL*, Rob Markman, October 2009.
2   Ibid.
3   Ibid.
4   Ibid.
5   Ibid.
6   Ibid.
7   Ibid.
8   Ibid.
9   Ibid.
10 Ibid.
11 Prodigy: An Infamous Walk Down Memory Lane, PlanetIll.com, Ipoppedoff, January 26, 2010.
12 Nas Vs Jay-Z Grade-A Beef, MTV.com, 2001.
13 Ibid.
14 Ibid.

Chapter Ten: Crazy In Love
1   Jay-Z Camp Refutes Tupac-Biting Claims, MTV.com, October 9, 2002.
2   Ibid.
3   Deja Feud: Jay-Z, Toni Braxton Tracks Sample Same Tupac Song, MTV.com, October 8, 2002.
4   Jay-Z Camp, MTV.com, 2002.
5   Ibid.
6   Backbiting, *Entertainment Weekly*, Gary Susman, October 15, 2002.
7   *Decoded*, Jay-Z, 2010.

Chapter Eleven: Blackout
1   Oprah Winfrey interview, O, October 2009.
2   Men Of The Year issue, GQ, 2011.

Chapter Twelve: The Boardroom Years

1   *Fade To Black*, Roc-A-Fella Films, 2004.
2   Jay-Z, R Kelly Part Ways As Best Of Both Worlds Tour Collapses, MTV.com, Shaheem Reid and Robert Mancini, October 20, 2004.
3   Jay-Z And Linkin Park Show Danger Mouse How It's Done, MTV.com, Jon Wiederhorn, October 28, 2004.
4   Ibid.
5   *The Making Of Collision Course* DVD, 2004.
6   *Observer*, Sylvia Patterson, 2007.

Chapter Thirteen: Return Of The King

1   Jay-Z And Nas Officially Dead Beef, Allhiphop.com, Seandra Sims and Houston Williams, October 27, 2005.
2   Behind The B'Day Videos, MTV.com, Jennifer Vineyard, 2007.
3   Jay-Z, Kingdom Come, *Observer*, Karl Wilkinson, November 12, 2006.
4   The Cat Who Got The Cream, *Guardian*, Chris Salmon, November 9, 2007.

Chapter Fourteen: Godfather Of America

1   A Conversation With Rapper And Entrepreneur Jay-Z, CharlieRose.com, November 9, 2007.
2   Jay-Z Delivers The Goods On American Gangster, HipHopDX.com, Andres Vasquez, October 9, 2007.
3   Ibid.
4   The World's Biggest Rap Star Reveals All, *Clash*, Adam Park, September 8, 2009.
5   The Cat Who Got The Cream, *Guardian*, Chris Salmon, November 9, 2007.

Chapter Fifteen: World Leaders And Wedding Bells

1   Inside Barack Obama's iPod, *Rolling Stone*, June 25, 2008.
2   World's Greatest, *Observer*, Alex Blimes, July 13, 2008.
3   Ibid.
4   *The Wall Street Journal*, John Jurgensen, October 21, 2010.

5   Ibid.

6   World's Greatest, *Observer*, Blimes, 2008.

7   *Observer*, Luke Bainbridge, November 29, 2009.

8   World's Greatest, *Observer*, Blimes, 2008.

9   Ibid.

10 The World's Biggest Rap Star Reveals All, *Clash*, Adam Park, September 8, 2009.

11 Ibid.

Chapter Sixteen: Completing The Blueprint

1   RealTalkNY.net video interview, June 12, 2009.

2   Jay-Z Looks At 'Blueprint 3' Leak As 'A Preview', MTV.com, Shaheem Reid and Jayson Rodriguez, August 31, 2009.

3   'Empire State Of Mind' Co-Writer In Disbelief Over Song's Success, *Billboard*, Muriel Concepcion, December 11, 2009.

4   Ibid.

5   Alicia Keys 'Grateful' To Jay-Z For 'Empire State Of Mind', MTV.com, Jocelyn Vena, October 29, 2009.

Chapter Seventeen: Ascending The Throne

1   Inside The Recording Of Bono And Jay-Z's Haiti Single 'Stranded', *Rolling Stone*, Brian Hiatt, January 21, 2010.

Discography

Jay-Z has appeared on over 1,000 tracks, singles, albums, compilations and mixtapes as main, guest and featured artist. This discography covers only those releases where he is a lead artist. For a full list of all of Jay-Z's recorded appearances, go to the Jay-Z discography on Wikipedia. Release dates quoted are international release dates, so please note that individual territories may vary.

Albums

Reasonable Doubt
Roc-A-Fella Records/Priority Records/Freeze Records
(CD/LP/2XLP/2XLP Promo; June 25, 1996)

Can't Knock The Hustle (featuring Pain In Da Ass, Mary J Blige)/ Politics As Usual/Brooklyn's Finest (featuring Notorious B.I.G.)/Dead Presidents II/Feelin' It (featuring Mecca)/D'Evils/22 Two's/Can I Live/Ain't No Nigga (featuring Foxy Brown, Big Jaz)/Friend Or Foe/ Coming Of Age (featuring Memphis Bleek)/Cashmere Thoughts/ Bring It On (featuring Big Jaz, Sauce Money)/Regrets/Can't Knock The Hustle (Fools' Paradise Remix)★/Can I Live II★★/Can't Knock The Hustle (Fools' Paradise Remix Instrumental)★★★/Can't Knock The

Hustle (Acappella)★★★★/Can't Knock The Hustle (Hani Remix)★★★★/ Can't Knock The Hustle (Instrumental)★★★★

★Bonus track on Northwestside Records' UK version only
★★Bonus track on 1998 US reissue only
★★★Bonus track on Northwestside Records' 2004 UK reissue including 10" limited edition vinyl and Music On Vinyl's 2010 Netherlands reissue including 10" limited edition vinyl
★★★★Bonus tracks on Not On Label's 2010 2XLP UK reissue

In My Lifetime, Vol. 1
Roc-A-Fella Records/Def Jam Recordings
(CD/2XLP/2XLP Promo; November 4, 1997)

Intro/A Million And One Questions/Rhyme No More/The City Is Mine (featuring Blackstreet)/I Know What Girls Like (featuring Puff Daddy, Lil' Kim)/Imaginary Player/Streets Is Watching/Friend Or Foe '98/Lucky Me/(Always Be My) Sunshine (featuring Foxy Brown, Babyface)/Who You Wit II/Face Off (featuring Sauce Money)/Real Niggaz (featuring Too Short)/Rap Game/Crack Game/Where I'm From/You Must Love Me/Wishing On A Star★/Wishing On A Star (Instrumental)★/Wishing On A Star (TV Version)★/Wishing On A Star (Acappella)★/Wishing On A Star (D Influence Remix)★★/Wishing On A Star (Track Masters Remix)★★/Wishing On A Star (D Influence Full Vocal Remix)★★★

★Bonus tracks on Northwestside Records' 3XLP UK release only
★★Bonus tracks on Northwestside Records' European and UK releases
★★★Bonus track on Northwestside Records' UK release only

Vol. 2… Hard Knock Life
Roc-A-Fella Records
(CD/2XLP/Cassette/2XLP Promo; September 29, 1998)

Hand It Down (Intro, featuring Memphis Bleek)/Hard Knock Life (Ghetto Anthem)/If I Should Die (featuring Da Ranjhaz)/Ride Or Die/Nigga What, Nigga Who (Originator '99) (featuring Big Jaz,

Amil)/Money, Cash, Hoes (featuring DMX)/A Week Ago (featuring Too Short)/Coming Of Age (Da Sequel) (Featuring Memphis Bleek)/ Can I Get A... (featuring Amil, Ja Rule)/Paper Chase (featuring Foxy Brown)/Reservoir Dogs (featuring Sauce Money, Beanie Sigel, The LOX)/It's Like That (featuring Kid Capri)/It's Alright (featuring Memphis Bleek)★/Money Ain't A Thing (featuring Jermaine Dupri)★

★Bonus tracks on all re-releases

Vol. 3... Life And Times Of S. Carter
Roc-A-Fella Records
(CD/2XLP/Cassette; December 1999, Europe)

Hova Song (Intro)/So Ghetto/Do It Again (Put Ya Hands Up) (featuring Beanie Sigel and Amil)/Dope Man/Things That U Do (featuring Mariah Carey)/It's Hot (Some Like It Hot)/Snoopy Track (featuring Juvenile)/S. Carter (featuring Amil)/Pop 4 Roc (featuring Amil, Beanie Sigel, Memphis Bleek)/Hova Interlude/Big Pimpin' (featuring UGK)/ Is That Yo Bitch (featuring Missy Elliot, Twista)/Come And Get Me/ NYMP/Hova Song (Outro)/Anything/Jigga My Nigga★/Girl's Best Friend★

★Bonus tracks on the CD version only

Vol. 3... Life And Times Of S. Carter
Roc-A-Fella Records
(CD/2XLP; December 28, 1999, US)

Hova Song (Intro)/So Ghetto/Do It Again (Put Ya Hands Up) (featuring Beanie Sigel and Amil)/Dope Man/Things That U Do (featuring Mariah Carey)/It's Hot (Some Like It Hot)/Snoopy Track (featuring Juvenile)/S. Carter (featuring Amil)/Pop 4 Roc (featuring Amil, Beanie Sigel, Memphis Bleek)/Watch Me (featuring Dr Dre)/Big Pimpin' (featuring UGK)/There's Been A Murder/Come And Get Me/NYMP/ Hova Song (Outro)/Jigga My Nigga★/Girl's Best Friend★

★Bonus tracks on the CD version only

The Dynasty Roc La Familia (2000–)
Roc-A-Fella Records
(CD/2XLP; October 31, 2000)

Intro/Change The Game (featuring Memphis Bleek, Beanie Sigel)/I Just Wanna Love U (Give It 2 Me)/Streets Is Talking (featuring Beanie Sigel)/This Can't Be Life (featuring Beanie Sigel, Scarface)/Get Your Mind Right Mami (featuring Memphis Bleek, Snoop Dogg)/Stick 2 The Script (featuring Beanie Sigel)/You, Me, Him And Her (featuring Beanie Sigel, Amil, Memphis Bleek)/Guilty Until Proven Innocent (featuring R Kelly)/Parking Lot Pimpin' (featuring Beanie Sigel, Memphis Bleek)/ Holla (featuring Memphis Bleek)/1-900-Hustler (featuring Memphis Bleek, Beanie Sigel, Freeway)/The R.O.C. (Featuring Memphis Bleek, Beanie Sigel)/Soon You'll Understand/Squeeze 1st/Where Have You Been (featuring Beanie Sigel)/I Just Wanna Love U (Give It 2 Me) (DVD)★/Change The Game (DVD)★/Guilty Until Proven Innocent (DVD)★

★Additional DVD content accompanying the German release only

The Blueprint
Roc-A-Fella Records
(CD/2XLP/2XLP Blue Vinyl/2XLP Promo; September 11, 2001)

The Ruler's Back/Takeover/Izzo (H.O.V.A.)/Girls, Girls, Girls (featuring Biz Markie, Q-Tip, Slick Rick)/Jigga That Nigga/U Don't Know/ Hola' Hovito/Heart Of The City (Ain't No Love)/Never Change (featuring Kanye West, uncredited)/Song Cry/All I Need/Renegade (featuring Eminem)/Blueprint (Moma Loves Me)/Breathe Easy (Lyrical Exercise)★/Girls, Girls, Girls (Part 2)★

★Hidden bonus tracks on the CD version only

The Blueprint^2: The Gift & the Curse
Roc-A-Fella Records
(2XCD/4XLP; November 12, 2002)

The Gift: A Dream (featuring Faith Evans, Notorious B.I.G.)/Hovi Baby/
The Watcher 2 (featuring Dr Dre, Rakim, Truth Hurts)/'03 Bonnie &
Clyde (featuring Beyoncé)/Excuse Me Miss (featuring Pharrell)/What
They Gonna Do (featuring Sean Paul)/All Around The World (featuring
LaToya Williams)/Poppin' Tags (featuring Big Boi, Killer Mike, Twista)/
Fuck All Night/The Bounce (featuring Kanye West)/I Did It My Way
The Curse: Diamond Is Forever/Guns & Roses (featuring Lenny
Kravitz)/U Don't Know (Remix) (featuring M.O.P.)/Meet The Parents/
Some How Some Way (featuring Beanie Sigel, Scarface)/Some People
Hate/Blueprint^2/Nigga Please (featuring Young Chris)/2 Many Hoes/
As One (featuring Beanie Sigel, Memphis Bleek, Young Gunz, Freeway,
Peedi Crakk, Sparks, Rell)/A Ballad For The Fallen Soldier/Show You
How*/Bitches & Sisters*/What They Gonna Do Part 2*

*Denoted 'bonus tracks'

The Blueprint 2.1
Roc-A-Fella Records
(CD; April 8, 2003)

A Dream (featuring Faith Evans, Notorious B.I.G.)/Hovi Baby/The
Watcher 2 (featuring Dr Dre, Rakim, Truth Hurts)/'03 Bonnie & Clyde
(featuring Beyoncé)/Excuse Me Miss (featuring Pharrell)/All Around
The World (featuring Latoya Williams)/Guns & Roses (featuring Lenny
Kravitz)/U Don't Know (Remix) (featuring M.O.P.)/Meet The Parents/
Some How Some Way (featuring Beanie Sigel, Scarface)/The Bounce
(featuring Kanye West)/What They Gonna Do Part II/La La La (Excuse
Me Miss Again)*/Stop*/Beware... (Jay-Z Remix)*/Blueprint 2**/
Bitches And Sisters**

*Bonus tracks on US, UK and Europe versions
**Bonus tracks on UK version only

The Black Album
Roc-A-Fella Records
(CD/2XLP/2XLP Promo*; November 14, 2003)

Interlude/December 4th/What More Can I Say/Encore/Change Clothes (featuring Pharrell)/Dirt Off Your Shoulder/Threat/Moment Of Clarity/99 Problems/Public Service Announcement (Interlude)/ Justify My Thug/Lucifer/Allure/My 1st Song

★An acappella version of *The Black Album*, featuring all the original album tracks, was also released

Kingdom Come
Roc-A-Fella Records
(CD/2XCD/2XLP/2XLP Promo/CD+DVD; November 21, 2006)

The Prelude – Oh My God/Kingdom Come/Show Me What You Got/Lost One (featuring Chrisette Michele)/Do You Wanna Ride? (featuring John Legend)/30 Something/I Made It/Anything (featuring Usher, Pharrell)/Hollywood (featuring Beyoncé)/Trouble/Dig A Hole (featuring Sterling Simms)/Minority Report (featuring NeYo)/Beach Chair (featuring Chris Martin)/44 Fours (Live From Radio City Music Hall)★/Politics As Usual (Live From Radio City Music Hall)★★/Can't Knock The Hustle (Live From Radio City Music Hall) (featuring Beyoncé)★★/Can I Live (Live From Radio City Music Hall)★★/DVD: Live At The Royal Albert Hall★★★/Behind The Scenes Of Show Me What You Got And Video★★★

★Bonus track on the UK CD version only
★★Bonus tracks on the US CD versions only
★★★Bonus content on CD/DVD version only

American Gangster
Roc-A-Fella Records
(CD/2XLP★; November 6, 2007)

Intro/Pray/American Dreamin'/Hello Brooklyn 2.0 (featuring Lil Wayne)/No Hook/Roc Boys (And The Winner Is)/Sweet/I Know (featuring Pharrell)/Party Life/Ignorant Shit (featuring Beanie Sigel)/ Say Hello/Success (featuring Nas)/Fallin' (featuring Bilal)/Blue Magic (featuring Pharrell)★★/American Gangster★★

*An acappella version of *American Gangster*, featuring all of the original tracks, was also released.
**Credited as bonus tracks on some versions

The Blueprint 3
RocNation
(CD/2XLP/CD Promo; September 8, 2009)

What We Talkin' About (featuring Luke Steele)/Thank You/D.O.A. (Death Of Auto-Tune)/Run This Town (featuring Rihanna, Kanye West)/Empire State Of Mind (featuring Alicia Keys)/Real As It Gets (featuring Young Jeezy)/On To The Next One (featuring Swizz Beatz)/ Off That (featuring Drake)/A Star Is Born (featuring J. Cole)/Venus Vs Mars/Already Home (featuring Kid Cudi)/Hate (featuring Kanye West)/Reminder/So Ambitious (featuring Pharrell)/Young Forever (featuring Mr Hudson)

Collaboration albums

The Best Of Both Worlds – Jay-Z and R Kelly
Roc-A-Fella Records
(CD/2XLP; March 26, 2002)

The Best Of Both Worlds/Take You Home With Me A.K.A. Body/ Break Up To Make Up/It Ain't Personal/The Streets/Green Light (featuring Beanie Sigel)/Naked/Shake Ya Body (featuring Lil' Kim)/ Somebody's Girl/Get This Money/Shorty/Honey/Pussy (featuring Devin The Dude)

Unfinished Business – Jay-Z and R Kelly
Def Jam recordings/Roc-A-Fella Records/Jive/Rockland/BMG
(CD/2XLP; October 26, 2004)

The Return/Big Chips/We Got 'Em Goin' (featuring Memphis Bleek)/ She's Coming Home With Me/Feelin' You In Stereo/Stop (featuring Foxy Brown)/Mo' Money (featuring Twista)/Pretty Girls/Break Up (That's All We Do)/Don't Let Me Die/The Return (Remix) (featuring Doug E. Fresh, Slick Rick)

Watch The Throne – Jay-Z and Kanye West
Roc-A-Fella Records/RocNation/Def Jam Recordings
(CD/2XLP/MP3; August 8. 2011)

No Church In The Wild (featuring Frank Ocean)/Lift Off (featuring Beyoncé)/Niggas In Paris/Otis (featuring Otis Redding)/Gotta Have It/New Day/That's My Bitch/Welcome To The Jungle/Who Gon Stop Me/Murder To Excellence/Made In America (featuring Frank Ocean)/ Why I Love You (featuring Mr Hudson)/Illest Motherfucker Alive★/ H.A.M.★/Primetime★/The Joy (featuring Curtis Mayfield)★★

★Bonus tracks on 2012 2XLP picture disc edition, US and European digital deluxe editions and US CD edition
★★Bonus track on US and European digital deluxe editions

Live albums

Jay-Z: Unplugged
Roc-A-Fella Records
(CD/LP; November 18, 2001)

Izzo (H.O.V.A)/Takeover/Girls, Girls, Girls/Jigga What, Jigga Who/ Big Pimpin'/Heart Of The City (Ain't No Love)/Can I Get A.../Hard Knock Life (Ghetto Anthem)/Ain't No★/Can't Knock The Hustle/ Family Affair (featuring Mary J Blige)/Song Cry/I Just Wanna Love U (Give It 2 Me) (featuring Pharrell)/Jigga That Nigga/People Talking

★The amended title of Ain't No Nigga
(Note: The German vinyl version also included a bonus studio track)

Remix albums & EPs

The Black Album Remix
Roc-A-Fella Records
(LP; 2003)

Intro/Encore (Remix)/Change Clothes (Remix)/Dirt Off Your Shoulder (Remix)/Justify My Thug (Remix)/Threat (Blend)/99 Problems (Blend)/Lucifer (Remix)/Allure (Remix)/Moment Of Clarity (Blend)

Collision Course – Jay-Z and Linkin Park
Roc-A-Fella Records/Def Jam Recordings/Machine Shop/Warner Bros.
(CD+DVD; November 30, 2004)

CD: Dirt Off Your Shoulder/Lying From You/Big Pimpin'/Papercut/ Jigga What/Faint/Numb/Encore/Izzo/In The End/Points Of Authority/99 Problems/One Step Closer
DVD: 1. The Once-In-A-Lifetime Performance – Documentary/2. Live Performances: Dirt Off Your Shoulder/Lying From You/Big Pimpin'/ Papercut/Jigga What/Faint/Numb/Encore/Izzo/In The End/Points Of Authority/99 Problems/One Step Closer/3. Special Features: MTV Ultimate Mash-Ups/Photo Gallery – 5.1 Surround Sound

Singles

For clarity, except in cases where singles were only released outside the US, versions listed are primarily US releases and don't include promo, non-label or unofficial pressings or tracks which charted via online sales or airplay without receiving a dedicated release, unless otherwise stated. Track listings of releases in territories outside the US differ widely in terms of the versions included – a full international discography can be found at discogs.com/artist/Jay-Z.

In My Lifetime/I Can't Get Wid Dat
Roc-A-Fella Records
(Vinyl; 1994)

In My Lifetime/In My Lifetime (Radio Edit)/In My Lifetime (Instrumental)/I Can't Get Wid Dat/I Can't Get Wid Dat (Radio Edit)/I Can't Get Wid Dat (Instrumental)

In My Lifetime
Payday
(CD/Vinyl/CD Maxi; July 25, 1995)

In My Lifetime (Original Ski Radio Version)/In My Lifetime (Original Ski Street Version)/In My Lifetime (Skistrumental)/In My Lifetime (Big Jaz Radio Remix)/In My Lifetime (Big Jazmental Remix)/I Can't Get Wid Dat (DJ Clark Kent Version)

Dead President$
Freeze Records/Priority Records
(CD/Cassette/Vinyl; February 20, 1996)

Dead Presidents (Clean Version)/Dead Presidents (Album Version)/Dead Presidents (Instrumental)/Ain't No Nigga (featuring Foxy Brown) (Album Version)/Ain't No Nigga (Instrumental)

Ain't No N!gg@ (featuring Foxy Brown)/Dead Presidents
Roc-A-Fella Records/Priority Records/Freeze Records
(Vinyl; March 26, 1996)

Ain't No N!gg@ (Commercial Clean)/Ain't No N!gg@ (Mixshow Clean)/Ain't No N!gg@ (TV Track)/Dead Presidents (New Lyrics – Dirty)/Dead Presidents (New Lyrics – Mix Show Clean)/Dead Presidents (New Lyrics – TV Track)/Politics As Usual (Snippet)★/Feelin' It (Snippet)★/Can I Live (Snippet)★/Can't Knock The Hustle (Snippet)★/22 Two's (Snippet)★

★Tracks which appeared on a pressing of the single backed with Jay-Z's Listening Party, which omitted the Ain't No N!gg@ mixes.

Can't Knock The Hustle (featuring Mary J Blige)
Roc-A-Fella Records/Priority Records
(CD/Vinyl; August 27, 1996)

Can't Knock The Hustle (Clean)/Can't Knock The Hustle (Album Version Dirty)/Can't Knock The Hustle (TV Track)/Can't Knock The Hustle (Instrumental)/Can't Knock The Hustle (Acappella)★/Can't Knock The Hustle (Fools Paradise) (Clean)★★/Can't Knock The Hustle (Fools Paradise) (Dirty)★★/Can't Knock The Hustle (Fools Paradise) (Instrumental)★★/Can't Knock The Hustle (Fools Paradise) (LP Version)★★

★Track on the US 12" DPRO-30086 pressing only
★★Tracks on the Fools Paradise remix version

Feelin' It (featuring Mecca)
Roc-A-Fella Records/Priority Records
(CD/Vinyl; April 15, 1997)

Feelin' It (Video Version)/Feelin' It (TV Track)/Feelin' It (LP Version)/ Friend Or Foe

Sunshine (featuring Babyface and Foxy Brown)
Roc-A-Fella Records
(Vinyl; September 16, 1997)

Sunshine (Radio Edit)/Sunshine (LP Version)/Sunshine (TV Track)

The City Is Mine (featuring Blackstreet)
Roc-A-Fella Records
(CD/Vinyl; February 3, 1998)

CD: The City Is Mine (Radio Edit)/The City Is Mine (TV Track)/A Million And One Questions (Radio Edit)

Vinyl: The City Is Mine (Radio Edit)/The City Is Mine (LP Version)/ The City Is Mine (TV Track)/A Million And One Questions (Remix)/A Million And One Questions (Remix) (TV Track)

The City Is Mine (featuring Blackstreet)/Face Off (featuring Sauce Money)
Roc-A-Fella Records
(Vinyl; February 3, 1998)

The City Is Mine (Radio Edit)/The City Is Mine (Dirty Version)/ The City Is Mine (Instrumental)/Face Off (Dirty Version)/Face Off (Instrumental)

Wishing On A Star (featuring Gwen Dickey)
Northwestside Records
(CD/Vinyl; March 11, 1998 – UK and Europe only)
CD Maxi: Wishing On A Star (Radio Edit)/Wishing On A Star (Trackmasters Remix)/Wishing On A Star (D Influence Remix)/ Brooklyn's Finest (featuring Notorious B.I.G.)/Wishing On A Star (Trackmasters Acappella)
European CD: Wishing On A Star (Radio Edit)/Wishing On A Star (Trackmasters Remix)
UK CD 1: Wishing On A Star (Radio Edit)/Wishing On A Star (Trackmasters Remix)/Brooklyn's Finest (featuring Notorious B.I.G.)/ Wishing On A Star (D Influence Full Vocal Mix)
UK CD 2: Wishing On A Star (D Influence Full Vocal Edit)/Wishing On A Star (D Influence Remix)/Feelin It/Wishing On A Star (D Influence Full Vocal Mix)
European Vinyl: Wishing On A Star (D Influence Remix)/Wishing On A Star (Radio Edit)/Wishing On A Star (Trackmasters Remix)/ Imaginary Players/Wishing On A Star (Trackmasters Acappella)

Can I Get A... (featuring Ja Rule and Amil)
Roc-A-Fella Records
(Vinyl; September 1, 1998)

Can I Get A… (Radio Edit)/Can I Get A… (LP Version)/Can I Get A… (TV Track)/Can I Get A… (Acappella)

Hard Knock Life (Ghetto Anthem)
Roc-A-Fella Records
(CD/Vinyl; October 27, 1998)

CD: Hard Knock Life (Ghetto Anthem) (Original Version) (Radio Edit)/Hard Knock Life (Ghetto Anthem) (Remix) (Radio Edit)/Money, Cash, Hoes (featuring DMX, Beanie Sigel and Memphis Bleek) (Remix) (Radio Edit)
Vinyl: Hard Knock Life (Ghetto Anthem) (Single Version Clean)/Hard Knock Life (Ghetto Anthem) (LP Version)/Hard Knock Life (Ghetto Anthem) (Instrumental)

Money, Cash, Hoes (Remix) (featuring Beanie Sigel, DMX and Memphis Bleek)/Jigga What?
Roc-A-Fella Records
(Vinyl; February 23, 1999)

Money, Cash, Hoes (Remix) (Radio Edit)/Money, Cash, Hoes (Remix) (Dirty Version)/Money, Cash, Hoes (Remix) (Instrumental)/Jigga What? (Radio Edit)/Nigga What, Nigga Who (Originator 99) (featuring Big Jaz)/Jigga What? (Instrumental)

Nigga What, Nigga Who (featuring Big Jaz and Amil)
Northwestside Records
(CD/Vinyl; November 30, 1999 – UK and Europe only)

CD: Nigga What, Nigga Who/Ain't No Nigga (featuring Foxy Brown)/Bring It On
Vinyl: Nigga What, Nigga Who/Ain't No Nigga (featuring Foxy Brown)

Do It Again (Put Ya Hands Up) (featuring Beanie Sigel and Amil)
Roc-A-Fella Records
(Vinyl; December 14, 1999)

Do It Again (Put Ya Hands Up) (Radio Edit)/Do It Again (Put Ya Hands Up) (Instrumental)/Do It Again (Put Ya Hands Up) (LP Version)/So Ghetto (Radio Edit)/So Ghetto (LP Version)/So Ghetto (Instrumental)

Things That U Do (featuring Mariah Carey)
Roc-A-Fella Records
(Vinyl; February 15, 2000)

The track-listing of this release is unconfirmed

Anything/Big Pimpin' (featuring UGK)
Roc-A-Fella Records
(Vinyl; February 29, 2000)

Anything (Radio Edit)/Anything (LP Version)/Anything (Instrumental)/Big Pimpin' (Radio Edit)/Big Pimpin' (LP Version)/Big Pimpin' (Instrumental)

Big Pimpin' (featuring UGK)
Roc-A-Fella Records
(CD Promo/Vinyl Promo; April 11, 2000)

CD Version 1: Big Pimpin' (Radio Edit)/Big Pimpin' (Clean LP Version)/Big Pimpin' (Instrumental)/Big Pimpin' (Call Out Research Hook)
CD Version 2: Big Pimpin' (Radio Edit)/Big Pimpin' (Instrumental)/Big Pimpin' (Call Out Research Hook)

Vinyl: Big Pimpin' (Radio Edit)/Big Pimpin' (LP Version)/Big Pimpin' (Instrumental)/Watch Me (Radio Edit)/Watch Me (LP Version)/Watch Me (Instrumental)

I Just Wanna Love U (Give It To Me) (featuring Pharrell)/Parking Lot Pimpin' (featuring Memphis Bleek and Beanie Sigel)
Roc-A-Fella Records
(Vinyl; October 17, 2000)

I Just Wanna Love U (Give It To Me) (Radio Edit)/I Just Wanna Love U (Give It To Me) (LP Version)/I Just Wanna Love U (Give It To Me) (Instrumental)/Parking Lot Pimpin' (Radio Edit)/Parking Lot Pimpin' (LP Version)/Parking Lot Pimpin' (Instrumental)

Change The Game (featuring Beanie Sigel and Memphis Bleek)/You Me, Him And Her (featuring Amil, Memphis Bleek and Beanie Sigel)
Roc-A-Fella Records
(Vinyl; January 9, 2001)

Change The Game (Radio Edit)/Change The Game (LP Version)/Change The Game (Instrumental)/You, Me, Him And Her (Radio Edit)/You, Me, Him And Her (LP Version)/You, Me, Him And Her (Instrumental)

Guilty Until Proven Innocent (featuring R Kelly)/1-900 HUSTLER (featuring Beanie Sigel, Freeway and Memphis Bleek)
Roc-A-Fella Records
(Vinyl; March 13, 2001)

Guilty Until Proven Innocent (Radio Edit)/Guilty Until Proven Innocent (LP Version)/Guilty Until Proven Innocent (Instrumental)/1-900 HUSTLER (Radio Edit)/1-900 HUSTLER (LP Version)/1-900 HUSTLER (Instrumental)

IZZO (H.O.V.A.)/You Don't Know
Roc-A-Fella Records
(Vinyl/Blue Vinyl/Clear Vinyl; June 22, 2001)

IZZO (H.O.V.A.) (Radio Edit)/IZZO (H.O.V.A.) (LP Version)/IZZO (H.O.V.A.) (Instrumental)/You Don't Know (Radio Edit)/You Don't Know (LP Version)/You Don't Know (Instrumental)

Girls, Girls, Girls/Takeover
Roc-A-Fella Records
(Vinyl; October 2, 2001)

Girls, Girls, Girls (Radio Edit)/Girls, Girls, Girls (Album Version)/Girls, Girls, Girls (Instrumental)/Takeover (Radio Edit)/Takeover (Album Version)/Takeover (Instruental)

Jigga/Renegade (featuring Eminem)
Roc-A-Fella Records
(Vinyl; January 16, 2002)

Jigga (radio Edit)/Jigga (LP Version)/Jigga (Instrumental)/Renegade (Radio Edit)/Renegade (LP Version)/Renegade (Instrumental)

Song Cry
Roc-A-Fella Records
(CD; May 8, 2002 – Europe only★)

Song Cry (Radio Edit)/Song Cry (MTV Unplugged Version)/Song Cry (Album Version)/Song Cry

★Only a CD promo of Song Cry was released in the US

'03 Bonnie & Clyde
Roc-A-Fella Records
(CD/Vinyl; October 10, 2003)

CD: '03 Bonnie & Clyde (Radio Edit)/U Don't Know (Remix) (featuring MOP)/'03 Bonnie & Clyde (Instrumental)/'03 Bonnie & Clyde (Video)

Vinyl: '03 Bonnie & Clyde (Radio)/'03 Bonnie & Clyde (LP Version)/'03 Bonnie & Clyde (Instrumental)/'03 Bonnie & Clyde (Acappella)

Hovi Baby/U Don't Know (Remix) (featuring MOP)
Roc-A-Fella Records
(Vinyl; November 2002)

Hovi Baby (Radio)/Hovi Baby (LP Version)/Hovi Baby (Instrumental)/
U Don't Know (Remix) (Radio)/U Don't Know (Remix) (LP Version)/
U Don't Know (Remix) (Instrumental)

Excuse Me Miss (featuring Pharrell)/The Bounce (featuring Kanye West)*
Roc-A-Fella Records
(Vinyl; February 4, 2003)

Excuse Me Miss (Radio)/Excuse Me Miss (LP Version)/Excuse Me Miss (Instrumental)/The Bounce (Radio)/The Bounce (LP Version)/
The Bounce (Instrumental)

*Some sources claim a US CD version of Excuse Me Miss was printed with a track-listing of Excuse Me Miss (Radio)/Excuse Me Miss (Explicit)/Excuse Me Miss (Instrumental)/The Bounce (Clean)/Fuck All Nite - Album Version (Clean)

Stop/Excuse Me Miss Again (Featuring Pharrell)
Roc-A-Fella Records
(Vinyl; 2003)

Stop (Radio)/Stop (LP Version)/Stop (Instrumental)/Excuse Me Miss Again (Radio)/Excuse Me Miss Again (LP Version)/Excuse Me Miss Again (Instrumental)

Change Clothes (featuring Pharrell)/What More Can I Say
Roc-A-Fella Records
(Vinyl; November 28, 2003 – US release date)

Change Clothes (Radio Edit)/Change Clothes (Album Version)/Change Clothes (Instrumental)/What More Can I Say (Radio Edit)/What More Can I Say (Album Version)/What More Can I Say (Instrumental)

Dirt Off Your Shoulder/Encore (featuring John Legend, Don Crawley, Kanye West and Leonard Harris)
Roc-A-Fella Records
(Vinyl; March 2, 2004)

Dirt Off Your Shoulder (Radio Edit)/Dirt Off Your Shoulder (LP)/Dirt Off Your Shoulder (Instrumental)/Encore (Radio Edit)/Encore (LP)/ Encore (Instrumental)

99 Problems/My 1st Song
Roc-A-Fella Records
(Vinyl; April 13, 2004 – US release date)

99 Problems (Clean)/99 Problems (Main)/99 Problems (Instrumental)/ My 1st Song (Clean)/My 1st Song (Main)/My 1st Song (Instrumental)

99 Problems/Dirt Off Your Shoulder
Roc-A-Fella Records
(Vinyl; April 27, 2004)

99 Problems (Explicit)/99 Problems (Clean)/Dirt Off Your Shoulder (Explicit)/Dirt Off Your Shoulder (Clean)

Show Me What You Got
Roc-A-Fella Records
(CD/Vinyl Pic; October 30, 2006 – UK and Europe only)

CD: Show Me What You Got/Can't Knock The Hustle (Live from Radio City Hall) (featuring Beyonce)/Show Me What You Got (Instrumental)★/Show Me What You Got★

Vinyl: Show Me What You Got (Clean)/Show Me What You Got (Dirty)/Show Me What You Got (Instrumental)

★Tracks on maxi CD only

Lost One
Roc-A-Fella Records
(Vinyl Promo; December 2006)

Lost One (Clean)/Lost One (Dirty)/Lost One (Instrumental)

Oh My God/Kingdom Come
Roc-A-Fella Records
(Vinyl; 2006)

Oh My God (Clean)/Oh My God (Main)/Oh My God (Instrumental)/
Kingdom Come (Clean)/Kingdom Come (Main)/Kingdom Come
(Instrumental)

30 Something/Lost Ones
Roc-A-Fella Records
(Vinyl; January 8, 2007)

30 Something (Clean)/30 Something (Main)/30 Something
(Instrumental)/Lost Ones (Clean)/Lost Ones (Main)/Lost Ones
(Instrumental)

Blue Magic (featuring Pharrell)
Roc-A-Fella Records
(Vinyl, Blue; September 20, 2007)

Blue Magic (Clean)/Blue Magic (Main)/Blue Magic (Clean)/Blue
Magic (Main)

Roc Boys (And The Winner Is)...
Roc-A-Fella Records
(Vinyl; October 10, 2007 in Europe, November 23, 2007 in US)

Roc Boys (And The Winner Is)... Clean/Roc Boys (And The Winner
Is)... Main/Roc Boys (And The Winner Is)... Clean/Roc Boys (And
The Winner Is)... Main

D.O.A. (Death Of Auto-Tune)
RocNation
(File/Vinyl; June 23, 2009)

File: D.O.A. (Death Of Auto-Tune)
Vinyl: D.O.A. (Death Of Auto-Tune) (Explicit Album Version)/D.O.A. (Death Of Auto-Tune) (Instrumental)/D.O.A. (Death Of Auto-Tune) (Amended Album Version)/D.O.A. (Death Of Auto-Tune) (Instrumental)

Run This Town (featuring Kanye West and Rihanna)
RocNation
(CD/Vinyl; July 24, 2009)

CD: Run This Town/D.O.A. (Death Of Auto-Tune)

Vinyl: Run This Town (Explicit Album Version)/Run This Town (Instrumental)/Run This Town (Amended Album Version)/Run This Town (Instrumental)

Empire State Of Mind (featuring Alicia Keys)
RocNation
(Vinyl; October 20, 2009)

Empire State Of Mind (Explicit Album Version)/Empire State Of Mind (Amended Album Version)

On To The Next One/Young Forever (featuring Mr. Hudson)
RocNation
(Vinyl; April 12, 2010)

On To The Next One (Explicit)/On To The Next One (Amended)/ Young Forever (Explicit)/Young Forever (Amended)

Collaboration singles

It's Alright (featuring Memphis Bleek)/The Doe – Jay-Z/Diamonds In Da Rough
Roc-A-Fella Records
(CD/Vinyl; August 19, 1998)

CD/Single: It's Alright (Clean Version)/The Doe
12" Vinyl: It's Alright (Clean Version)/It's Alright (Dirty Version)/It's Alright (TV Track)/The Doe (Clean Version)/The Doe (Dirty Version)/The Doe (TV Track)

Can I Get A…/Bitch Better Have My Money/And You Don't Stop – Jay-Z/Jah/Wu Tang Clan
Def Jam Recordings
(Vinyl; 1998)

Can I Get A… (Radio Edit)/Bitch Better Have My Money (Radio Edit)/And You Don't Stop (Radio Edit)/Can I Get A… (TV Track)/Bitch Better Have My Money (TV Track)/And You Don't Stop (TV Track)

Jigga My Nigga/Memphis Bleek Is…/When Will U See/What A Thug About – Jay-Z/Memphis Bleek/Rell/Beanie Sigel
Roc-A-Fella Records
(CD; June 15, 1999)

Jigga My Nigga (LP Version)/Memphis Bleek Is… (LP Version)/When Will U See (LP Version)/What A Thug About (LP Version)

Jigga My Nigga/What A Thug About – Jay-Z/Beanie Sigel
(Vinyl; 1999)

Jigga My Nigga (Radio Edit)/Jigga My Nigga (LP Version)/Jigga My Nigga (Instrumental)/What A Thug About (Radio Edit)/What A Thug About (LP Version)/What A Thug About (TV Track)

20 Bag Shorty (featuring Frody, Gotti and Niela)/Why You Trying To Play Me (featuring Christopher Wallace) – Jay-Z and Aaron Hall
BMG Arista
(CD; 2001 – Germany only)

20 Bag Shorty/20 Bag Shorty (Instrumental)/Why You Tryin To Play Me

Honey – Jay-Z and R Kelly
Jive
(CD/Vinyl; 2002 – UK and Europe only)

Honey (Radio Edit)/Honey (Dirty Album Version)/Honey (Instrumental)★

★Track on vinyl and some CD pressings only

Take You Home With Me A.K.A. Body/Get This Money – Jay-Z and R Kelly
Def Jam Recordings
(Vinyl; 2002)

Take You Home With Me A.K.A. Body (Radio Version)/Take You Home With Me A.K.A. Body (LP Version)/Take You Home With Me A.K.A. Body (Instrumental)/Get This Money (Radio Version)/Get This Money (LP Version)/Get This Money (Instrumental)

Big Chips/Don't Let Me Die – Jay-Z and R Kelly
Roc-A-Fella Records/Jive/Def Jam Recordings/Island Records
(Vinyl; October 19, 2004)

Big Chips (Radio)/Big Chips (LP)/Big Chips (Instrumental)/Don't Let Me Die (Radio)/Don't Let Me Die (LP)/Don't Let Me Die (Instrumental)

Numb/Encore – Jay-Z and Linkin Park
Roc-A-Fella Records/Warner Bros. Records
(Vinyl/2XVinyl; November 16, 2004)

Numb/Encore (Explicit)/Numb/Encore (Radio Edit)/Numb/Encore (Instrumental)/Numb/Encore (A Cappella Explicit)/Numb/Encore (A Cappella Radio Edit)/Bonus Beat

Swagga Like Us – Jay-Z and T.I. featuring Kanye West and Lil Wayne
Roc-A-Fella Records
(File/Vinyl; September 6, 2008)

File: Swagga Like Us
Vinyl: Swagga Like Us (Clean)/Swagga Like Us (Main)/Swagga Like Us (Clean)/Swagga Like Us (Main)

Stranded (Haiti Mon Amour) – Jay-Z, Rihanna, Bono and The Edge
N/A
(File; January 23, 2010)

Stranded (Haiti Mon Amour)

H★A★M – Jay-Z and Kanye West
Roc-A-Fella Records
(File; January 12, 2011)

H★A★M

Otis/Niggas In Paris – Jay-Z and Kanye West
Roc-A-Fella Records/RocNation/Def Jam
(Vinyl; August 8, 2011)

Otis/Niggas In Paris

Niggas In Paris – Jay-Z and Kanye West
Roc-A-Fella/RocNation/Def Jam
(File; September 13, 2011)

Niggas In Paris

Why I Love You – Jay-Z and Kanye West
Roc-A-Fella/RocNation/Def Jam
(File; September 13, 2011)

Why I Love You

Gotta Have It – Jay-Z and Kanye West
Roc-A-Fella/RocNation/Def Jam
(File; December 6, 2011)

Gotta Have It

No Church In The Wild (featuring Frank Ocean and The-Dream) –
Jay-Z and Kanye West
Roc-A-Fella/RocNation/Def Jam
(File; March 20, 2012)

No Church In The Wild

Soundtrack singles

Who You Wit (from the motion picture *Sprung*)
Qwest Records
(Vinyl; May 20, 1997)

Who You Wit (Clean Version)/Who You Wit (Album Version)/Who You
Wit (Instrumental)/Who You Wit (A Cappella – Clean Version)

Girl's Best Friend (from the motion picture *Blue Streak*)
Epic
(CD Promo/Vinyl Promo; October 19, 1999)

CD: Girl's Best Friend (Radio Version)/Girl's Best Friend (LP Version)/
Girl's Best Friend (Instrumental)

Vinyl: Girl's Best Friend (LP Version)/Girl's Best Friend (Instrumental)/ Girl's Best Friend (Radio Version)/Girl's Best Friend (Acappella)

This Life Forever (from the motion picture *Black Gangster*)
Lightyear Entertainment
(Vinyl; 1999)

This Life Forever (Radio Edit)/This Life Forever (Album Version)/This Life Forever (Instrumental)/This Life Forever (Acappella)

Hey Papi (featuring Memphis Bleek and Amil) (from the motion picture *Nutty Professor II: The Klumps*)
Def Jam Recordings/Def Soul
(Vinyl; July 18, 2000)

Hey Papi (Radio Edit)/Hey Papi (LP Version)/Hey Papi (Instrumental)/ Hey Papi (Acappella)

Index